DYING TO BETTER THEMSELVES

DYING
TO BETTER
THEMSELVES

WEST INDIANS AND
THE BUILDING OF THE
PANAMA CANAL

Olive Senior

The University of the West Indies Press
Jamaica • Barbados • Trinidad and Tobago

The University of the West Indies Press
7A Gibraltar Hall Road, Mona
Kingston 7, Jamaica
www.uwipress.com

A catalogue record of this book is available from the National Library of Jamaica.

ISBN 978-976-640-457-4 (print)
978-976-640-465-9 (Kindle)
978-976-640-473-4 (ePub)

Book and cover design by Robert Harris.
Set in Adobe Garamond Pro 11/14.5 x 27
Printed in the United States of America.

Frontispiece: Construction of the Panama Canal, Isthmian Historical Society, *c.*1913 (Wikimedia Commons).

When the war was done – when they came home, when they looked at what had been accomplished . . . the great fact remained that they had played their part like men among men; that they had borne themselves so that when people asked what they had done of worth in those great years all they had to say was that they had served decently and faithfully in the great armies.

—President Theodore Roosevelt, speech to American ("gold") workers at Cristóbal, Panama, 1906, referring to the American Civil War.

The construction worker gave everything he possessed to the U.S. Government; in regards of work, we worked in rain, Sun, fire, Gun powder, explosions from dynamite; in house and out Side, we had to be hiding for our lives, Yellow fever, Bad water, long hours, in some jobs, no overtime, ten cents an hour, but our interest was to see the Canal finish cause we came here to build it You see most of us come here with the same Spirit as a Soldier going to war.

—West Indian Prince George Green, referring to his days as a construction worker ("silver") on the Panama Canal.

CONTENTS

ILLUSTRATIONS

MAPS

FIGURES

TABLES

PREFACE

PANAMA, "CROSSROADS OF THE WORLD": for centuries, that craggy isthmus blocked the path of world trade and exploration, taunting freebooters and sober traders, until, inevitably, human energies forced a way to link the great oceans here: uncounted lives, incalculable treasure and extreme efforts of back-breaking labour, ingenuity and social upheaval joined Atlantic to Pacific one hundred years ago. Today, the Republic of Panama exists as a wealthy, modern country overseeing this waterway.

This book is not about modern Panama.

Instead, it explores the days before, those days from which modern Panama arose. It tells the tale of the hands that dug and laid its miles of railway, that constructed roads, sluices, trenches, dams, and lakes while blasting rock and primeval forest to clear the way. It charts the rise of Panama's railway and canal through the lives of the workmen who gave body and mind to the immense enterprise. It examines the task they fulfilled, the price they paid and the rewards they won. It tells the tale of the people who literally carried out the work. Without them, modern Panama would not exist. This book chronicles the contribution of the largest ethnic group within Panama's workforce, a majority far outnumbering all other nations who shared in the great endeavour.

This majority were West Indians of mixed African descent: Barbadians, Jamaicans, St Lucians, French Antilleans and others from all the islands. The destiny of these islands was closely bound up with the destiny of Panama, and strong connections between the two areas continued until weakened by time. Today, such ties with the West Indies are ephemeral, echoing memories of a place where a relative had gone, or had come from, remembered in family tales only in words such as "fever", "gold" or "dynamite".

The expected flow in world trade arising from new locks enlarging the Panama Canal sets Panama once more as a focus of international interest. In nearby Jamaica, there is talk of a new logistics hub to handle shipping. Just as the shape of Panama's isthmus determined its history, so too the central position of Jamaica in the Caribbean Basin (only 550 miles from Colón, Panama) has always made it the gateway to Panama and Central America. Few people today, however, know how deeply linked were Panama and the Caribbean over the last five centuries.

Within the Caribbean Basin, and in what was once known as the Spanish Main, invading Europeans fought each other, allied with each other, fought and traded with native Americans, brought in captive Africans to strengthen their hold on territory as the territory fought back with malaria, yellow fever, hurricanes, drought, torrential rains, and inhospitable mountains and swamps. For four centuries, Panama blocked expansion westwards: undoing this barrier created a maelstrom of human energies, transforming millions of lives, changing the West Indies forever.

As a child I knew nothing of this, although like many West Indians of my generation, I grew up in a household of people who had "gone to Panama": my great-uncle Edward Rupert Peart of Manchester, Jamaica, and his sister Isobel (who had joined him in Panama and later in New York) returned to Jamaica and settled at Haddo, Westmoreland. My maternal grandfather Lewis Arnold Peart had also gone to Panama at the time of canal construction, but he died long before I was born. I have no knowledge of his life there. This book represents both a search for and a tribute to the composite "grandfather": the legendary forefather who vanished, or who came home crippled, as well as the one who brought home "Panama gold" and used it to better himself.

"Panama" formed a recurring motif in my Jamaican childhood: in conversations, in books, in photographs and from visitors who "knew Panama", punctuated by letters with return addresses that seemed exotic, terminating with "RdeP" or "CZ": at the time I did not know that these stood for "Republic of Panama" and "Canal Zone".

Nor did I know that the Canal Zone was an outpost of American imperialism in the Caribbean and Latin America, or that in the Zone, racial segregation and discrimination ran as deep as that in the American South. In my childhood and over the many years since of talking and listening to people who had indeed "gone to Panama", no one talked about Jim Crow in Panama. Everyone had, however, felt its shadow.

I discovered this fact only when I too went to Panama, impelled by a growing desire to find out what our people had done there, since those I had known personally had died without my ever asking the questions which later came to haunt me. In the 1970s, I spent months going through the archives in the Canal Zone library and meeting Panamanians of West Indian descent. On subsequent visits I interviewed many Jamaicans who had gone to Panama at the time of canal construction, both in the urban areas of Panama and Colón, and in the banana zones of Bocas del Toro province. On my return to Jamaica, my tape recordings were stolen before I had time to transcribe them: in this book I cite only the few that were transcribed. This loss left me unable to acknowledge some informants, people who were enormously helpful to me, as their names and contextual information had also disappeared. Fortunately, my main notebooks were untouched.

I then wrote articles on the Panama railroad and the French canal construction that were published in *Jamaica Journal*, but the Panama manuscript remained unpublished as I turned my attention elsewhere. In the meantime, some excellent books addressing the topic were published in the 1980s: Velma Newton's *The Silver Men: West Indian Labour Migration to Panama, 1850–1914*; Michael L. Conniff's *Black Labor on a White Canal, Panama 1904–1981*; and Bonham C. Richardson's *Panama Money in Barbados, 1900–1920*.

With the forthcoming centenary of the opening of the Panama Canal in 2014, I knew I had to "tell our story". Revisiting my notes, I was overcome with the need to tell the canal's most essential tale: that of the men and women whose physical labour made it a reality. Innumerable books discuss its construction, detailing problems in mining, engineering, project management and medical innovations. Few speak of the reality of daily life and work by the so-called silver workers. Few recognize the immense contribution of physical labour. The blatant racism of many of the early accounts truly shocked me. It is only in recent times that American and other scholars are beginning to take an approach to the Panama Canal construction that finally acknowledges the significant role played by West Indians, who were never less than two-thirds of the labour force. This time around I intend – as much as possible – to let the voices of those workers speak for themselves alongside the official accounts. I have succeeded to a limited extent only: I regret not making earlier efforts to capture these voices in Jamaica as well as in Panama when people of the construction generation were still with us.

I am aware that while this book deals with the West Indian experience, it is at times heavily weighted towards Jamaica. One reason is that, at the start, here lay my main interest as I pursued my research in Jamaica's archives and libraries. Richardson's work cited above (as well as Newton's book) deals extensively with the Barbadian experience. Barbadian and other West Indian voices are prominent, however, in the oral accounts cited in this book, thanks to the work of the Isthmian Historical Society and Ruth Stuhl, who organized a competition, transcribed the respondents' letters, and so preserved them for posterity. These and much else are now more widely accessible at the Digital Library of the Caribbean at the University of Florida.

The wave of migration to Panama and elsewhere starting in 1850 can be said to constitute a major component of our West Indian epic, the story of our forebears' struggles to transcend their brutal inheritance of slavery, poverty and neglect in order to better themselves. While large numbers emigrated to other countries, Panama in legend and actuality was the crucible for subsequent events: "Panama Man" or "Colón Man" remains the mythical embodiment of the traveller of those times.

The Panama emigration opened our eyes to many issues that are still with us: poverty, wage labour, emigration, population, race, development, globalization, British colonial neglect, American imperialism, as well as environmental challenges and gender relations. Also, given its sex-selective nature, "going to Panama" raises issues of manhood and success. I hope that more accounts will come from the other islands from whence so many men and women travelled to the isthmus, and that the centenary will fire the interest of younger generations in delving deeper into our Panama narrative.

ACKNOWLEDGEMENTS

I HAVE ACCUMULATED SO MANY debts over the years this project has been in gestation that I am aware that I might fail to acknowledge many who have been helpful to me, but I assure them that I am eternally grateful for all the goodwill and support that have come my way.

My first thank you should be to Tony Russell, who kept on urging me to get it done. I am grateful to those who took on the task of reading some or all of the manuscript at various times including Rupert Lewis, Velma Pollard, Nesta Scott, Vanessa Spence. My biggest debts are to Jean D'Costa for her meticulous reading and unflagging encouragement and to Jean Handscombe for huge assistance with picture search and invaluable editorial advice. Thanks to Alford Alphonse, Emelda Brathwaite, Cecile Eistrup, Alvin Fong-Tom, Elizabeth Harry, Jolien Harmsen, Rosemary Kavanagh, Dennis Ranston, Jackie Ranston, Tricia Spencer, Sandero Panama and Margaret Cezair-Thompson, who assisted with images and or information as did Veerle Poupeye and O'Neil Lawrence of the National Gallery of Jamaica. A special thank you to Panama Canal historian William P. McLaughlin for generously allowing me to use pictures from his invaluable collection. Thanks to Thera Edwards for her maps; Tricia Evelyn for assistance with the pictures and Margot Gibb-Clarke for her translations from the French. Cheryl Ryman's help in locating material at a critical stage was invaluable.

Libraries and archives have of course been the foundation of this work and I still owe a great debt to the helpful librarians at what was the Panama Canal Library (now part of the Library of Congress) as well as the Jamaica Archives. The National Library of Jamaica and the Institute of Jamaica have been nurturing institutions for me over the years, and I am thankful that I have continued to benefit from the assistance of the current staff under Winsome Hudson, national librarian, and the current director of the Institute of Jamaica, Anne-Marie Bonner. Yvonne Fraser-Clarke and the research librarians at the National Library of Jamaica were also most helpful. Shirley Maynier Burke was the first to publish my Panama material when she was editor of *Jamaica*

Journal, and I wish to acknowledge that as well as her continued interest in this project. I am also grateful to Bernard Jankie and the staff of the African-Caribbean Institute of Jamaica for access to the Jamaica Memory Bank material. Thanks also to the literary executors of Louise Bennett-Coverley for their permission to quote from her poem "Amy Son".

Many others over the years have offered suggestions and encouragement, including Bridget Brereton, Mike Conniff, Marguerite Curtin, Fred Hickling, Hilary Hickling, Richard Hilton, Rita Hilton, Denise Inglis, Annette Insanally, Keith Lowe, Ifeoma Kiddoe Nwankwo, Leah Rosenburg, Norma Stanley. Several were helpful at various stages of my research but did not live to see the ending, among them Neville Hall, Mary Hanna, Fay Harrison, Herman McKenzie, Ann Spackman of Jamaica, Oscar Savage and George Westerman of Panama.

Thanks as ever to my agent Daphne Hart, to Linda Speth, director of the University of the West Indies Press, Shivaun Hearne, editorial and production manager, and the rest of the team, as well as book designer Robert Harris, for their creativity and commitment in bringing this project to fruition.

A NOTE ON TERMINOLOGY

THE TERM "CARIBBEAN" IS WIDELY used today in identifying the islands and Central American territories surrounding the Caribbean Sea. In this book I have used the term "West Indies", which was current during the period covered. In the past, "Caribbean" was used to denote the entire region and its varied language groups, while "West Indies" was the term used for the English-speaking islands.

Figure 1.1 Opening lower guard gates, Miraflores Locks, Panama Canal. (Courtesy of William P. McLaughlin, www.czimages.com.)

1. "TO SHRINK THE WORLD BY HALF"

The Chagres has never gone anywhere, but it has seen just about everything. . . .
Then, when George Washington Goethals had finished his locks and ditches and
dams, the Chagres sent its water plunging in, to grow into the lakes, to surge
through the turbines, to fill the locks, to raise and lower ships, to shrink the world
by half.

  —John Easter Minter, *The Chagres: River of Westward Passage.*

AT EXACTLY 2:00 P.M. on 10 October 1913, the president of the United States
pushed a button in Washington to send a telegraphic signal that triggered a
massive explosion in another country two minutes later and some 1,850 miles
away. It was not a signal to start a war but to signify the near ending of one:
a battle of man versus nature that had been raging for four centuries across
the strip of land now known as the Isthmus of Panama. What President
Woodrow Wilson signalled was America's triumph in accomplishing the
world's greatest feat of engineering: the successful construction of the Panama
Canal. Amazingly, the canal was completed within the deadline established
ten years earlier. The total cost was to be $375 million,[1] more than double the
$135 million projected in 1903, but no one was complaining. One writer
estimated that it cost American citizens $4 per head.[2] In terms of manpower,
it cost the lives of 350 white Americans and 4,500 non-American lives, mainly
black workers, as recorded by the hospitals, though countless other deaths
went unrecorded.[3]

  The actual opening of the canal was still some months away but that took
place only two weeks after a real war was declared in Europe, so the passage of
the first ship through the Panama Canal on 15 August 1914 was something of
an anticlimax. It was the October 1913 event that attracted the world's attention. Crowding the east bank of the canal was the vast army of workers who
had made it possible, along with a significant portion of the population of
Panama, American politicians, international journalists and tourists. They had

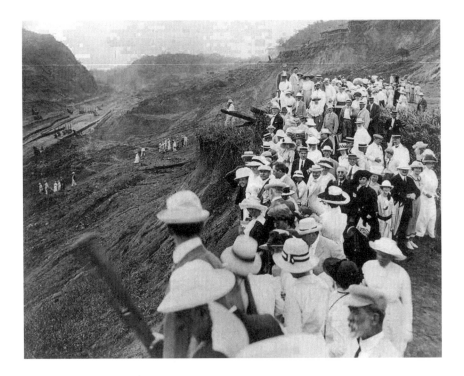

Figure 1.2 Tourists in Culebra Cut, February 1914. (Courtesy of William P. McLaughlin, www.czimages.com.)

made the ten-year-long construction project one of their must-see sights, arriving on the trains called the "rubberneck specials".[4]

On 10 October 1913, all eyes were on the deep nine-mile ditch or "cut" that had been dug through the mountain at Culebra to channel the water that would flow when the president's signal blew up Gamboa dike across Gatún Lake, which had held back the waters of the volatile Chagres River. Tamed and buttoned up in a man-made lake the size of the island of Barbados, then led into manageable channels, with three pairs of mighty lock gates set along the length of the canal to regulate its flow, this torrent would be the last mighty gush for a river that had fought savagely against human encroachment. So it had been ever since 1513 when Europeans – in the person of Vasco Núñez de Balboa – encountered a western ocean, later called the Pacific. So it had been ever since newcomers began to traverse the dangerous passage across the narrow neck of land dividing the Pacific from the Atlantic, later called the Gold Road. And so it was ever since visionaries began to dream of creating a passage for ships through the narrow strip of land connecting North and South America.

The excitement on that October day was palpable: the event would be captured in photographs and breathless prose on the front pages of newspapers everywhere. But the mood most comes alive in the words of one who had worked on the actual construction. Edgar Young, an American engineer, recalled,

It was Sunday morning late in the Fall. Every man who was not actually working at the time gathered along the Cut to see the water go through. . . . I remember the bottom of the Cut that morning, three hundred feet wide and flat with a deep drainage-ditch in the exact centre. . . . A yawning gash nine miles long and over six hundred feet deep at Gold Hill, a great scar into the very vitals of Nature.

Everyone held their breath. Many held pocket watches in their hands, mesmerized by the second hand moving to zero hour.

Boom! Boom! Boom-boom! Boom-boom-boom! came the muffled reports of the dynamite bombs that had been placed along the face of Gamboa dike. The water shot upward in a foaming cataract, visible for miles. Then came the coffee-colored flood raging through the Cut.

Cheer on cheer. Men were screaming mad with joy. Their shouts welded together in a mighty roar that echoed above the roar of water tearing through the Cut. Their cries ran the full length of Culebra and back again many times.

To the reverberating human cries the great mechanical voices of industry lent their sounds:

The great sirens on the power-houses were booming as hysterical men yank, yank, yanked on the ropes until arms grew numb and they tied them down to blow until steam ebbed from the mighty boilers. Ships of all nations lying in the harbors of Colón and Panama were giving tongue to their joy in huge blasts, tugs in the channels, five hundred locomotives along the P.R.R., every industrial plant in Colón and Panama, pleasure launches, everything that boasted a whistle was lending volume to the roar that rose in a crescendo to the very heavens and echoed back again and again.[5]

Figure 1.3 Gamboa dike explodes, 10 October 1913 (Panama Canal).

Among the actors and witnesses – but largely ignored in the stories pouring out of Panama into newspapers and in the hundreds of books written afterwards – stood one vital component that had made canal construction possible: West Indians who provided at least 60 per cent of the workforce for the entire construction period, part of the vast army of workers from ninety-seven different countries. When the dike exploded that morning, some thirty-eight thousand West Indians were still on the job. Few left written records of this momentous event; when they did, their pride was evident.

Daniel T. Lawson, a Jamaican who had started work on the canal in 1906, recorded his role as an assistant to the man who spliced the submarine cable between Panama and America, enabling the push button operation to work. Lawson's low-key narrative embodies the palpable pride of every man who had ever worked on the canal, sprayed with mud, drenched with rain, covered in dust almost every day of their working lives.

> My boss, learning that a special train was to have ran on the occasion for the white Americans entreat me to board the train with tool bag and other pieces of tools. It was a packed train, I had was to stand between two coaches on the platform. I was not opposed. The great Governor Goethals was on the scene, thousands of spectators with wrist watches and cameras were all alert watching and waiting for the final minute, the specified time was less than two minutes, then the blast, water and dirt were hurled into the air, coming down spraying everybody in its wake.[6]

Charles Booth who operated star drills proudly remembered that on the day they blasted the dike, "one of the great man of U.S.A. send me Chas Booth, an 2 others" to make fast the cable to a flood pipe at the bottom of the canal; the men ran back up as the water gushed forth while "on top of the bank of the canal they catch our pitchur".[7] Wesley Clarke, standing in another location, "watched the water coming down looking for it to come with plenty power but it didn't. It took its own time and came down gradually."[8]

To the Americans present and those at home, the successful completion of the canal confirmed their belief in their country as the world's greatest superpower. On the official opening, the cable from Washington to General George Goethals, the man in charge, captured the collective feeling that "a perpetual memorial to the genius and enterprise of our people has been created".

Yet to many West Indians and Panamanian residents, the end of construction still came as something of a surprise. Some believed the work would never end; others seriously doubted that they would ever see water in the cut. They had good reason for scepticism, for as one worker said of the most formidable work at Culebra, "today you dig and it grow tomorrow beside it slides every day the Government wash down the hill give it a bath night and day until the hill catch cramp then blass it up with dannimite".[9] George Martin confessed long afterwards that,

> while working, some of our good bosses would find some encouraging talk for us, they would say to us, boys, are you saving your money, it won't be long from now, we will see water into the Cut, but we just take it for a joke.
>
> I personally would say to my fellow men, that could never happen, my children would come and have children, and their children would come and do the same, before you would see water in the Cut, and most all of us agree on the same.[10]

John Prescod humorously recalled how "Big Boss Mr. Hagon say who the hell tell you to put that machine up there   take it down   Canal is finish. I say what the heel I am going to do now   no money only the pay check that coming   now one man in the gang eating flour dumplin drop out of his mouth   what sir!   the canal finish   I have no money."[11] (The spaces used in place of punctuation were replicated in the original transcription and have been retained throughout.)

Figure 1.4
Jamaicans operating a compressed air drill (Abbot, *Panama*, 209).

Long-time residents in what became the Canal Zone had watched bemused as this new set of strangers came in to again attempt the impossible. The oldest had seen the French, under Ferdinand de Lesseps, attempt for years to dig a canal and fail, and they had no greater confidence in the Americans. When the villagers of Gatún were warned that they would have to move because their village would soon be submerged by a man-made lake, many refused to believe it, saying the French had told them the same stories thirty years before.[12] One old man confidently said that his village would not be flooded since the Lord had promised to send no more floods.[13] On the opening of the canal, Mrs Mary Couloote, a St Lucian at Miraflores, recorded almost casually how "my husband was working at the tunel and I use to do sewing for people at home, then it happen a white man came and give every body notice that we have to live for the water is coming throw the canal and I move to Panama [City] the year of 1914".[14]

While the "ditch diggers" from the islands were proud of the part they had played and had cheered at each successful demonstration, they were enveloped in sadness too. Each step towards completing the canal represented for them a step closer to unemployment and displacement. On the Canal Zone, not only were the actual workers affected, but so were the large settlements of those who did not necessarily work for the Panama Canal but whose lives were closely bound up with its activities. There were peasant farmers, petty traders, higglers and artisans – barbers, shoemakers, tailors, seamstresses, domestic workers, photographers, teachers and preachers, doctors, pharmacists, businessmen large and small. As the canal neared completion and the floodwaters came, they were forced to abandon everything – their homes, farms, churches, schools, villages, so as to start life afresh elsewhere. By 1913, all settlements on the west bank of the canal were abandoned.

Those who stayed on in Panama were to look back on construction days as their best times on the Canal Zone, for while the United States had accomplished the world's greatest feat of engineering, the man in the bottom of the ditch had a different perspective: "The completion of the water way Brought great Desolation on the W.I. Employees. Some of us were transferred to other places. others were Sent Home to different Islands. The wage small during the Canal Conscruction was so small that we could not put by any saving in the Bank hence the majority of ous left Empty handed. to lived or die. of which many died from a weak heart."[15] Prince George Green, who had been a driver for Governor Goethals on his yellow inspection car, observed with some bitterness in 1954, the year of his retirement from the Panama Canal, that "I live to See the foundation we have laid down become a living paradise for those who are enjoying life to its heights on the Canal Zone today, while we who

Figure 1.5 Delivering ice to the cold-storage plant at Cristóbal, 1910 (Panama Canal).

laboured as hard as hell to help complete it can only pass through and look at it and say I have worked here and there in the construction of the Canal".[16]

Sadder commentaries came from other letters written by former workers and entered in the competition for the best "true stories" of construction days fifty years after the canal opened. St Lucian Albert Banister wrote in the midst of a largely enthusiastic narrative: "on account of high cost of living I am not in a possition of a little money to perchase writing paper to write all that I remember. I there-fore beg Uncle Sammy to remember the disability releaf retirree . . . we will soon dead out but while we alive please give us a little to eat."[17] And Clifford Hunt (who came in 1906) inscribed what might be called "The Lament of the Old Construction Worker":

> I work with ever thing that come to put thrue the Canal   Men in my gang tell the Boss I am going out to ease my bowels and they die in the bush and nobody look for you   I cry sometimes to see how I work to put this Canal through   up to now they don't pay us no mine today men are walking in and have everything sweet   I am one up to the time they retire me in 1950 and the little small pension we are dying for Starvation. but I ask God to open you all hearts and have mercy on us.[18]

As Prince George Green concluded, "most of us come here with the same spirit as a Soldier going to war." As in a war, some returned home heroes – or paupers; some remained and continued work on the canal or elsewhere in Panama; some went to other places where new jobs beckoned; many died or simply disappeared, and some remained broken forever, many suffering from what is now called post-traumatic stress disorder.

Nevertheless, over the years, the construction had also seen a vast movement of people back and forth between Panama and the islands as workers arrived

Figure 1.6 West Indian bakers at work (Panama Canal).

Figure 1.7 Casting concrete (Panama Canal).

and stayed for longer or shorter periods. While uncounted numbers died or contracted debilitating disease or lost limbs, sight or sense in the frenzied atmosphere where the only deity was work, many islanders were to use work on the Panama Canal to better themselves, acquiring skills and funds to set them on the ladder to upward social mobility back home.

PANAMA GOLD

Long contact with Panama had embedded in the West Indian imagination the notion of that location as a source of gold. Starting with the Spanish conquistadores, continuing with buccaneers such as Henry Morgan bringing plunder to Jamaica's "wicked city" of Port Royal, the dreams of adventurers who sailed from the West Indian islands down to the Spanish Main had always been sustained by the myth of El Dorado.[19] Poverty-stricken working men and women, all those heading to the isthmus this time around, were also driven by that ancient dream: they too would lay their hands on "Panama Money".

On the American canal, West Indians did not sing of gold: they were paid in Panamanian silver, gold being reserved for white Americans. But they did sing of Panama as a place where "money grew like apples on a tree". Back home on the islands, the icon of the times was Jamaica's strutting "Colón Man" or the "Panama Man" of Barbados. "I love you, yes I do, you know it's true", the young troubadours of Barbados sang as they wielded their pick-axes or shifted a train track.

> I'm going to Panama to work and send for you.
> And when you come to Panama how happy you will be
> Cause money's down in Panama like apples on a tree.[20]

The construction of the Panama Canal (1904–14) and its maintenance thereafter was in fact the third industrial undertaking in that country to be built by West Indian labour. Jamaicans had provided much of the workforce for the Panama Railroad Company (1850–55) and were joined by other West Indians for the French effort spearheaded by de Lesseps to construct the Panama Canal (1881–89). These workers, followed by their families and others, led to the development of large enclaves of British subjects in the heart of Latin America. The flood of work-hungry West Indians began in the nineteenth century and continued as opportunities opened up: they spread to Costa Rica, Honduras, Mexico, Brazil, Guatemala, Ecuador and finally on to Cuba when that country surpassed the British islands as the world's largest sugar producer. Emigrants also flowed into the United States until checked by restrictive legislation in 1924 and the economic downturn caused by the Great

Depression. This epic of migration was to continue in cycles with large movements later to England, Canada and the United States: today, more West Indians live overseas than at home, many pushed and pulled by the same factors that were operating in their great-grandfathers' time.

So fifty years before the American canal builders arrived, a flood from the islands had already begun that would soon expand into a tide as rich, as challenging and as volatile as the Chagres River, a tide that the West Indian plantation owners and the British authorities tried in vain to hold back, a tide that flowed into a convenient pool from which the growing capitalist construction projects throughout Latin America could pluck cheap labour and baptize in a nascent globalized culture. Especially during the US canal construction, Panama became the mothership for all these later journeys, riding the crest of a "demographic tidal wave" of an estimated 150,000 to 200,000 islanders pouring in.[21]

This narrative, then, tells the story of the building of the Panama Canal from the other side, the underside. It tells of the impact on the islanders who supplied the manpower and the impact on their homelands. So many young men of reproductive age came from the islands and British mainland territories that the construction of the Panama Canal might be called the most effective birth-control device of its times. The birth rate in the islands fell and continued to do so until the 1920s; when large numbers of emigrants returned home, the birth rates soared. That effect was only one consequence of the huge emigration beginning in the second half of the nineteenth century to Panama and elsewhere in Central and South America which resulted in a net loss to the islands of a quarter million people. Viewed within the worldwide movement of peoples, this appears minuscule, until seen as a ratio of total population which, in 1911, was below two million.[22] Or when viewed another way, it can be seen as a flood of West Indian migrants into Central American territories that were then undeveloped and sparsely populated.

For the islanders, "going to Panama" was the greatest event of its time, imprinting itself on the consciousness of a generation. Today, it conjures up vague images of "gold", "fever", and a grandfather, great-uncle or -aunt who went there, some to be lost forever to family narratives, some returning enriched, and others remembered only for the snakeskin or alligator-skin bags they brought back along with their gold teeth and seemingly tall tales.[23]

Yet the story of West Indians' connection to Panama and the construction projects which ended with the Panama Canal is truly an epic, filled with superlatives, with peaks and shadows and larger-than-life heroes. As with all epics, however, we must ask ourselves: Where do the tall tales end and the real stories begin?

GEOGRAPHY SHAPES HISTORY

For Panama, shape is destiny. The narrow waist of land called the isthmus was immediately attractive to the first European men who crossed it, their eyes gleaming with the possibilities of trans-global trade. A scant eleven years after the Spanish Balboa discovered the land bridge linking the Atlantic and Pacific Oceans, discussion began of cutting a canal across it. In 1524 the Holy Roman Emperor Charles V of Spain commissioned a survey to establish its feasibility but his successor, the more religious-minded Philip II, concluded that piercing the land in such a manner would be sacrilege. As a Jesuit scholar had advised, "I believe there is no humaine power able to beate and breake downe those strong and impenetrable Mountains, which God hath placed betwixt the two Seas." Even if men were able to do so, "they should fear punishment from heaven, in seeking to correct the works" of the Creator.[24] When the subject was raised again by scientists in the nineteenth century, preachers continued to thunder at the sacrilegious nature of an interoceanic canal, warning, "What God has joined together, let no man put asunder." So it seemed there was some defiance in the motto adopted by the Panama Canal Company in 1913 and triumphantly carved on the administration building in the Canal Zone: "The land divided the world united."

Panama's importance derives from its geographic location but its orientation can be somewhat confusing. The Isthmus of Panama is the narrowest point on the land bridge connecting North and South America but it does not run north–south. Curled like a flattened letter S, it runs east–west and so must be crossed from north to south. Thus the Caribbean Sea (Chagres, Colón) lies to the north and the Pacific Ocean (Panama City, Balboa) lies to the south. This is why in 1513 Vasco Núñez de Balboa named it the South Sea, and why the Panama Railroad and the Panama Canal run not east to west, as some imagine, but north to south.

The Panama Canal was not the first "watery link" between the oceans as some suppose. Millennia ago, North and South America were totally separate

Figure 1.8
"The Kiss of the Oceans", 1915, one of a series of popular posters and postcards celebrating the opening of the Panama Canal (author's collection).

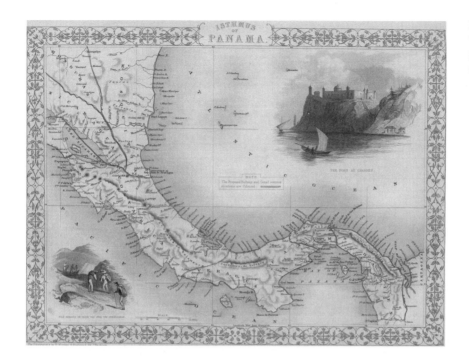

Map 1.1
The Isthmus of
Panama (Wikimedia
Commons).

and the waters of the Atlantic and Pacific Oceans mingled freely. The first epic event associated with Panama, then, was the creation of the isthmus itself, the narrow strip of land connecting two continents. Over millions of years, underwater volcanic activity and plate tectonics had been throwing up islands that eventually emerged above the sea and continued to grow from geological convulsions. Massive amounts of sediment from North and South America filled the gaps between the islands and, about three million years ago, the Isthmus of Panama assumed its present form.

Scientists regard the formation of this land bridge as one of the most significant geological events of the last sixty million years. It separated the oceans, rerouted ocean currents in both the Atlantic and Pacific and established their present pattern, including the Gulf Stream. The isthmus greatly affected global climate, including the formation of an Arctic ice cap. Finally, by facilitating the passage of plants and animals between the north and the south, it affected biogeography, causing the astonishing biodiversity of the Americas.[25] The geologic upheavals had also thrown up a formidable mountain range that combined with equatorial heat to create what was considered the wettest place on earth, the rain supporting festering jungles and feeding volatile rivers like the Chagres, which made the creation of any kind of crossing seem an impossible task.

The Panama Canal construction crews were to find ample confirmation of the oceanic and geologically disturbed origins of the country through which they were digging the big ditch, such as fossils and seashells and coral on hilltops. The most treasured find for a West Indian worker on the canal works was

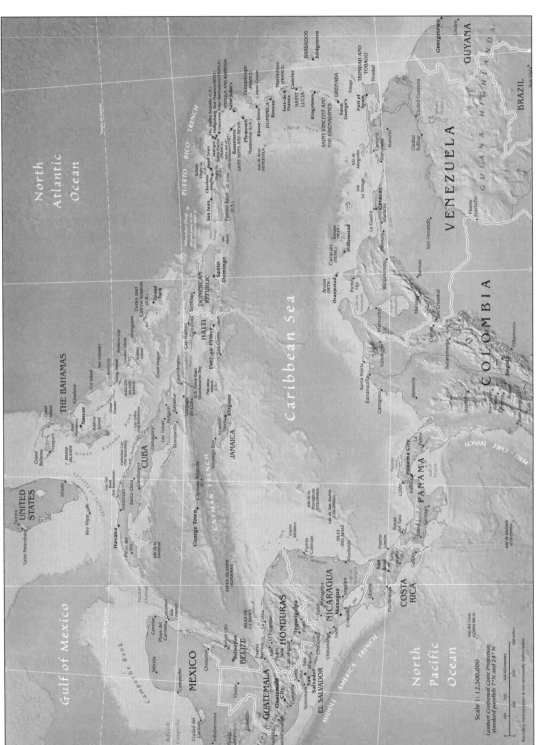

Map 1.2 The Caribbean Basin (CIA, *The World Factbook 2013–14*, https://www.cia.gov/library/publications/the-world-factbook/docs/refmaps.html)

a shark's tooth, which could be mounted in gold and hung from his fob watch chain as a talisman. Reginald Beckford, a jeweller, was at first sceptical when construction workers brought him sharks' teeth which they said had been taken out of a rock in the Culebra diggings. But he did in time come to mount many of these teeth in gold. He described them as "large, the size of a man's wrist watch in diameter, and larger".[26]

THE ANTILLEAN ARC

That West Indians should pour into Panama seeking work is not surprising. While to most nineteenth-century North Americans the lands of Central America betokened dark and unknown territory, these coasts were long familiar to the islanders, associated with romanticized tales of pirate sorties, military derring-do and fabulous treasure, all part of conquest, settlement and rivalries among the European powers.

But much earlier, the Antillean arc in the Caribbean Sea provided a prehistoric bridge to continental America, the islands emerging as stepping stones to the Central American mainland, or what became known in the West Indies as the Spanish Main. Biogeographers have concluded that "the earliest Palaeolithic societies to disperse throughout the New World were perfectly capable of navigating from proximate points on the mainland to every Caribbean island, and back . . . only modest navigational skills would have been needed to follow rhumb lines traced by flocks of migrating waterfowl".[27]

We do know that those indigenous inhabitants of the Caribbean who entered "history" at the time of Columbus's arrival, the Kalinago or Carib and the Taino, were noted for their sea-going canoes and seamanship. Long before European penetration, they had made themselves masters of the seas between the islands and the American mainland where, indeed, they are believed to have originated.

For several hundred years after European settlement, the Caribbean Sea would be as busy with watercraft as the Mediterranean Sea to which it is likened: from dugout canoes to trading sloops to men-o'-war and laden treasure ships assembling in convoy to sail across the Atlantic and from pirate ships to those of merchant marines and navies. And above all, there plied the unmistakable slave ships, bringing millions of captured Africans across the Atlantic for forced labour on the New World plantations. Construction of the Panama Railroad began only twelve years after the ending of black slavery on the British islands in 1838.[28] The first migrant workers would have included many of the formerly enslaved and their descendants, with nothing to sell but their labour power.

Figure 1.9 "Balboa taking possession of the Pacific Ocean", eighteenth-century Spanish engraving (Wikimedia Commons).

West Indian connections with Panama then did not begin at this time but might be considered part of an endless Antillean conveyor belt for plants, animals and humans. As historian Franklin Knight was to observe, "In days of sailing ships, the transit from Europe or Africa to the Americas could not be done without first calling at some Caribbean port or the other. . . . The early Caribbean gave to the mainland colonists a steady supply of people, not only of European origin, but also from Africa and Asia."[29] It is within this long history of migration in the Caribbean basin that the story of the West Indian workers on the Panama Canal should be understood.

Written records of these connections date back to Balboa's effort to reach the Pacific Ocean almost exactly four hundred years before the blowing up of Gamboa dike. In view of the future development of the isthmus as attracting a polyglot, multicultural population, it is perhaps symbolically significant that the European adventurer was led there by native Americans and that a man of African descent, Núflo de Olano, stood beside him at that critical moment.

European mapping of the isthmian coast had begun with Columbus and his fellow conquistadores, to be followed by conquest and settlement. Jamaica was strategically situated as a take-off point for many of these excursions to the Spanish Main and remained the connecting point between Central America and Europe until the nineteenth century. The seminal document of Latin American liberation, "Carta de Jamaica" by Simón Bolívar, an early proponent of an interoceanic canal, was written while he was in exile in that country in 1815.[30] The island served as a strategic location and communications hub for the wars of Spanish-American independence.

Willis J. Abbot listed the Port of Kingston as "the front door to Panama".[31] Jamaica lies only 550 miles north-east of Colón, Panama, and a fast-sailing ship could make the journey in about a week, helped by the prevailing trade winds. However, the return journey meant beating up against the wind, and could take as long as six weeks. Steamships reduced the time during canal construction to thirty-six hours.

When Jamaica was a Spanish colony, the island served as a provision depot for the conquistadores travelling to and from the Spanish Main, supplying horses and meat, cassava bread, and lard. Among those provisioned by the colonists was Balboa himself, though it is claimed that he never did pay for the supplies. By 1521 Jamaica was supplying meat to the new colony of Panama,[32] which in time would become the funnel for all the goods that would flow between Spain and its colonies. Excepting Brazil, which belonged to Portugal, Spain's New World empire would stretch from present-day Texas in North America to Patagonia in South America and included most of the Caribbean islands.

The Panama Railroad and later the canal were to exploit a route which existed from these times, the so-called Gold Road. Spanish treasure ships laden with gold, silver, pearls and other riches sailed from Callao in Peru to the Pacific city of Panama. There the treasure was loaded on to hundreds of pack mules for the journey across the isthmus on the overland trail which became known as the Gold Road and ended at Cruces on the Chagres River. Here, the precious shipments were again transferred – from the mule train on to the flat-bottomed boats (from that time called *bungos*) – to be poled down the river to the Caribbean port of Chagres guarded by Fort San Lorenzo. At Chagres, the goods were loaded on to the treasure ships which then sailed a few miles

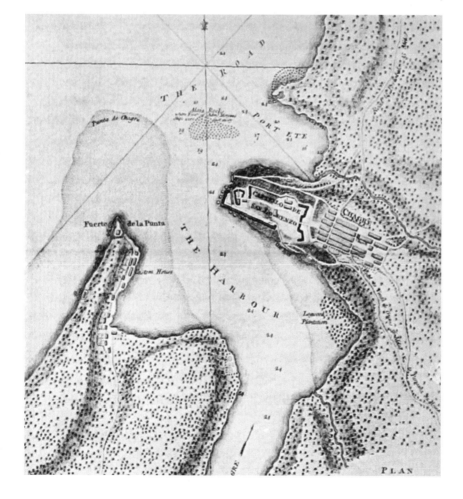

Map 1.3 Plan of Chagres showing the river mouth and the fort guarding it (Wikimedia Commons).

Figure 1.10
Fort San Lorenzo overlooking Chagres guarded the trade route between 1626 and 1741 (Weir, *Conquest of the Isthmus*, 50).

down the coast to Portobello, to travel in heavily guarded convoys (called the Plate Fleet) across the ocean to Seville. Every moment of the Chagres route was perilous.

Spain's power was challenged by the English, French and Dutch, who all encouraged piracy to further their national interests. Panama's wealth and location made it a favourite target. The Jamaican city of Port Royal became a hub for contraband trade and a base for privateering raids. The island had its own sloop fleet of about one hundred in 1679. By the 1680s, Port Royal was the busiest port in the English Caribbean, attracting close to two hundred ships a year.[33] It was from Port Royal that buccaneer Henry Morgan sailed to attack Spanish settlements on the isthmus, taking Portobello in 1668. Lacking enough men to storm the fortress, he sent nuns and monks captured in the town to ascend the scaling ladders first and take the brunt of the assault. Two years later, he again headed for Chagres and marched his men across the Gold Road to sack the city of Panama, or what was left of it after a violent attacks, flight of the inhabitants, fire and pillage lasting nearly a month. Morgan's nine-day march to Panama is a classic example of the hazardous nature of the isthmus crossing, even to hardened pirates, as described by Alexandre-Olivier Exquemelin, the starving men reduced to eating their boot leather.[34] Even more alarming to the Spaniards was the attempt in the 1690s by some four thousand Scots to establish a beachhead on the isthmus at Darién, on the Caribbean coast, to be referred thereafter as the "Darién Disaster".[35] The aim was to set up a wealthy colony as the centre of global trade using the land bridge linking the oceans, but the adventure ended in the deaths of most of the colonists from starvation and disease. Scotland went bankrupt, a disaster which led to the union with England in 1707. While England and Spain were at peace for a while (during which England had failed to help the Darién colonists), England continued to cast envious eyes at the isthmus and its control of the route to Pacific trade. English incursions continued with the attempt by Admiral Edward Vernon to take Portobello in 1739. After this, the Spanish colonists abandoned the Panama route and the Plate Fleet started to sail around Cape Horn, leading to the decline of Panama City, once one of the richest in the New World. Panama was now attached to the Vice-Royalty of New Granada in Bogotá, Colombia.

Figure 1.11 Pirate Henry Morgan. (Courtesy of the National Library of Jamaica.)

Constant traffic between Jamaica and Central America continued by way of locally built sailing ships of small tonnage belonging to logwood cutters, turtle fishermen and the like, some of whom formed permanent settlements on this coast and on the islands of San Andres and Providencia. The fact, too, that English settlements along the Bay of Campeche were for a short time under the jurisdiction of the governor of Jamaica further facilitated Jamaican–Central American contacts.

Over the centuries too, Jamaican fishermen made their way westwards in ever increasing numbers, establishing coastal settlements in Panama (Bocas del Toro), Nicaragua (Miskito coast), the Talamanca coast of Costa Rica, among others.[36] The Bocas settlement, one of the earliest, dates from the early eighteenth century, at least, and originally consisted of turtle fishermen, some of whom later settled Talamanca.[37] There are also legends on this coast of settlements of shipwrecked enslaved Africans escaping from Jamaica.[38]

By the early eighteenth century, the route between Jamaica and the English settlements on the Caribbean coast of America had become a well-beaten path for illicit trade with the Spanish colonists. When such trade became legal by peace treaty in 1766, Jamaica became a free port and trade increased rapidly after the Napoleonic Wars. British businessmen rushed to establish offices in Kingston and it was as a trans-shipment port that Kingston at this time recorded its greatest period of activity. Convoys of schooners, sloops and brigs would assemble at Port Royal or Negril to sail under the protection of British men-o'-war for the Atlantic ports of Rio de la Hacha, Portobello, Chagres or Santa Marta to cash in on the Latin American markets.[39]

However, as the Spanish colonies began to secure their independence in the early nineteenth century, they were free to trade elsewhere and these business connections were reduced, especially since the Jamaican merchants had on the whole supported the Royalists in the independence struggles. Some merchants moved to establish their base in the city of Panama, situated on the Pacific route serviced by British steamships. But the bulk of Panama's trade continued to be with Jamaica,[40] leaving behind in both countries strong business connections. Thus, from earliest times there was constant sea traffic between the West Indies and Panama, and Jamaican fishermen, seamen and traders were as familiar with these ports as were their Latin counterparts with the northern Caribbean, or those of Barbados and the islands to the south with the eastern Caribbean and South American mainland.[41] However, all these early connections between the West Indies and Central America were based strictly on plunder, trade and social intercourse, cemented by settlement and marriage ties. It was not until the mid-nineteenth century with the birth of venture capitalism and the incursion of the United States into Central America that the first efforts were made to attract wage labour from the islands.

PART 1

THE PANAMA RAILROAD

"Its principal asset was hope."

—*Tracy Robinson,* Panama: A Personal Record of Forty-six Years, 1861–1907

Figure 2.1 The Panama Railroad train steams through the jungle with monkeys in the trees and crocodiles in the swampy ground (Wikipedia).

2. THE PANAMA RAILROAD, 1849–1855

It is true to say that, in Panama, all the forces that drove the world at the end of the 19th century converged – a scientific revolution and an intensified industrial revolution, a transportation revolution, mobility of capital and labour, and the expansion of world commerce. The assertion of imperial power by the United States succeeded in converting the Caribbean definitively into its fifth frontier, and opened the door to China.

—Patrick Bryan, "The Background to the Canal", *Regional Footprints.*

THE "DOOR TO CHINA" IS what Columbus sought when he sailed westward in 1492 and encountered the Americas instead. It took another four hundred years for America to insert the key that opened that door: the Panama Canal. The initial step in that direction, however, was not to China but to the city guarded by a Golden Gate: San Francisco. Through pure serendipity, the California gold rush coincided with the construction of a railroad across the isthmus. The subsequent tide of gold-seeking passengers made the railroad's completion possible, adding drama and excitement to what started as a purely commercial enterprise. The Panama Railroad in turn would provide the means to move the men and material that facilitated the successful construction of the Panama Canal.

Both the railroad and the canal were linked by the same factors: the application of American finance capital and technology to Latin America and the provision of labour largely by West Indians. And both enterprises, on the surface, offered one of the main staples of robust romance: man versus the elements. Man ultimately was the winner. But not before Nature in all its fullness laughed and clawed and chomped and spat out the bones of many of those who dared to challenge it.

Over the centuries, private groups as well as nations had made proposals for a railroad or canal across the isthmus. Survey parties set out from time to time, across Mexico, Nicaragua and Panama, some to be lost forever. By 1850,

United States interest in such a route marked the growing stature of a young nation less than eighty years old. America's raw New World energy would – in time – eclipse the Old and shift to itself the balance of power in Latin America previously held by Europe.

Britain, the last remaining European power in the region, had sought to safeguard its Central American interests by establishing settlements in Nicaragua, one of the countries vying for the construction of a canal. But American diplomatic action in Colombia had already given it the advantage. Colombia was then called the Republic of New Granada, one of several countries that had freed themselves from Spain under the leadership of Simón Bolívar and united as the Colombian confederation.[1] Panama was the sparsely settled, northernmost province of New Granada, with the impassable Darién jungles barring the way to the mountain capital of Bogotá, at eighty-seven hundred feet one of the most inaccessible cities in the world. No roads connected them. Communication was by sea, then by boat for nine days on the Magdalena River from Barranquilla to Honda, a tiny village, followed by three more days by horseback, mule or wagon.[2] The journey could take three to four weeks. Panama residents, oriented to the sea, chafed under this remote connection to the centre, and revolutionary and separatist activities flared up from time to time, to be fully exploited later by American interests.

The Frenchman Philippe Bunau-Varilla, whose intrigue contributed greatly to the separation of Panama from Colombia and the negotiation of a new treaty in favour of the United States in 1903, was to write of Bogotá that "the echoes of the outer world that arrived thither were all weakened by distance". He claimed: "All foreign questions appear at Bogotá to be purely theoretical, abstract and remote . . . without any regard for tangible realities and their material consequences."[3]

This attitude might have contributed to the signing in 1846 of a treaty between the United States and the government in Bogotá, negotiated by a new American chargé d'affaires, Benjamin A. Bidlack. In exchange for guaranteeing the "perfect neutrality" of the Isthmus of Panama and New Granada's sovereignty over it, the United States secured the right of free and uninterrupted transit from sea to sea across the isthmus, a concession of land over four hundred square miles. Events would soon show just what a prize the Bidlack-Mallarino treaty was. Britain's annoyance at this intervention in what it considered its sphere of interest[4] was mollified by the Clayton-Bulwer treaty of 1850 it signed with the United States by which both countries agreed they would cooperate in building and controlling jointly a Central American trans-isthmian canal.

Over the next fifty years, however, an increasingly belligerent United States challenged that treaty, citing "manifest destiny" and the Monroe Doctrine.[5]

Finally by signing the Hay-Pauncefote treaty in 1901, which gave the United States exclusive rights to any trans-isthmian canal, Britain acknowledged its reduced influence in Latin America and the rise of the new world power.

America's interests in a passage across Central America were strategic as well as commercial. Thanks to the Mexican-American war (1848) California became the Pacific rim of the United States, now a vast country extended between two oceans. To travel the thirteen thousand miles from New York to San Francisco by sea took three months at least around the tip of South America via Cape Horn.[6] Until the opening of the transcontinental railroad in 1869, it took just as long to cross North America by land (an even more dangerous crossing than by sea). Wanting to speed up postal service, the US government offered subsidies to shipping companies to provide Atlantic as well as Pacific steamers linked by land passage across the isthmus.

The United States Mail Steamship Company undertook to provide two sailings monthly between New York and Chagres on the Caribbean coast of Panama, with stops at New Orleans and other ports. As there was hardly any western settlement, there was not much interest in taking up the offer for the Pacific side, with one monthly sailing from Panama City to Oregon and return. Then William H. Aspinwall, a wealthy New York entrepreneur and co-owner of a clipper ship service, stepped in and established the Pacific Mail Steamship Company, incorporated in 1848. A visionary who thought globally, Aspinwall had an interest in building fast ships to facilitate his trade connections around the world, which included China.[7]

Figure 2.2
William H.
Aspinwall (www
.panamarailroad.org).

Wall Street was at first not impressed by his latest move. The Pacific Mail Steamship Company, one writer sniffed, "was looked upon by the generality of businessmen as a sequestration of a large amount of property for an indefinite time, with a faint prospect of profit; and the wonder seemed to be that so sound a man as Mr. Aspinwall should have engaged in it".[8] But Aspinwall would end up making a fortune from this decision, for his real aim was to build a railroad across the isthmus linking ocean to ocean. In 1845 the New York State Legislature granted Aspinwall a charter for the formation of a joint stock company: the Panama Railroad Company.[9] In this enterprise he was assisted by John L. Stephens, an experienced Central American traveller. Stephens had discovered the half-buried Mayan city of Copán in Honduras, and he published the still highly rated book (with drawings by the artist Frederick Catherwood) *Incidents of Travel in Central America, Chiapas and Yucatan*. Returning to New York, Stephens developed an interest in steam navigation and was a director of the Ocean Steam Navigation Company, which built the first ship in the United States to utilize the new technology. In the 1840s Stephens had roamed off the beaten track surveying possible rail and canal routes, and he would guide Aspinwall in terrain that was new to the investor.

Figure 2.3
John L. Stephens
(www.panamarailroad
.org).

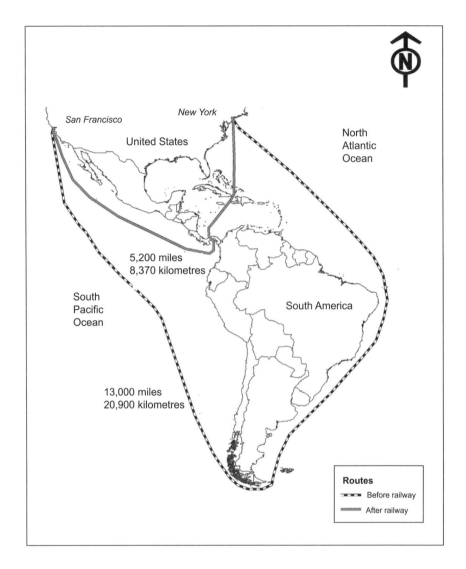

Map 2.1 Sketch map showing routes and approximate distances before the construction of the Panama Railroad and, later, the Canal across the Isthmus. (Map prepared by Thera Edwards, Department of Geography and Geology, University of the West Indies, Mona.)

San Francisco

New York

United States

North Atlantic Ocean

5,200 miles
8,370 kilometres

South Pacific Ocean

South America

13,000 miles
20,900 kilometres

Routes
Before railway
After railway

Fluent in Spanish, Stephens negotiated a contract with the government in Bogotá on the company's behalf for the concession to build the railroad across its territory. In 1848, Stephens was severely injured when he fell off a mule on the journey to Bogotá and conducted communications with the government while prone and immobile on a bed, in intense pain. He got back down to the coast lying on a specially designed cushioned chair, carried by bearers all the way to the steamer on the Cartagena River.[10] But this was a man who had fearlessly travelled off the beaten track throughout the world (having been advised by his doctor as a young man to travel for reasons of health), and he remained an active working director of the railroad, spending two years in Panama, living in a cottage he built on the bank of the Chagres, supervising surveys and overseeing preliminary work, until his death from fever in 1852, age forty-six. The third and lesser-known partner in the Panama Railroad Company was Henry L. Chauncey, said to be in the West Indian trade, operating out of Valparaiso, Chile. Although all three were men of vision and experience, little did they know what they were attempting in what would come to be called "the unhealthiest place on earth".

Relying on inefficient surveys, the promoters were overly optimistic regarding the task ahead; the thinking in 1850 was that the railroad could be built in six months at a cost of one million dollars, the amount of capital the company had raised. Instead, they found a seemingly bottomless morass that devoured men and money; a rainy season lasting from June to December with week-long cloudbursts; blistering heat between January and May; endless jungles devoid of timber that could be used for railway construction; no local labour; no food or shelter available. In short, everything would have to be imported: men, provisions and materials.

THE GOLD RUSH

Shortly after the United States took California from Mexico at the end of the Mexican-American War, an enormous gold strike was made at Sutter's Mill in January 1848, not far from the fledgling town of San Francisco. The news took some time to travel to America's east coast, and Aspinwall and the State of New York were unaware of it as they negotiated. Aspinwall formally chartered his Pacific Mail company in April of that year, and launched the first of his steamers in May with its departure for California via Cape Horn set for October. The *California,* like the two other ships to follow, was a wooden paddle-wheel steamer of some one thousand tons, and about two hundred feet in length, propelled by two boilers supplying steam, augmented by three sails. The small fleet was expected to maintain monthly mail service between Panama City and San Francisco, the mail from Oregon to be transported by other means to that city. Meanwhile George Law founded the US Mail Steamship Company to serve the Atlantic ports.

Figure 2.4
Advertisement aimed at the gold-rush traveller (Wikipedia).

To fulfil its contract, Law's company chartered the *Falcon*, a small steamer, to make the first run from New York to Chagres. It sailed with only twenty-nine passengers on 1 December 1848. While the *Falcon* was sailing down the Atlantic coast to Chagres and Aspinwall's *California* was making its way up the Pacific coast of South America, news of the fabled gold in

California finally spread back east, confirmed by President Polk in his State of the Union address on 5 December 1848. This fabulous wealth took tangible form when the War Office in Washington displayed a small chest with gold from the strike. America was instantly seized by gold fever. News travelled fast around the world, setting off a mad scramble for transportation. At the ports of New York and New Orleans, every imaginable object that floated would be pressed into service – fishing smacks, schooners, whalers, harbour boats or ferry tugs; shipyards abandoned all else but the building of the vessels that would take the seekers at least as far as Chagres where they would be left to make their way as best they could the fifty miles across the isthmus to Panama City on the Pacific. A later traveller described these packed ships as "floating herring boxes",[11] but the instant guide books to California and shipping company advertisements promised "a pleasant voyage to Panama, stroll across the fifty miles of Isthmus to the Pacific, and, after another easy sea voyage, find yourself in San Francisco".[12]

When the *Falcon* reached New Orleans it was overrun by California-bound gold seekers, who bullied the captain into packing them in. It sailed on 18 December 1848 – to be followed by others equally overcrowded – and dropped anchor about a mile offshore at Chagres on 27 December, unable to go further because of a sandbar at the mouth of the river. The sleepy little village came awake long enough for its more enterprising citizens to put off in boats to ferry about two hundred passengers from ship to shore, where they waded through the mud and stared about them, as dumbfounded perhaps as the locals were at the sight of these scruffy, bearded Yankee men laden with picks, shovels, bedding, money belts and chests to carry home the gold.[13] Neither spoke the other's language. "Panama!" the Americans shouted and pointed, trying to convey their need. Many carried rifles, pistols and bowie knives which they were not above using to force the *bungo* boatmen to pole them up the Chagres River which, they discovered, was the next stage of the journey. The arduous river passage of some thirty miles landed them at Gorgona, four and a half miles from Cruces, a journey possible by boat or on foot, depending on the season and the height of the river. From Cruces they took the overland trail by foot, mule, or seated on a *sillero*[14] for the twenty miles to Panama City, there to board a boat for California, the entire overland trip lasting (with luck) five to eight days. The trek across the isthmus would bring – for a few years at least – profit to those along the route who provided transport, food, and accommodation for the travellers.

Aspinwall's *California* was destined to be the first steamer on the next phase of this epic journey. The boat had sailed almost empty from New York three months earlier. Word of the discovery of gold had reached the captain at Callao in Peru, and some one hundred Peruvian gold seekers had boarded. Arriving in Panama City on 17 January 1849, the captain was stunned to find over a thousand passengers clamouring for passage – by then other boats had been discharging passengers at Chagres – and ordering him to get rid of the Peruvians.

The frenzied actions of these first travellers, overcome by their rush to get to the gold fields, prefigured a great deal of what would happen over the next few years. They besieged the ticket office, offered bribes or threatened physical harm to the ticket agents, smashed furniture, and fired guns into the ceilings. They even laid siege to the ship at anchor off the harbour island of Taboga, "boatloads of frantic supplicants waving money at the uniformed officers on the bridge. Occasionally, a group brave with alcohol would storm the rails of the ship. The mates and boatswains would grab clubs and belaying pins to fight them off. During these forays the water around the ship seethed with fully clothed men, gasping and splashing about, trying to claw up the side of the steamer or get back into their boats."[15]

The steamship agent held a lottery for tickets at two hundred dollars per passage (which winners willing to wait sold on to others for one thousand dollars). The *California* was registered to carry 150 passengers but in response to a message from Aspinwall to "crowd a little", it finally sailed with 365 passengers and 36 crew, setting the pace and standard for future voyages in which some passengers would even be bedded down in the lifeboats. The ending of the voyage is also instructive – stowaways were found and, along with some mutineers, put ashore before reaching San Francisco; the coal supply ran out and the ship was stripped of anything that could burn to feed the fire box. As the crippled ship entered San Francisco harbour a month after leaving Panama, 145 days from New York, the entire crew, except for one engine-room boy, joined the passengers in the rush to get off. It took the captain three months to assemble another crew.

By the end of May 1849, some four thousand passengers had been landed at Chagres by every device that could float, with the link between the US east coast and San Francisco now reduced to about forty days. Thousands were to keep coming back and forth – people from all over the world seduced by gold-lust. Among them were West Indians, some of whom had come looking for work on the Panama Railroad but kept on going until they too reached the golden shores of California. We have only glimpses of their experiences there, but there were enough of them to establish a community, as Errol

Figure 2.5 Men from every nation rushed to join the search for gold in California (Wikimedia Commons).

Hill noted from an 1874 advertisement in a San Francisco paper catering to the black community: "Belvedere and Brokins Party" to be given as soon as the first steamer arrived from Panama in September "with materials and fancy fixins".[16] "Bruckins Party" was an annual celebration by formerly enslaved Africans in Jamaica marking the emancipation of 1838.

THE START OF THE RAILROAD

Plans were executed and contracts for building the Panama Railroad were signed in 1849 with Colonel George M. Totten hired as chief engineer. The next year, on 20 May 1850, engineer John C. Trautwine and his assistant, James L. Baldwin, symbolically chopped down the first tree to begin construction, Colonel Totten being away on a recruiting mission. The chronicler of the railroad, F.N. Otis, presents this moment in romantic fashion: "Two American citizens, leaping axe in hand, from a native canoe upon a wild and desolate island, their retinue consisting of half a dozen Indians who clear the path with rude knives, strike their glittering axes into the nearest tree; the rapid blows reverberating from shore to shore, and the stately cocoa crashes upon the beach." Otis concluded: "Thus unostentatiously was announced the commencement of a railway which, from the interests and difficulties involved, might well be looked upon as one of the grandest and boldest enterprises ever attempted."[17]

Topography and climate presented the two biggest challenges to the fulfilment of man's dreams on the isthmus, divided as it is lengthwise by the central mountains of the Continental Divide with peaks rising to twelve thousand feet. From the cloud-capped mountain ridges, numerous rivers flow steeply to the coast, surges in the rainy season sometimes filling the narrow valleys and sweeping all before in sudden floods. The Chagres was the mightiest of the rivers flowing to the Caribbean and could rise fifty feet in a few hours in its narrow canyons and drop as rapidly; during the dry months it could become a trickle then suddenly turn into a roaring torrent from rain upstream. Panama's early reputation for having the highest average rainfall in the world comes from its mountainous nature and its location only nine degrees north of the equator. Heavy rainfall occurs

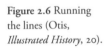

Figure 2.6 Running the lines (Otis, *Illustrated History*, 20).

from June to December when the sun is directly overhead and lifts warm water vapour, which then condenses in the cool upper atmosphere, returning to earth as rain. For over four centuries, the rainfall, rivers and the rugged jungle terrain had proved formidable obstacles to travellers, but their experience could be considerably modified if they attempted the crossing in the dry season from February to April, when the rich tropical verdure and scenic mountain backdrop, birds and exotic wildlife could bring forth cries of delight.[18] Yet few of those who crossed the isthmus in these times would have noticed or cared about the scenery. Until the opening of the railroad in 1855, the strip of land represented no more than a perilous obstacle to be crossed. When surveyors for the railroad found a gap in the mountains at Culebra of 286 feet, this feature largely determined the route of the railroad and later of the canal. The railroad surveys also put paid to the belief that there was a difference between the levels of the oceans. The difference lay in the height of the tides; up to 20 feet on the Pacific side but no more than a foot on the Caribbean.

From the Continental Divide the land falls steeply to the Pacific, ten miles away. The Caribbean side is wetter, low-lying and swampy near the coast. It was in this swamp that the Panama Railroad began. The engineers could not have chosen an unhealthier spot to plant a railroad than the one-square-mile Manzanillo Island. The name itself foreshadowed what was to come, for *manzanillo* in English is manchineel, a deadly tree of the coastal region of the Americas famous for its poisonous apples and its caustic milky sap. The latter can cause serious burns, blisters and even blindness, and many a pirate or castaway sailor died from eating the attractive "apples", fruit of the "poison tree". The native Indians used manchineel to tip their poisoned arrows.[19]

On the islet, the very air was toxic, the rotting, hitherto undisturbed vegetation exuding "putrid miasmata", swarming with vapours from the black ooze awash with crocodiles that slid over its surface, disturbed sandflies and mosquitoes blotting out the air. Manzanillo Island lay below water level most of the time, enclosed by the towering stilt roots of mangroves interlaced with huge vines, thorny scrub and the manchineel, making it impenetrable until the first workers from coastal Colombia moved in with their slashing machetes.

Surveys had shown that the best choice for a landing place was closer to Fort San Lorenzo above the village of Chagres, but that land was unobtainable due to the machinations of Aspinwall's rival in the steamship business, George Law, who optioned some seven or eight miles of coastline, all the land from Chagres to Navy Bay (also called Limón Bay) in order to force the railroad company to put him on its board of directors. They refused and decided to build their docking facilities and railroad terminus on the offshore island across from Navy Bay.

Manzanillo Island was cleared, the swamp filled in, a settlement began to grow there, protected by an earthen embankment at high water mark and all buildings on stilts. Linked at first to the mainland by a causeway that became permanent, it eventually ceased to be island. It would soon eclipse Chagres as the principal Atlantic port. The town that grew there was named Aspinwall, in honour of the promoter, but the Colombians wanted the name Colón to honour Christopher Columbus (Colón in Spanish), who had sailed into Limón Bay in 1502. The controversy continued for the next thirty-eight years until Colombian authorities enforced their name in 1890, mainly by refusing to deliver mail addressed to Aspinwall. By then the raucous town had already assumed its identity as Colón.

"A Dead Worker for Every Tie"

The little one-track broad gauge railroad, its wooden carriages pulled by puffing steam engines, was built at extreme cost in men and money (an estimated six thousand men and eight million dollars). It crossed Panama along a vital trade route of the Spanish empire, now fallen back to the jungle. The difficulties involved in throwing up just 47.6 miles of rail across such inhospitable terrain would make the Panama Railroad infamous, contributing to the legendary "dead worker for every tie" railroad construction story. Among the dead would be untold numbers of black men from coastal Colombia and the West Indian islands, especially Jamaica. Hundreds were to be Chinese.

No one knows the truth about the death rate since no reliable statistics were kept by the company. Though mortality was extremely high, the claim of one dead worker for every tie is absurd, since someone has counted seventy-four thousand ties. Estimates of the death rate range from 35 to 40 per cent of an annual average workforce of six thousand. Some cite six thousand as the likeliest number of total deaths. The engineer in charge of the project claimed that the total deaths for one year was 835 of which 295 were whites, 140 were black and 400 Chinese. Statistics given to Robert Tomes showed the death ratios as: natives 1:50; East Indians and foreign Negroes 1:40; Europeans 1:30; Chinese 1:10.[20] On the other hand, another source claimed that no statistics were kept for the black workforce.[21]

The work environment would prove so daunting that men of any race could instantly vanish unnoticed – dragged down by crocodiles into the black ooze in which the men worked for most of the time, swept away in deadly rivers, bitten by poisonous snakes, or simply dropping where they were from illness and exhaustion. Whether or not the workers heard the horror stories from afar, they came in their thousands anyway, driven by hunger and need.

There was no question of recruiting local people. In the 1851 census, the isthmus had a scattered population of 138,108, many hidden away in the jungle, in small hamlets or subsistence farms. The province of Panama (which included Panama City and the transit route) totalled 52,322, but most residents preferred to retain their independent status as providers of services to travellers. Already, a feeling was hardening among the American entrepreneurs that would be explicitly stated later: white men could not labour in the tropics. Non-white labour would have to be found.

The company had turned to the coastal town of Cartagena for their first recruits. With their machetes, these black and mixed-race Colombians became the advance guard who first slashed at the jungle vegetation and cleared the ground. As time went on, adventurers and soldiers of fortune attracted by posters advertising "Money Adventure Women" and shiploads recruited by the company poured in from all over the world – Irish from Ireland, "Coolies from Hindostan, Chinamen from China, English, French, Germans, and Austrians",[22] but none of these efforts was successful. Many died within a few hours of landing; others deserted after a few days of the "green hell"; still others committed suicide, as did many of the Chinese; Irish navvies recruited from Cork died in such numbers that the rest were shipped to New York. The Panama Railroad found Jamaicans and labourers from neighbouring provinces best able to "resist the influence of the climate".[23]

So the company came to rely mainly on black workers – from the coastal Colombian towns of Cartagena and Santa Marta, from St Thomas, Virgin Islands, Saint-Domingue (Haiti), and, ultimately, Jamaica. Of 1,590 workers on the payroll in 1853, 1,200 were black, and people from the Caribbean continued to provide the bulk of the labour force. The tone of the official "History

Figure 2.7 Chinese workers aboard a ship bound for California, 1850s (Wikimedia Commons).

Figure 2.8 Chinese gold miners (*at right*) in California (Wikipedia).

of the Panama Railroad" site captures the stereotyped attitude towards the West Indian workmen that would persist and harden into outright racism during the US canal construction years: "In the end, the company discovered that for heavy work in the tropics, no race of men could match West Indian Negroes. Slow-moving, accustomed to heat, resistant to the fevers, these cheerful and humble people played a most honorable part in the realization of man's dreams on the Isthmus."[24] Still, they could not fill the railroad's insatiable need for workers as the pace of work quickened: some one thousand Chinese were among those recruited. The swift and dramatic nature of their deaths was to immortalize them in Panama Railroad legend more than any other: ("a Chinaman buried underneath every cross tie") and also, incidentally, established the earliest Chinese–Panamanian–Jamaican connection as the survivors were shipped to Jamaica.

The Chinese at Matachin

The Chinese workers were brought in near the end of the project – less than a year before the finish, at a time when the railroad company was pushing to complete a particularly difficult stretch and wanted to flood the site with labourers. By the end of February 1854, some nine thousand workers toiled on the eighteen-mile stretch between the Obispo River and Panama City. The company consistently downplayed the dangers of death and disease, leading to the claim in the *Star and Herald* that, "as to all the nonsense about malaria, fever, pestilential swamps and the thousand other ills that are charged to the Isthmus, we report again, they exist no more than in any other tropical climate, and that prudence and ordinary precaution is all that is required on the part of unacclimated newcomers to our sunny shores".[25]

Early on the morning of 30 March 1854, the clipper *Sea Witch,* with towering masts and a black dragon figurehead, entered Panama Harbour sixty-one days from Swatow (Shantou) in southern China. It disgorged men from every nook and cranny. The *Herald* newspaper (later *Star and Herald*) of 1 April 1854 reported that the *Sea Witch* landed "701 in good health and 4 invalids", remarking that "they are fine looking men and we are told conducted themselves remarkably well on the voyage". Once ashore, dressed alike in dark silk pyjama suits and conical hats, the men formed themselves into a long line, marching silently with heads bowed, ignoring the crowds of chattering, curious onlookers who followed them across the city.[26] Aspinwall owned the *Sea Witch*, the fastest and most famous clipper of the day, and she brought 705 Chinese contracted for work on the railroad, to be followed by two smaller ships bringing the total number of labourers to 1,040. The Chinese were placed at a camp called Matachin, a name that later writers would erroneously claim was derived from *matar chinos* – "to kill Chinese". The place name in fact translates as "butcher" and it appears on maps as early as 1678.

Also at the Matachin camp were Malays and other nationalities as well as a large number of Irish labourers, who had arrived in 1854. The Irish regarded the incoming "heathens" with so much hostility that they were placed as far apart as possible. The railroad company had paid labour contractors in Canton twenty-five dollars a month for each man and the contractors supplied the passage and food, paying the workers four to eight dollars per month. The contractors also provided cooks, for whom the railroad commissary stocked dried oysters, cuttlefish, bamboo sprouts, sweet rice crackers, salted cabbage, vermicelli, tea and hill rice. Joss houses and opium were also provided for in the Chinese contract.[27] It was claimed that these workers – unlike other Chinese who were being sent to the Caribbean and elsewhere at the time – were not agricultural labourers but were city men who could have been sculptors, wood workers, calligraphers, musicians, and the like. Mortality among them was great from the start – sixteen had died on the voyage, sixteen more on arrival, and eighty more in less than a week. Many were soon prostrate from fevers and other illnesses. Those still standing nevertheless fell to work with a will and impressed everyone with their industry, labouring steadily without breaks except for brief moments when the Chinese cook brought tea, toiling in mud and swamps up to their necks like other workers, hacking at rocks all day long and carting huge loads of fill in baskets on their heads. All went well, until one of the Irish labourers wrote a letter to a Catholic priest in New York referring to the opium and accusing the railroad company of trafficking in drugs. The letter appeared in the New York *Herald*. Once an investigation led the company to realize that the opium it imported was costing it fifteen cents per man per day, it ordered no more supplies.

There has so far been no reliable recounting of exactly what next happened. Although the popular story is quoted on the official website of the Panama Railroad Company, the actual dramatic details of the suicides are open to dispute, fabricated, some say,[28] by later writers. Without the opium, the Chinese were said to have fallen into a state of misery and prostration and stopped working. But the deadly fevers could not end their misery fast enough and they began to commit suicide en masse.[29] Two weeks after the drug supply ran out, the chief engineer, Colonel Totten, on his sick-bed was awakened early one morning by an urgent call. He staggered outside to be rushed by handcar to Matachin. "Should I live to be as old as Methuselah, I shall never forget the sight that met my eyes that morning," the Colonel is quoted as saying. "More than a hundred of the coolies hung from the trees, their loose pantaloons flapping in the hot wind. Some had hung themselves with bits of rope and tough vines. Most, however, used their own hair, looping the long queue around the neck and tying the end to a tree limb."[30] Crumpled bodies were scattered on the ground. Some had tied stones to themselves and jumped into the water, some sat silently in shallow water waiting for a freshet to drown them, some threw themselves on pointed sticks, some bargained with the Malays to kill them. There is no real count of how many died in such ways, though the construction foreman's report of over four hundred seems a gross exaggeration. Some of the Chinese ran away from the works and remained in Panama but at least two-thirds of the arrivals perished from disease, accident or suicide. Although this dramatic rendering of mass suicide is attributed exclusively to opium withdrawal, newspaper reports of the time suggest that many Chinese fled from the work because of conditions there, and several in Panama who experienced loss of face also chose suicide. This choice, the reports claimed, reflected their "peculiar notions" regarding insult or chastisement, and cited several instances where "punishment has been inflicted or where insult has been offered" and the aggrieved party killed himself.[31] Perhaps the Chinese workers had more to contend with as far as the working conditions and their treatment were concerned. Those who were caught deserting were sent back by the police but a number seemed to have escaped.

The *Star and Herald* reported the arrival in early September 1854 of a Chinese gentleman from Jamaica "whose object, we have been told, is to effect an exchange with the railway company, and furnish them with an equal number of Jamaican labourers for such of his countrymen who are able bodied and in good health". The paper added that "the climate of Jamaica agrees well with the Chinese, and they are found to be useful agricultural workers there".[32]

In November, the company shipped the survivors to Jamaica where a shipload of indentured Chinese had arrived from Hong Kong on the *Epsom* in July. The schooner *Vampire* brought 195 and 10 came on the *Theresa Jane*, 205 survivors in all, many found to be in a state of extreme emaciation and unfit for labour. On the isthmus, the surviving Chinese at the start lived out a beggar's life, with frequent newspaper reports of them ill and even dying on the streets,[33] but some survived and even thrived, to be joined later by other Chinese who settled in Panama and developed into a large and prosperous enclave.

RUNNING THE LINE

The earliest workers on Manzanillo Island lived on derelict boats anchored in the swamps until enough ground could be cleared to build shacks on stilts. They spent sleepless nights under attack by the pitiless insects; those escaping to sleep on deck were drenched by rain and nauseated by the ceaseless movement of the vessels. Most soon fell from exhaustion and fevers.[34] The workers included American engineers and technicians, some white American and Irish labourers, machete men from coastal Colombia who had the task of clearing the site, and some early arrivals from Jamaica. In the same month the first tree was felled, one hundred young men left Kingston for Chagres, finding work as soon as they arrived,[35] and by the end of the year some three thousand departures were officially recorded. Many of them were carpenters and they were put to work erecting buildings as soon as lumber started to arrive from the United States.

Figure 2.9 The first shanty (Otis, *Illustrated History*, 53).

The labourers' first task was to erect a wooden trestle bridge or causeway across the swamp to connect Manzanillo Island to the mainland at Navy Bay. They worked waist deep in stinking mudflats, sometimes crawling on their hands and knees, dragging chains with their teeth. Those who strayed too far from the group could run into the waiting jaws of a crocodile. The swamp was found to be so deep that in places over two hundred feet of gravel backfill was dumped to build up a roadbed on which to lay the tracks. From Navy Bay,

Map 2.2 Route of
the Panama Railroad
(www.panamarailroad
.org).

the first two miles of track took the line to solid ground at Monkey Hill (later
rechristened Mount Hope), and there the first cemetery was established. From
there the line again crossed swamps to an area near the Mindi River where,
after a bridge, it ran on firmer ground to Gatún. Up to four hundred men
struggled for a full year to cover the few miles from Monkey Hill to Gatún. At
times the swamps seemed bottomless, and the engineers had to keep dumping
enormous – and costly – quantities of wood, earth and rock to build up cause-
ways to literally float the tracks over the swamps. Although their numbers were
reduced daily by death, sickness and desertion, the crews persisted, and the
first train of working cars drawn by a locomotive travelled from Navy Bay to
Gatún on 1 October 1851.

By this time, men were arriving from all over the world, induced by attractive offers from recruiters. Much of the work depended on sheer man-power
since the steam revolution was just beginning. The power equipment in use
included a steam-driven pile driver, steam tugs, and steam locomotives
equipped with gondolas and dump cars for carrying fill material. For the rest,
it was machete, axe, pick, shovel, black powder and mule cart.[36]

As the men carried the line farther into the interior, they were also plunging into a dark, fecund and largely undisturbed world of nature that lashed them at every turn, the vegetation opening a path before them only with the slash of machetes as ticks and spiders rained down from the leaves on to their heads. The world's deadliest snakes – bushmasters, coral snakes and fer-de-lance – coiled ready to spring. Stinging insects and mosquitoes covered every inch of their exposed bodies. The white men wore pith helmets and gauze veils to protect themselves; the black and native labourers worked without protection. Chigoes bored into their skins. Sudden river surges swept the men away. They hacked their way through jungles so thick their eyes could not penetrate the gloom beyond. They were almost always wet. Their clothes mildewed in the perpetual dankness and their shoes turned green overnight. At nights, their sleep was broken by the howls and screeches of unfamiliar wildlife, the monkeys that chattered and threw nuts at them; the pumas, ocelots and jaguars which in the islanders' imaginations became fierce lions and tigers immortalized in place names along the railroad such as "Lion Hill" and "Tiger Hill". The rest of the fauna was equally varied and strange – wild turkeys, tapir, opossum, anteaters, peccaries or wild hogs, sloths, deer, bears, cougars, and some varieties of tiger cats. Iguanas grew to monstrous sizes, as did tarantulas, land crabs and scorpions.

Though the vegetation was tropical, for the islanders who would make up the bulk of the workforce, this place was nothing like home; this watery world of muddy seashores, swamps, treacherous rivers and endless, pelting rain was like nothing they had experienced. In the steamy conditions, even familiar trees became transformed into unrecognizable giants – enormous palms scarcely lifting their trunks from the ooze sending out leaves half a dozen yards in length; tropical cedar towering for hundreds of feet; monstrous vines covered with parasites blotting out the sunlight. Only occasionally would the beauty of the country reveal itself with colourful flashes and chatter of disturbed parrots or flocks of egrets suddenly taking flight if one stumbled into an unexpected clearing.

Despite the workers' valiant efforts, only eight miles of track were laid after twenty months of work. Much of the company's one million dollars had been used up in filling the swamps. Near bankruptcy, the company laid off workers. The project seemed doomed to failure. Then came a happy coincidence. In November 1851 during heavy storms, two ships were unable to land at Chagres, the usual disembarkation point, and put in instead at Navy Bay. Over a thousand gold seekers waded ashore and immediately commandeered the working cars of the railroad, riding them to Gatún where they disembarked to board the *bungo* boats to be poled up the Chagres River. To discourage the rail passengers, Colonel Totten set the rate at fifty cents a mile and three dollars for each hundred pounds of baggage. Within a short time he had collected seven thousand dollars, and the relentless tide of passengers soon propelled the project onwards and swept Panama Railroad stocks to new heights. Though many of the workers were in the habit of taking off to join the gold seekers, new workers were always arriving and as quickly as they pushed on through the swamps to lay the tracks, passengers followed.

By July 1852 the line had reached the Chagres River, which promptly washed away the first wooden bridge built when it rose over forty feet in a single day. A massive three-hundred-foot-long iron bridge was to prove more lasting. In all, the railroad required the construction of over three hundred bridges and culverts along its route, a factor that contributed to its status as the most expensive ever built per mile.

Work on the other end of the line was started at Panama City and eleven miles were laid from there under less harsh conditions. Workers from the two ends met at the summit at Culebra where the mountain had been dug down to forty feet. At midnight, in pouring rain, by the light of sputtering whale oil lamps, Colonel Totten used a nine-pound maul to drive the last spike. This act marked the completion of the line and the inauguration the next day, 28 January 1855, of the world's first interoceanic railroad. Suddenly, the world's most dangerous transit was reduced from a week or more of hardships to three hours. The first train's arrival in Panama City was viewed with as much surprise by the native population "as Cortez exhibited on beholding the Pacific for the first time", a newspaper claimed. When the engineer opened his steam whistle, women and children ran away screaming. After the initial shock, however, people crowded the train so closely it could scarcely move upon the track.[37]

Figure 2.10
Aspinwall at the start
(Otis, *Illustrated History*, 57).

The railroad brought unimaginable wealth to Aspinwall and his company, which charged twenty-five dollars in gold for a one-way ticket across the isthmus. The company also had sole right to carry mail and goods. It was to make seven million dollars profit in its first six years after completion and at one time was the highest priced stock on the New York Exchange. However, the line had been built so hurriedly that a great deal of work continued over many years to rebuild and replace tracks and rolling stock with more durable material.

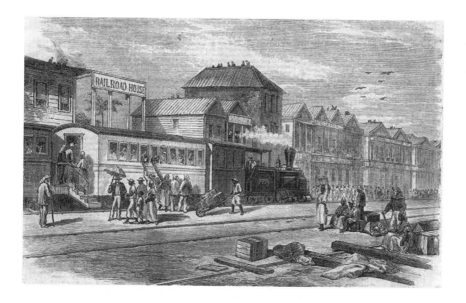

Figure 2.11
Aspinwall in 1855
(www.panamarailroad
.org).

Panama was not the first railroad outside Europe and North America to be opened to traffic. The Jamaica Railway had opened in 1845. And it was increasingly to workers from that country that the Panama Railroad Company had turned to complete theirs.

ISLAND WORKERS

Why were so many Jamaican men willing to go to a place where the earliest news travelling back home was that almost certain death awaited them? The short answer might well be the push of desperation, the pull of money wages. These same impulses propelled them over the next half-century to seek work on equally dangerous railroad projects in Central and South America, including the Madeira–Marmora on the Amazon, the Guayaquil–Quito in Ecuador, and railroads in Guatemala, Honduras, Mexico and Costa Rica.

By 1850 decay had settled on an island that fifty years earlier had been the brightest jewel in the British Crown. Soon – like those other gold seekers – men from the colony would be fighting to get on to any transport that would take them to a place that offered the possibility of earning a livelihood. On the sun-bleached streets of Kingston or in abandoned cane fields, idle men lounged with an air of helplessness, hungry and destitute. With the decline of the sugar industry, formerly the mainstay of that island, there was little work for carpenters, masons, bricklayers and other artisans, and news of work in the offing travelled fast the 550 miles across the Caribbean Sea. Carpenters in particular were in great demand and their going to Panama had a marked effect on the wages and availability of such workers at home. A newspaper claimed that Jamaicans were receiving six to seven dollars a day as carpenters in Panama, given the huge demand for building construction at Aspinwall and elsewhere.[38]

There was no real count of how many went to Panama.[39] Small fishing boats slipped away with uncounted passengers on board, some with women and children, as they had done for centuries. Little schooners or sloops left from the outports around the island, such as Falmouth on the north coast, anchoring overnight at Port Royal before heading across the Caribbean, the larger ones carrying up to forty passengers. Those who could afford it bought deck passage on the vessels which regularly stopped at Kingston on the journeys between New York and Chagres. Kingston was a coaling station and regular port of call for Panama-bound ships, and in 1842 the Royal Mail Steam Packet Company[40] began a regular route from England to the West Indies, North and South America, putting its first ship – a wooden paddle steamer – on the Panama route in that year. By 1851 the first iron ship was added and when steam began to supersede sail in the 1870s, the timely introduction of considerably larger ships enabled the Royal Mail Company to pack on larger shipments of labourers for the Panama Canal.

Deck passengers could not attempt to rise above their station. The Royal Mail line was strict in its regulations which stated that those belonging to the "superior classes" of society were expected to travel in regular accommodation – and pay five times the deckers' fare. As for the deckers, "only troops, common sailors, labourers and others not superior to those classes of society, to be conveyed as deck passengers; to find their own provision and bedding, and not admitted abaft the chimney".[41]

The Panama Railroad Company offered a bounty of one pound sterling to ships' captains for each labourer they brought. By 1854 the company had hired a recruiter – Hutchins and Company – to recruit and ship labourers from Jamaica,[42] suggesting perhaps that the voluntary flow was inadequate to meet their needs as the pace of work quickened.

To the job seekers, any inconveniences of travel or rumours of dire working conditions were tempered by the fact that in Chagres, there was the promise of work, something that had become increasingly scarce at home. Artisans earned two to three dollars a day, labourers eighty cents a day for work and thirty cents for keep.[43] Converted at three shillings and two pence, this rate was more than double the daily wage for plantation labourers in Jamaica.

While wages and adventure were pulling many to Panama, most were being pushed out of their island homes by poverty, hunger and destitution stalking even those who might have had a comfortable existence in former times. The opening of work on the isthmus coincided with a period of severe economic depression in the British West Indies.

These tiny West Indian islands had been the richest jewels in the imperial crowns. Sugar, along with some lesser crops (grown by enslaved labour on rich virgin lands), formed the basis of their wealth. Thanks to centuries of imperial rivalries and constant warfare between the colonial powers, these islands were also considered of the utmost strategic importance, guardians of maritime gateways between the Americas and Europe. Wars were fought over them.

In their heyday, an enormous portion of the world's wealth was extracted from these tiny specks of land or steamy continental outposts. In 1805, Jamaica was England's richest colony; half a century later it was a backwater, cast away on the changing tides of commerce. The fate of Kingston was similar to that of Panama City. Both in their times had been flourishing centres of commerce and vital transportation hubs that fell into disrepair and disuse as the imperial powers turned to new obsessions: Spain to lick its wounds for the loss of its American possessions, England hoping to shed the now importuning, unprofitable islands in favour of new riches proffered by India, the Far East or North America.

The British West Indian plantations were first established in the seventeenth century, reached their peak in the late eighteenth century and were in decline by the nineteenth. The decline accelerated as the century progressed, hastened by cheaper beet sugar introduced to the European markets, the ending of the slave trade by Britain in 1807, the emancipation of the enslaved Africans in British colonies in 1838, and the introduction of tariffs such as the Sugar Duties Equalization Acts of 1846 which no longer gave West Indian sugar a monopoly in England. The inefficient plantations could not compete. In the late eighteenth century, the British West Indies supplied one-fifth of all British

Figure 2.12 Harbour Street, Kingston, circa 1835. (Courtesy of the National Library of Jamaica.)

imports. By the 1850s they produced less than one-twentieth. The sugar islands were still ruled from London but were now regarded as weights around the body politic instead of sparkling jewels. Since enslaved people had been classified as property, the slave owners were compensated financially for their loss; the newly freed Africans received nothing. They were left to fend for themselves, beset with increasingly onerous taxes and stringent legislation of all sorts aimed at keeping them firmly in their places in the racial hierarchy of the islands.

Populations shifted with the abandonment of sugar-cane fields, plantations and factories. Where there was land available, as in Jamaica, many formerly enslaved Africans left the lowland sugar plantations – so tainted with evil memories – and established free communities in the mountains. Others drifted into the towns or into somnolence on the edges of old abandoned estates. By 1850 the ruin of the plantations in Jamaica's monocrop economy meant hard times for everyone. Wages to field labourers fell, as did demand for their services or those of skilled workers. Those formerly enslaved who had started to grow provisions on their own plots found their markets reduced for there were fewer to buy. There was so little coin in circulation that merchandising trade came almost to a standstill.

People of all classes began to leave Jamaica. Some headed for Panama, others joined the flood of travellers to the gold fields of California; still others set out to settle in Australia.[44] In commenting on this exodus, a local newspaper noted that "all the Commissions that the British Government may send out cannot gainsay what they prove – the impoverished condition of a country in which all classes are vieing with each other in quitting as soon as possible".[45] Many persons were forced to leave their homeland out of sheer necessity. A newspaper editor claimed, "We could name many persons who were walking the streets of this City for a long period of time, – literally starving because they could not get employment, – who are now doing well in Chagres."[46]

A more telling picture was provided in the 1870s by William Lee, a Kingston auctioneer giving evidence before the Commission on the Condition of the Juvenile Population in Jamaica. He reminisced that "after that sugar bill came into operation, say in 1846 and 1847, there was not a day's work to be found for a carpenter or a bricklayer throughout the length and breadth of this city. Many thousands of tradesmen and labourers were forced to seek employment elsewhere; they went to the Isthmus and completed the Panama Railway, and nearly all of them died there, indirectly the victims of the free traders and the sugar refiners of England."[47]

But an event even more traumatic than economic depression forced many to flee Jamaica's shores. This was a cholera epidemic, the first ever experienced by the island and "probably the greatest catastrophe ever visited upon the population".[48] For the nineteen months it raged (September 1850–March 1852) an estimated twenty to fifty thousand persons died.[49] The epidemic was followed by a smallpox outbreak, then less virulent outbreaks of cholera and scarlatina (scarlet fever). Cholera left deserted villages and wasted fields, abandoned houses, homeless and wandering people, destitute orphan children, and emotional scars on the entire population which are difficult to comprehend at this time.

Whereas during slavery the estates provided doctors for the enslaved Africans, virtually no formal medical services were available to the newly freed population. The period was one of acute poverty, distress, suffering and fear, so much so that many were willing to take the risk of migrating to "the unhealthiest place on earth". The irony is they were going to a place where cholera had raged on and off since it was brought to the isthmus by the first set of gold seekers in 1849 – from the same source as the Jamaican infection – a ship from the port of New Orleans.[50]

MARY SEACOLE: "THE YELLOW WOMAN FROM JAMAICA"

Once the railroad opened, travellers crossed the isthmus easily. But during the five years of construction, the transit route became a gold mine of another sort for those who could provide accommodation, transportation and other services for the gold-rush travellers and construction workers. Into the jungle villages and hastily built camps came cooks, tailors, shoemakers, traders, clerks, hoteliers, farmers, doctors, lawyers, newspapermen, photographers, printers, and higglers, quacks and conmen. Jamaicans, the largest ethnic group, were in the thick of it. Some were businessmen already long established in Panama City. Many came and went, taking advantage of the sudden and highly profitable entrepreneurial possibilities.

Figure 2.13 Mary Seacole. (Courtesy of the National Library of Jamaica.)

Among these Jamaicans was Mary Seacole, an energetic woman who later achieved lasting fame through her best-selling autobiography, *Wonderful Adventures of Mrs Seacole in Many Lands*, published in 1857. Her arrival on the isthmus in a time of cholera was fortunate: she had gained experience treating patients during the epidemic in Jamaica. Mrs Seacole was not a trained medical doctor but she came from a long line of women traditionally called "doctoress" in Jamaica, a self-taught medicine woman whose knowledge of tropical disease and treatments at the time often surpassed those of doctors trained exclusively in European medicine and who often acknowledged their debt to native healers.[51]

Her greatest fame lay ahead on the muddy battlefields of the Crimean War in 1854–56.[52] In Panama, Mary Seacole was "the yellow woman from Jamaica with the cholera medicine". She laboured in mud. We have our first glimpse of her arriving in Panama in late 1851,[53] a stout brown woman in a drenched bonnet shouting orders to her servants, Mac and Mary, who are trying to assemble a mountain of trunks, bags and baskets of goods unloaded from the rickety little train at Gatún while trying to protect them from the grasping hands of would-be porters and the shoves and curses of fellow travellers. A steamer from Kingston and the train have brought them this far at the height of the rainy season; torrential, jungle-spitting outbursts sending sheets of water cascading down the travellers' backs before abruptly ceasing, then starting up again.

Her goods secured and portered precariously up a muddy cutting from the railway embankment, Mrs Seacole follows, slithering and sliding in the mud until she reaches the river bank above. In the brief lull before the skies open again, she lands amid the usual riotous uproar. Impatient American travellers are fighting each other to get into one of the *bungo* boats to take them up the Chagres River, and if shouts, fists and knives do not work, a Colt revolver thrust at the boatman's head will speed him along in their rush to California's gold fields. Landing at Navy Bay, they must now cross the Isthmus of Panama to the Pacific where, they hope, another ship awaits. They are fearful that others will arrive before them and there will be no gold left.

Mary Seacole is travelling a shorter distance, ostensibly to visit her brother who operates the Independent Hotel at Cruces, on the overland trail, but really to scout out her own business opportunities. She successfully negotiates with the black *padrón* (captain) of one of the boats and, securing the *bungo* exclusively for her little party, she installs herself on board in the captain's hammock, closing her eyes to the semi-naked condition of the four boatmen who laboriously pole them upstream as the *padrón* steers. Only later will she ruefully observe how that morning at Navy Bay she had dressed so carefully for the journey, donning "a delicate light blue dress, a white bonnet prettily trimmed, and an equally chaste shawl" – now drenched in mud.[54]

Her insouciance is typical of the woman who knew how to laugh at herself and survive this and thirty more years of adventures.[55] In rainy Panama, however, she was far from the fame she would later achieve. But her objective would remain the same – to have an adventure while exploiting business opportunities as caterer, hotelier, trader, and practising her best-loved activity, that of healer. Now with the construction of the railroad and the passage of gold seekers, the isthmus suddenly became the perfect place to explore those options. Perfect, that is, except for the climate and environmental hazards: "It seemed as capital a nursery for ague and fever as Death could hit upon anywhere", were Mrs Seacole's first observations.[56] And she it was who identified that most dreaded carrier of Death when it made its appearance at Cruces.

Cholera and "Panama Fever"

Cholera was a new and mysterious disease when it came to the West in the nineteenth century. Originating in India's Ganges delta, it was spread by travellers in world-wide pandemics. Cholera was most virulent among populations lacking immunity acquired through long exposure. In 1883 it was established that the disease is caused by a bacterium that attacks the intestine and is excreted in human waste, spreading mainly through contaminated drinking water. Until the cause was identified, cholera was attributed to miasmas, God's will and depraved habits, especially because it attacked the poor who lived in the vilest conditions. Only much later would sanitation be recognized as the best preventative.

Figure 2.14 Cholera as deadly reaper is captured in this 1912 French magazine cover (Wikimedia Commons).

The United States first experienced cholera in the 1830s, when New Orleans, Chicago and Detroit were devastated. It returned with the gold rush, brought by the first travellers departing for Panama from the ports of New York and New Orleans in 1849. The hot, steamy isthmus provided an ideal incubator for this disease; an estimated quarter of the local population and untold numbers of travellers died in the first onslaught. Throughout the gold-rush years, cholera lessened and then reappeared sporadically in less virulent forms.

The mere word "cholera" struck terror because, without rhyme or reason, the disease came suddenly, stopped suddenly, often after wiping out entire populations. Its action on the individual was no less uncanny and frightening. As George W. Groh, an American author succinctly puts it: "A man might set out in the morning in seeming health and vigor and be stricken by noon. In the next few hours he might suffer diarrhea, spasmodic vomiting, painful cramps, burning thirst, and complete prostration. That same night he might die in convulsions."[57]

This fate befell a friend of Mrs Seacole's brother who had dined with him at the Independent Hotel at Cruces

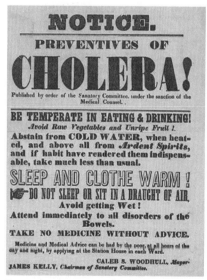

Figure 2.15 Instructions for preventing cholera were plentiful, such as this handbill from New York City (Wikimedia Commons).

when cholera flared up there in 1851. His sudden illness and death caused the man's relatives to suspect poison at the hotel. When Mrs Seacole rushed down to see the corpse, "A single glance at the poor fellow showed me the terrible truth. The distressed face, sunken eyes, cramped limbs, and discoloured shrivelled skin were all symptoms which I had been familiar with very recently."[58]

She was correct in her diagnosis of cholera and thereafter claimed to be the only source of medical attention for the Cruces residents and travellers, recording horrible death scenes in her autobiography, working as tirelessly to save those who could "reward her handsomely" as she did for those who had nothing to give her but thanks. It was the same attitude that she was to take to the Crimea when cholera broke out there among the troops a few years later; she was more knowledgeable about the disease than most, having even secretly conducted a post-mortem on a child's body to learn more.[59]

She lost some of her patients but saved others with her traditional remedies: "by dint of mustard emetics, warm fomentations, mustard plasters on the stomach and the back, and calomel, at first in large then in gradually smaller doses".[60] This regimen sounded slightly less destructive than treatments prescribed by doctors at the time,[61] and far more efficacious than that noted on the flyleaf of the diary of a young gold digger from Maine embarking for Panama: "Recipe for Cholera, one tablespoon salt, 1 teaspoonful red pepper, mixed in ½ pint boiling water."[62]

Cholera took a terrible toll on railroad workers and gold-rush travellers alike. In the first epidemic soon after construction started, only two were left of the first group of fifty American technicians, draughtsmen and engineers; most of the line workers died where they were, unburied and unrecorded. Among the passengers, the worst recorded fatalities occurred with the American Fourth Infantry en route to California (a group that included a young lieutenant and US-president-to-be Ulysses S. Grant). They contracted the cholera in Cruces; it raged with such virulence that 150 men, women and children of the party died en route to Panama City.[63]

Cholera, while dramatic, was a disease that came and went. Yellow fever inhabited the isthmus. Known throughout the Caribbean and southern United States, it came to be called "Panama fever" because of its prevalence there,[64] the most violent outbreaks alternating with cholera epi-

Figure 2.16 Start of Las Cruces Trail in the old town of Cruces. (Courtesy of William P. McLaughlin, www.czimages.com.)

demics. Yellow fever started with severe and intense headache and violent pains all over the body, pain so intense that in most cases it produced delirium, followed by vomiting of blood. At that stage, most sufferers died. Pernicious malaria was also widespread, the Panama variety becoming known as "Chagres fever".

The isthmus provided an ideal environment for mosquito-borne diseases such as yellow fever and malaria, a process unknown until forty years later. Typhoid, dysentery, smallpox, hookworm and cutaneous infections were endemic. Crossing from east to west or west to east brought equal hazard. Gold seekers returning home were almost equally at risk from death and disease. Although little documentation exists, the large "gold-rush graveyard" that was opened up in Kingston, Jamaica, the first port of call for ships leaving Panama for American eastern ports, suggests epidemic fatalities.[65]

The Jamaican workers had gained a reputation for hardiness; they were supposedly immune to yellow fever (as were most people who grew up where it was endemic). However, Jamaicans readily succumbed to typhoid and malaria, and especially to pulmonary infections, tuberculosis and pneumonia. They had no immunity to infectious pneumonia and many contracted it and died as soon as they arrived.

OTHER HAZARDS ON THE ISTHMUS

Death came from fever and environmental hazard but also at the hands of humans. Before the railroad opened, workers and travellers arriving on the isthmus plunged into a lawless, violent, dangerous world. Crossing the isthmus it was every man for himself and only the boldest of women travelled unprotected. In this ramshackle, makeshift environment, everything was hurriedly thrown up to meet the travellers' needs, and those who catered to them prayed only to make as much money as possible in the shortest time. Unhealthy conditions added to hazard, as did the continuous revolutionary rumblings in this province, so far from Bogotá, the seat of government: political tensions in Panama remained high during construction years, crime flourished in the absence of law and order, and racial tension often exploded in violence and riot.

Figure 2.17 The hazards for gold-rush travellers crossing the isthmus, 1849 (Wikimedia Commons).

Figure 2.18 Some travellers resorted to a *sillero*, a seat on the back of a human carrier, common elsewhere in South America, as this engraving of a traveller crossing the Andes shows (Sullivan, *Our Times*, 64). Human carriers on the Cruces trail can also be seen in the right foreground of figure 2.17.

The City of Panama on the Pacific side was once a major colonial city, the only civic settlement on the isthmus. After Peruvian gold no longer travelled across it to Spain, the jungle swallowed the gold road and the city was cut off from the rest of the world, its only means of access by sea or via the mule and *bungo* boat trail to the Caribbean coast. American Tracy Robinson, who arrived in 1861 and stayed for sixty years, noted how at the time of the gold rush, the "once proud city had fallen into a state of apathy. It had no foreign commerce and little domestic trade. . . . Life had slowed down to a snail's pace."[66] Its citizens received a rude awakening from the "Yankee" travellers who were stuck there, sometimes for weeks, as they awaited transportation to California. The Caribbean coast was even more dismal, or "lively", depending on point of view. Chagres was described as a miserable little collection of bamboo huts and thatch houses with earthen floors "surrounded by heaps of filthy offal, and greasy, stagnant pools bordered with blue mud".[67]

Newcomers with an eye to chance remained in Panama to provide services to travellers – a lucrative business as some four thousand passengers had landed at Chagres by 1849. At the river mouth on the opposite bank from "Native Chagres", "Yankee Chagres" soon sprang up around the wharf of the American steamship companies, a hastily built Wild West American town providing ramshackle hotels and drinking, gambling, and carousing, day and night. Yankee Chagres burned brightly for less than two years and disappeared as soon as the Panama Railroad established the town of Aspinwall/Colón seven miles eastwards at Navy Bay as the landing place for passengers. At the start, the character of this new town hardly differed from the old.

On her arrival from Jamaica, Mary Seacole was immediately struck by the unhealthiness of Aspinwall. As her steamer docked, "a steady downpour of rain was falling from an inky sky; the white men who met us on the wharf appeared ghostly and wraith-like, and the very negroes seemed pale and wan". She saw men "dying from sheer exhaustion" beneath leaky tents, damp huts and under broken railway wagons.[68]

In 1855 when the railroad was completed, the American author Robert Tomes was told by the company doctor that no one who remained on the isthmus for over two months escaped the "fever" (that is, malaria). The first attack would either result in death or in recovery attended by habitual fever, ague and mental depression. Complete recovery during residence on the isthmus was impossible. Even the little Jamaican children told him: "Me no like dis country, berra bad country; me hab de feber ebry oder day."[69]

Tomes found, "A walk in the streets was painfully convincing of the fact that I was among the sick and the dying. The features of every man, woman or child, European, African, Asiatic or American I met had the same ghastly look of those who suffer from the malignant effects of miasmatic poison. I do not believe there is a wholesome person in all Aspinwall."[70]

Often people sickened and died without funeral rites or decent disposal. The luckiest would be put on a funeral train; it ran daily to the Monkey Hill cemetery, which the railroad had established. The bodies of the unfortunate ones – and they included both labourers and travellers crossing the isthmus – were often thrown into the river along with other refuse and garbage where, it was hoped, they would be carried out to sea. If they were not, their bodies merely added that much more to the general stench pervading the settlements.[71] If they died in the company hospital, their bodies were pickled and the cadavers sold by the company doctor to medical schools all over the world, which paid handsomely. This thriving business made the hospital self-sufficient during construction years.[72]

Tents, Lean-tos and Bamboo Huts

Until the completion of the railroad, scrounging for food and shelter occupied travellers and workers alike. The first railroad workers lived aboard boats anchored in the swamps of Navy Bay, ate sailor fare and drank rain water. Building material, food, and everything else, was imported. When lumber was shipped in from the United States, the workers carried the boards on their backs through the swamps to the highest point – Monkey Hill – where they erected shanties.[73] As the work progressed, they threw up huts of thatch and bamboo or wattle and daub with earthen floors, similar to the ones occupied by the natives or, indeed, by the poorest Jamaicans at home. The houses were usually unfit to resist the rainy season and equally unsuitable for the dry. Whole towns such as Gorgona on the bank of the Chagres were subject to frequent flooding. When the dry season came, the highly combustible building materials provided tinder for the fires that periodically roared through the settlements. Some of these flimsy shanty towns supported large numbers of people. When Gorgona was destroyed by fire in 1851 it had a population of nearly one thousand.[74]

Figure 2.19
The village of Paraiso (Otis, *Illustrated History*, 23).

Even the most substantial structures in the towns, the so-called hotels, were ramshackle structures slapped together to meet the demand for accommodation. Indeed, Jamaican businessmen developed a profitable business in the export of prefabricated wooden houses to Panama. A Kingston newspaper reported in 1850 that "many persons of capital of this City have embarked large sums in the building of frame-houses, some of which have already been sent on to Chagres; and, upon this speculation, they expect to realise large returns. Mr. Delapenha and Mr. Mordecai have entered largely into that business and the sloops . . . which left the harbour yesterday crowded with passengers carried many of them."[75] Some were not content to simply ship out houses. The paper mentioned, "as an instance of the success of some of our fellow townsmen", the case of "Mr. Ariano, a person well known in this community, [who] had a frame-house put together in this City, and the same being pulled to pieces by the withdrawal of the temporary pegs by which the building was kept together, he carried it with him to Chagres; he could not have expended more than a couple hundred dollars up on this building; and on his arrival in Chagres he had offers of purchase for it; he refused six hundred dollars".

The "wide-awake" Mr Ariano acquired land near to where passengers landed at Chagres and erected his building. Small as it was, it proved "superior" to the others on that side of the river, "the houses being mere huts". He named it the Washington Hotel, from which, according to the paper, he soon expected to amass some wealth.[76]

Mr Ariano had probably established his hotel at Yankee Chagres. Several hotels built there were soon surrounded by "tents, lean-tos and bamboo huts – housing saloons, gambling houses and brothels" operated by foreign entrepreneurs for the entertainment of the gold-rush travellers. Drinking, gambling, prostitution and other diversions were readily available, all designed to part the travellers or workers from their money at the heavily inflated isthmus prices. Women were as freely available as liquor. The drink of choice for the colourful saloon hostesses of every nation was a Blue Moon – coloured water – which cost their escort a dollar and they charged two dollars a dance – once around the room only. They carried their money on their persons and they packed their guns, even when plying their trade.

The hotels were unpainted wooden structures with wide porches circling both floors. The rooms were filled with cots renting for four dollars a night. During crowded periods hammocks were hung from posts on the porches and between the cots.

Mrs Seacole's brother, Edward, owned one of the two hotels at Cruces, the overnight stopping place on the trail to Panama City. Edward had come over from Jamaica in 1850 and his hotel seemed the same as the Americans'. "The

Independent Hotel", she tells us in her autobiography, was "a long, low hut, built of rough, unhewn, unplaned logs, filled up with mud and split bamboo", with a sloping roof and a large veranda. Downstairs, the entire floor was occupied by a huge dining table covered with green oilskin cloth. Upstairs was for sleeping. At the entrance to the hotel

> sat a black man, taking toll of the comers-in, giving them in exchange for a coin or gold-dust (he had a rusty pair of scales to weigh the latter) a dirty ticket, which guaranteed them supper, a night's lodgings, and breakfast . . . as the evening wore on, the shouting and quarrelling increased . . . while some seated themselves at the table, and hammering upon it with the handles of their knives, hallooed out to the excited nigger cooks to make haste with the slapjack.

Amid all this confusion, Brother Edward was "quietly selling shirts, boots, trousers, etc., to the travellers; while above all the din could be heard the screaming voices of his touters without, drawing attention to the good cheer of the Independent Hotel".[77]

Four crowds passed through Cruces each month, coinciding with the movement of the steamers; their coming brought frenetic activity. So crowded was her brother's hotel the night of Mrs Seacole's arrival that she created bed space for herself and her young maid beneath the dining table, once the dinner was cleared, her brother sleeping on top of the table for her protection. In between the steamers, Cruces and the other towns were quiet places. When Mrs Seacole herself started the British Hotel opposite her brother's, she described it as a "tumble down hut" of wattle and daub. Another hotel which she started later at Gorgona (devoted to the entertainment of ladies and care of the sick), was a "miserable hut".

Described as even more miserable were the huts of the native families which offered travellers shelter along the trail, although their nights could be sometimes made lively by the local women dancing the *fandango*. From Cruces, travellers could hire mules and drivers for the one-day journey to Panama City, or they could walk it over two or more days along a rutted, rocky, muddy, back-breaking trail.[78] In Panama City where they awaited berths on the ships for California, many idled their time away in drinking, gambling and other indulgences in the shanty town (known as El Arrabal) that sprang up in Santa Ana outside the city walls. One young traveller, disgusted by the "unbridled lust" of his fellow Americans, wrote to his mother complaining that "good young men raised in God-fearing homes go to the dogs at a fast clip doing the clutch-and-hug dance in the arms of the painted females of the hurdy-gurdy halls".[79] Other women passed the time in more respectable money-making activities such as sewing clothes for fellow travellers. Jamaicans and other West Indians were no doubt among those providing services to the travellers; from newspaper and other reports, the islanders seem to have become involved in almost every aspect of life.

Monkey, Iguana and Snake Stew

The food on the isthmus at first was as questionable as the accommodation. Jerky – thin strips of beef hung on lines and dried in the sun – was an isthmus staple then as later, as were, in the American hotels "dried beans, hard tack, mouldy bread and coffee". The fare at the Independent seemed more hearty. 'Slapjack' – "a thick substantial pancake of flour, salt and water" – was followed by pork, strips of beef stewed with dumplings, hams, great dishes of rice, jugs of molasses and treacle for sauce, with quantities of tea or coffee.[80] But this was fare for the travellers who could afford the expense. Chickens and eggs were such luxuries that the hoteliers would hang a chicken outside their establishments to show their availability. On the whole, food was scarce and expensive, and some of the travellers, like the workers, soon learned to eat monkey, iguana or snake stew in order to survive.[81]

After 1851, the railroad established commissaries at Aspinwall and along the line towns, and cooked food at the work camps. Fortunately for the workers, many familiar tropical fruit such as coconuts and guavas grew wild and others, such as plantains, scorned by the northern travellers, became increasingly available. Whether the labourers earned enough to eat properly is questionable for even drinking water was sold, at ten cents a crock (three gallons), carried around by vendors. But if water was scarce, drink was plentiful and cheap, and the constant spectre of sickness and death made many imbibe freely and recklessly: "The American mechanics and the better-paid railroaders of other nationalities restored themselves periodically from the wastage of the fevers . . . by going on a regimen of champagne cocktail, using quinine for bitters."[82]

As time went on, the little white schooners that brought the labourers in from Jamaica and Cartagena also carried on board provisions for sale such as yams, plantains, turtles, chickens and livestock. They also brought plants and seeds. Some enterprising Jamaicans set out for the bush and started cultivations,[83] and soon Jamaican women at railway stations were selling to the travellers bananas, green coconuts and oranges which came from these fields.[84]

Thus some Jamaicans began doing in Panama what they had done for centuries in the island and wherever they went throughout Central America: taking possession of a piece of ground and planting food crops. Meanwhile their women – heads loaded with trays of fruit or cooked food to sell – were imprinting their presence on the landscape like the famed itinerant higglers or hucksters of their homeland, images that were to persist until well into the twentieth century.[85] By the time the railroad opened, ice brought from Boston was a welcome luxury, and Tomes recorded that natives were getting used to the luxury of "sherry-cobblers and ice-cream, which latter is now cried nightly in the streets of Panama, in English, by Jamaican Negro women".[86]

VIOLENCE AND JUNGLE JUSTICE

While the Jamaicans in Panama tried to replicate home as much as they could, one habit acquired on the isthmus and unknown in their colonial homeland at the time was the acquisition of a gun and the gun-play that went with it. By all accounts, to dare to put foot on the isthmus at this time was to dance with Death. No one had immunity from the violence which came in many forms – disease, accident, act of God or the wilful acts of men. However, law-lessness of isthmian society and the frequent episodes of violence in which Jamaicans became involved presented a picture that was in direct contrast to the situation in their homeland at this time. The reports of the colonial police in Jamaica show very little crime, most of it limited to praedial larceny (theft of crops), disorderly conduct and vagrancy, and the reports over time comment on the "good order and sobriety" of the populace.[87] Tensions might have been simmering beneath the surface but a white newspaper editor in 1900 could aver, "Negroes continue to be the most law-abiding people in the Empire."[88] He added that "any white person of either sex, young or old, may walk alone from one end of the island to the other, and meet nothing but courtesy and kindness",[89] a view confirmed in many travel memoirs then and later. In Panama, by contrast, many Jamaican males soon acquired the popular acces-sories of a gold watch, a gun and matching attitude. Returnees brought their guns and attitude back home too, so that Latin American countries were soon to be perceived as schools for violence until well into the twentieth century, a view reinforced by the revolutionary political activity of the times.

Much of the man-made violence on the isthmus was shaped by ethnicity, nationality and, above all, by race. One of the main antagonisms of the period was between foreigners in general and the local populations, and, specifically, between Jamaicans and coastal Colombians. Overlaying all social relations, however, was the acute hostility between white Americans and everyone else, including the Panamanians, arising mainly from the uncouth treatment of all non-Caucasians by the Yankees (as all Americans came to be called). This hos-tility culminated in what is known in Panamanian history as the "Watermelon War" of 18 April 1856, an incident over a slice of watermelon that ended in a near-massacre of all white Americans trapped inside the railroad building in Panama City.[90]

Figure 2.20 An engraving of the time showing "an attack on whites" during the Watermelon War of 1856 in Panama City (Wikimedia Commons).

The behaviour and attitude of the Americans to the "natives" was estab-lished by the first shiploads of gold-rush travellers, no doubt emboldened by their country's recent annexation of one-third of Mexico. One Theodore T. Johnson, arriving in 1849, reported his fellow passengers as shouting, "Whip the rascal, fire his den, burn the settlement, annex the Isthmus",[91] remarks directed at the local boatmen who could never act fast enough for the trav-ellers. At first, few of the boatmen or those who provided porterage or mule services along the trail understood English, but the intent was always made clear with threats or a gun to the head. Mrs Seacole recorded, "Terribly bullied by the Americans were the boatmen and muleteers, who were reviled, shot, and stabbed by these free and independent filibusters, who would fain whop all creation abroad as they do their slaves at home."[92]

The boatmen at first made fifteen dollars or more for the trip to Cruces, but for people constantly reviled as "lazy", it was astonishingly hard, daunting work, pulling against the heavy current, for thirty constantly twisting miles, the mood of the river unpredictable and dangerous. Each boat was about twenty-five feet long and three feet wide, a flat-bottomed dugout made from a single log. It usually had a bit of thatched awning for shelter called a *toldo*. The *padrón* was the steersman, and a crew of four propelled the boat by paddles or by poles where the river was shallow. The picture presented by a gold-rush traveller evoked a boating tradition which went back many hundreds of years:

> Taking their stand upon the broadened edges of the canoe on either side, one end of their pole upon the bottom of the river, and the other placed against their shoulder, smoking with perspiration, their deep chests sending forth volumes of vapor into the vapory air, their swollen sinews strained to their utmost tension, and

Figure 2.21 A native bungo boat with sails (Otis, *Illustrated History*, 191).

Figure 2.22 Boatmen and passengers. Detail of a painting by Charles Christian Nohl (1850) titled *The Isthmus of Panama at the Height of the Chagres River* (Wikimedia Commons).

keeping time to a sort of grunting song, they step steadily along from stem to stern, thus sending the boat rapidly over the water, except where the current is strong. The middle of the channel, where the water is deep and the current rapid, is avoided as much as possible, yet with every precaution the men frequently miss their purchase and the boat falls back in a few minutes as great a distance as it can recover in an hour.[93]

Every hour the men tied up their craft and plunged into the river to cool off, taking long draughts of *anisou* or *aguardiente*.[94]

The *bungo* boatmen were native Indians, Spanish-speaking blacks and mestizos, and they were joined at the time of the gold rush by blacks from Jamaica and Haiti. But while the Yankee invasion at first brought some wealth into their hands and that of other locals who provided services, this benefit soon passed into the hands of Americans, who took over much of the transportation system including the transit from ship to the landing at Chagres and passage up river. Individual Americans acquired their own boats to ferry passengers from the ships and were not above using violence and intimidation against the competition. Companies brought in steamers that carried passengers up the Chagres to Gorgona, or as far as they could go, then riverboats, which carried hundreds at a time; fifty lifeboats were brought in as river transport. By 1853, foreign firms were organizing integrated ocean-to-ocean transit for passengers – by rail, river and passage to the ship at either end. By 1854 the crossing could be completed in seven hours.

These innovations wiped out local earnings from transit services, and some of the former independent boatmen hired on with the large companies. Others, however, maintained their independence fiercely and competition among the boatmen led to price wars, violence and intimidation on both sides. When a riot between Americans and other boatmen (including men from Jamaica and Haiti) erupted as it did at Chagres in 1851, it expended itself in bloody anti-American feeling. According to the *Star*, thirty to forty Americans were killed in the ensuing melee that lasted several days, during which the blacks shot up the town. Some fourteen natives were also killed. These figures might be an exaggeration, but there is no doubt that anti-American feeling ran high: the US mail could be put on board a steamer only under the protection of the British flag. Two-and-a-quarter million dollars in gold dust was also put on the ship the same way, and "as the last box was removed the negroes fell on the boat and in a few minutes cut it in pieces". The newspaper (owned and operated by a white American) complained that "an American scarce dare own himself as such now in the neighbourhood of the Chagres, else he will have a whole horde of semi-savages upon him to cut and hew him to pieces. His only safety is to deny his country, and say he is an Englishman or a Frenchman."[95]

The American travellers were coming from a society in which slavery was still a flourishing institution (the US Civil War was ten years away), and their behaviour partly reflected this fact. Their attitude also simply reflected a belief in the superiority of Americans, which they expressed in every way. But the locals were just as deprecating of the often drunken Yankees who took over their city as they camped out waiting for their ships and showed no respect for the Panamanians and their customs.

The anti-American feeling was induced by proximity to "ugly Americans" and was also actively encouraged by many formerly enslaved Africans from America who resided in Panama and, in many cases, had risen to positions of prominence and power, occupying public offices.[96] Mrs Seacole informs us that many of these blacks were fugitives from the American South who sought refuge in Central American countries. These "self-liberated Negroes" were generally "superior men" and in time came to occupy positions of prominence in the priesthood, army and municipal offices. They were described as "bold" with white Americans, and the locals soon followed their examples. When white Americans crossing the isthmus brought their enslaved Africans with them, the people of the towns and villages frequently connived with the enslaved to escape. When they did, the authorities refused to aid in their recapture. Similar anti-slavery activity was reported in Jamaica at this time also, the newly liberated Africans there taking enslaved black seamen from American ships in the harbour and bringing them before local magistrates who declared them free. So widespread was this practice there that the US consul noted in a despatch of 1853 that "such is the power and audacity of the Negro population here just now, heightened by the plentiful distribution of *Uncle Tom's*

Cabin, that they would take any of their colour out of an American Vessel, be they free or otherwise".[97]

In Panama, however, there existed yet another layer of antipathy: that between Jamaicans and the local people and especially the coastal Colombians from Cartagena and Santa Marta. The original reason for this hostility is lost in time, but it can be assumed that linguistic, religious and cultural differences were at play. The mutual antagonism was clearly deep-seated: serious and bloody confrontations between the two groups continued during the French canal construction. This particular antagonism also contributed to the stories being circulated in Jamaica about the violent nature of life on the isthmus.

Such forces of law and order as existed in Panama at this time of acute tension and political instability clearly showed their bias towards the Colombians – unless modified by lavish bribery. This fact is repeatedly emphasized in contemporary accounts.[98] Mrs Seacole described the soldier-police of New Granada as a "dirty, cowardly, indolent set, more prone to use their knives than their legitimate arms, and bore old rusty muskets, and very often marched unshod". As far as justice was concerned, "you might commit the grossest injustice, and could obtain the simplest justice only by lavish bribery. . . . I generally avoided claiming the protection of the law whilst on the Isthmus for I found it was . . . rather an expensive luxury."[99] Additionally, facilities for speedy apprehension and trial did not exist.

Sometimes the violence escalated, as it did following a fight between Jamaicans and Colombians at a dance given by a señorita at Yankee Chagres. The Colombians apparently got the worst of it and they ran to the river and called for help from the native town. According to the newspaper, reinforcements armed with their machetes surrounded the house.

> The Jamaicans attempted to escape and ran for their boats. Many were cut down at the first attempt, others were followed to the river where they plunged in and drowned. In this manner 6 or 8 were killed. The rest made their escape, some severely wounded. The house was literally gutted of everything. During the night crowds of highly excited natives went around the streets stopping whoever they met and asking, "Are you American?" If the reply was yes it was all-right and the reply was "Bueno Americano, Muerto a los Jamaicanos."[100]

Of course Jamaicans were also frequently perpetrators of violence against others and among themselves. The *Star* headed an article "An Outrage": "On Thursday, a Jamaican negro, a servant man of Sr. Maximo Perez, we believe, attacked a servant girl of Mr. Benjamin in the street, and beat her severely with a cart whip. He was sentenced to 14 days in jail. Soon after his master made application for his immediate release and this was done."[101] Jamaicans also figured prominently in reports of other criminal activities such as theft and robberies[102] and some were to be caught up in the vigilante justice that came to prevail.

Since the jungle trail was also once again the carrier of immense wealth in gold, officially or unofficially, along with personal baggage, commercial cargo and the US mail, it became infested with robbers, highwaymen, outlaws and cut-throats from all over the world. The robbers were collectively called the Derienni (presumably from "Darién"), harking back to an earlier name for local highwaymen. By 1851, some five thousand passengers from thirteen regular ships were in constant movement across the isthmus, those going to California equipped with their "stake", those returning, with their gold. To facilitate goods and passengers, a number of express companies sprang up, operating mule trains. Frequently, "Guns would bark in the jungle and the next day mules without riders or packs would turn up at Gorgona or Cruces. The Derienni massacred boatloads of travelers on the Chagres and looted their dead bodies. Buzzards wheeled in the skies above the green jungle, marking the end of these little dramas."[103]

To counter these highwaymen, the railroad secured from the governor of Panama absolute power over those traversing the territory, and in 1851 secretly brought in a Texas ranger named Randolph (Ran) Runnels,[104] who organized the Runnels Express Service as a cover for the secret organization named the Isthmus Guard. They managed to identify and round up the leading criminals and administer Texas justice, hanging thirty-seven of them at one time on the Panama City sea wall. Citizens and travellers alike stared silently at the dangling bodies, asking no questions. Over the next few years, similar vigilante justice was administered to some two hundred people. Thereafter, although criminal activity was not eradicated, the trails grew safer, with the Isthmus Guard numbering some Jamaicans among its multicultural ranks – as well as among those detained.[105]

In general, the restraining influences of the legal, cultural, or social institutions of an established society were largely non-existent. The Federation of New Granada was experiencing constant political turmoil and was unable to provide effective government in Panama. Thus the whole society lived in a state of actual or perceived anarchy. The boldest among the immigrants adopted the values of the society and swaggered about with gun and gold chain. The more circumspect attempted to graft on to Panamanian soil their own institutions and values.

The Final Years

But swiftly, this first cycle of high times and low, of prosperity or death, ended with the opening of the railroad, many returning to their homelands or leaving for more promising climes. The foreign inhabitants of the isthmus during rail-road construction years were of every variety of race, shade, colour and nationality, stratified along the same lines, according to Robert Tomes. Rail-road officials, steamboat agents, foreign consuls, and a score of Yankee traders, hotelkeepers, billiard markers and bartenders comprised all the whites – the "exclusive few" he tells us. The "better class of shop-keepers are Mulattoes from Jamaica, St. Domingo, and the other West Indian Islands, while the dispensers of cheap grog, and hucksters of fruit and small wares are chiefly negroes". The main body of the population was made up of "laborers, negroes from Jamaica, yellow natives of mixed African and Indian blood, and sad, sedate turbanned Hindoos, the poor exiled Coolies from the Ganges".[106]

Most of the Jamaicans were labourers, but the isthmus attracted Jamaicans of every class. Among those migrating to Panama and other places during the cholera epidemic were some described as the "best blood".[107] Many of these people already had commercial and family ties with Panama. Some were Jamaican Jews who had gone over in 1849 at the beginning of the gold rush, among them A.N. Henriques, who remained on the isthmus for fifty years and became a recruiter of Jamaican labour for French canal officials. The activity connected with the building of the railroad and the constant passage of gold-seekers flocking west enhanced opportunities for business among old established firms. There were also many enterprising new traders, such as Mrs Seacole, who functioned on the isthmus at various times as hotelier and store-keeper and who on trips to and fro carried goods for trade and profit in the respective countries. White Jamaicans also occupied high status positions in commerce, on the Panama Railroad[108] and in the professions.

Although most poor Jamaicans came to find work on the railroad, many soon found alternative sources of employment or "scuffled" as they would have done at home. They filled positions as household servants, hotel and restaurant employees at all levels, as porters, boatmen and coachmen, their understanding of English an obvious advantage. Some Jamaicans squatted on lands in the bush and became cultivators while their women became higglers, in the pattern of rural Jamaica. Thus from the middle of the nineteenth century a Jamaican presence was established on the isthmus with Jamaicans stratified according to race and occupations much as they would have been at home.

We have little information on the social activities of the Jamaicans who came at the time of the railroad but it seems reasonable to suppose that these earlier emigrants established rudimentary churches, schools, banking and social security systems (through "pardners",[109] mutual aid societies and the like) as later arrivals did. We do know that they made a valiant effort to tame the hostile environment through agricultural endeavours, and some became settlers. Many got caught up in the excitement of the gold rush and continued to California.

Jamaicans continued to work on the railroad after its opening. Since the line had been thrown up so quickly to accommodate the travellers, much of it was temporary and reconstruction continued for many years afterwards. However, once travellers could transit the isthmus without stopping, the prosperity which they had brought to the line towns and villages soon vanished. Most of the local people lost their means of livelihood, businesses and hotels closed, and the apathy into which much of the isthmus was sunk soon returned.

Yet clearly, the memory of the isthmus as a hell-hole did not last long and might have been outweighed by the lasting benefits of that first migration. For a generation later, Jamaicans would be stampeding to get to Panama once again, and this time they would be joined by other West Indian islanders in large numbers, especially from Barbados, St Lucia, and from the French islands of Guadeloupe and Martinique. They were electrified by the news that a French syndicate was to begin construction of a Panama canal.

PART 2

THE FRENCH CANAL

Quel Panama!

—*French expression meaning "What a mess!", which became popular
after the French canal disaster.*

Figure 3.1 West Indians promenade on Front Street, Colón, during prosperous times. (Courtesy of William P. McLaughlin, www.czimages.com.)

3. THE FRENCH CANAL, 1881–1904

THE JAMAICAN EXODUS TO COLÓN during the attempt led by Ferdinand de Lesseps to construct a canal across the Isthmus can be described only as a stampede: men, women and children fought to get on to the ships making the run. During the eight years of construction by the Compagnie Universelle (1881–89), at least eighty-four thousand Jamaicans left their homeland for Latin America, though this is an estimate only. Few formal records exist for this period but demographers agree that at least twenty thousand of those who left never returned.[1] A few thousands scattered to Costa Rica, Mexico, Guatemala, Honduras, Ecuador, Brazil[2] and elsewhere in Latin America, but the vast majority headed for Colón.[3]

Some 3,144 left at the start of construction in 1881–82; the next year recorded 32,958 leaving while 14,962 returned. After 1884 returning residents began to outnumber emigrants and by 1888 when work by the Compagnie Universelle had almost ceased, only 1,861 left while 10,958 returned.[4] Although more than 7,000 were officially repatriated in 1889 (and many undoubtedly returned home on their own steam), a considerable number of Jamaicans must have remained, consolidating what was already becoming a permanent West Indian presence on the isthmus. American businessman Minor C. Keith hired "boatloads" of labourers in Colón to complete his railroad in Costa Rica.[5]

While they dispersed along the line of canal works following the railroad across the isthmus, it was the little Atlantic port of Colón, still called Aspinwall by some, that became romanticized as the goal of the migrants. They would come to be referred to in their homeland as the Colón people, and Colón Man became the age's symbol of glamour – and ridicule. The song "Colón Man" survives as a popular staple of Jamaican folk song repertoire:

> One two three four
> Colón man a come
> With him watch chain a lick him belly
> bam bam bam

Ask him for the time
and he look upon the sun
With him watch chain a lick him belly
bam bam bam

What set these Colón people apart from later emigrants was perhaps a kind of heady liberation that they experienced and expressed in the French construction years, a mode of being later lost forever as travel became more circumscribed by rules. In contrast to the US military approach to canal construction and social engineering yet to come, the French enterprise was a stop-and-start affair as investors wrestled with problems of financing, engineering, mismanagement, geology, climate and the death rate. In these wild days on the isthmus, virtually every man packed a gun, liquor flowed and "licentious living" was the norm. High-priced French courtesans flourished and brothels offered women of every nation. While the French lived separate lives with superior facilities to the black workforce, there was not the rigid racial segregation that was introduced later by the Americans. And, for a while, money flowed: the French payroll was over one million US dollars per month.

After the French canal's failure, both the Jamaican authorities and the American imposed tighter regulations, the former – in part – as a reaction to the French debacle and to the sudden flood of repatriations that it caused. Coupled with this disaster were stories of maltreatment and stranding of Jamaican workers in Ecuador, Mexico and other places.[6] By the turn of the twentieth century, Jamaicans seeking work abroad would find it harder and more expensive to leave their country.

COLÓN: "THE NEW JAMAICA"

As with the first migration in the 1850s, this second wave in the 1880s affected every class of people. Jamaicans of all colours and walks of life flocked into Colón. So many came that by 1884 Colón was being called "the new Jamaica".[7] For most of the construction period, Jamaicans outnumbered not just all other nationalities there, but they almost swamped the native population as well,[8] providing the majority of labourers for the canal and many of the self-employed and professionals. Jamaican doctors, druggists, veterinary surgeons, pastors, teachers, photographers, translators, newsstand dealers, newspaper compositors, proofreaders and editors are recorded for this period, as well as merchants, many of Jewish origin, including Isaac Brandon and Company and S.B. Delvalle and Company. The *Star and Herald* noted the celebration of the Jewish High Holiday of Yom Kippur in Colón by persons well known in Jamaica: Charles Alberga, Mr Martinez, Michael Delevante, David Lindo and Isaac Symons.[9] Frenchmen who had settled in Jamaica, some coming via Haiti, were also prominent, including Adolfo Maynier, a veterinary surgeon; Henri Duperly, a photographer who worked there around 1884; and Charles Gadpaille, who became the Compagnie Universelle's chief recruiting agent in the West Indies.

Because of the traditional linkages between Jamaican and Panamanian merchant houses, enhanced by increased demand for Jamaican products such as rum, folk medications, livestock and ground provisions, traders or "travelling representatives" became a ubiquitous presence.[10] Together with the railroad workers, clerks and domestic servants, they presented a wide cross-section of Jamaica's population and gave this alien society the feel of a Jamaican outpost. Proximity and ease of communication meant that Jamaicans could still continue to participate, even vicariously, in the life of home. When a fire destroyed most of Kingston in 1882, the first overseas subscriptions to the fire fund came from Panama. Jamaican ministers of religion frequently came to the isthmus, as did entertainers. Among the latter was the humourist Andrew C. Murray, who, as his father Henry G. Murray had done earlier, made more than one tour. By 1883 he had collected enough material for new comedy sketches to be presented in Jamaica titled "The Panama Canal" and "Uncle Dober in Colón".[11]

Panama's newspapers regularly carried Jamaican news, including the results of the Kingston races, and there was even talk of providing a Colón purse for these races. Calabar College in Kingston was advertising for student boarders from Central America – a start of what would later become a regular connection between Jamaican educational institutions and Latin America. Obituary notices in Panama carried the note "Jamaican papers please copy", which Jamaican papers reciprocated. Ease of transit between the countries was such that some of the services verged on the ludicrous: Jamaican washerwomen regularly travelled back and forth taking clothes from the isthmus to be laundered in Jamaica, a practice that was finally prohibited as a health hazard by the City Council of Kingston in 1885.[12]

MASS DEPARTURES

We know little about the impact of the returning Panama Railroad workers on their homelands though this influence was undoubtedly significant. Those of the 1880s imprinted themselves on private and public consciousness because of their sheer numbers, and because many came from and returned to the smallest hamlets in every corner of the island. The Colón Man embodied everything that was both feared and envied: a dream of personal independence – incredibly – made flesh.

As a Jamaican newspaper pointed out to its readers at the height of the emigration in 1883:

> Men are to be seen in the different parishes who never wore a whole pair of britches or knew a pair of boots, strolling fully dressed, with an umbrella, a gold, brass or plated chain, a brass or silver watch, rings to give away and a nucleus of cash in five dollar gold pieces in their possession and at sight of these irresistible inducements, away flock cane hole diggers, wood cutters, trenchmen, wain men, all able hands to the El Dorado.[13]

Most of those who left for Panama in the 1880s probably saw the venture as temporary, a way of making quick money and returning home. No passport or papers were required – all one needed was money to buy passage on a boat and company recruiters offered free passage to labourers. Deck passage on a steamer from Kingston was twenty-five shillings one way and could be purchased at dock side. Traffic by schooner and other small craft prospered. The Royal Mail line ran regular fortnightly service, and every few days a British or American steamer called at the Port of Kingston en route to Colón.

At first it was people from Kingston, the capital city, who got into the boats, but as company recruiters sent runners around Jamaica's countryside and the news spread, rural people began to migrate in droves. Sometimes mass departures by labourers heightened excitement in Kingston as happened, for instance, when seven hundred rural people wanting to travel came in by train at one time.[14]

In January 1882 a newspaper noted that on the departure of labourers on the Royal Mail steamer that week, "the lower part of Duke Street and the wharf premises were so crowded by the vast number of men who were thus emigrating to a foreign and sickly clime to earn a livelihood, that the scene could not fail to strike one with astonishment".[15] On another occasion, in 1883, Duke Street from Harbour Street down to the sea was "utterly impassable to pedestrians and wheeled traffic". So dense was the crowd on board that the steamer was delayed two hours beyond sailing time.[16]

A similar scene was reported in January 1884. Although the clerks in the ticket office warned the crowd that the ship could not accommodate them all, they expressed themselves satisfied with having standing room only for the whole voyage. At ten o'clock the gates were thrown open and a stampede took place: men with trunks on their backs, women with little children tugging through the crowd, all trying to get on board. In a few minutes the deck was so crowded that the crew could scarcely move about. The captain told the agent to stop the embarkation:

This was the signal for an extra rush and the energies of the officers of the ship, the Inspectors of Constabulary, the Constables, Water Police and Detectives (of which there was a good muster) were severely tried in keeping the stage clear. The notice bell was rung and those who managed to get on board before were not allowed to leave the ship and their baggage was consequently left behind, while others who had put their trunks etc. on board could not get aboard and the steamer carried these away. When the last bell rang and the stages being drawn off, consternation arose and the people cursed the company for selling more tickets than the accommodation. The captain and others reasoned with them that the *Belize* would leave in a day or two and tickets could be used for her – the women with tears in their eyes called attention to the quantity of perishable articles which would spoil.

About five hundred people were left behind. Some made a rush for the company's office where those who wished had their tickets redeemed; others had them altered for the next steamer. The ship sailed with an estimated twelve hundred on board, including crew.[17]

As before, the travellers were packed on the open decks without shelter from wind or weather. They squatted on top of their possessions and made themselves as comfortable as they could for the trip to Colón. When the weather was fine they sang at nights. When the weather was bad, they cowered sick and shivering. Sometimes they sang the songs that were being made about the grand enterprise in which they were participating: "Isaac Park gone to Colón / Colón *bolow* a go kill dem bwoy." Or,

> Mass Charley say wan' kiss Matty
> Kiss him with a willing mind
> Me ra-ra boom oh
> Colón money done.

At other times the plaintive sound of Moody and Sankey hymns rose above the hissing wind and creaking machinery. One out of every four would never see Jamaica again. For survivors, however, Kingston-to-Colón became a circular route with frequent travel back and forth. By the end of the first year it was estimated that a significant number of the migrants had already come back to Jamaica, "bringing with them money with which they arrange their affairs and aid their families. Many of them return to the Canal works taking others with them."[18] By 1884, the peak year of French construction, it seemed "a regular course for the men after earning a fair amount to return to Jamaica to visit their families and friends and after a short time to return to the Isthmus to work again".[19]

Returning home to celebrate holidays such as Christmas, Easter and Queen Victoria's Birthday was a regular practice, interfering, incidentally, with the progress of the work. "The Easter holidays", the French canal *Bulletin* complained in 1887, "have stripped the canal works of a great many labourers, almost all from the Antilles, who have gone home for a vacation. For a long time the company has been calling the contractors' attention to the evils resulting from . . . the ease with which workmen can return to their own countries in a few days."[20] Many workers also abandoned the works during the rainy season, presumably heading for home.

A report from the Jamaican parish of St Thomas where, it was claimed, all able-bodied men had left for Colón, described the migrants' activities on returning home: "They return periodically with coin, pay their taxes, and spend their earnings on their families who with themselves go about seeking pleasure until their cash is nearly exhausted, then return to Colón to work for more, but during their stay here will work for no one."[21]

Although these biased views are those of the elite, the image of Colón and the symbols of life there were nevertheless highly visible through the frequent visits of well-dressed Colón Men, igniting ambitions and dreams of those left behind. As a newspaper noted, "No repressive measures will prevent men leaving the Island so long as the returning toilers continue to land in Kingston dressed in black cloth suits, brilliant with cheap jewellery, and proud of the possession of a watch and a revolver."[22]

So many left for Colón that large areas of the Jamaican countrywide were – reportedly – depopulated. Parts of the eastern coast, especially, took on the appearance of almost total desolation as men deserted their families, their jobs, their crafts, their fishing boats, their homes or provision grounds to join the exodus. Whole villages or estates were abandoned. Lack of jobs and adverse weather might compel everyone in a given area and drive them to try their luck

Figure 3.2 The rural poor, Jamaica, at the end of the nineteenth century. (Courtesy of the National Library of Jamaica.)

overseas; groups of relatives and friends might decide to go off together, or they might be contracted for the same sailing by recruiters for the canal contractors, Gadpaille and Company, who became quite extravagant with their promises. After a while, their work probably became unnecessary as returning migrants became walking advertisements for the advantages of travel. As a planter faced with a labour force disappearing in the direction of Costa Rica had complained, "Now and again you see a great swell with a watch and gold chain, a revolver pistol, red sash, big boots up to his knees, who swaggers about for a week or two then disappears. Of course that has the effect of making others go."[23]

Such visible signs of individual success cancelled out all the tales of disease, death, poor living conditions, massacres and other negative news. Even those who seemed to the planters most settled and stable joined the rush from home: "One well-to-do man who has continual employment as a Headman superintending labourers on the roads, and other employments of trust giving him good wages, who had his house and land, owns a good horse, and with a wife and family, goes along. The infatuation to go seems to have taken hold of the whole of them who are able to go."[24] While the pull of money wages and the glamour of travel or thirst for adventure should not be overlooked, most people continued to be pushed out of their homelands by adverse social and economic conditions.

The first emigrants came, as stated earlier, from Kingston with its huge numbers of unemployed, thereafter followed by the depopulation of the countryside. Between 1871 and 1881, the total number employed in agriculture fell by over twenty thousand; many drifted into the city.[25] A disastrous fire in Kingston in December 1882 destroyed over 570 buildings, leaving six thousand homeless. Many of these were tenement dwellers who emigrated. The government's medical report of 1884 notes that Kingston's mortality rate had dropped, not from improvements in health but from emigration among that section of the population in which the deaths would have occurred.[26] So many people left Kingston that shopkeeping became a "precarious business".[27]

By 1883 the "unbroken stream of migrants" caused a labour shortage and rising prices in Kingston.[28] Opportunities were scarce for everyone. For the young women thrown out of work as seamstresses

Figure 3.3 Clerking in a store offered one of the few white-collar jobs for males. Customers (*seated*) and clerks in the shoe department of a high-end store in Kingston in the late nineteenth century (Johnson, *Jamaica, the New Riviera*).

by the newfangled sewing machines, prostitution or emigration seemingly offered the only means of livelihood.[29] The business of tailors was also affected. And for many young men aged between sixteen and eighteen, there existed little alternative employment to labouring in the fields or clerking in the stores.[30] The commission looking into the condition of the juvenile population noted that

> the class of young men that are not fit for labourers are about the most difficult to deal with. Some become bookkeepers and others clerks; but there is not room for all of them. If they once lose their situation in the store it is very difficult for them to get another, and they are obliged to hang on for a long time before they can find employment.
>
> When the young men are driven to starvation point they leave the island, and it is gratifying to know that we often hear of their succeeding and doing well in other countries.[31]

In the long run, however, most of the labour for the Panama Canal was provided by Jamaica's rural folk: unemployed peasant youth; landless family men who found it impossible to feed their families on wages of one shilling a day; and frustrated peasant proprietors burdened under oppressive taxation, unpredictable crop yields, adverse weather, unrewarding markets, and plots of land too small to sustain themselves and rising generations.[32]

Attempts were also made to attract workers from the other West Indian islands and many came from the French island of Martinique, and from Barbados and St Lucia. The flood of workers from these and other islands would come later, during construction of the American canal.

Figure 3.4 The French digging of Culebra Cut, 1885 (Wikimedia Commons).

DE LESSEPS'S GRAND ENTERPRISE

New life surged into the isthmus in 1881 with the coming of the Compagnie Universelle du Canal Interocéanique. It was the start of a grand debauch:

> In the course of twelve months rents of buildings quadrupled, the prices of land were more than doubled, and the most sober-minded residents were seized by a mania for speculation. French contractors came in, with adventurers, profligates, and gamblers close behind them. For nine years, there were high prices, feverish excitement, business activity, hard drinking, and general demoralisation. Champagne flowed and diamonds flashed. Improvidence in canal management was matched by reckless play in the gambling hall. Corruption, bribery and immorality were rampant.[33]

Such was the reign of the French as seen through English Victorian eyes. It tells only half the story. Despite the panache the French brought to *La grande entreprise*, yellow fever continued to make the Isthmus of Panama a hell on earth: two out of every three Frenchmen collapsed and died soon after arrival. At times empty ships sat at the company's pier in Colón harbour, the entire crew having died from yellow fever.[34] For every eighty employees who survived six months on the isthmus, twenty died. Although the French "doctored" their medical statistics as they did their other data, thus obscuring the true death rate, the American physicians who later took over calculated that at least twenty thousand canal employees died during the French construction years. A significant number would have been West Indians, who made up the majority of the workforce.[35] Reputations also died, including that of France's revered Ferdinand de Lesseps, a sad fate after his triumph as builder of the Suez Canal.

Figure 3.5 Ferdinand de Lesseps in 1880 (www.canalmuseum.com).

While the earliest survey of an isthmian canal route was made in 1524 on the orders of Charles V of Spain (followed by many others over the centuries),[36] it was a private French syndicate that began construction. In the 1870s, a group of Frenchmen undertook surveys, decided on the Panama route and obtained concessions from the Government of New Granada to construct a canal. De Lesseps lent his prestigious name and enormous energies to the enterprise. Because of the rich returns their compatriots had earned from investments in the Suez Canal, tens of thousands of French citizens purchased stock in the Compagnie Universelle, which also promised a lavish return. The initial public offering at five hundred francs

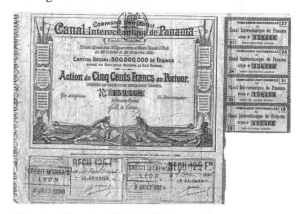

Figure 3.6 Compagnie Universelle share certificate (www.canalmuseum.com).

per share was oversubscribed, much of it coming from ordinary men and women for whom the investment represented half their annual wages. Later, even when it was clear that the bankers and rich investors were pulling out, the public continued to support more and more stock offers, so great was their faith in de Lesseps. These humble investors lost everything, even when the plutocrats profited highly and mysteriously.[37]

De Lesseps – seventy-four years old at the start but still capable of dancing all night and looking "fresh as a daisy" next morning[38] – glossed over many of the difficulties inherent in a project of such magnitude, and in the face of much scientific opposition, he announced that he would build a sea-level canal. "The Grand Frenchman" was a towering figure, to all accounts an honest and honourable man, but he was neither an engineer nor a financier. He was a charismatic and confident optimist but he was unable to see through the financial schemers surrounding him.

De Lesseps also made the mistake of seeing the Isthmus of Panama through the prism of Suez, although in terms of climate and geographical configurations they are dramatically dissimilar. Construction of a Panama Canal succeeded only after its American builders recognized the entirely new, unforeseen problems presented by the isthmus and took a pragmatic approach.

The French effort was doomed from the outset. Although French engineers were acknowledged as the best trained in the world, and they marched off by their hundreds to their deaths in Panama, the project was ill-conceived. Quotations and projections were not only unrealistic but the statistics were continually doctored to keep shareholders and new investors in Paris happily subscribing funds. Lavish expenditure, mismanagement, corruption and bribery characterized the enterprise.

The company crashed in 1889 amid a scandal that blackened de Lesseps's name and ending in trial and imprisonment in France for some of the bankers and company executives. The biggest financial and political upheaval of its time, it aroused so much anger among French citizens that residents of rue Panama in Paris, a street named during the glory days of the venture, sought in vain to change its name. "*Quel Panama!*" became a popular French expression, meaning "What a mess!" Panamanians, for their part, came to refer to the days of the free-spending French as "*le temps de luxe*".

In 1894, the Compagnie Nouvelle du Canal de Panama was formally incorporated to carry on the work so as not to lose the concession from New Granada while exploiting American interests in buying it out. It undertook work in fits and starts, hampered by the perennial problems of funding and disease, and by almost continuous civil war throughout Colombia. The War of a Thousand Days lasted from 1888 to 1902 and ended when, with American collusion, Panama declared its independence.[39] When the Compagnie

Nouvelle sold out to the United States government in 1904, it had a workforce of only seven hundred labourers, mainly Jamaicans.[40]

While the French effort had failed miserably, a considerable amount of preliminary work and excavation for the canal was undertaken. Some of the French equipment and material left behind was usable and, above all, the French maps, surveys and plans and information on rainfall, weather and topography proved invaluable. More important though, the failure of the French paved the way for the Americans, who carefully avoided their predecessor's mistakes, including, above all, elaborate ceremony.

They could not have failed to note the symbolism attending the inauguration of the French ceremonial "turning of the first sod" on New Year's Day, 1880, with de Lesseps, his wife, and distinguished guests sipping champagne as they set off on the launch *Taboguilla* from Panama City towards the mouth of the Rio Grande three miles away. Here, de Lesseps would dig his shovel into what was scheduled to become the Pacific entrance to the canal. Crowds of latecomers so delayed departure that receding tides prevented the party from reaching the site in Panama Bay. It was left to de Lesseps's seven-year-old daughter to launch the enterprise by thrusting a ceremonial pickaxe brought for the occasion into sand in a champagne box on deck.

The French effort consumed money and lives until the inevitable end, but not before some $260 million was spent. The venture hit highs and lows on the Paris bourse; bouts of frenzied activity followed by listless uncertainty on the Panama construction sites. There, even the best engineers and contractors had to contest with natural and man-made disasters: fires, floods, earthquakes,

Figure 3.7
Montage of the French arrival in Colón
(www.canalmuseum
.com).

political insurrections, massacres, strikes, labour shortages, labour surpluses, and, above all, disease and death. For the French, it was the best of times, it was the worst of times, a narrative of heroism and despair. Investors in France were told little of what was happening on the isthmus; those on the isthmus knew little of what was happening in Paris. As in the chaotic days of the Panama Railroad, into this melee were to pour tens of thousands of West Indians in continued pursuit of the dreams of the optimistic dispossessed.

THE COURSE OF CONSTRUCTION

Construction during the French years was to be so buffeted by internal and external circumstances that it is best to see it unfolding as it happened. On 30 December 1879, de Lesseps, his wife, three of their young children, and a team of engineers and financiers arrived in Panama and officially inaugurated the project on New Year's Day 1880. De Lesseps then set forth with vigour to raise the necessary funds.

The Compagnie Universelle was officially incorporated in Paris on 3 March 1881 with de Lesseps as president. On 29 January of that year, some forty engineers had arrived in Panama aboard the *Lafayette*. Armand Réclus, agent supérieur, led the operation and Gaston Blanchet (who had conducted surveys in Panama) was chief engineer for the main contractor Couvreaux and Hersent and director of works. A few of the men brought their wives. Although they arrived in the dry season, the shock of pulling into Colón must have been great, but they were taken by train immediately to Panama City, where they stayed initially at the Grand Hotel, later to become French headquarters. Its enormous lobby provided the only diversion in a city without concert hall or café, featuring a vast bar, where "most of the business in Panama was conducted while standing and gulping down cocktails",[41] and a roulette wheel with the croupier calling the numbers in three languages. Opposite the hotel stood the cathedral, where bells tolled continuously as funeral processions passed through the narrow cobbled streets.

The Frenchmen wasted no time. On 1 February 1881 Réclus telegraphed to de Lesseps "*Travail commencé*" – work has started – and the news was immediately transmitted to newspaper readers all over France. Blanchet organized work camps along the line and rushed constantly from one to the other. The newcomers were billeted in barracks until prefabricated houses arrived from the United States. These houses were erected on high pilings and coated with tar to repel snakes, each room furnished with a chair, a table, and a hammock. Although French delicacies were later imported, the first men out in the bush sampled local dishes, such as ragout of freshly killed armadillo. By May, the rainy season brought on malaria, or "the shakes" as the Americans called it, and the men got used to heavy doses of quinine daily.

Blanchet had decided that the first two years should be spent in preparation: in mapping and surveying; in clearing a strip running the entire length of the canal, and in construction of housing. By February 1881, men pouring in from Jamaica were building barracks for workers and cottages for the white employees; and the towns of Gatún and Emperador (later Empire) were established, the latter becoming the headquarters of the French canal works. Other Jamaicans were working alongside coastal Colombian Indians and blacks, using machetes and axes to chop down trees and bushes and clear Blanchet's fifty-yard strip (later to be expanded to three hundred yards) alongside the railroad from Colón to Panama City. The work was hard and dangerous, the men hacking through dark, matted jungle with enormous trees that had to be felled and taken out by hand, and contending with wild animals, poisonous snakes, marshes and floods, the route crossing the volatile Chagres River fourteen times. They accomplished the task by May, though only one in ten of newly arrived workers remained on the job for over six months. For, as the rainy season arrived, the first deaths from yellow fever struck and deaths from typhoid, malaria and other diseases also soared. Among the casualties was the moving force behind the entire project, the chief engineer Gaston Blanchet. Labourers were said to be dying at the rate of two hundred a month, but there was no shortage of replacements as men were arriving on every ship.

Despite the well-publicized loss of life, adventurers came from all over the world as they had done during the building of the Panama Railroad. One of them was the French painter Paul Gauguin, who worked as a labourer on the canal before he ran afoul of the Colombian police and left in disgust for Martinique.[42] Volunteers, could not, however, provide the core of a reliable labour force, and contractors recruited African Americans from New Orleans, workers from Ireland, China, the Kru coast of Liberia, the Caribbean coast of Colombia, the French West Indian islands of Guadeloupe and Martinique, and the British islands of St Lucia and Barbados as well as Jamaica.

In the first five months of actual operation (February to June 1881) the French company had a workforce of 588. By the next year the force had expanded to 2,652 and by 1884 it had reached a peak of 19,000 employed. In 1885, of 12,875 labourers on the payrolls, 10,844 were British West Indians: 9,005 Jamaicans, 1,344 Barbadian, and 495 St Lucians. There were 800 from Martinique.[43] In 1886 it was estimated that there were 4,000 St Lucians on the isthmus and some 30 to 40 per cent of adult men from that island were in Panama (or about 10 per cent of the entire population).[44] From 1883 onwards, however, the vast majority of the labour force consisted of Jamaicans.

Labour contractors on the islands provided free passages to the fittest and promised wages of $1.00 day. Unskilled workers earned $1.00 to $1.75; artisans $2.50 to $2.75 for a ten-hour day lasting from 6:00 a.m. to 6:00 p.m. with a two-hour break from 11:00 a.m. to 1:00 p.m. The French also instituted a system of task work which the West Indians preferred since, working on their own time, unskilled labour could earn over $2.00 a day. At the then existing rate of exchange, one silver dollar equalled three shillings and three pence sterling, or roughly three times the usual daily rate for male plantation labour in Jamaica.

THE OFFICIAL START, 1882–1883

On 20 January 1882, seventy-four days after Blanchet's death, the actual digging of *La Grande Tranchée* was launched at Emperador, where throngs turned out to watch the first dig; the city of Panama staged a grand fete to celebrate. Excavation began at other levels, using steam shovels as well as men with picks and shovels, later with dynamite, so as to dig down to sea-level, mountains and all.

Equipment poured in via Colón, much of it requiring assembly. The lack of standardization and the fact that and much of the equipment proved too light for the heavy work of the isthmus contributed to the French failure. A pile-up of the vast quantities of equipment and material at Colón at first created chaos, partly because the French company had no control over the American-owned railroad (the only mover of men and materials), leading to frustrations and delays. In June 1881 the Compagnie Universelle bought out the Panama Railroad shares for over twenty million dollars, though not the railroad itself, since the United States remained the guarantor of Panamanian sovereignty according to the 1846 treaty with Colombia.

In Colón, workers were busy erecting sawmills and facilities for storage and shipping as well as housing for the French workers along the salubrious seaward side with its white coral beach. The little French residential area of Christophe-Colómb arose next to the houses of railroad employees and other white residents, its neatness, landscaped green lawns and palm trees contrasting with the chaos and squalor of Colón. The West Indians worked as well on the construction of hospitals, a large one at Ancón overlooking Panama City, a smaller one at Colón, and a sanatorium for convalescents at Taboga Islands.

As soon as they arrived, the labourers were sent to places along the line wherever work was needed. Up to 1884 little provision was made for them – there was frequently no accommodation, no tools or appliances. But they adapted:

These circumstances have little effect upon the final general distribution of these nomads, who have a way of shifting for themselves and selecting their own masters and places of work that the company could scarcely have contemplated. Frequently they are not to be found twenty-four hours after arrival upon the ground where they are originally sent to work, but go about from section to section wherever they can best suit their own particular ideas as to wages and other circumstances. The best of the men at once fall to and begin earning money, while the worthless and shiftless, and these are many, are always on the move until sickness prostrates them, or hunger or necessity compels them to quit their idleness.[45]

The workers were strung out in twenty-five villages along the line from Colón to Panama City. Labourers were at first housed in temporary ranchos or thatched huts with earthen floors until wooden barracks with galvanized iron roofs were constructed in the work camps. The barracks accommodated forty to one hundred men sleeping on two-tier bunks in two rows.[46] Separate accommodation was provided for blacks and whites; bathrooms were provided only for those above the rank of labourers; labourers had pit latrines. Where workmen were quartered free they were expected to feed themselves. Many made arrangements to eat at the cantines or boarding houses run mainly by the Chinese while native and West Indian women supplied food, as they had done before.

At the start, all the work was being undertaken by a single French contractor, Couvreux and Hersent, but in 1882 they withdrew, thereafter functioning as consultants and the work was parcelled out among many smaller companies, including some American. The contracting out of work to some two hundred poorly coordinated firms resulted in high expenses and low efficiency and was another contributor to the French failure. The Compagnie Universelle now had to directly supervise all aspects of the operation and hire and oversee the contractors. Workers were paid by the individual contractors but housing was the responsibility of the canal company.

Larger rumblings were ahead, for everyone was shaken by a massive earthquake on 7 September 1882, which severely damaged the railroad and buildings and cut cable communications with Jamaica and the United States for a month. Consequently, the news was slow to spread to the outside world. When it reached Paris, Panama stock devalued, but de Lesseps placated investors by telling them there would be no more earthquakes. In Panama City, Wolfred Nelson, a Canadian physician, noted how people had rushed in terror out of their houses and filled the plazas, as lesser shocks followed. "While nobody was afraid", Nelson recorded, "the sociability was intense".[47]

As if these problems were not enough, the contractors had to contend repeatedly with disturbances among the workers themselves. Racial, linguistic and cultural factors continued to set the West Indians apart, and the local population no doubt felt threatened by their sheer numbers. In an atmosphere where death through sickness, criminal or revolutionary activity awaited just around the corner, life was excessively cheap. Distrusting such forces of authority as existed, people frequently took the law into their own hands. Lack of peacekeeping forces in the towns and villages also contributed to the absence of harmony. So delicate was the balance between the peoples who shared the line towns, especially between Jamaicans and Colombians, a simple quarrel between individuals of different nationalities could escalate into "tribal wars" embracing several communities. As happened in March 1883.

A dispute over money between a Jamaican and a Colombian at Matachin ended in riots and reprisals which lasted for ten days along an entire section of the line, leaving twelve dead and scores injured. The initial quarrel had escalated into a war between the two nationalities. The Jamaicans left en masse for reinforcements from Gorgona, a largely Jamaican town. When they returned to Matachin, they found the Colombians all armed and Colombian soldiers present. Then came skirmishes in several towns up and down the line during the following days and soon, fearing reprisals, men fled into the woods to spend the nights with their women and children. Jamaicans started to leave the towns for Colón, where they felt they would be safe. The unrest slowed down work in these areas, as the contractors could not get the men to work until the state government dispatched troops. Soon after, the families at Matachin were back in the woods, this time the town was accidentally destroyed by fire.[48]

Despite the start of construction there was yet no overall plan for the canal. In March 1883 Charles de Lesseps arrived on the isthmus as representative of his father, along with a new chief engineer and director general, Jules Isidore Dingler, a highly rated engineer and organizer, who spent the next two years trying to put things in order. Visiting Panama the previous year, Dingler had made a survey of all the works, and now he laid out a master plan for the construction. The canal should start on the Atlantic end in Limón Bay (Colón), run through the Chagres River valley for twenty-eight miles to Obispo, cut through the mountains for seven miles, then follow the Rio Grande valley to Pacific deep water in the Bay of Panama. Building a huge dam across the Chagres river valley at Gamboa would control the flow (with a reservoir to store part of the floodwaters), the excess to flow in channels on either side out to sea. De Lesseps confidently predicted that the canal would be finished in 1888. Dredges were by now heavily at work at both Atlantic and Pacific canal entrances. Drilling and blasting of Culebra mountain at Matachin began.

CONDITIONS IN COLÓN, 1883–1884

Panama at this time seems awash in contradictions. On one hand, there were reports of champagne flowing freely and of high, even licentious, living. On the other, there was news of disease, death and destitution. The truth probably included all of these experiences. During the French canal era, Panama was a prosperous place for commerce as it was for those who obtained work. Panama also attracted, however, far more people than the jobs available. Moreover, the infrastructure simply could not cope.

The year 1883 saw an "unbroken stream" of job-seekers arrive and the population of the line towns and terminal cities swelled with incomers. When dock workers struck in Colón, one thousand newly arrived Jamaicans were put to work in their stead. By the end of 1883, the workforce numbered thirteen thousand, which still left a considerable number of unemployed.

Colón continued to shock the arriving travellers. Outside of the main Front Street overlooking the railroad terminus, Colón floated on a sea of mud, tattered and disillusioned. The majority of people lived in the back alleys lacking roads, sidewalks, running water, sewers or street cleaners. Dust covered everything in the dry season; clouds of mosquitoes swarmed in the wet. The streets were craters filled with the refuse tossed from the houses on either side.

Half of the residences were tenements and rent was astronomical. "New comers crowd into the place with little money and few friends. They sleep on the sidewalks, in door spaces, on the open wharves – wherever they can find room. Among the poor people the death rate is startling."[49] In 1882 it was estimated that probably eight hundred persons had no other habitations than the open wharves, the sidewalks and vacant railcars; in times of depression the numbers sleeping in the open climbed to the thousands.[50] In the dry season, such a life might just be bearable. In the wet season, from May to November, many died where they lived, huddled in doorways and underneath railcars. It was said that the three industries that thrived most in Colón were "gambling houses, brothels, and coffin manufacturing".[51]

Many who came in the 1880s found service jobs on the isthmus as earlier migrants had done. West Indian domestics, cooks, porters, railway conductors and store clerks were common. Others continued to be simply "scufflers". The governor of Jamaica later noted that "there are a considerable number of men from Jamaica who . . . lead an independent life, trying to earn a living in various ways".[52] The Panama *Star and Herald* commented that many preferred to "pick up a precarious living in the vicinity of the docks, hotels, etc. to going in for steady work".[53] It seemed as if the very poorest city dwellers from Kingston had merely shifted their misery from one location to another.[54]

Nor were the black population the only ones in this situation. The French canal, like the railroad construction, had attracted adventurers from all over, men and women wanting to try their luck in what was still essentially a wide open frontier. A newspaper correspondent found that many white men "who rely on their supposititious intellect rather than upon their muscle – are today to be found in Panama and Colón literally starving". He added, "Most of them are swindlers or clerks. The former class, unless they are expert gamblers, find little scope for the exercise of their talents; and the latter oscillate between feeble efforts to emulate the unremunerative practices of the former and a fruitless beggary, until they die in the street or stow away on some homeward-bound vessel. It is no unusual matter, either, this sad spectacle of educated men starving in the streets of Panama."[55]

Although the French had constructed fine hospitals at both Panama and Colón, the medical facilities were inadequate to serve the entire workforce. Responsibility for sending workers to hospital lay with contractors, and since they were liable to pay a fee of one dollar a day for each labourer in the hospital, some contractors dismissed sick men to save the money. Sometimes those in charge of work camps simply put sick workers on a train with no provision for care or access to hospital; many arriving in the towns received medical attention only by the charitable act of some sympathetic person.[56] Hospital facilities for non-employees were virtually non-existent; the foreign hospital seemed not to have admitted non-whites.[57] In the rainy season especially, the hospitals overflowed; many patients suffered from dysentery caused by bad water, unwholesome meat, and filthy conditions of the yards and streets.

Better-off workers from France were not spared; many fell dead almost as soon as they arrived. The yellow fever casualties in the autumn of 1883 included three of director Dingler's family – his daughter, his son and his daughter's fiancé. By the summer of 1884, forty-eight officers of the Compag-

Figure 3.8 French excavator at work in Culebra Cut (www.czbrats.com).

Figure 3.9 Jamaicans at work (Wikipedia).

Figure 3.10 French workers – the pick-and-shovel brigade (www.czbrats.com).

nie Universelle had died of yellow fever; an American naval officer estimated the mortality rate overall as two thousand per month.[58]

So many Canal workers died from yellow fever that a floating hospital was set up in the Colón harbour to deal with the overflow from the hospital there. The sick rate was estimated at one-third of all workers. (In 1884 construction had reached its peak with 19,243 employees at work in October, of which 16,249 were black workers.) Other troubles included widespread political instability, while continuous mudslides at Culebra and elsewhere led to serious damage to the works and equipment, and considerable loss of life as men were often buried in the mud flow. The cost of living also rose enormously. The *Star and Herald* complained of the excessive prices in Panama's market because speculators bought produce from the arriving schooners and sold it at inflated prices. The "smallest fowl" cost one dollar, eggs were fifty to seventy-five cents per dozen, and plantains two and a half cents each.[59] By 1889 when work on the canal ceased, inflation from the booming canal payroll had caused rent and food prices to rise 500 per cent over pre-canal days.[60]

YEAR OF TRAGEDIES, 1885

The year 1885 was to bring horrors for everyone. It opened with shocking news: Madame Dingler had died on New Year's Eve of yellow fever.[61] Dingler would soldier on for another year, but the grand house he had built for his family on Ancón hill would be left unoccupied, to be known for a long time after as "Dingler's Folly".

Meanwhile, unemployment on the isthmus had risen so high that in early

March the governor of Jamaica issued what was to be the first of several proclamations against going to Colón. But at home, floods, hurricane and a smallpox
epidemic were only some of the factors that continued to drive Jamaicans
abroad.

Pedro Prestán's Revolt and the Burning of Colón

In Colombia, political discontent was bubbling and what the British consul
Claude Mallet described as "a revolution" (in a despatch to London) broke out
in the city of Panama on 16 March 1885. Although Panama was a part of the
Colombian confederation, like other provinces it had its own parliament and
universal suffrage through a treaty known as the Rio Negro Constitution,
which provided for a more decentralized regime. The dictatorial actions of
President Rafael Nuñez, a former Liberal now turned Conservative, led to fears
that he would abrogate the Rio Negro treaty (as indeed occurred in 1886).
Protests increased across Colombia and the provinces. Raphael Aizpuru, a
former president of Panama and now a deputy, decided to act in Panama's
interests and with 250 men, he seized control of the city on 16 March
when government troops stationed there were rushed elsewhere to stamp out
insurrections.

His ally in Colón was Pedro Prestán, a young mulatto lawyer and fellow
Liberal, a former deputy for Colón. When troops stationed in Colón were
rushed by train to Panama City, Prestán mobilized a small band of followers
and seized control of the barracks. Over the next few days he tried to impose
some sort of order on the city and on the rag-tag army he had assembled. It
was a motley collection of all races, poorly armed with handguns, shotguns,
rifles and machetes; the blacks and mulattoes were formed into a brigade called
the Foreign Legion, reflecting their multinational origins. The legion was
under the command of Antonio Pautrizelle, a Haitian mulatto who was said
to have been a general in the Haitian revolutionary army; other leading supporters were Leopold DeCaille, another Haitian, and George Davis (known
as Cocobolo), a Jamaican and former canal worker who began to mobilize his
compatriots. Soon, hundreds of volunteers rallied behind Prestán. All they
lacked was arms.

When a ship arrived at Colón with guns Prestán had ordered from New
York, the American Pacific Mail superintendent refused to hand the shipment
over. The rebels took as hostage five Americans, including the consul, to force
compliance, but the attempt failed. In the meantime, troops from Bogotá had
landed in Panama; Aizpuru surrendered on 24 March and on 30 March, the
troops arrived in Colón and engaged the rebels in fighting at Monkey Hill.
By the end of the next day, however, the remnants of both armies scattered in

disarray as fire broke out in Colón. Fanned by winds from the north-east, it raged for twenty-four hours and consumed the town, leaving only four buildings standing. From the start, Prestán would be accused of starting the fire, although no evidence supported this conclusion or even revealed how the fire started. During the fighting in Colón, Aizpuru regrouped his forces and on 1 April declared himself military and civil chief of Panama. By this time American warships had assembled on both sides of the country and used the railroad to facilitate the movement of Colombian troops. Until these troops arrived in Panama City, twelve hundred US marines landed and secured key positions. Aizpuru later surrendered to the Colombian troops.[62]

Figure 3.11 Artist's rendering of the burning of Colón, 1885 (Wikipedia).

In Colón, hundreds of Prestán's followers were rounded up by government troops while he and a small group escaped on foot to Portobello, later joining the Colombian rebel army in Barranquilla.[63] Meanwhile, there was a witch hunt for anyone suspected of being a Prestán supporter, which included West Indian blacks. Suspected followers, including the innocent, were arbitrarily arrested and languished in jail, and many were executed after summary justice. Leopold DeCaille was shot by firing squad and Antonio Pautrizelle and George Davis were hanged, among the fifty-odd to be executed for their part in "Prestán's uprising". Prestán eventually would be captured, brought back to Colón and after a swift military trial would be hanged on 18 August 1885 from a scaffold erected in the middle of Colón, witnessed by a vast crowd.

Prestán was thirty-two years old when he died. He was born in Cartagena, son of a Colombian woman and a sailor described in several accounts as from the British West Indies.[64] His father died when he was young and his mother took her family to Colón to seek a better life. Prestán struggled to overcome his early poverty and became a lawyer and politician, well known and respected in his native city by most of the population – until he was accused of burning them out. One hundred years after his death, his reputation would be rehabilitated; he is now viewed as a hero in Colón, the black man who struggled for the rights of his fellow citizens and the sovereignty of his country.

Race clearly played a role in these events and shaped the image of Pedro Prestán as a crazed, power-hungry black hater of all whites. The Liberal Party,

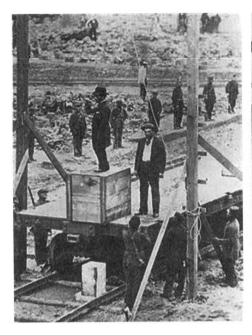

Figures 3.12–3.13 The hanging of Pedro Prestán, Colón, 18 August 1885. In figure 3.12, Prestán stands on a box on a specially created platform above the Panama Railroad line with the noose around his neck; in figure 3.13 Prestán is shown with his coffin on the line (Panama Canal).

which attracted a number of men of colour such as Prestán and the light-skinned Aizpuru, was anathema to the Americans. Americans on the ground would eventually be ordered to take control of the isthmus and restore order, as they were expected to do by the terms of the Bidlack-Mallarino treaty that gave them right of passage across the isthmus in exchange for defending the interests of the government in Bogotá. The Panama railroad authorities facilitated the movement of Colombian troops and the Pacific Mail port authority denied Prestán delivery of the guns.

Mindful of the Monroe Doctrine, the French stayed aloof from all the activities but the disturbances and fire caused incalculable damage to the canal operations. While the section of the city in which the foreigners lived was spared, the Panama Railroad headquarters and the Compagnie Universelle's docking facilities and repair yards were totally destroyed, along with equipment and supplies.

The fire left Colón's ten thousand inhabitants homeless, and many were given temporary shelter on ships in the harbour. Those who could, fled to Jamaica. So serious did the situation become that the British vice consul recommended wholesale repatriation of Jamaicans on the isthmus and a British gunboat stood by. But an official sent by the Jamaican governor found that "there was no necessity for the measure", though a small number of destitute Jamaicans were given free passage home.[65] However, the insecurity caused by revolutionary activities, the entry of Colombian soldiers to the isthmus, and the perceived involvement of West Indians in Prestán's uprising[66] were to create dangerous situations for the remaining workers, culminating in what became known as the Culebra Massacre.

The Culebra Massacre

On 3 May 1885, a circus tent set up near to a work camp at Culebra. The men had just been paid and there was a fiesta atmosphere. The mayor requested soldiers to keep order, and five men were sent. They were newly arrived from Colombia and, as Consul Mallet later reported, they were ignorant of isthmian affairs, "animated only by a blind prejudice against all people who did not speak their language".[67] The soldiers tried to pass through camp number 4 to reach the circus but were turned back by the West Indian camp watchmen as there was a rule against arms in the camp. Their rifles were also seized as the watchmen had no proof they were soldiers. The men returned to their base in Emperador and reported what had happened. Incensed, their commanding officer ordered out his whole force and set out for Culebra, joined by a mob of Colombian citizens armed with machetes and guns. They reached the camp about two o'clock in the morning and first attacked the watchmen, chopping them with machetes. The soldiers then attacked the barracks, firing into the building where the men were sleeping, cutting down with machetes those who tried to flee. They then entered the barracks, killed those who remained, rifled the men's possessions to steal their valuables and attempted to set fire to the building. They were to leave behind eighteen men dead and twenty seriously wounded.

Arthur Webb, who witnessed the initial attack on the watchmen from outside the barracks, fled into the night and hid. He returned the next day and later testified that he found twenty-three Jamaicans hacked to pieces on the ground and in their bunks. "Some of them had their legs and arms chopped off, and many had their skulls split in pieces. Many of the dead appear to have been killed while attempting to dress."[68] The floor was awash in blood and the contents of the workers' bags and possessions were scattered everywhere.

The Colombian authorities were to claim that the Jamaicans had been the aggressors, but this allegation was contradicted by the statements compiled by British diplomats, especially since no weapons were found among the workmen. An American contractor told Claude Mallet, "I have never before witnessed anything so horribly sickening as the scene of butchery at the camp."[69]

Jamaicans in the other camps immediately fled Culebra, and other nationalities got ready to leave as serious disturbances broke out along other sections of the line. The governor arrived from Panama with a force sufficient to restore order. The Panamanian authorities continued to blame the Jamaicans and were tardy in responding to requests for an investigation. Mallet wrote, "The poor negro has been the legitimate prey of Executive and Judicial outrage of the gravest and most serious character. The records of this Consulate are made up largely with the story of their wrongs." He also took aim at "the powerful Companies that bring them", accusing them of taking little interest in the workers' welfare, claiming they "make no active efforts in their favour when they fall into the hands of the authorities".[70]

The British government formally lodged a protest with the Colombian government over the incident and the Colombians eventually paid thirty-three hundred pounds sterling in settlement of claims. In 1887 the Government of Colombia announced that the officer in command of the soldiers involved in the killings at Culebra, and who had previously been acquitted by court martial, was tried by the Supreme Court of Bogotá, which reversed the decision. He was sentenced to loss of appointment, six years banishment from the republic, to be deprived of all public office, appointment or employment, of pension, suspension of political rights during banishment, and payment of all costs and of an indemnity for all loss and injury resulting from commission of the crime.[71] A *Jamaica Gazette* proclamation was issued warning Jamaicans against going to Colón.[72] Those who remained were busily arming themselves and otherwise preparing for defence against those who viewed them as hated *chombos*, the derogatory name for blacks.

These events did not prevent new workers from arriving from Jamaica, despite a proclamation by Governor Sir Henry Norman warning them not to go. But the Compagnie Universelle was desperate for workers, and a letter from acting chief engineer Buneau-Varilla to Mallet assured him that labourers coming would find work as soon as they arrived, that pay that could reach two dollars a day or more for those doing piece work and that hospital treatment for the sick was assured.[73]

Figure 3.14
Payday for workers
(Wikimedia
Commons).

This assurance resulted in an increase in Barbadian labourers, lured by attractive offers in that country from company recruiters Gadpaille and Company:

A trip to Colón?
Wanted immediately!
10 000 labourers
for the
Panama Canal Company.
No indenture. Passengers returning when they like.
Both passage and food given.
$1.50 to $3.00 per day.
Medical care given when sick.
Apply to Charles Gadpaille
Hincks Street,
Agent, Panama Canal Company.

The shipping companies also offered to take labourers' wives and children at greatly reduced prices. There were also at the time hundreds of African Americans from New Orleans working on the canal, established at Emperador, and they were said to fraternize freely with the Jamaicans.[74]

WEST INDIANS AND VIOLENCE

The tragic events at Culebra were indicative of a deep-seated fear of the other that had developed on both sides and determined the adversarial relationships between the Jamaicans and their hosts, and led to the increasing adoption by the islanders of a violent mode of life such as had prevailed during the Panama Railroad days. The issue was of concern to the colonial authorities at home. A year before the massacre, a French-speaking government official despatched to the isthmus to report on conditions there had submitted a confidential report which, on the whole, reported favourably on the conditions of Jamaicans in Panama. Nevertheless, the governor concluded in his despatch to the secretary of state that "at present crimes of violence are rare in Jamaica and it is possible that this may not continue when Jamaica has several thousand returned emigrants accustomed to the lawless habits which prevail at Colón".[75]

Since violence continued to be a prominent feature of life on the isthmus during the French canal years, it was astonishing that there were no reports of violence or gun crimes included in the Jamaican police reports even after thousands were repatriated in 1889, although, in later years, the increasing use of knives in cutting and wounding cases would be attributed to those who had returned from the isthmus.

While a great deal of the violence took place at a time of political tension, at least some of the organized violence during the French canal years carried racial overtones. For instance, an Englishman living in Jamaica recounts the following story of organized assassination:

> A coolie who was there [that is, on the isthmus] described to me the proceedings of one night when the "panish" (by which is meant any straight-haired people) went out in a band and murdered every woolly-haired man they met. They began at one end of the camp, a straight line of barrack huts. Some of the victims were shot through the windows, others slashed with cutlasses. When there were no lights the assassins passed their hands over the strangers' heads and if they felt wool, revolver or cutlass did its work. Straight-haired coolies, that is to say East Indians, were allowed to go unharmed.[76]

This story cannot be verified; it certainly contains elements of incidents such as the Culebra massacre embellished by the perception of race at its heart. Some labourers who returned to Jamaica from Colón gave as their reason for returning the fact that they did not wish to be "carved up like fowls" by the "Cartagena devils".[77] Colombians armed themselves with machetes, Jamaicans acquired guns. Jamaicans and Colombians frequently tried to reduce the threat of violence by refusing to live or work with each other. In July 1884, two hundred Colombians arrived on the works and were assigned quarters at Culebra. Overnight, every single one disappeared: they refused to work with the Jamaicans.[78]

Although the *Star and Herald* acknowledged the racism directed at black workers, the newspaper went on to suggest, within a few months after the Culebra massacre, that the racial problems were aggravated by the personal behaviour and character of some Jamaicans:

> We know of very few cases in which Jamaicans who are quiet, sober and industrious men, have not succeeded here to a much greater extent than was, or is possible, in their own country. We know men who have been here for years; done good, hard, honest work, day and night; conducted themselves in such a manner as to win the respect of all their neighbors, and who have no more dread of their Colombian associates, or less confidence in Colombian law than have the natives of the country themselves.[79]

The paper went on to attribute the upsurge of racial prejudice and armed hostility to "the excessive use of rum and other vile liquors", claiming that "sober men, law-abiding and God-fearing men who are not habitués of the pulpería; or cockpit or gambling room, are here on the Isthmus as living witnesses of the hospitality of Colombians to those who do well, but who do on occasion rise in terrible reprisal against the noisy, turbulent and vicious".

Many migrants did indeed lead a dissolute life. Workmen were paid on

Saturday afternoons and, it was claimed, "Sunday is usually a day of dissipation . . . Monday one of recuperation, and by Tuesday he is generally at work."[80] Drunkenness among Jamaicans on the isthmus stood in startling contrast to the contemporary standards in Jamaica when officials frequently commented on the remarkable sobriety of the majority.[81] The police report for the island for 1886–87 showed only fifty-six cases of "drunk and disorderly" conduct and sixty-five in 1887–88.[82]

On the isthmus, by contrast, liquor flowed freely and cheaply – some said it was a great deal safer to drink than the water. Brandy could be had at $1.50 a quart, champagne at $1.50 to $3.00; gin from $0.40 to $2.00; rum from $1.00 to $2.00; whiskey $0.80 to $2.00. Jamaican manufacturers did a brisk business supplying the isthmus not only with rum, but with counterfeit J. Wray and Nephew wrappers to be put on lesser-known brands. When the *Star and Herald* noted this counterfeiting in 1887, it remarked that such sharp practice was as old as the popularity of the rum.[83]

While evidence shows that certain elements were provocative by their behaviour, there is also no doubt that discrimination existed against the *antillanos,* as the black West Indians were called, when they were not called by the more insulting term *chombo.* Part of the prejudice against them could have arisen simply because they came in such overwhelming numbers and shared a different language and culture from those of the host society.

While one section of the population displayed continuously "respectable" behaviour, another segment attracted unfavourable attention by conduct that was clearly at odds with prevailing norms. These transgressions included drunken mourners riding to and from the cemetery on the funeral trains and the custom of keeping dead bodies over forty-eight hours to pass the hat for a "grand funeral", as well as "nine-nights" or wakes, the latter having been banned in Jamaica (under law 27 of 1873).[84] Another source of criticism was indecent language[85] and the use of what became known as "forty-shilling words", the fine levied in Jamaica for their utterance in public. There were also complaints – repeated many years later – that Jamaicans were noisy at night when others were in bed. Their engagement in public brawls was also noted.[86] An overstocked labour market undoubtedly led many to habitual idleness, and its consequences stoked anxiety regarding the "hundreds of men out of employ, without means, and with no fear of the law before them".[87] Gun ownership continued to contribute to violence, "every man of a certain class and even small boys" carried pistols, and scores and quarrels of the most trivial kind settled by a gun. In 1884, there was a murder every three or four days in Colón. Jamaicans figured prominently in gun crimes, both as perpetrators and as victims.[88]

As before, Jamaicans complained of their unequal treatment under the law or the arbitrary manner in which justice was administered. Bribery and corruption continued along with petty harassment of the workers. Jamaicans argued that they were singled out for the collection of a poll tax and for a special tax on persons found on the street after dark, a rule which was sometimes enforced in Colón. The ones who fell victim were usually those who came to Colón from the night before their boat sailed and were forced to sleep on the sidewalk. Those who refused to pay were "taken to jail on some false charge in which case a fine would be imposed which in nine cases out of ten would take away every cent the victim possessed and in many cases prevent his leaving the country".[89]

Blatant abuse of the law sometimes had even more serious consequences, such as murder, but Jamaicans also fought with police to prevent arrest of their countrymen. The police themselves were usually outnumbered and untrained. The Colón police consisted of "men and boys armed with rifles when they should not be – [who] can never be found when needed".[90] Colombia's soldiers were a mixture of regulars and of poverty-stricken, barefoot conscripts. For instance, the Cali troops responsible for the Culebra massacre had been brought to Colón in response to the Prestán uprising and included many conscripts described as peasants dressed in rags and without weapons, outfitted after they arrived.

White Americans, Britons and other foreigners were also victims of the country's lawlessness. Regarding justice, Wolfred Nelson commented of his time on the isthmus, "The laws on the statute book are excellent, but it will be true to say that justice there, like kissing, is a matter of favouritism. At other times, renderings in court are brought about, by a magical influence that I shall not dilate upon."[91]

Not surprisingly, Jamaicans featured in the criminal statistics of the isthmus. On at least two occasions, those who had spent long terms of imprisonment there were forcibly repatriated at the expense of the Panamanian authorities: thirty-one men and fifteen women were repatriated in January 1889 and forty-two persons in February.[92] Imprisonment could have been imposed for a variety of offences, varying in severity, including "fighting and scandal" and for ill-treating a horse.[93]

From the outset, however, the migration had included a criminal element. In 1881 the official Jamaican government reports recorded a decrease of 20 per cent of the prison population over the previous years, partly attributable to a decrease in praedial larceny and partly to "the considerable emigration to the Panama Canal works of that class which contributed to the prison population".[94] In 1883 the island recorded 150 fewer habitual criminals under surveillance than in the previous years. "It is believed that the attraction of high wages on the works of the Panama Canal has relieved the island of many of these men", the governor's report noted.[95] In 1884 a Panama newspaper complained that prior to canal construction, a judge in Jamaica spent four or five days clearing dockets of cases of petty theft and other minor charges: "Now a day will suffice – they have gone to the Isthmus."[96]

It is interesting that over the construction years when there was considerable travelling back and forth, the decrease of criminal statistics on the island continued be recorded. The authorities both in Colón and Jamaica blamed the absence of any moral force or authority on the isthmus for the unrestrained behaviour of some: "Freedom degenerating almost into licence is theirs continually, much different from what they find things at 'home'."[97]

Unrestrained freedom might well have held true for that segment of the population which was underage. Alarm over the situation of the under-twenties in Jamaica had led in 1879 to a commission to enquire into the condition of the juvenile population, a large segment of which seemed to have turned vagrants on the streets of Kingston and the towns. According to evidence presented, young people fourteen to eighteen years of age formed roving gangs of labourers on the estates, were leading lives free from parental guidance as early as age twelve, and were without school or church influences. Child labour on many estates was still common and twelve appears to have been the

Figure 3.16 West Indian labourers on a raft used for underground placement of dynamite prior to dredging (Panama Canal). They first bored holes for the dynamite charges with long steel drills according to a predetermined pattern.

age at which wages were paid directly to young workers. Apprentices also seemed to have been in the habit of setting themselves up as independent at very young ages.[98] Within the island these young people were highly mobile and their spirit of independence might have carried many of them to Colón.

The Emigrants Protection Law of 1885 was in fact designed to protect young persons under sixteen years of age, who were no longer allowed to emigrate unaccompanied or without parental permission and was intended to stop the traffic in children who were being sold into bondage in Haiti.[99] It might have served to inhibit the movement of other youthful emigrants, though many undoubtedly slipped through the net and landed up on the isthmus. There, their lives would be shaped for good or ill, depending on the circumstances into which they fell.

GOOD TIMES GONE, 1886–1889

For the French canal company, it was as if nature itself conspired with the man-made violence of 1885 that destroyed Colón and the company's facilities there and, on top of that, the Culebra massacre that caused thousands of workers to flee the works, effectively halting construction. As a *New York Tribune* correspondent in Panama wrote in May, 1885, "In going over the canal route, one gets the impression that the work is practically stopped, and from the best information to be got at here, I believe such to be the case. The last revolution here, of course, has had something to do with this state of affairs, for when bullets fly, spades drop."[100]

There were also leadership problems. Dingler resigned as chief engineer and his successor, Maurice Hutin, was almost immediately struck down with yellow fever after his arrival and returned to France soon after, in September 1885. Into this leadership vacuum had stepped Philippe Buneau-Varilla, twenty-seven years old, burning with ambition and patriotic fervour as great as de Lesseps's, and now appointed acting chief engineer.[101] Buneau-Varilla had to cope with yet another natural disaster: Just as the company was trying to get back on its feet, on 2 December 1885, a severe storm destroyed the waterfront and sank eighteen vessels in the harbour; the Chagres rose to thirty feet in a few hours, burying works and equipment in mud including rail tracks and spoil cars of the Panama Railroad; train service was suspended.

Figure 3.17 Philippe Buneau-Varilla (Wikimedia Commons).

In Paris, however, de Lesseps glossed over the difficulties, played down the damages, reported confidently on the progress of excavation at the annual meeting of the Compagnie Universelle. He promised to go to the isthmus himself to inaugurate "the final stage of construction". On seeing his projections, the *Tribune* correspondent wrote to his paper that the figures "are simply astounding". William Kimball, an American lieutenant who toured the works and sent a secret despatch to Washington, estimated that only one-tenth of the work had so far been completed.

To support his bid for more financing, which included a much revised and higher estimate for canal construction, the eighty-year-old de Lesseps visited Panama again at the start of 1886, receiving a "warm welcome" from the black workers in Colón amid the fire-blackened hulks of buildings that remained after Prestán's revolt in March 1885. Despite the fireworks and fetes surrounding his stay in Panama, the rest of the news was unre-

Figure 3.18 Panama was *en fête* for de Lesseps's visit in 1886 (www.canalmuseum .com).

lieved gloom. Destructive fires raged along the line at the start of the year; March saw the most serious accident of the construction years: the powder magazine at Rio Grande Superieur with thirty-three thousand pounds of powder exploded. Nineteen Jamaicans were among the wounded and five among the dead.[102]

In September 1886, a change of contractors led to a stoppage and threw many out of work, and the yellow fever trains were running to Monkey Hill cemetery two to four times a day, full of dead workmen. John Bigelow, who accompanied de Lesseps as a representative from the New York Chamber of Commerce, observed that human life is about the cheapest article to be purchased on the isthmus. A new chief engineer, Léon Boyer, had arrived in January 1886 bringing sixty engineers. By the end of the year, he and virtually all of them were dead from yellow fever and Buneau-Varilla soldiered on as the chief officer.

By 1887 it was clear that the good times were over, but canal construction limped along. The year as usual began with floods, and the canal company recorded about ten deaths a day among white employees. Food became scarce, and while steamship companies reduced their fares, only 1,861 migrants arrived from Jamaica; so parlous was the state of affairs for the immigrant population that the governor of Jamaica despatched an investigator to the isthmus, though he reported no cause for alarm.

Nevertheless, the problems were piling up although the dirt was not – the excavation at Culebra was seriously behind schedule; only an estimated 10.5 million cubic yards had been dug of the 157 cubic yards estimated for a sea-level canal. Most of the money had been spent, and back in France, investors balked. Panama stocks hit a new low when an exposé in London revealed conditions on the isthmus. Finally, de Lesseps with much reluctance in 1887 announced that a lock canal would be built instead of the sea-level canal which had been his dream, but one which was not supported by technical advice. However, the announcement came too late. He announced his intention to borrow six hundred million francs more to complete the work on a lock canal and the focus throughout 1888 was to be on the efforts to raise more funds through a lottery scheme. The scheme was a failure and by 14 December the newspapers were headlining the "Great Canal Crash". Despite his own optimism, de Lesseps could not raise the funds required to continue and the company went into receivership.

On 4 February 1889 in Paris the Compagnie Universelle was dissolved and a liquidator appointed. Work on the isthmus was to be halted by 15 May. When the news reached Panama, troops were posted along the line and British, French and United States warships converged on the isthmus in case of disturbances, but there were none. Many at the time believed that the problems were only temporary.

However, without the Panama Company payroll, the economy imploded. Workers and contractors laid down their tools; many without the train fare made their way on foot to Colón. Small shops were the first to go out of busi-

Figure 3.19
The Compagnie Universelle liquidation court in Paris, 1891 (www.canalmuseum .com).

ness, but by March, with no money circulating, the large commercial houses shut down and the merchants started to leave. Prices fell drastically and rents were substantially reduced, but the circulation of money on the isthmus had dried up. At Colón, Culebra and La Boca, the storing of Compagnie Universelle equipment began. People began to dismantle some company buildings and take them into the woods to erect shanties. West Indians, like others, were plunged into starvation and destitution, and thousands had to be repatriated by their governments. Some went to other parts of Latin America in search of work; a few hundred continued in their employment on the railroad and the canal; and many were left behind. Colón, the lodestar of their dreams, was to remain a burned-out, half-empty shell, its canal an evanescent vision.[103]

Figure 3.20
Abandoned French machinery covered in bush (Panama Canal).

"GREAT DISTRESS IN COLÓN"

Immediately following the crash of the French company in February 1889, the British consul general at Panama had telegraphed the secretary of state for the colonies, Lord Knutsford, who in turn cabled the governors of the British West Indian colonies to get in touch with the consul general. The home governments, however, perhaps not fully understanding the gravity of the situation, acted in leisurely fashion.

On 29 January 1889 the acting governor of Jamaica had informed Knutsford that the government surveyor who was about to visit the isthmus would make "quiet enquiries" about the Jamaicans there. On 13 and 18 February, acting on the consul general's report, the secretary cabled that several thousand Jamaicans were in danger of complete destitution. Not until 25 February did the governor, Sir Henry Blake, despatch Dr Christopher Gayleard of the Island Medical Service to investigate. He was also authorized to provide for the relief and repatriation of Jamaican labourers "as may be absolutely necessary".[104]

By early March, Gayleard had arrangements well underway for repatriation. However, many were so poor they were unable to get from the towns to Colón to board the ships. Arrangements were made for special trains to convey people to the docks free of charge. By the end of March, 2,197 persons had been repatriated to Jamaica (of a total of 3,112 returning). Then Gayleard left Panama and repatriation ceased. The reason might have been that the governor had so far been acting with the advice of the Privy Council but without the approval of the legislature for the expenditure.[105] In any event, some administrative strategy was involved. "I have reason to believe", said the governor, that "so long as passages are provided by this government the labourers now on the Isthmus will not pay their own way. I have little doubt that now that the issue of free passage has been suspended those who have money and the desire to return to Jamaica will do so at their own expense. The destitute residuum can then be repatriated and in the meantime the expenditure can be laid before the Legislative Council for sanction." While a session of the legislature held 24 and 25 April endorsed Blake's actions, the legislators required that the baggage of repatriated persons should be detained until the passage money was repaid.[106]

But while the authorities dickered, those Jamaicans left behind on the isthmus were actually starving. The rector of Christ Church found hundreds at Culebra who had not eaten for days. The British consul in Colón was feeding one thousand people (he had been granted two hundred pounds by the Jamaican governor to relieve cases of destitution). These were people who had been flocking into Colón from the line and were being accommodated in an empty lumber yard. Other destitute people were housed in empty barracks.[107]

On 10 April, Blake wrote to Knutsford that he had just had a visit from the British consul general based in Panama City, who said that he had travelled across the isthmus and saw no signs of suffering or starvation. He accused the consul at Colón, Claude Mallet, of being led astray by sympathy. The people, Blake concluded, were much better off than imagined.[108]

Knutsford in London was probably better informed because he took the initiative away from the Jamaican authorities, telegraphing the governor on 24 April 1889: "Great distress at Colón. I have guaranteed maintenance of Jamaicans payable from Colonial funds for a few days longer. Make arrangements for taking passages to Jamaica at once, sending by first opportunity special Commissioners to identify. Instruct Consul by telegraph."

On 13 April, Gayleard was again sent to Colón where on arrival he "was the object of an enthusiastic ovation from some 1,400 people", and he proceeded to arrange further repatriation under the new arrangements laid down by the legislators. On 22 April, a further 1,415 persons arrived in Jamaica from Colón.[109]

In early May it was announced that the final shipload would leave on 10 May. The retreat from Colón mirrored the order of the arrivals, for in the days when the French company had first started work, it was the fittest, the most youthful, who first left the West Indies. In the scramble to leave, the fittest were the first to depart and it was the weakest who made up the last pitiful remnants awaiting the final ship home. In the city of Panama, where three hundred free tickets had been issued for passages on the railroad to Colón, Jamaicans described as "crippled and infirm old men, many just handed over from the hospital, and women with children" waited until night at the station without food or water. But the train or chartered ship never arrived, and they disbanded and picked up such charity as was available, resting under galleries and piazzas.[110] They, along with another 2,300 destitute ticket holders along the line, lived like this for another eight days. The Jamaican government undertook to feed them until another ship arrived. On 17 May, the *William Cliff* sailed with 1,126 adults and 111 children. A few days later the *Avon* sailed with 1,358. Although the ship waited all night, large numbers holding tickets never showed up. When the *Avon* sailed at dawn, it marked, for the West Indians as well as the host society, the end of variable times on the isthmus.

In all, 7,246 Jamaicans were repatriated under varying conditions. The first 2,197 seem to have been allowed in without conditions; 3,632 had their luggage detained until they repaid the passage money; and 1,417 were repatriated under bond to repay the cost of passage after arrival in Jamaica.[111] When repatriation ceased, it was estimated that 6,000 Jamaicans had been left behind on the isthmus.[112] The editor of the *Star and Herald*, Tracy Robinson, in his memoirs was to note that

> after the French canal failure, a number of the laborers employed, mostly Jamaicans, preferring to remain, took up small bits of land near the line of the railroad, which they have cultivated after a fashion, thus contributing in a measure to the general welfare. They have certainly changed the appearance of the country through which the railroad passes; for now one may, from the train, form some idea of the lay of the land; while in former days the jungle shut in the track, or shut out the adjacent country as effectively as if the rails had been laid between two parallel walls.[113]

The Return Home

On arrival in Kingston, many returnees could not afford to redeem their luggage. Hundreds loitered about Kingston for weeks awaiting the opportunity to get their clothing and effects. The incidence of breaking and entering rose dramatically. The cause was not hard to find. The police discovered that in nearly every case "the perpetrators were men who had recently returned from Colón" and they stole articles of clothing. Out in the countryside, larceny of crops and small stock increased and was attributed to the "Colón people".[114]

Many questioned the destitution of those who had returned. The *Colonial Standard* claimed that those who came on the *Nile* had brought over one hundred tons of luggage, and quoted "a gentleman of the gangplank" who said that of seven hundred disembarking he did not see more than half a dozen who, judging from their dress and absence of parcels, could be judged distressed. The Panama paper queried the truth of the statement, pointing out that on the occasion referred to, only eighty-seven Jamaicans returned, eighteen of whom were children. To each, one parcel of effects was allowed. The luggage belonged to four hundred St Lucians on board who, when repatriated, had consented to pay their passage money either in cash or in work on their return home.[115]

Certainly the medical reports from both city and countryside showed that many persons came home in a debilitated condition, taxing the slender medical resources of the island. At the Kingston Public Hospital, records disclosed a number of very serious cases, many of them the repatriated Colón people. Dr Gifford from the parish of St Mary reported that he had in his care – both at hospital and in private practice – several persons who had returned from Colón either at their own or at government expense: "They all appeared to have been victims of great privations and hardships to judge of their ill nourished frames. Phthisis [a wasting disease such as pulmonary tuberculosis] proved fatal in several cases." The Island Medical Report concluded that rates for mortality and disease were prejudicially influenced by Jamaicans returning from Colón "saturated with malarial poison and in a very debilitated condition".[116]

Other repercussions were felt throughout the society. Exports fell dramatically. During the French canal construction, the total export trade to Panama stood at one hundred thousand pounds a year. This official figure omits, of course, the extensive unofficial and invisible trade carried on, for example, by owners of small cargo boats called droghers. Droghers still made daily trips around Jamaica's small ports and bays. They made a profit carrying rum, sugar and ground provisions to Panama,[117] and extensive smuggling should not be overlooked. There was considerable trade in horses and mules, cattle and small stock, fruit and vegetables, cigars and other tobacco products, including "jackass rope",[118] and in sugar, rum, and folk medication, all of which were now seriously affected by the canal failure.

The collapse of the export market affected not only the major merchant houses, but also the "small man" of rural Jamaica, such as the people of Hanover parish who "abandoned nearly every industry for yam cultivation for the Colón trade" and suffered dire hardships when yam exports fell to one-quarter of what they had been.[119] In the peak year 1887 yam brought in just under sixteen thousand pounds to local growers with thirty-two thousand hundredweight exported. In 1889 this sum had dropped to three thousand pounds.

The Government Savings Bank suffered an increase in withdrawals and a drop in savings, and throughout the whole island there was a shortage of specie because less foreign money came in. In 1885 when work on the canal temporarily ceased, the amount of money in circulation in Jamaica was recorded as nearly twenty-two thousand pounds less than the previous year, a reduction attributed to this cessation of work.[120] Not all of these effects could be directly attributed to the emigrants, since there were also strong commercial ties between the two countries. In 1904 the colonial secretary noted that when the French canal works had been in full swing, Jamaican labourers were bringing back about one thousand pounds a month, apart from remittances.[121]

For many in Panama, to accumulate any surplus at all was difficult, especially when they had to pay an inordinate amount to convert their wages. Payment was in depreciated silver currency (Frenchmen received their pay in drafts or francs) but the standard of exchange was gold. There was no organized banking system on the isthmus and a worker who wanted to remit money abroad, convert his wages or buy a ticket home was charged at the rate of $1.30 to $1.50 Colombian silver for $1.00 gold by the merchant houses that acted as bankers.[122]

Not surprisingly, in 1899 the post office recorded a dramatic decline in overseas mail and the registrar general recorded as unaccounted for, some twenty thousand Jamaicans who had emigrated.[123]

In April 1889, the inspector-general of police began to furnish the colonial secretary with reports on the condition of returning Jamaicans throughout the island. In these reports he could state only that the returnees had settled down quietly, were behaving well and that many were already working, "though there is, as might be expected, some objection to the necessarily lower rates of wages than they have received on the canal. There has been no increase in crime since their return."[124]

It is the very ordinary that is extraordinary here: the fact that people who had gone away and experienced so much could return and settle back so quietly into life at home. Although the Compagnie Nouvelle du Canal de Panama continued work on the canal on a much reduced scale over the next few years, the era of Colón Man was done, at least until the next awakening of the Isthmus of Panama.

The Compagnie Nouvelle was incorporated in France in 1894 so as not to lose the concession from New Granada and, until its sale to the American government in 1904, recruited workers from Jamaica. All laboured in an atmosphere of continuous political instability as the War of a Thousand Days (1898–1902) raged around them. A Jamaican carpenter was among those who experienced first hand the dangers to non-combatants. He was laid up for half a year after getting shot in both feet in 1899 during an exchange of gunfire between Liberals (holed up at Culebra) and the Conservatives stationed at Empire.

"Neither party dared to go where the other one was, but they fired at each other all night at long range. We shut ourselves up in the houses and kept dark" he reported, "but it was not safe then. A man was killed in the next house." He himself was standing in the middle of the floor "when a ball fired by the Conservatives passed through the wall and flew down and struck my feet". No one could come to his aid so he had to wait until morning (when the firing ceased) to be taken to the doctor; he spent the next three months in Ancón hospital.[125]

Jeremiah Waisome, who lived in Panama as a child during the war and who later worked for the US canal, recalled that the cheapest items in those days were guns and bullets, there were no restrictions on their purchase, and they were all American-made. Every man owned a gun, he claimed. At election time, Panamanians packed up and left the urban areas where most of the fighting took place. "Before the election my Mother would stock up supplies in her home . . . when the shooting start we had to lay flat under our bed pretty near a week, you could hear the bullets rolling off the roof tops when everything cleared off . . . when my Mother comes out in the morning you could see bullits holes through the side of the buildings, and a lots of corps laying around."[126]

The declaration of independence by the Republic of Panama in 1903 and the takeover of the canal by the Americans finally established a state where law and order prevailed; widespread violence ceased at last to be a feature of isthmian life. Nevertheless, as we shall see, nothing would change the British authorities' opinion of Latin American republics as "schools for violence".

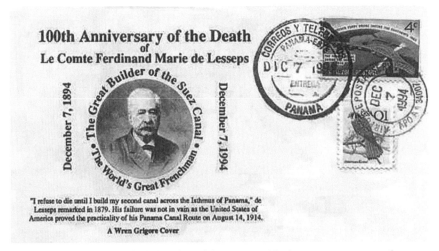

Figure 3.21 The "great Frenchman" Ferdinand de Lesseps and his brave attempt were not forgotten in Panama. This first-day cover in Panama honoured him in 1994 on the hundredth anniversary of his death (www.canalmuseum.com).

PART 3

THE US CONSTRUCTION OF THE PANAMA CANAL, 1904–1914

Figure 4.1 Arrival of SS *Ancon* with fifteen hundred contract labourers from Barbados at the port of Cristóbal, Colón (www.canalmuseum.com).

4. WHO WENT, HOW AND WHY

By the time the post-1904 wave of emigration to Panama was in progress, foreign travel was accompanied by such an aura of accomplishment, that it came to be regarded as a necessity in order to "become a man", to know the world, and to understand life. Thus . . . emigration became highly desirable and sought after, even for its own sake.

—Velma Newton, *The Silver Men*

BY 1904, THE PANAMA RAILROAD and the French canal had become vague memories for most West Indians, despite the impact these events had in their time. It would be the work on the US canal that conferred status and authority on those who went there, lingered in their memories, and passed on to their descendants powerful images of trials and triumphs in a strange land. In Barbadian George Lamming's classic novel *In the Castle of My Skin*, the old man Pa, fearful of the future and in dialogue with his wife, reminds himself: "Time wus when money flow like the flood through these here hands, money as we never ever know it before. We use to sing in those times gone by 'twus money on the apple trees in Panama. 'Tis Panama my memory take me back to every now an' again where with these said hands I help to build the canal, the biggest an' best canal in the wide wide world."[1]

Like many narratives of Panama, the reference to money easily flows into what seemed even more important, the pride West Indians felt in contributing to what was then the world's greatest endeavour "with these said hands". Though Pa by the time of the story is old and poor, his community's views and his own memory that he was "great once", due to his Panama sojourn, affirm his dignity. That a heavy price would have been paid in the process is not something that the old workers liked to talk about. They left for Panama as boys and returned as men, fired in the crucible of back-breaking labour and racial discrimination. For West Indians of the time, "Panama" became the ultimate test of manhood.

In 1906, a Colón newspaper commented that "the first fortnight's residence virtually settled the future of every man who comes to Colón".[2] Mothers back home probably knew this too. A Jamaican interviewed many years later confessed, "When I leave Jamaica I was a young green boy. My mother cry and my mother kissed me and my mother say to me, Boy: you are going oversea be careful. Please don't make your eye red for everything you see."[3]

To be "red eye" in the West Indies is to be greedy or envious, and greedy for adventure and experience is probably what these boatloads of mostly young men were. Albert Peters of Nassau, Bahamas, then twenty-one years old, recalled reading in the newspapers that "they were digging a Canal from ocean to ocean on the Isthmus of Panama and needed thousands of men". He and two of his friends decided to go as they were "eager for some adventure and experience". His parents cautioned against it. "They told me about the Yellow Fever, Malaria and Small pox that infested the place but I told them that I and my pals were just going to see for ourselves."[4]

In stepping off the boat, the young worker stepped into a new world. Not only was this world organized in ways that were strange, but he had to learn to understand its many languages. There was the Spanish language of his Panamanian hosts (which he hardly bothered to learn), the American English of his employers and his own dialect or creole. A newspaper character quoted a newcomer speaking in West Indian creole, "Dis seems to be a bery funny place. Two shillins dem call it dalla, den kall rum seco, den wen de teamer was cuming longside de waff we yerri say we gwine a de dock."[5] The confusion worked both ways, as a book entitled *Maid in Panama* consisted mainly of anecdotes marking the linguistic and cultural divide between West Indian workers – mostly female household helpers in this case – and white American employers.[6]

But the newcomer was also forced to learn other, more subtle languages. One morning, without telling his mother, thirteen-year-old Jeremiah Waisome decided to sneak off from school and get himself a job on the American canal.

> I approach a boss. . . . I said good morning boss, he retorted good morning boy. At that time he had a big wad of tobacco chewing. I ask him if he needs a water boy, he said yes, he ask what is your name, I told him. I notice that my name did not spell correctly as Jeremiah Waisome, so I said excuse me boss, my name do not spell that way. He gave me a cow look, and spit a big splash, and look back at me and said you little nigger you need a job? I said yes sir, he said you never try to dictate to a white man, take that bucket over there and bring water for those men.[7]

Jeremiah Waisome had entered a world called the Canal Zone, where black men of all ages would be addressed by white men of all ages as "Boy".[8]

THE CANAL ZONE

The Canal Zone was an extension of the United States, a ten-mile-wide strip of land across Panama's national territory. Panama ceded it to the United States to construct and maintain an interoceanic canal in exchange for America's help in declaring its independence from Colombia on 4 November 1903.[9] The new Republic of Panama[10] gave to the United States in perpetuity, the "use, occupation and control" of the Canal Zone. Within this territory the United States held sovereign status and Panama retained no rights or authority there. In return, Panama received $10 million in cash, the annual sum of $250,000 to commence nine years after the signing of the treaty, and the guarantee of its independence by the United States. Ratifica-

tion of the treaty by America on 23 February 1904 cleared the way for the French Compagnie Nouvelle du Canal de Panama to dispose of its rights and assets to the US government, which it did for $40 million. This sum represented the largest real estate transaction in history up to that time.

Map 4.1 The towns on the route of Panama Canal (Wikimedia Commons).

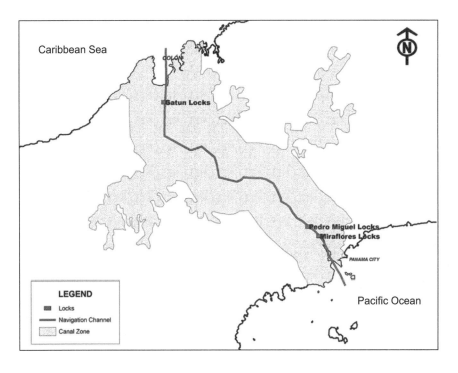

Map 4.2 Extent of the Canal Zone. (Map prepared by Thera Edwards, Department of Geography and Geology, University of the West Indies, Mona.)

At 7:30 on the morning of 4 May 1904 at the old headquarters of the French canal company at Cathedral Plaza in Panama City, all the property and equipment of the Compagnie Nouvelle were officially handed over to a representative of the US government, a young lieutenant of the American army, Mark Brooke. Following instructions from the secretary of war, he signed, along with a representative of the French company, a receipt that was written in French, Spanish and English, shook hands all round, and hoisted the flag of the United States to the top of the flagpole. The US Canal Zone was to last for ninety-six years. In 1977 (by the terms of the Torrijos-Carter treaties), Panama was granted sole jurisdiction over the canal, and on 31 December 1999, the American Canal Zone ceased to exist.

Scar, New York *Globe.*

Figure 4.2 Cartoon of President Theodore Roosevelt with his "big stick" (Wikimedia Commons).

The Stars and Stripes flying over the Canal Zone signalled the imposition there of American mores and values. Jim Crow, the racial segregation of the American South, took hold of the Zone with a single difference: on the Zone "black" and "white" signs were never used. Instead, the Isthmian Canal Commission (ICC), the government body charged with the construction of the canal,[11] used the terms "gold" and "silver" since these currencies represented

Figure 4.3 "Gold" and "silver" workers in strictly segregated groups; the house in the background was being moved from areas to be flooded by the canal and re-erected elsewhere (www.canalmuseum. com).

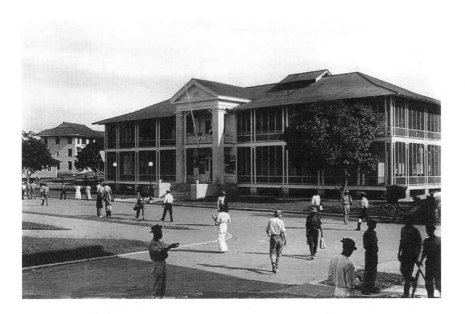

the metal in which the workers were paid and symbolized their status. US citizens were paid in gold; non-US citizens were paid in Panamanian silver. All gold employees were white and were paid considerably more than silver workers even for the same work. African Americans were considered "silver".

The ICC exercised complete jurisdiction over the Zone's 436 square miles of territory. At the Atlantic end adjoining Colón they constructed the American town of Cristóbal, and adjoining the City of Panama on the Pacific, they built the town of Ancón. By simply crossing a street, a person became immediately subject to a different language, a different set of laws and regulations, a different prevailing religion, a different culture, and a different way of life. The Canal Zone became a segregated North American enclave in the heart of a Latin country.[12]

The ICC built special towns for the "gold" employees, set apart from the "native" town where Panamanians, West Indians and other settlers from the past were living along with the new "silver" workers. But strict distinctions also regulated gold employees: they inhabited a rigid hierarchical system where everything, in the beginning at least, was determined by the size of the man's pay cheque. American Harry Franck noted,

> Caste lines are as sharply drawn as in India. . . . The Brahmins are the "gold" employees, white American citizens with all the advantages and privileges thereto appertaining. But – . . . the Brahmin caste itself is divided and subdivided into infinitesimal gradations. Every rank and shade of man has a different salary, and exactly in accordance with that salary is he housed, furnished, and treated down to the least item, – number of electric lights, candlepower, style of bed, size of bookcase.[13]

While there was camaraderie among Americans on the job, Franck observed that

> D, who is a quartermaster at $225, may be on "How-are-you-old-man?" terms with G, who is a station agent and draws $175. But Mrs. D never thinks of calling on Mrs. G socially.... Mrs. X, whose husband is a foreman at $165, and whose dining table is a full six inches longer and whose ice-box will hold one more cold-storage chicken, would not think of sitting in at bridge with Mrs. Y, whose husband gets $150. As for being black, or any tint but pure "white"! Even an Englishman, though he may eat in the same hotel if his skin is not too tanned, is accepted on staring suffrance. As for the man whose skin is a bit dull, he might sit on the steps of an I.C.C. hotel with dollars dribbling out of his pockets until he starved to death – and he would be duly buried in the particular grave to which his color entitled him.[14]

Distinctions divided the silver workers too. Europeans from Spain, Italy, and Greece, for instance, were classified as silver and treated as inferior to white Americans but superior to black workers as to pay, living and other conditions. Europeans were segregated from the black workers.

Building the canal forged the only unifying link among the workers. It was no accident that the project fell under the portfolio of the War Office and ultimately was run by military men. In time, Zone dwellers occupied a self-contained enclave that was being built around them in which – like the military – they had to accept total control of every aspect of their lives. The Zonian, if he chose, need not go into the terminal cities at all. Under paternal Uncle Sam he could, eventually, obtain in the Zone everything he needed: there were commissaries, schools, hospitals, churches, post offices, fire departments, hotels, entertainment and sports, as well as courts, prisons and mental asylums. Gambling, public drinking and cohabitation without marriage would all be prohibited.

Apart from the separation in work and living conditions, the silver worker saw his children placed in separate, inadequate schools run exclusively by black teachers. He shopped at the commissary in restricted hours (and eventually in separate commissaries). He joined a separate line when he went to buy stamps at the post office; drank at separate water fountains; attended separate churches or services at different hours from the gold workers; and he entered white clubs, hotels or homes only as a provider of services. When sick, he occupied a separate hospital ward and when dead he was buried in a separate part of the cemetery. With the abandonment of the Zone towns on the west bank of the canal as they were drowned by Gatún Lake, he became segregated in completely separate "silver towns" constructed for him: La Boca, a new town built in 1912 on the Pacific side, and Silver City (later renamed Rainbow City) near the Atlantic.

As writer Sydney Roberts saw the Canal Zone:

"Silver" and "Gold" divide the human race
Here where a fountain's polluted by a stare,
A "silver" man must keep his silver place;
He waits in silver lines, eats silver fare.
Each licks a postage stamp within the pale.
Each has his ghetto according to his hue.
Only at midnight when all colours fail,
What law has done, Freud's children will undo.
And in "gold" churches what do preachers tell
Their congregations in the pews of gold:
Of gentler burnings in the golden hell?
Of dimmer heavens for the silver fold?
But heaven is here: Gold homes, gold jobs, gold schools
And in the heaven of gold latrines, gold stools.[15]

The West Indian worker knew that the separate facilities provided him were grossly unequal: housing, schools, social amenities. Benefits provided by the ICC administration for its workers averaged out at $750 a year for gold workers, $50 for the West Indian. By the time the Zone became organized, gold roll workers and their families were provided with well-equipped clubhouses and playgrounds, hotels, Young Men's Christian Associations and other facilities catering to their wants; the silver workers – West Indians, Europeans and others – were thrown on their own resources.

The service provided to the West Indian workers was also intentionally inferior, a notion endorsed by the ICC. In 1914, for instance, an official order went out to commissary workers – no doubt in response to complaints – as to how they should act towards customers. It noted in part that the silver workers (who made up at least three-quarters of the clientele),

> cannot be handled with the same nicety that is expected to characterize the service on the gold side. Their number, the physical limitations of the commissaries, and the prime necessity of getting them served in the short time allotted them by their working hours for the making of purchases precludes this. They must, however, be treated with politeness and every effort made to show them goods, and to see that they get what they want. No discrimination must be shown against them in the matter of wrapping their purchases.[16]

Themselves having immutable racial notions of black and white, the Americans strove to cope with the subtleties of West Indian race relations or, for that matter, the gradations of "shade" prevailing in Panama. In a book permeated with his own racism, Harry Franck reviled a Panamanian census taker who agonized over how to list his own relatives in the box for "colour" which required "W, B or Mx.". Franck claims that after considerable consideration, the census-taker set down his relative as "Color; – A very light mixture" – for which he was fired.[17]

Another visiting American writer, Willis J. Abbot, recorded that at Ancón hospital, "The question of color was often an embarrassing one. The gradations of shades between pure white to darkest African is so exceedingly delicate in Panama that there is always difficulty in determining whether the subject under consideration belongs to the 'gold' or the 'silver' class, for the words black and white are tactfully avoided in the Zone in their reference to complexions." Colonel Mason, the hospital chief, had a plan: "On certain days the patients are allowed visitors. When the color of the inmate is problematical, as is usually the case with women, I ask if she wants her husband to visit her. If she does and he proves to be a negro, she goes into the colored ward. If she still insists that she is white, she can go into the white ward, but must dispense with his visits."[18]

Many an American woman set out to police the racial boundaries of the Zone,[19] often questioning the whiteness of some foreigners residing there. Cohabitation between white Americans and anyone perceived as non-white meant exclusion from Zone residence, and while it could not be forbidden in the Republic itself, male workers who indulged in such practices were seen as having "gone native", and worse, and would be dropped from the workforce.

Zonian notions of racial segregation also began to permeate the terminal cities, a fact that was particularly galling to those who had lived in Panama before the Americans came. For instance, when the Colón Jockey Club organized a race meeting for 4 July 1906 in Cristóbal (the American town), the gatekeepers attempted to exclude black people. All were admitted only after the racehorse owners (mainly prominent West Indians and Panamanians) refused to race if anyone was excluded.[20] Churches and schools also became segregated after the American takeover. Some took the situation humorously in their stride. When a notice advertising a function at Cristóbal Young Men's Christian Association which stated "white public invited" was posted, a joker went around and wrote on the poster, "When you does doan wan to invite black people you mus print wid white ink."[21]

FROM THE ISLANDS, AGAIN

While the eyes of the world were turned in 1904 to the new Republic of Panama and the circumstances of its founding, for the people of the West Indies these events heralded only one thing: work. Thousands did not even bother to wait for the formal US takeover of the Panama Canal, so eager were

Figure 4.5 *Croptime*, by Albert Huie. This painting shows the background of many of the canal workers – the sugar cane fields and factories of the West Indies. (Courtesy of the National Gallery of Jamaica.)

they to try for Panama gold. In the year the new treaty was signed and before any work began, some six or seven thousand Jamaicans flocked to Colón, and other Caribbean islanders soon followed. This new wave grew and gained momentum up until the 1920s. For after Panama, other destinations beckoned: Costa Rica, Mexico, Nicaragua, Honduras, Colombia, Venezuela, Ecuador, Cuba and the United States itself. For a long time, however, Panama remained the mother ship from which West Indians launched themselves, "Panama money" providing both cash and confidence for further journeying.

In the forty years between the censuses of 1881 and 1921, some 146,000 Jamaicans left their homeland and never returned.[22] We do not know how many actually left since migration figures covering the whole island began only in 1910. For Barbados, between 1860 and 1920, the net loss has been estimated at 104,000.[23]

In many ways, the impact of these movements on the home societies reverberates still, as if the Panama Railroad had set in motion a ghost train that has never stopped, still carrying West Indian wanderers far beyond the confines of their countries so that today, more West Indians live abroad than at home, many pushed and pulled by the same factors that were operating in 1850:

> Never seen
> a man
> travel more
> seen more
> lands
> than this poor
> path-
> less, harbour-
> less spade.[24]

At the turn of the twentieth century, the Caribbean shared in the momentous changes that were taking place throughout the world. The rapid decline and reorganization of the sugar industry in the British West Indies had the greatest impact on the islanders, but many other factors contributed to emigration. Although Jamaica contained about 40 per cent of the British West Indian population, it would provide more than half of the net emigration from the area between 1881 and 1914 and so become the "primary Caribbean source of labour supply for the rest of the Americas".[25] Between 1904 and 1915, almost ninety thousand departures from the island to Panama were recorded.[26] Barbados was not far behind, nor were still smaller islands such as St Lucia, which had sent "about 10 per cent of the entire population" consisting of adult males to work on the French canal between 1885 and 1890[27] and a significant number during the period of US construction.

Earlier Panama experiences had ended in disaster but had also brought visible improvements in the lives of many West Indians who returned home. In Jamaica, monies acquired in Panama during the French construction had contributed to the rapid expansion of the landowning class and to financial independence for some individuals. Purchases of land, houses, buggies, livestock and goods, together with the means to set themselves up in independent trades and business, were some of these visible results. There is no doubt that between the emigration of the 1880s and the turn of the century, there were also great improvements in Jamaica's social and economic life and in infrastructure. Kingston now boasted new water, sewerage and gas works as well as a tramway system. Communications were expanded by the building of mountain roads, the extension of the railroad, the expansion of post offices and an island-wide steamer service. Increased shipping and the growth of tourism were brought about by the banana trade. By the end of the nineteenth century, seventeen steamship lines were sailing to Jamaican ports from the eastern seaboard ports of the United States.

Between 1880 and 1902 the area under cultivation in Jamaica grew by two-and-a-half times and land ownership of holdings between five and fifty acres doubled. Much of this reflected the growth of the banana industry and the use of money earned on the French canal to buy land. The government had also started land settlement schemes by which large tracts of idle land were acquired and sold in small lots to farmers. The shift from ownership of large estates by a few to small plots by the many was reflected in a reduction of sugar estates from 700 to about 120 and the growth of peasant proprietors from ten thousand to over eighty thousand.[28]

But despite these positive statistics, the post-emancipation problems persisted: the existence of surplus labour and the inability of the workers to earn a "living wage". Winston James notes that "nominal – not to mention real –

Figures 4.6–4.8 Jamaica became a tourist destination from the late nineteenth century, promoted by the United Fruit Company with its "Great White Fleet", which offered "every convenience" to travellers on its boats which also took bananas from the island back to the United States (Wikipedia).

agricultural wages had remained stagnant over three generations. . . . African Jamaicans had left the realm of chattel slavery only to enter a world of wage slavery – with hardly any wages at all . . . in certain respects conditions were worse in the post-slavery period than they were during the years of bondage."[29]

With sugar's steady decline only thirteen thousand were employed in that industry in 1911, and most of them seasonally; despite the growth in banana cultivation, it was far less labour intensive than sugar. This dramatic fall in agricultural employment left the workforce with no alternatives.

Women intensified their efforts in trading and in domestic service to keep food on their tables. Some turned back to agricultural labour on their own account, a circumstance which no doubt suited the plantations, since women were paid far less than men for the same work. But it was to emigration that their men had to turn, especially when nature itself conspired to bring an endless series of natural disasters. In Jamaica, these troubles included a disastrous hurricane of 1903, one of the worst to hit the island up to then, the destruction of provision grounds and fruit trees leading to outright starvation. A traveller

Figure 4.9 On the wharf in Kingston, tourists (*to the right*) disembark, narrowly avoiding the streams of young people, mainly women, who load up (*left*) with thirty-pound baskets of coal on their heads to refuel the ships (author's collection).

in the parish of St Mary (where the banana cultivations were destroyed) commented: "Many of the men who apply for employment on the relief works are gaunt and emaciated, and if given a task are scarcely able to complete it."[30] The hurricane was followed by serious drought, which affected exports. A major earthquake and fire destroyed most of Kingston in 1907. In that year, widespread drought (which continued in the southern parishes for another two years) took heavy toll, leaving the south a disaster zone and the greatest areas of out-migration. Flooding caused widespread damage in November 1910,

Figure 4.10 Gangs of women also loaded the banana boats with green bunches of the fruit carried on their heads. (Courtesy of the National Library of Jamaica)

Figure 4.11 A Jamaican yard and its occupants, around 1910, with their banana cultivations in the background (Abbot, *Panama*, 18). The well-dressed young man holding the baby was most likely a returnee from Colón.

another hurricane hit in 1912, followed by others during the rest of the decade, which was further convulsed by the First World War.

Jamaican writer Claude McKay (who became a leading light in the Harlem Renaissance) described the impact of such events on the lives of the poor in his novel *Banana Bottom*. After the 1903 hurricane,

> the transient Negro workers had had a fat season of work clearing away the wreckage and debris of the hurricane and flood. And when there was nothing left to do they used their savings to take ship to Panama. The Panama Canal was the big hope of

Figure 4.12 Jamaican market traders or "higglers" were the backbone of the domestic economy, keeping their children and the country fed as their men laboured abroad or not at all. (Courtesy of the National Library of Jamaica.)

the poor disinherited peasant youths of Jamaica and all those islands of the Caribbean Belt that were set in the latitude of hurricanes and earthquakes – all those who did not like to sport the uniform of the army and police force.[31]

To the people of Jamaica's southern plains, the effect of three years of drought coming on top of the earlier shocks of earthquakes and hurricanes led to widespread depression and apathy. Among the population of St Elizabeth, especially, local preachers saw in these events signs presaging the end of the world. When the acting governor visited the area, he reported that many of the able-bodied men had left to seek work in Panama or Costa Rica, and a committee appointed by the legislative council confirmed that migration had become the response to these natural disasters.[32] Although figures on emigration from the southern plains are not available, heavy depopulation did occur. After four successive hurricanes levelled cultivations in the banana parishes of St Mary, St Ann and Portland, these parishes contributed 37 per cent of total net emigration after 1911.[33] Other factors – including taxation – continued to drive emigration. At the turn of the century, 29.6 per cent of total revenue came from direct sources, 70.4 per cent from indirect. This meant that the poorest people (the majority) paid the largest portion of the tax since it was derived from items they consumed most: food and textiles. The working class also felt the heavy taxes on land and houses. Overall, Jamaicans earning the average daily wage of one shilling per day paid five shillings and sixpence per head in direct taxation per annum and no less than thirteen shillings in indirect taxes.[34] An official report noted that "it is hardly possible for any one to spend a quatty [one and a half pennies] in Jamaica on anything except native grown food without contributing at least a farthing [quarter-penny] to the revenue".[35] Although no direct evidence was found to show that taxation was a major precipitating factor in emigration at this time, sufficient evidence abounds from the French canal days to suggest that it constituted an important grievance among those who did emigrate. Prison was still a real possibility for defaulting taxpayers, regardless of their ability to pay.

For many young men, acquiring a technical skill held their sole hope of advancement, and fathers readily sent off their sons (whose schooling ended at fourteen) to learn a trade, with the carpenter, the shoemaker, tailor, cooper or blacksmith. It is striking that so many interviewed in Panama had acquired multiple trades in such fashion and that over five thousand Jamaican artisans were employed on building construction and infrastructural works by the Panama Canal in its first two years. Tradesmen in Jamaica found little or no market for their skills. In any Jamaican village at the turn of the century,

> no one . . . expected a trade to support him. A man might be a shoemaker, but he couldn't live by a trade since most people in the district wore no shoes at all, and

most of those who did wear shoes walked with the shoes in their hands and put them on when near the church door. There wasn't a tailor in the district who could live by tailoring – he too had to depend on what passed for farming – for the limited amount of clothes possessed by any villager was often bought at the nearest biggish market and was faithfully worn until it could be worn no more.

This was the life and people lived it because to the best of their knowledge if they didn't get a chance to emigrate to Panama or somewhere, well – that was the life.[36]

Even those fortunate enough to have regular jobs were waking up overnight to find the jobs gone. The most serious of such blows was the closure of the British naval dockyard at Port Royal in 1904–5 as Britain shifted its maritime interests. This withdrawal represented not only immediate loss of wages but cut off career opportunities for promising Jamaicans. Other occasional public works employed the artisans' skills briefly. In between, there was nothing. A severe blow to educated black Jamaicans was the ending by the colonial government of competitive exams for positions in the civil service. The examination that was introduced in 1885 had given opportunities to bright black Jamaicans, while the new system of selection after 1911 was found to favour the white and light-skinned.[37]

The need to feed one's self by one's labour led to flexibility in many ambitious people, a pragmatic approach known on the islands as "turn-hand", the ability to turn one's hand to something new, including relocating. By the time the United States builders arrived in Panama, West Indian freedmen and women already had over fifty years of migration experience. Though a positive trait, flexibility resulted in the transient lives led by many of the emigrants as they shifted from one job to the next, or from country to country as opportunities arose. Their skills and adaptability also demonstrated that, far from the stereotype branding all the incoming West Indians as lazy, ignorant and inept, many who arrived in Panama carried with them multiple skills acquired at home along with the burning ambition to better themselves.

In the drive to leave home, social factors were sometimes as compelling as the economic: the desire for a better quality of life, or escape from the stifling nature of small island colonial society. Leaving home could provide an opportunity to breathe a different air as well as transcend the brutal poverty of their parents. Though official racial segregation did not exist in the islands, racial stratification certainly did, and it was clearly identified as a factor that limited opportunities for personal advancement, especially for ambitious, dark-skinned individuals. The people of the West Indies still lived in a repressive culture where opportunity for advancement bore a direct relationship to skin shade. Many retired Jamaicans interviewed in Panama cited some specific instance in which they felt they had been insulted, humiliated or passed over for advancement as the precipitating factor in their decision to leave Jamaica.

In Panama, some sixty years after he left home, one old gentleman recalled precisely such an event. As an employee at a parochial office in Jamaica, "I was a clerical assistant, then the assistant clerk was an elderly man and they promised that when he goes out of office I would be appointed in his place but he went off and when the appointment came, they appointed a white boy, they appointed a white fellow in his place and I didn't feel satisfied. I had an aunt in the Canal Zone and I wrote to her asking if I could come."[38]

Of course some compelling reasons for leaving might be classified under the category of flight. Fleeing to Panama presented the ideal opportunity to escape from difficult or embarrassing situations – desertion of families and other responsibilities, escape from criminal prosecution or debtors' prison, evading personal or social humiliation, escaping parental dominance or discipline. In the short stories of Claude McKay or of Eric Walrond (who was himself taken to Panama by his mother in search of an errant father), Panama is portrayed as just such an escape route.[39] Or, as in the novel *Susan Proudleigh*,[40] set at the time of canal construction, it offered a door for young men and women who had little going on in their lives and who simply saw Panama as an opening to an adventure. For those who already had a relative or other connection abroad, "being sent for" became something to look forward to, making one an object of envy among one's peers.

For some young women, though, being "sent to Panama" could signify trauma, the route for those who shamed their "respectable" families by getting pregnant out of wedlock. These women would be sent to friends or relatives in Panama or Costa Rica to have the child and avoid disgrace at home. In some cases, a husband would be found for them abroad.[41]

RECRUITING THE LABOUR FORCE

The ICC had raised the hopes of Jamaicans in their first annual report. As with previous contractors, the ICC noted that perhaps "the greatest difficulty to be encountered in the construction of the canal will be the procurement of an adequate force of labourers and the preservation of their health and efficiency". The commissioners knew just where to turn:

> It is stated by Mr. Bunau-Varilla, at one time chief engineer of the old Panama Canal Company, that out of one hundred individuals sent to the Isthmus, not more than twenty, at an average, could remain there, and even these lost a part of their value. The negro alone could perform manual labour; the white man must supervise and direct. After costly and fatal experiments with other races, the company ceased sending to the Isthmus as labourers any but native Colombians and negroes from the British Antilles, particularly Jamaicans.[42]

So it was to the British colony of Jamaica that the ICC first turned for labourers, wanting to recruit ten thousand men in the first instance.[43] They ran into a roadblock in the person of the English governor, Sir James Alexander Swettenham, who derived his rather arbitrary authority from the system of government in effect at this time. Following the Morant Bay Rebellion of 1865, the frightened Jamaica House of Assembly, after two hundred years as a fiercely independent law-making body, felt unable to deal with the crisis and surrendered its power to the Crown. Jamaica thus became a Crown Colony, with direct rule from Britain, and other West Indian colonies followed. The assembly was replaced by a governor answering directly to the Colonial Office in England, and a legislative council was appointed to rubber-stamp his decisions. Much, thereafter, depended on the personality and dynamism of each governor.

Figure 4.13 Governor James Alexander Swettenham. (Courtesy of the National Library of Jamaica.)

So even as thousands of Jamaicans were streaming to the new Republic of Panama in the hope of finding work and thousands more were dying to go, the United States was to spend two futile years trying to recruit labour officially in Jamaica, frustrated at every turn by the governor. Swettenham was conceded to be a man of great rectitude, a Victorian gentleman of upright though totally unyielding character who carried his desire for "correct form" to such extremes as to seem eccentric.[44] A Jamaica *Gleaner* editorial complained that "his belief in himself is profound, is illimitable; and apparently it is accompanied by an equally profound and illimitable contempt for the ideas and opinions of other persons".[45]

On 9 December 1904, just two months after Swettenham first arrived on the island, US secretary of war William Howard Taft was sitting in the governor's office in Kingston and sweating, notwithstanding the tropical breeze blowing through the louvered windows and the ceiling fans turning overhead. Taft's discomfort arose not just from the heat and his enormous size, but from the governor having just informed him that the US government would have to pay to the island treasury twenty-four dollars (five pounds sterling) for every Jamaican they recruited for work on the canal.

Figure 4.14 William Howard Taft (Wikipedia).

"JAMAICAN GOVERNMENT SELLING WORKERS", the *New York Sun* headline screamed.[46] Since the Americans had come to Jamaica with the expectation of recruiting ten thousand workers in the first instance, and they wanted to make it a government-to-government arrangement to ensure a steady supply of workers, Taft and his colleagues were taken aback. Especially when the governor assured them that although it might be imagined that there was a labour surplus in the island, Jamaica's employers held a very strong opinion to the contrary.[47] The governor's statement represented the attitude of one segment of the ruling class to the question of emigration. Behind it were the old surviving planter interests and their desire to maintain a surplus pool of cheap labour. But it was also, allegedly, a signal from the American United Fruit Company, the new player, which had started to establish large banana plantations on the island and was already the largest single employer of labour.[48]

Swettenham imposed one other condition for the recruitment of labour: that the US government should agree to defray the cost of repatriation of every labourer contracted, whether or not he fulfilled the terms of his contract. Other than that, the governor washed his hands of the Jamaican workers. The US government, he said, was free to make whatever arrangements it chose with the labourers; his government wanted no part of it.[49]

One wonders how the fate of workers might have been affected had he also accepted Taft's proposal for the appointment of a special agent from Jamaica to liaise between the workers and the British consulate in Panama and to handle disputes on the spot, his salary to be paid by the ICC. Swettenham said no one in Jamaica's civil service could be released for the post.

Swettenham reiterated his position at a further meeting on 12 December with J.F. Wallace, chief engineer of the Panama Canal. Present at both meetings was Claude Coventry Mallet, who was by then the British representative in Panama, and who strongly urged that arrangements for the workers be made on a government-to-government basis.[50] This view also had the support of the secretary of state for the colonies.[51] Swettenham stuck to his hard line and two days later temporarily suspended all licences for recruiting agents for Panama, such licences being required under the Emigrants Protection Law.[52]

Emigrants Protection Laws

Since 1885, the Jamaican government had enacted a series of laws[53] called the Emigrants Protection Law and law 23 of 1902 consolidated previous legislation on the subject. The main clause stated that the governor had the power to "proclaim" any country to which the law would apply. Names of countries were added as a demand for Jamaican workers arose there. Proclamations were issued for Brazil, Costa Rica, Colombia, Cuba, Ecuador, Guatemala, Haiti, Liberia, Mexico and Nicaragua. Workers going to these countries and those recruiting them had to fulfil certain legal requirements, mainly that recruiting agents had to be registered and workers had to secure exit permits.

As the US takeover of the Panama Canal appeared certain, moves were made by British colonial authorities to draft a new law to regulate the expected exodus of workers. However, at the time of the meeting with Taft, the first bill had been disallowed in England and a revised law was being drafted. Swettenham chose to adhere neither to the old law nor to proposals contained in the new, and his position was uniquely his own. He not only suspended the licences of recruiting agents but he also instructed the police that, before granting exit permits, they ensured that would-be emigrants could provide reliable sureties from bona fide property owners with property sufficient to pay the sum of ten pounds.[54] This condition discriminated in particular against impoverished emigrants. Swettenham was attacked by the *Daily Gleaner*,[55] roused by the fact that it (and the rest of Jamaica) had learned about the terms of the agreement from US sources.

Meanwhile, the revised new Emigrants Protection Bill was rushed through the legislature and passed into law on 21 March 1905, despite much public outcry, including well-supported public meetings and island-wide protests. The official justification alleged that labourers were irresponsible and, when they abandoned or failed to support families left behind or themselves returned home sick or unable to work, they became a drain on the public purse. Such claims implied a level of social support not borne out by facts. Nor did the claims take into consideration the value that the entire country derived from remittances, from the export of island products that followed emigrants, and also from the social and material progress that attended the various waves of emigration.

A new and significant clause was added to the law. Labourers wishing to go to a proclaimed place now needed a permit and also had to deposit money (twenty-five shillings) to the island treasury, though that sum was to vary, depending on destination, reaching as high as ten pounds for Mexico. Agents had to be registered and bonded. The deposit was to be returned to a labourer on his return or used to repatriate him if stranded.

Over the next two years the US government continued to send emissaries to reason with Swettenham, to no avail. Swetttenham possibly had a problem dealing with Americans, but in relation to those from the ICC and their urgent need to solve the labour question, the situation resembled negotiations between the tortoise and the hare. These Americans were all men of action – President Theodore Roosevelt was exhorting them to "make the dirt fly!" As for Swettenham, the *Daily Gleaner* suggested that his years as an administrator in the East had slowed him up: "even at critical moments he would prefer writing little essays in political philosophy to showing the readiness and initiative which we would expect from a capable administrator".[56]

What followed could be considered high comedy, were it not that poor, jobless Jamaican working men were victimized. Many would find their way to Panama at great financial sacrifice to themselves and their families, but what was lost was the opportunity for an organized recruitment policy that would have afforded them, as British colonial subjects, the protection of that government.

The American emissaries to Jamaica after the initial meeting with Taft found the governor's attitude obstructionist and insulting. First, he refused to treat with anyone but Taft, and the American officials were left to pass their time in government offices and hotel rooms. Swettenham refused to see the special labour agent sent by the Panama Railroad, Thomas H. O'Connell, who was informed by the colonial secretary that "the Governor deems it his duty, in courtesy to Mr. Taft, to abstain from opening fresh negotiations or listening to overtures from any person purporting to represent the Canal Commission".[57] O'Connell had been despatched to recruit for the Panama Railroad (itself part of the ICC) some three thousand men and foremen, as well as carpenters, locomotive machinists and others.

After his frosty reception, O'Connell withdrew a letter he had written regarding proposed terms and conditions for the recruitment and was recalled to Panama. The man who had despatched him, Henry Burnett, acting manager of the Panama Railroad then came himself, believing that O'Connell had bungled the negotiations by antagonizing the governor.[58]

Burnett started out confidently with a long letter setting out the views and desires of the ICC with regard to employing Jamaicans. The reasons for preferring Jamaican labourers and artisans, he stated, included the nearness of the source of supply and the low cost of transportation, and the law-abiding habits of the Jamaicans which made for maintenance of order on the works. The US government would offer guarantees regarding repatriation upon completion of service and under certain other conditions, such as alleged violation of contract or abuse of workers by employees of the commission. He suggested that a maintenance order by a court in Jamaica could be served on the ICC which would deduct the amount from the worker's wages – this was in lieu of the deposit required by the Emigrants Protection Law. One objection to the payment of the fee was that it would automatically require long-term contracts and labourers would be unable to return home annually, since a new contract would be required for each trip. Burnett also said that the ICC objected to the fact that, according to the law, contracts could be enforced in Jamaica or place of employment "at the option of the emigrant". The right to elect the tribunal should be given to both parties in the contract. Finally, since the ICC felt that many other provisions of the law were onerous, they wanted its operations suspended for recruitment to the Panama Canal. They were prepared to enter into a formal contract which would conform to the major guarantees required by the Government of Jamaica.

If the ICC's proposals had been accepted they would certainly have been of greater benefit to the Jamaican worker than the Emigrants Protection Law. Every single worker recruited would have been provided with some measure of protection against, among other things, abuse at the workplace. The contract provided by the ICC would have fulfilled all that the Jamaican government hoped to achieve by the law: the safeguarding of the welfare of families left behind and the guarantee of return passage.

The governor again refused to negotiate, insisting that he was still awaiting word from Taft. Stevens, the chief engineer of the ICC, at this stage decided to force the governor's hand and cabled Burnett from Panama to break off negotiations and apply for independent labour. Burnett sent a copy of the advertisement with a request for the governor to instruct the police to cease intimidation of ICC employees as well as the labourers desirous of emigrating. The governor expressed frigid disapproval of the advertisement and, defeated, Burnett left Jamaica.[59]

The Americans made one last effort, in late 1906, sending ICC quartermaster Jackson Smith to negotiate. Smith at least got to see Swettenham, but took cold satisfaction from the meeting, reporting to his chief engineer that "if I had not felt it was your desire for me to exercise extreme caution and repression, I would have refused to continue the interview further".[60] Smith called the whole experience "humiliating", especially when the governor opened the discussion by referring to the case of Martinique women whom the ICC had been accused of bringing to the isthmus for the purpose of prostitution (discussed in chapter 7) and accused Taft and other high-ranking canal officials of lying about the issue.[61]

Smith said he talked "to many of the representative men of the Island in all branches of trade and agriculture" and found them generally favourable to emigration. Their reasons did not arise from disinterest: "These people . . . assure me that the men return to them better laborers, and better prepared to do satisfactory work than before their engagement by us, it being explained to me that the class which shows a disposition to go to the Isthmus are the younger ones and those who constitute Jamaica's surplus labour population." Perhaps even more compelling though was the fact that his business informants recognized "the value of the Isthmus as a market for their surplus products, and are anxious to build up a trade with us as well as to continue friendly relations with the U.S. which furnishes them 90% of their tourist trade, and takes fully 95% of all the bananas exported from this Island".[62]

Here Smith thought he had found the leverage, the "stringent retaliatory measures" that would bring the governor "to his senses", by ruining Jamaica: hitting bananas and tourism (both went hand in hand as the tourists travelled via the banana boats). He proposed a tax of one hundred dollars on every ticket to Jamaica and a tax of one dollar on every bunch of Jamaican bananas imported into the United States. On his return to the Canal Zone, Smith urged pressure on the US Congress to impose a tariff on bananas from Jamaica.[63]

Such measures did not become necessary, for the ICC gave up all attempts to recruit from Jamaica. One might ask why they persisted for so long. The short answer was economy: Jamaicans would have been the cheapest workers available. As an official explained, "the expense to us of putting the laborer on the Isthmus, including the fee to the Jamaican Government, transportation, medical examination, vaccination and photography, would be only $9.73 per head, as against $15 which we have been paying for transportation only to bring men from Martinique, and as against approximately $75 to $100 per head which it would cost us to bring Chinamen and repatriate them".[64]

One hundred Jamaicans were recruited by the ICC, mostly for work on the railroad. The majority of them came via Costa Rica and Bocas del Toro (Panama), only forty-seven coming directly from Jamaica. The Americans had rightly reasoned that Jamaicans would still travel to the isthmus on their own and add to the pool of labour there, which is what happened. In the end Jamaicans did become a significant part of the workforce on the canal and formed the majority of foreign residents on the Canal Zone with uncounted numbers residing in Panama as well. (See tables 7.1 and 7.2.) Because they had to pay their own passage and deposit a similar amount to the island treasury, a process of economic selection took place, notwithstanding that a Jamaican newspaper claimed that "quashie" could always find money for a wedding, a funeral, or a passage to Colón.[65]

Jamaicans who went to Panama after passage of the Emigrants Protection Law were of a higher social stratum than contract workers recruited elsewhere and who were mainly labourers taken free of charge. Labourers in Jamaica would have been hard-pressed to find the sum required to leave the country, plus the fifteen dollars in gold required of arrivals in Panama who did not come on contract (though this fee was dropped if they were hired immediately). The majority of Jamaicans who went initially were of the white-collar or artisan classes, and small peasant proprietors and the like, men who could somehow raise the fare and deposit (usually by pooling family resources or selling all they had). Flooding into Panama then were Jamaican artisans, craftsmen, clerks, soldiers, policemen, teachers and the like; in short, skilled and educated workers. They could command white-collar jobs and earn the highest wages being paid to black employees, and they formed, to a large extent, the elite of the West Indian workforce in Panama. While white-collar workers and artisans also came from the other islands and many Jamaicans were of the labouring class, the political stance of Jamaica's governor had effectively screened the emigrants from the start. Thanks to Swettenham, Jamaica's poorest would have to wait for relatives already in Panama to send for them.

FROM BARBADOS: "GLAD TO GO BUT SORRY TO LEAVE"[66]

While Jamaica's governor dithered, the planters and governors of the other islands proved more amenable to recruitment, and the ICC concluded satisfactory arrangements elsewhere. They established their chief recruitment centre on the island of Barbados, and the diplomacy and efficiency of their recruiting agent William J. Karner were to prove highly successful. He first gained the support of the island's governor, and although he was disappointed with the response of contract workers to the initial sailing on 18 January 1905 on the *La Plata*, his offer of free transportation and food on board, a contract with the ICC, and the option of free passage home after five hundred days was to prove irresistible. His assistant had labelled as "timid men" the first batch of workers who returned in 1905 with complaints about conditions in Panama. But the song,

> Fever and ague all day long
> At Panama, at Panama,
> Wish you were dead before very long
> At Panama, at Panama[67]

far from discouraging others, would become a kind of shipboard anthem. By early 1906 the men returning with money were themselves effective recruiting agents, setting off what was described as a "craze" and a "frenzy" to go. As Bonham Richardson described it, "Departing men walking to Bridgetown from the farthest points of the island stopped en route at the chattel houses of friends who also were going, and their numbers swelled accordingly as the groups of walking men approached town."[68] It was claimed that as a group of workers passed a sugar-cane field where others were working, one called out, "Why you don't hit de manager in de head, and come along wid we!"[69] As they abandoned the plantations, they sang provocatively,

> We want more wages, we want it now
> And if we don't get it, we going to Panama
> Yankees say they want we down there,
> We want more wages, we want it now.[70]

The men of Barbados were coming from a milieu unlike that which prevailed in Jamaica and the other islands, their circumstances shaped by geography. Most West Indian islands are mountainous, their wild hinterlands unsuitable for sugar cane, and offering a refuge for the formerly enslaved Africans to escape plantation labour. No such refuge existed in flat, open Barbados, where in the census of 1891, an estimated 182,300 occupied 166 square miles – a density of over one thousand persons per square mile.[71] Barbados is a low-lying coral island with gently rolling hills, washed by both the Atlantic Ocean and the Caribbean Sea, all of it ideal for growing and processing sugar cane; sugar and its products formed 97 per cent of exports in 1897. A Royal Commission of that year noted that "the condition of Barbados is markedly different from that of any other Colony in the West Indies. It is very thickly populated. . . . There are no Crown Lands, no forests, no uncultivated areas, and the population has probably reached the maximum which the island can even under favourable circumstances support."[72] Barbados's planters controlled both land and government – in 1911 only 1,986 persons met the landholding or educational qualifications for electors.[73]

While the rural poor in the other islands were able to grow some food and collect fuel from the forests, Barbados was denuded of forests and firewood was imported along with most food. The majority of black Barbadians still lived on rural plantation "tenantries" where their "tiny subsistence gardens normally were rented from the estates, and access to these garden plots was contingent upon their working (usually exclusively) on the same estates".[74]

The planters at first were fearful of the impact emigration would have on labour and were mainly opposed, but their attempts to stop it were short-lived, outweighed by their fears that the frustrated would-be emigrants would riot. External migration was nothing new to the Barbadians and had proved an effective safety-valve to overpopulation and an escape from impoverishment. Large numbers of Barbadian emigrant workers had settled in nearby West Indian islands, such as Trinidad, and in British Guiana. Barbadians had even gone as far afield as the Belgian Congo and the Putumayo (Peru) during the rubber booms there. Later, they had joined workers from Jamaica and other Caribbean islands recruited for work on plantations and railway construction in Mexico, Peru, Ecuador and elsewhere. But these emigrations were usually a gradual outflow or in relatively small numbers. Nevertheless, as Richardson argues, "by the turn of the century, recurring migrations had established a migration precedent for black Barbadians, and this precedent had become a hard-earned, informal right to migrate".[75] It was this informal right that the authorities were unwilling to challenge.

Barbados had passed an emigration act (of 1904) which offered protection of workers and registration of agents without payment of a fee.[76] Over-population was so acute that the planters withdrew their initial objections and the first group of contract workers left the island in the summer of 1905. By 1907, Barbados had contributed 13,175 of the 23,000 contract labourers on the isthmus. In all, 19,000 contract labourers of the 31,071 recruited from the West Indies came from Barbados. Fitness and strength rather than birth certificates were required. Many simply put down their age down as twenty, the minimum age set by the Americans. From Barbados, everyone went who could. Women and children later joined the early workers and although only the contract workers were officially counted, it is estimated that some 45,000 Barbadians went to Panama during the construction years.[77]

Although their reasons for going varied, some clearly saw the "call" to Panama almost in the nature of a religious crusade. In 1964 George Martin recalled his arrival from Barbados in 1909,

> I were only 18 years   a school boy, with a thinking ability, a voice from a great people saying Hearken ye, people of a different tribe. Let not your heart be troubled, and so we were invited; at this age with the others I accepted, for this people, no other than the American people promised strong protection, and so I leave father and mother, brothers, and relatives, away in the land of the Indies, in the west, and came to this strange land now 54 years ago.[78]

As early as 1906, the ICC was aware of the effect that the migration from Barbados was having on that island, and commented that it had depleted the population to a large extent so far as able-bodied labour was concerned. Recruiting work became difficult, and the ICC saw that in time recruiting from that island would have to be suspended,[79] which finally occurred in 1911. Approximately 10 per cent of the total population and 30 to 40 per cent of adult males are said to have left Barbados for the Isthmus of Panama.[80] Like Jamaicans, many of the islanders who were unable to secure a contract came on their own in search of work and in later construction days, a number came as bona fide immigrants.[81]

Men and women also came from the other islands: about fifteen hundred men from Grenada answered the call from an agent there in 1906, leading to "an exodus of labourers". However, they arrived in Panama at the worst possible time, the year of the highest death rates there, and some eight hundred returned home that same year "absolutely ruined in health", suffering from "Panama fever", an especially virulent form of malaria. The returnees were said to have transmitted it throughout the island. Nevertheless, hundreds more migrated from Grenada to Panama over the next eight years,[82] as did workers from the other islands. Most sailed from Barbados officially, having arrived there as deck passengers on steamers or on the inter-island schooners before embarking on the larger Panama-bound vessels.

In addition to workers from the British islands and mainland territory of British Guiana, a total of seventy-five hundred men were recruited from Guadeloupe and Martinique before permission was withdrawn by the French government in 1907. The summons by recruiting agents had seemed especially alluring: "500 days to make a fortune in the best place in the world".[83] After the ban by the government, French islanders continued to travel secretly to Panama, mainly via St Lucia, Barbados and Trinidad, where some of them remained, while others continued on to the canal. Although the de Lesseps years evoked bad memories, many could not wait to go on this new adventure. Joseph Jos notes that in the clandestine movement, many men anglicized their names to obtain contracts and a number of women disguised themselves as men in order to go.[84] Emmanuel Aliker of Martinique recalled how he yearned to follow his elder brother while, "in innumerable modest homes, Caribbean baskets waited under beds for a trip to Panama", and "our lives took on the rhythm of waiting for letters from Panama".[85]

Although recruits were usually referred to as contract labourers, the term was merely one of convenience as, in the words of the chairman of the ICC, no formal contract existed between the government of the United States and the labourers: "such a contract, if made, would on the face be unequal; one party being a responsible government, abundantly able to fulfil its obligations, and the other party an irresponsible labourer, for whom no penalty could be exacted" if he failed or refused to perform his part of the contract. The "contract", said the ICC, merely set out the conditions under which men desirous of working for the ICC would be admitted. The terms provided free transportation with the privilege of repatriation after five hundred working days with the canal. Payment was at the rate of ten cents per hour with housing provided in specially constructed labourers' barracks.

On acceptance of the conditions, the workman was expected to perform his duties "faithfully, to the best of his ability, and to observe the regulations which have been adopted by the Commission for the conduct of the work". The ICC regarded as sufficient reason to terminate employment the following: if a labourer refused to obey the orders of his foreman; if he shirked his duties, was lazy or unwilling to work; if he was an agitator and engendered discontent among his co-labourers; and if he voluntarily, without good reason, quitted the work for which he was engaged.[86] Few of those streaming into Panama would have paid attention to the wording. For, as the song assured, "money's down in Panama like apples on a tree".

THE SCREENING

In Barbados, strings of men walking across the island headed for the recruitment centre in the capital of Bridgetown where huge crowds gathered from early morning. Here, the men were subjected to a rigid screening process that ruled out all but the fittest. As in a war, the healthiest would be chosen. Policemen keeping order outside the recruitment centre admitted the men in batches, so a hundred at a time lined up against the wall in a large empty room as the doctor made his rounds: "First, all those who looked too old, or too young, or too sickly were picked out and sent away. . . . [The doctor] went over the whole line again for trachoma, rolling back their eyelids and looking for inflammation. Seven or eight fell at this test. Then he made them strip and went over them round after round for tuberculosis, heart trouble and rupture. A few fell out at each test."[87] The visitor to this examination found only twenty men left of each hundred that were examined and concluded that they were "certainly a fine lot of men".[88] The men chosen would show their joy by bursting into song and slapping one another on the back. They were vaccinated and signed their one-page contract which was also signed by the ICC recruiter and witnessed and signed by a police magistrate before they went prancing downstairs to spread the good news to their friends in the square.[89]

A labour contractor was paid $6.50 for every worker he produced. This fee was reduced in 1909 to $2.00 per head.[90] Those rejected could still purchase their own passage on one of the Royal Mail vessels and hope to find work on arrival in Colón. Others boarded sailing vessels or schooners that regularly made the run, packed with ground provisions, fruits, animals and people.

While the schooners might slip away from Bridgetown harbour without much ado, the sailing of a batch of contract workers turned the place into an uproar. Mothers, fathers, girlfriends, wives, sisters and aunts all turned out for the departure of the loved one. The sailing (which usually took place a week after the lucky one passed his physical) was attended with much weeping and wailing and parcels of food and drink to see him through the journey. Some workers were wearing shoes for the first time, along with finery for travelling bought on the promise of future earnings. As each number was called, the labourer stepped out of the crowd, and a wail went up. He was medically examined again, especially for signs of the vaccination he received on recruitment, as sometimes a healthy recruit would pass the first examination and then sell his contract.[91] The men boarded lighters to be ferried to the ship out in the harbour and, once on board, were again checked to see that they corresponded to the numbers on their contracts. From henceforth, as a Canal Zone worker, this number became his identity.

As their forefathers had done on similar voyages, the recruits occupied every square inch on deck. Many carried musical instruments and singing broke out even before the boat sailed. In the crowded conditions, fighting would sometimes erupt, and the captain would have the ringleader put in irons and thrown into the brig.

On arrival at Colón, after a twelve-day journey from Bridgetown, everyone's temperature was taken and they were examined for trachoma. Those whose vaccinations had not taken were vaccinated again. A representative of the ICC quartermaster's department (responsible for assigning men to jobs and housing) came to oversee the men on board a train from which they were dropped off at various camps along the line. They were given a hot meal and the chance

Figure 4.15
Barbadian contract
workers line up on
arrival in Colón to
await transportation
to their work sites on
the canal (Panama
Canal).

to rest for a day or two before joining the canal's army of workers. The men
had no idea what to expect, and if bad weather or other conditions delayed
the journey, they were ravenous on arrival. Harrigan Austin endured thirteen
days of bad weather on a ship with "sparing meals". On landing on the docks
the men saw a pile of bags of brown sugar, and "the whole crowd of us like
ants fed ourselves on that sugar without questioning any one, and no one said
anything to us either".[92]

When Edgar Llewellyn Simmons arrived in 1908, he and others of his batch
were transported by train to San Pablo where they were met by white Americans and some silver workers. The first problem occurred when they had to
walk across a little swinging bridge over the Chagres River. "We were scare to
death, couln't make it until the same watchmen and jaunitors came and release
us of our grips and bags and shew us how to walk on the bridge   At any rate,
we got over trembling of fear, because the little bridge was swining from side
to side." Next morning, "after a whistle blew, we turn out only to meet some
white faces again. This time they had time books, pads, and brass checks, and
also meal tickets, etc. etc. We were lined up in two long lines clad to the best
of our ability. They began to pick every other until they had about 12 or fifteen
men, handing them picks and shovels, so, off they went."[93]

Still waiting to be assigned, Simmons was pleased when a smiling West
Indian man came and picked him and several others for, he believed, he would
be faring better than with pick-and-shovel work. He was surprised to be given
a spade and taken to a railroad car. "It was loaded with coal, he made us put

the coal on one side, then knocked off a ring around a link of chain, and not aware of what would happen, suddenly I was up to my knees in coal." He went on to shovel coal into a steam shovel all of his first day. "Next day we were off laying ties for track lines. We completed another day." His friends heard where he was, came for him and "by seven oclock that evening I was in Tabernilla".[94] They took him to their boss, who took him on. This shifting of work location was a common occurrence among the workers, especially in the early days as they tried to find the most congenial environment.

Vaccination

Most of the labourers were in the habit of working on the canal for a while, returning home, then accepting another contract. As time went on, virtually every worker arriving had contacts with friends or relatives already on the Zone. Such workers soon disappeared from the work camps to which they were originally assigned and distributed themselves as best it suited them, frequently joining work gangs in which they already had friends. Such independence did not please the ICC which, in 1909, instructed its labour agent in Barbados not to recruit any worker who had previously been on the isthmus. Such workers were easily identified by their vaccination marks. Of course, this did not prevent workers returning to the isthmus on their own steam.

Vaccination against smallpox was obligatory for everyone arriving on Panamanian soil and was then relatively new, so many of the arrivals were frightened of it. The dread of vaccination by labourers recruited in Martinique precipitated a shipboard riot on their arrival on the *Versailles* in October 1905. The labourers refused to be vaccinated, believing it to be another form of branding as enslaved people were branded, a mark which would prevent them from ever escaping from the Zone. They would not disembark and the captain refused to take them back to Martinique. The stalemate continued despite the intervention of the French vice consul. Eventually the ship was stormed by police and the workers forcibly removed. In the melee, "scenes of wild excitement" occurred, according to a newspaper. Some of the men brandished knives or whatever weapon they could find. Some were clubbed by the police; some jumped overboard and were drowned. Eventually the labourers gave up resistance and were finally sent off to their work camps.[95]

Stowaways

Those unable to make it to Colón by other means adopted the final resort of stowing away. Stowaways were so numerous in the early construction days that the ICC regarded them as a large factor in the immigration movement; they were particularly numerous from Barbados. On one occasion, a vessel arrived from the West Indies with 288 stowaways on board, including women. In another case, 65 stowaways, 52 from Trinidad and 13 from Barbados arrived on one ship, the RM *Atrato*. Seven escaped on landing and the rest were employed by the ICC.

When labour was greatly in demand, the stowaways were allowed to land without showing the cash (fifteen dollars) required of all passengers who arrived on the isthmus without a contract, if they were immediately employed by the ICC. However, in later years when the labour market was glutted, the stowaways were returned home. In 1911, one group received particularly harsh treatment. Before leaving Trinidad, the crew of the *Thames* discovered sixty-five stowaways on board and put them ashore. Searches at other ports revealed another three. Before being landed, some of the stowaways had their faces painted with red lead by the crew as a highly visible warning to others.[96]

So desperate were men for a chance to get to Panama that Karner, the ICC recruiter who found it impossible to control them, reported seeing men paddle on fishing sloops and lighters out to where the ships were anchored and "scale the sides of the steamships, dangling from ropes and chains and asking for a hand from those already aboard".[97]

JAMAICA FAREWELL

In Jamaica, the scene at departure in Kingston was slightly different than in Barbados. Here the workers were travelling on their own initiative and no pre-screening took place. On the much larger island, the trip by boat was the culmination of a journey that might have started days before. The worker from the interior first had to make his way, usually on foot, to the nearest railway station or a port to catch the island coastal steamer for Kingston on the south-east coast of Jamaica. A worker from Hanover, in the north-west of the island, recalled his journey: "First of all I sail from Green Island. I take the island boat from Green Island to Montego Bay. And from St James I take a train and hit to Kingston", where he boarded a steamer for Panama.[98]

On sailing day, more than one agency showed an interest in those leaving and uniformed as well as plainclothes members of the police and military made up a large part of the crowd by the gangplank. They scrutinized each person about to board and sometimes plucked from the line a wanted man or an indentured East Indian or Chinese worker trying to break his contract, or a member of the West India Regiment trying to sneak away. Sometimes the police recognized someone they regarded as a particularly troublesome individual and heaved a sigh of relief at his departure.

As the deck passengers (deckers) came on board, burdened with packages, boxes, baskets, live birds and fowls in cages, plants, food and fruits, the ship's doctor inspected each one for trachoma. The deckers also brought their own utensils into which meals and water could be ladled. Experienced emigrants travelled with canvas-covered wooden folding chairs, as neither sleeping nor sitting facilities were provided. Selecting the most favourable spot and gathering their possessions around them, the passengers settled down as best they could for the forty-hour trip across the Caribbean, sometimes grouping according to religious denomination so that hymn-singing rivalry at times broke out around the decks. Most times the decks were so crowded that it was virtually impossible to move. More than one thousand deckers on a ship was not uncommon. If the weather was bad, they liberally applied Bay Rum[99] and other high-smelling antidotes against sea-sickness and "bad feeling". Before landing at Colón, those needing it were vaccinated. Many tried to prevent the virus from taking by rubbing the spot with lime juice and other preparations. All made ready for arrival.

Author Winifred James (who travelled in the Caribbean and Panama around this time), noted of the deckers that "on the day of arrival there is a great awakening. The parcels are undone, clean dresses and marvellous hats appear out of the brown-paper parcels." Although the men were equally vain about their appearance on landing, it was the ladies James noticed combing their hair and powdering their faces: "I have seen them make their toilet in the full blaze of morning light, with no more thought than if they were in the screened privacy of a jealously guarded bedchamber."[100]

An anonymous first-class passenger witnessed the deckers come aboard "carrying their canvas bags and cheap trunks on their heads. Some had concertinas, some had guitars, and each had a package of resin-perfumed mangoes. All were dressed in their Sunday clothes. The men wore high collars and absurd neckties while the girls were dressed in bright bandannas and print gowns, all in odd contrast to the black faces, daubed with white powder."[101] The deckers sang and made merry for most of the night when the weather was fine. When the weather was bad, another mood prevailed. On this sailing, a squall struck:

> The ship shivered. The sea lay flat and foamed like milk in the churning. A gray mist flung over the waters and drove the first class passengers to the shelter of the companionway. But the hundreds of negroes with their belongings were at the mercy of the storm, which pitilessly lashed them all night. . . . They cowered under the boats and in the lee of the deckhouses, but the rain found them out, washed the powder from the girls' faces and started the gay colors of their bandannas and frocks. The concertinas and the guitar essayed a merry strain now and then, but despair and misery and the tempest won the mastery.[102]

On this particular sailing, the doctor in the morning ordered a medicinal shot of whisky for the older men and women.

Deck passengers and their belongings were sometimes washed overboard in bad weather, as happened on the *Atrato* in June 1904. The women and children had to be taken off the deck and offered safe accommodation below. Mary Couloote, a St Lucian woman who came to Colón as a young girl, would never forget her voyage:

> I came with my sister on a ship by the name of la plata it live castries to jamaica then the ship left jamaica at 4 PM o'clock the ship was going to the gulf of Mexico it started to roll it had a storm heavy brize water came into the ship I [had] was to go down stairs to second class and stay their the sailor had chain around they waist and a pail emptying out the water when we reach Colón thy call everybody name 5 men were missing from jamaica the captain leg get broken when the life boat brak away and hit the captain on his leg and the life boat drop into sea he was send to the hospital 3 days after he died and we all was sorry.[103]

The newspaper report of the accident said that the *La Plata* had been hit by a tidal wave.[104]

Two young girls, Edmee and Hortense Joseph of Martinique parentage, would some eighty years later recall their voyage from Trinidad on the *Ancón* and the shock of their arrival in Colón in 1908, aged four and six, accompanied by their aunt. They remembered the interminable crossing in uncomfortable steerage, where personal needs were dealt with in a bucket one had to empty overboard oneself. Only the idea of being reconnected with their parents enabled them to withstand the pitching and the salt spray, the nausea, and the smoke that stung their eyes and noses as well as the foul odours and the din of the motor engine. The food they remembered was heavy, cooked in cheap oil: rice, beans, and bits of dried meat. To drink they had tepid, brackish water.

According to their memories (recorded by Joseph Jos), with them on the boat were some one hundred Martiniquans, "all men, young and old, solid farmers like their father, but also older men of whom one wondered if they would make it to the end of the voyage. Wearing old colonial caps or *bakouas*, dressed in threadbare suits, they held in rough bundles or at the bottoms of *paniers caraibes* a few photos in an envelope or in a notebook and broke the monotony of the trip in staring at them until they were worn or yellowed by spray."[105] The girls' first glimpse of Colón no doubt reflected the sentiments of many who came, accustomed to and expecting better. They were thrilled to actually land in American Cristóbal – "a paradise of paved streets and well-mown lawns", until their aunt saw the signs: Whites only.[106]

"A Total Stranger"

The contract workers often knew each other beforehand or bonded on their travels; some went to the isthmus because they already had friends and relatives there. But for others, the trip was a lonely adventure. Daniel Lawson left Jamaica 17 February 1906 and two days later took the train from Colón to Panama City, arriving

> a total stranger. . . . I knew absolutely no one who speaks the English language, all the money that I had in my possession was the value of three American quarter dollars. Some how or other I was able to secure the names of bread, sugar and water, in the Spanish language. Miraculously I existed on the three named for three days. I slept in an un-known man's horse stable in Panama City for two nights without his knowledge of my being there. . . . Very late in, and early out. Pressure started to bear.

He decided to retrace his journey on foot to Culebra, as he had been told in Jamaica that a younger brother had died in that section.

> Fortunate for me I found this place Culebra on a day never to be forgotten "WASHINGTON'S BIRTHDAY". I did not only find this place, but the Camp and Bunk, providence willed it. The camp laborers were all generous to me in every way. It was a general holiday and all at home and cooking. I got something to eat in a crude ware for the first time, cooked since my leaving Jamaica, then I was shown the bunk my brother had been sleeping in, took sick, taken out and died in the hospital. The bunk was un-occupied since his death for nearly two years I was told. That was mine. I took possession, slept there-in and felt at home.

Two days later he was absorbed into the canal workforce. Amazingly, eight years later, worker Lawson was able to record his presence at the effective ending of canal construction, the blowing up of Gamboa dike on 10 October 1913 which allowed water to flow for the first time through the Panama Canal.[107]

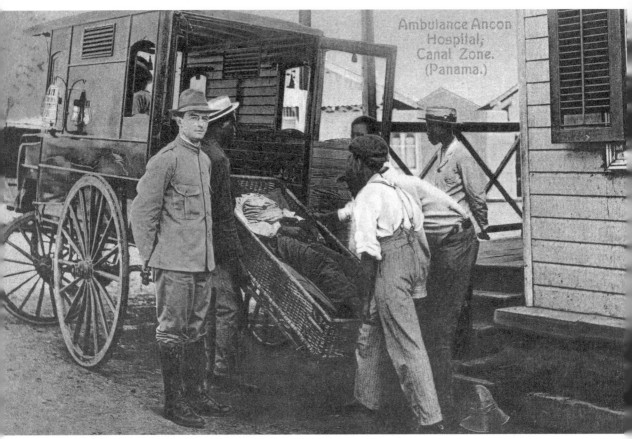

Figure 5.1 Postcard showing ambulance men, Ancón hospital – a common sight during early construction days. (Courtesy of William P. McLaughlin, www.czimages.com.)

5. WHAT THEY ENDURED, 1904–1907

"Most of us came from our homelands in search of work and improvement. We turned out to be pioneers in a foreign land."
—John O. Butcher, Barbadian contract worker

"PANAMA MEN" TOLD THEIR LOVED ones little about their experiences and their descendants were to remain ignorant of what they endured while working on the Panama Canal. Silence and fortitude might have been bound up with the code of masculinity on the construction zone and the goal of most simply was survive, make enough money, and go back home. The greatest suffering and hardships fell upon those who came at the start.

These early workers were to make a clear distinction between themselves, the "1904–1907 gang", and those who came after, as between troops who arrived in the heat of battle and subdued the enemy and latecomers enjoying the fruits of the conquered territory. Here, the enemy – as it had always been – was the environment. These first workers were both pioneers and victims. They were victims of many things, some fatal, but the most insidious in the early days of the Canal Zone was bureaucratic inefficiency. The first fifteen months were characterized by chaos and maladministration and it was the workers – black and white – who felt it.

One widely quoted book, *Make the Dirt Fly!* by Rose van Hardeveld,[1] the wife of an American worker from rural Wyoming, allows us to hear from her husband, Jan, in his first letter home, as he struggled alone on his very first night to find the bachelors' quarters in Culebra, "down by the railroad tracks", where he was assigned to sleep: "A heavy suitcase in each hand, no light anywhere, the sweat rolling down my face, I stumbled along the wet slippery track, which I had been told to follow until I found a place to turn off." Jan's anxiety was magnified by the water on all sides, his feet slipping from the ties landing in soft mud. "In the deep darkness I seemed to have walked miles," he continued, "and

Figure 5.2 President Theodore Roosevelt "letting the dirt fly" (Wikimedia Commons).

I never dreamed there could be such unearthly noises as came to my ears from all around. Thick croaking, hoarse bellowing, and strange squeaks and whines leaped at me from the blackness." The noisemakers were lizards, frogs and crocodiles, but to him that night they sounded like the howling of demons. "Well," he assured his wife as many others no doubt would do, "I decided that turning back looked almost as hard as going on, so here I am." Awful food, so much rain "my hat is getting mouldy on my head", and a bout with malaria were among his earliest news home.[2]

Thomas Gittens, who arrived from Barbados in 1905 as a nineteen-year-old contract worker also found it "ruff and tuff", as he recalled sixty years later: "when we got here we live in camps   we slep on chain bunks a pease of canvis tie with rope   no matress blanket sheet or piller jhus the cold cain bunk   it was ruff and tuff   no water   we had to get it where ever we could get it   we had to do our own washing on Sunday   we could only wash once a week   it was ruff and tuff from the start."[3]

The first Isthmian Canal Commission (ICC) was headquartered in Washington, DC, from whence it attempted to run affairs in Panama. The very structure of the organization worked against efficiency. The US Congress had voted the appropriations necessary for the construction of the canal and considerable public support arose for the project. The first commission consisted of seven members, all given equal authority – resulting in jealousy, obstruction and confusion. Each of the seven members of the ICC was a distinguished individual in his own field, but none had any experience whatsoever of organization on the scale required in Panama. In fact, no one did.

The civil service controlled operations in Panama which was soon smothered in bureaucratic red tape. In 1904, the fortnightly payment for the ICC's eighteen hundred workers involved the filling in of seventy-five hundred individual sheets of paper weighing more than one hundred pounds.[4] Approval for the smallest expenditure had to come from Washington. Washington bureaucrats, utterly ignorant of conditions in Panama, arbitrarily pruned requisitions or ignored urgent requests; delays in filling orders led to pile-ups on the wharves in Panama City and Colón.

Such was the fate of lumber urgently ordered for constructing the vast numbers of buildings required. Because of bureaucratic bungling, three ships arrived at the Pacific port at the same time with twelve million feet of lumber, all of which had to be unloaded by hand. The lumber was transferred from the ships to lighters and rafts, which tied up as close as possible to shore. Then "gangs of Jamaicans were ordered to wade into the knee-deep mud and bring the lumber in on their heads. In water up to their chests they struggled ashore with a few planks at a time, dropped them on the muddy banks, and went back for more – a vast army of Negroes slowly plodding back and forth across the mud flats."[5] The rafts piled high with lumber were moored along the shores of the Rio Grande, which suddenly rose and tore their moorings loose. The rafts floated out to sea where, in the narrow channels of the bay, they remained a menace to shipping. Many were recovered, "but expensive driftwood from Washington girded the shore at high tide for miles".[6]

The newspapers had a field day exposing Washington inefficiency and Canal Zone squalor. Workers were deserting as fast as they arrived and recruiters were finding it hard to replace them: this was when the Americans were still trying to negotiate for Jamaican workers with that government. The Americans seemed to be doing as badly as the French. There was clearly a crisis at Panama.

Secretary of war William Howard Taft saw the situation at first hand when he visited in November 1904, and he lost no time in communicating his fears to President Roosevelt. Roosevelt acted with characteristic dispatch and on 1 April 1905 appointed a new commission. This body still consisted of seven members, but three constituted an executive committee and two constituted a quorum. Each member was put in charge of a particular area of the Panama operations. In July 1905, a new chief engineer, John Stevens, a former railway-man, was appointed. Under his regime, order started to come to the Canal Zone as the "railway men" laid down the foundations and provided the necessary planning and infrastructure. After nearly two years of hardships the modern Canal Zone, as later workers came to know it, took shape and the Zone became a model of cleanliness and efficiency. The actual work of building the canal got underway in 1907 and the man in charge then was Colonel George W. Goethals, an army engineer. The "army men" saw the work to its completion.[7]

HATS IN THE AIR

When the first whistle blasted on 4 May 1904 to signal the start of work by the Americans, Amos Clarke, who was standing at Bas Matachin,[8] witnessed workers who had been toiling for the French company throw their hats in the air, dance and jump "about 2 feet high".[9] There were 746 employees of Compagnie Nouvelle on the day the United States took over, of whom 700 were labourers, many of them Jamaicans.[10]

At 7:45 a.m., the first group of men hired by the Americans were issued machetes and started slashing at the vines and bushes that covered the French works and material, the efforts of de Lesseps and his men having been reclaimed by the voracious jungle. Most of it effectively abandoned fifteen years earlier, work sites, camps and villages had almost disappeared from sight under exuberant tropical growth. All over the isthmus, machinery lay rusted and broken; vines and trees covered buildings; bats, spiders and lice had colonized the houses. Among the first group of workers slashing at the vines and creepers, Clarke recalled both black and white American adventurers who had poured in from the United States, dressed in "blue jungarees and khaki pants", with derby hats on their heads.[11] This is a rare glimpse of these men doing such work, mainly "tropical tramps", as they were called, or drifters; such men would later be discouraged from employment. The Canal Zone would never again be so democratic.

The men relied on itinerant vendors for food. At Clarke's job site two Jamaican women arrived with large trays on their heads bearing coffee, bread and butter, a breakfast that cost $0.10 (equivalent to one hour of the silver worker's labour). These women must have been well-known figures on the isthmus, for Clarke says one of them, Mrs Caroline Lowe, lived to 110 and the other, Mrs Marian Cunningson, lived to 75.

In 1904, though, order was still remote. Inadequate food and shelter continued to plague everyone. There was no surplus on the isthmus for thousands of new mouths. In November 1904 there were thirty-five hundred canal workers. In November 1906 this number had reached seventeen thousand employees on the canal along with four thousand on the Panama Railroad. With casual or seasonal labour added, there were about twenty-five thousand workers within the jurisdiction of the ICC and the Panama Railroad. In addition, thousands not yet employed had come to Colón, including women and children. The lack of locally available food was exacerbated by crop failures during the two previous years and abandonment of agricultural labour for work on the canal. For a time in 1905, food could not be imported from neighbouring provinces or from the Caribbean because an outbreak of bubonic plague locked the port of Panama in quarantine.[12]

Food shortages affected everyone, including white employees and the few wives who had so far joined them. They too were amazed to see strips of jerky hanging

Figure 5.3 Workers of "the 1904 gang" prepare food at their worksite (Panama Canal).

outside native huts, and although most turned up their noses at local food offerings, they were forced to patronize native stands to buy the local staples of black beans and rice, salted codfish, and fried plantain. They also came to rely on itinerant black women bearing huge baskets of fruit or vegetables on their heads or in hampers on mules, or the Chinese men selling fresh vegetables and greens from two baskets balanced on a pole across their shoulders. In ramshackle native villages along the railway line, were cantinas and native and Chinese shops stocked with a few goods, though, on entering one of these shops, Rose van Hardeveld found that "not one edible thing looked familiar".[13] Familiarity on both sides grew, and Rose later noted that, lacking small coin, Chinese shopkeepers gave a plug of tobacco as change: it could always be brought back on the next visit.[14]

In times of scarcity, prices soared, pushing many items beyond the means of the West Indian workers. Many had sold everything at home to pay for their passage and arrived penniless with only the clothes on their backs. Thanks to the general maladministration, they were paid irregularly; a monthly pay system was finally instituted in 1907. At first Chinese shopkeepers were happy to give the workers credit but when payday repeatedly failed to arrive, the credit ended.[15]

The ICC soon established commissaries to supply the American workforce with food and other goods. Silver workers were initially excluded, but in August 1905 commissary privileges were extended to all ICC and Panama Railroad workers; branch commissaries appeared along the route of the canal. This system ensured adequate supplies and brought prices down.[16] Until then, men foraged the swamps and jungles for food. Many lived on sugar cane.[17] Disturbances among the workers grew and many returned home in discontent. Others left in fear of the appallingly high death rate, which hit a peak in 1906 when over one thousand black workers died.

The situation was particularly dire for the newly arrived West Indians, many of whom came off the boat malnourished. Happily, there was no shortage of work; the challenge was surviving until payday. A worker recalled seeing "hundreds of men lying down in Colón streets dead   some pick up on arrival dead some 2 days after dead   all the report from the Doctor was starvation kill him   man hungry till he drop".[18]

Although exaggerated, this recollection was partly true. Before the early arrivals learned that prudence was the only course to adopt on the hazardous isthmus, many came with the notion of starving themselves in order to save as much as possible in the shortest possible time: "Some of the men try hard to save; buy 2 cents bread, 2 cents sugar, and go to work all trembling and cant lift a thing."[19] Many died because of this practice, before they learned the hard Zone lesson that the work regime and the toughness of the environment allowed only the fittest to survive. As one ninety-year-old explained some seventy years later,

> I remember when I was getting 13 cents an hour and a man was getting 10 cents and he was actually working under me for I was driving the waggonette for the hospital . . . and I ask the man how much he save and the man say about forty dollars and I say what! Out of that money? We don't feed weself, you see. Getting the little money and if you don't eat good you drop down you drop down to nothing. So therefore you got to eat good and drink something good and make you feel good and all the rest of it and that's what keep me till now.[20]

THE STENCH OF GUANO

Finding shelter – even the crudest place to lay one's head – became the arriving worker's second challenge. Those brought on contract were sent from the boat by train straight to assigned places along the line. So were many others hired right off the boat, especially in the early days when workers were in high demand. On the Zone, the new arrivals – black and white – were housed in tents, railway boxcars and some of the old houses abandoned by the French. On first entering these mouldy old buildings, the West Indian workers no doubt experienced, as did Rose van Hardeveld, "a penetrating stench, so vile it was almost unbearable", which struck her the instant the door was opened. It came from guano – the droppings from resident bats that covered the walls "by the hundreds".[21]

Soon, an army of West Indian builders began rehabilitating these houses and constructing new ones as well as barracks to house the workers. These later

Figure 5.4 Old boxcars such as this one provided housing for some of the earliest workers, black and white. (Courtesy of William P. McLaughlin, www.czimages.com.)

arrivals were provided with kitchens and offered three cooked meals a day. But the first arrivals were expected to shift for themselves. Their bodily strength was sapped by hunger, by lack of proper shelter, by an inhospitable climate and by the work regimen: ten hours a day, six days of a week of back-breaking labour, as well as insanitary conditions and the illnesses they caused. Jamaican David Crawford described the environment as "raw – just like a piece of land that is there but hardly anything around".[22]

The same old isthmus of rain, jungles, morasses and unpredictable rivers awaited the men, with twenty-seven ramshackle villages and whistle-stops along the now decrepit railway line. Most of the villages were simply clusters of shacks. At Culebra station (forty minutes by rail from Panama) there were "no sanitary arrangements of any kind, and lean black pigs wallow under the shacks and vie with the buzzards as scavengers".[23] Most of the people in this village were Jamaican, having lived there since the early days of the French canal, and they were all chronic malaria victims.

The terminal cities were little better. In 1906, Colón's back alleys were described as a "swamp in which all sorts of slimy things lived and which is covered with rank green weeds".[24] H.G. de Lisser, visiting editor of the Jamaica *Gleaner*, had shocking news for his readers back home: "imagine houses resting on piles driven into this swamp, and you have the greater part of Colón. . . . [Y]ou wonder how human beings can have consented to live amidst such frightful surroundings all those years." De Lisser repeated a doctor's statement that "fully sixty per cent of apparently healthy people in Colón have their blood simply swarming with malarial parasites, and that one day or another the victim will drop down unconscious, hardly ever to rally again". De Lisser concluded, as had many before him, that "to live in the back streets of Colón is to consign yourself to death".[25] By 1907, the United States government had made the streets of Colón habitable and rid the Zone towns of the breeding places of the disease-carrying mosquitoes. Such public health schemes came too late for those already infected: the deadly malarial organisms had already entered their bloodstream, there to reside for life. As late as 1909, the sanitary department of the ICC estimated that one-sixth of the entire population of Colón (many of them West Indian) suffered weekly malarial attacks. Blood samples from one Zone town showed that 80 per cent of its people were affected with malarial organisms, and this estimate could be generalized throughout the Zone.[26]

The chaos of the early years also applied to the work. Without proper plans, tools or equipment, men were sent hither and yon. Frequently, the calibre of men recruited from the United States was so poor that they could neither instruct nor lead the silver workers in their charge – their ignorance sometimes exceeded that of the men. With the restructuring of the ICC and of the local administration, however, order began to come to the Zone, order that would soon develop into rigid supervision of every aspect of the lives of Zone dwellers. From 1905 to 1907, emphasis was placed on providing the infra-structure that would create the proper working environment. During this time, also, the issue was settled once and for all as to what type of canal the United States would build: the US Senate voted thirty-six to thirty-one for a lock canal over a sea-level canal. All plans for construction could now be completed.

Activity in these early years was to centre on sanitation, on building construction and on civil engineering, all aimed at making the Zone habitable. Once these housekeeping matters were out of the way, the work of building the canal could start. But realization of the dream of a Panama Canal would never have been achieved had it not been for the first great American triumph in Panama: freeing the isthmus of disease.

THE WAR AGAINST MOSQUITOES

"Malaria was raging   yellow fever was raging   another fever was call tyfod fever raging in the matchin section. United States Citensin and West Indian lives and blood was taken to put through this Canal." So wrote silver worker Alfred Banister of the early years.[27]

In 1904 and 1905 American workers recruited in Washington would arrive on a boat, take one look around and board the same ship for an immediate return home.[28] Some might have been victims of a practical joke played on newcomers by old hands who shipped the coffins from the factory in Gorgona, timing them for the day the boat bringing new employees arrived. As they disembarked, they would be greeted by coffins neatly stacked at the railroad depot. Pranksters then approached the newcomers to take their measurements, assuring them they were being measured for their coffins – just in case. Some failed to see the joke.[29] Scare stories about Panama abounded: newspapers in America portrayed it as a hell on earth. This perception was not helped by the fact that the first chief engineer, John F. Wallace, brought coffins for his wife and himself among his personal belongings.

Figure 5.6 First-day cover, Canal Zone, 1962, marking "the world united against mosquitoes" (postcard, author's collection).

The Americans were perfectly aware that failure to control the disease-ridden environment had contributed to the failure of the French effort. At first, however, nobody paid much attention to Colonel William Crawford Gorgas, the small, white-haired army doctor who was head of the medical team for the Panama Canal. Gorgas preached that the two major endemic diseases on the isthmus, yellow fever and malaria, were both transmitted by mosquitoes and could be eradicated or controlled by the simple measure of destroying the mosquitoes and their breeding places.

At the time, theories and demonstrations revealing the role of mosquitoes as transmitters of disease were so new that most people had not heard of them. And if they had, they refused to believe such nonsense: Admiral Walker, head of the ICC, called it "balderdash". But Gorgas was a leading authority on the subject. Not long before, he had been one of the army doctors assigned to Havana during the occupation of that city by US forces following the Spanish-American war. There, the theory of yellow fever as a mosquito-borne disease was put to the test and it was Gorgas who worked out and applied the sanitation measures that rid Havana of the *Stegomyia fasciata* (later *Aëdes aegypti*) mosquito and the disease by 1901.

Figure 5.7 Dr Carlos Juan Finlay of Havana, Cuba, who identified the mosquito now known as *Aëdes aegypti* as the carrier of yellow fever (Wikimedia Commons).

A Cuban doctor working alone, Carlos Juan Finlay, had given the world the theory that a mosquito was the carrier or vector of yellow fever. Finlay identified the species but failed to give practical demonstration of his theory. This proof was completed by American doctors in Havana, led by Walter Reed. About this same time came the discovery by Ronald Ross, an English army doctor working alone in India, that the *Anopheles* mosquito was the carrier of another world-wide disease, malaria. In 1898 Ross succeeded in working out the pattern by which the disease was spread.[30]

Dr Gorgas arrived on the Zone 28 May 1904 as chief sanitary officer. From

Figure 5.8 Dr Ronald Ross who identified the *Anopheles* mosquito as the carrier of malaria, shown on the steps of his laboratory in India with his wife and assistants with cages for malarial birds in the foreground (Wikimedia Commons).

Figure 5.9 Colonel William C. Gorgas made the Isthmus habitable and canal construction possible by his sanitary measures which included mosquito control (Abbot, *Panama,* 253).

the start he wanted to apply the same concepts he had used in Havana to rid the isthmus of malaria and yellow fever. At first he was regarded as a slightly eccentric man who was plaguing the bureaucrats in Washington with requests for personnel and supplies to fight mosquitoes down in Panama. Washington replied by telling him to cut down on sending costly cables.

Support for Gorgas came in a macabre way. A yellow-fever epidemic broke out in November 1904, the first since the US takeover, and claimed as its first victims top-level employees working in the administration building. The hospitals were soon overcrowded and, as the death toll rose, piles of coffins were stacked in full view of the street and the bells of the funeral trains clanged shrilly as they headed for Mount Hope cemetery. Three-quarters of the American workforce fled the isthmus, their terror augmented, no doubt, by the ghastly spectre conjured up by the popular resident poet James Stanley Gilbert:[31]

> You are going to have the fever,
>   Yellow eyes!
> In about ten days from now
> Iron bands will clamp your brow;
> Your tongue resemble curdled cream,
> A rusty streak the centre seam;

Your mouth will taste of untold things,
With claws and horns and fins and wings;
Your head will weigh a ton or more,
And forty gales within it roar!

Although by this time many workers had already contracted malaria, it did not inspire the fear yellow fever did. One could "live with" malaria; yellow fever was a swift and deadly killer, especially of Caucasians. As in earlier times, it was believed that blacks and "natives" were immune to yellow fever because the incidence among them was comparatively low. As John Lindsay-Poland points out, "Doctors did not yet comprehend that yellow fever is like the measles: Mild cases during childhood produce individual – not racial or collective – immunity."[32]

In 1905 a new ICC commission gave Gorgas four months to rid the isthmus of yellow fever and the resources to do so. Chief engineer Stevens threw his full weight behind the sanitation project that Gorgas envisioned. First, the fight would be against yellow fever, then malaria. Each species of mosquito has a different lifestyle and habitat, so each must be treated differently. In both cases, it is the female mosquito that bites because she needs the blood to mature her eggs. If the person bitten is infected, the mosquito will pass the disease along to the next person she bites. *Aëdes aegypti*, the yellow-fever carrier, is a domestic insect that likes clean water only, cannot fly far and is found around places of human habitation. Thus the plan of attack was simple: destroy local sources of water that allow the insect to lay her eggs or her larvae to survive. Control of *Anopheles*, the malaria carrier, was more challenging. This species is found virtually everywhere and is remarkably prolific. The female will lay her egg in the smallest drop of water, dirty or clean, so that even water collected inside the leaves of plants provides a nursery. *Anopheles* could not be wiped out completely, so the challenge was to establish frontiers and keep the areas within as free of the insect as possible. Workers outside this frontier were always at risk, and when they returned to civilization and were bitten, they became new sources of the disease. Because of its liking for cities, and its limited range, *Aëdes aegypti* became the first object of attack.

The Sanitation Brigade

Gorgas's approach was military, multipronged, relentless and swift. Buildings were fumigated, mosquito habitats destroyed, swamps drained and rivers sprayed with pesticide; and for the cities of Panama and Colón, the American authorities installed sewage systems, paved the streets and piped in drinking water. The building of larger hospitals and the establishment of line hospitals

Figure 5.10
The "sanitation brigade" of 1905 (www.canalmuseum.com).

on the Zone were all part of the programme, along with relentless enforcement there of rigid sanitation rules.

In addition to their complete control over the Canal Zone, the Americans were also granted jurisdiction over roads, sanitation, water and sewerage supplies in the terminal cities of the Republic.[33] The citizens of Panama could only stand by and watch incredulously as their lives were turned upside down by an "army" that invaded their homes, while outside thundered pneumatic drills ripping up their streets to lay down paving and water pipes. Gorgas's "sanitation brigade" consisted of thousands (mainly West Indians), some little more than boys, assembled in July 1905 for every district of Panama and Colón.

Each was handed a ladder, a gallon of glue and long strips of paper three inches wide by six feet long. In a one-month blitz, they invaded and fumigated every building in Panama City. They sealed up every opening with the paper and glue so no smoke or insects could escape, then room by room they burned an insecticide consisting of pyrethrum or sulphur. It was a scandal to Panama residents, who had no choice but to endure it. Before piped water was connected, domestic water came from wells and was stored in barrels, jugs, pots and other containers. The sanitation crews entered every single yard, throwing out rubbish and emptying all containers that could possibly harbour mosquitoes. Not even the holy water in the font of the cathedral was spared, as the priest complained. Gorgas ordered it changed every day. Oil and insecticide were sprayed everywhere. The smell of sulphur hung like a pall over everything and "even the leaves of the trees curled up", a sanitation worker recalled.[34] In one year, the sanitation brigade used up 330 tons of sulphur and 120 tons of

Figures 5.11–5.12 A typical street ("Bottle Alley") in Colón before the sanitary crews arrived (*above*) and (*below*) D Street after installation of sewerage system and paving (Abbot, *Panama*, 36–37).

pyrethrum.[35] Other teams sprayed standing water in puddles or potholes or cisterns with kerosene to kill mosquito larvae. They cleared vegetation from around houses to prevent water pooling in leaves and providing a home for the insects. The aim now was to exterminate *Aëdes aegypti* by attacking the larvae.

Figure 5.13 Colón water carrier (Abbot, *Panama*, 39).

As Gorgas said on arrival, Panama was a "mosquito paradise". Colón was so low-lying that at high tide much of the town was under water. In the rainy season, the streets became rivers of mud, stagnant pools formed everywhere. By early July 1905, the sanitation effort was aided by the fact that running water was connected for Panama City, so water no longer needed to be stored around yards and houses. Meanwhile, West Indian crews were building reservoirs in the bush while others were constructing the streets and sidewalks, laying proper drainage-pipes and sewerage systems.

Once the main blitz was over, Panamanian doctors were recruited to carry out inspections. Residents were offered a reward of fifty dollars for reporting each case of yellow fever. Such cases could then be traced to the source of infection which could be eradicated. So successful was the campaign that Panama City had its last reported case of yellow fever on 11 November 1905. Colón's last case was in May 1906. Gorgas was right in announcing that Panama was free forever from yellow fever.

Ten-dollar Mosquitoes

Control and eradication of mosquitoes on the Zone itself proved much more challenging, especially of the malaria mosquito, *Anopheles*. Gorgas failed to get from the authorities the sort of support that had made the yellow-fever blitz possible. The new head of the ICC, Colonel Goethals, considered the sanitary department expenditure too extravagant. The following exchange between them was recorded by Mrs Gorgas: " 'Do you know, Gorgas,' Colonel Goethals said one day, 'that every mosquito you kill costs the . . . Government ten dollars?' 'But just think,' answered Gorgas, 'one of those ten-dollar mosquitoes might bite you, and what a loss that would be to the country!' "[36]

Controlling the environment in built-up areas was relatively easy, but it was much harder to control a working environment that extended through swamps and jungles in areas lacking safe water supplies or sanitation. Here, in such settings, many of the newly arrived West Indians were at work. Thousands were repairing the old French buildings on the Zone and constructing new houses. Over five thousand West Indians were employed by the Department of Construction and Engineering up to 1907 when the buildings on the Zone were completed. West Indians were also involved at many levels in the multi-faceted activities of the ICC – building machine shops, in locomotive pits, boiler shops, blacksmith and car shops, and foundries. One found them as well in the departments established to deal with meteorology, hydraulics, map-making, lithography, printing, and telephone and telegraph services.

The Panama Railroad had to be relocated and reconstructed, and many of these jobs lay outside of the sanitized zone. Those most at risk were toiling out in the jungles conducting surveys and quarrying the stones for street paving and building reservoirs, among other activities. Leslie Carmichael recalled, "Water to drink was very hard to get . . . after we had gone so far in the jungle there were times when we would lie on our stomach and drink whatever water in sight to quench our thirst, by drinking water that way a lot of the workers died from black [water] fever and yellow fever for there was no other way water could be acquired."[37]

In the built-up areas of the Zone, sanitation crews were beginning the mammoth task of clearing bush and eradicating breeding places for mosquitoes near all human dwellings. As order began to come to the Zone, every effort was made to protect the "gold" workers: their buildings were screened all around with mesh to keep mosquitoes out, the surroundings cleared and lawns established. No such screening or protection was offered to the silver workers, who nevertheless were also subject to the stringent public health laws that were passed and rigidly enforced. A perfectly law-abiding man or woman could find him- or herself spending a night in jail because he threw water outside the house at night or forgot to close the garbage bin. In 1907 alone, 650 arrests were made for violations of sanitary regulations. Emmanuel Aliker in his letters to his family in Martinique wrote frequently about the war on anything that could breed mosquitoes:

> Nothing more ordinary than throwing out of one's hut a sardine tin, a coconut shell or a piece of *coui*. But with the Americans it cost a disproportionate fine. Rain made these bits of waste into mosquito nests. It is only a sardine tin until one of the squadron of sanitary inspectors with his black-mounted DDT[38] spray gun inspects the perimeter of the hut metre by metre, and the garden and the outlet pipe to track down abandoned containers and charge the guilty.[39]

Figure 5.14
Mosquito control squad removing breeding places for mosquitoes underneath a house; Zone residents were fined for transgressing sanitary regulations (Panama Canal).

The Zone itself was divided into twenty-five districts, each in the charge of a sanitary inspector with a force of twenty-one hundred labourers. They cleared all the bush and undergrowth within two hundred yards of houses and villages and drained the ground within these areas. Pools and puddles were kept oiled with kerosene distributed from a can on a man's back. The can had a pump which the oilman worked by hand, forcing the oil through a nozzle. Photographs taken at this time show West Indians engaged in the variety of jobs involved in sanitation. We see them mixing huge vats of potent mosquito killer, mopping concrete drainage ditches with oil, heating the oil so it would run more easily through the sprayers, and carting drums of the oil through the jungles on mules along with the smaller sprayers on their backs. They used flat-bottom boats to spray the swamps; they saturated the marshes and set fire to the oil they sprayed on ditches to kill the mosquitoes. This dangerous, dirty

Figures 5.15–5.17
Oil for controlling mosquitoes in the bush was carried to their habitat in swamps and jungles by mule, backpack or boat (Panama Canal).

work was done without any protective clothing or devices. At its peak, the sanitation men distributed sixty-five thousand gallons of crude oil each month.[40] As Joseph Pennell, a visiting artist, recorded in 1912, "There was not a smell, or a mosquito, or a fly on Ancon Hill, but over it all was the odor of petroleum, with which the streams and marshes of the whole zone were sprayed almost daily."[41]

With yellow fever under control, the medical team did succeed in substantially reducing the death rate from malaria and keeping the incidence of disease in check. While in 1906 there were 233 deaths from malaria on the Zone, by 1913 only 12 malaria victims died. However, malaria was never eradicated and it contributed greatly to absenteeism and hospitalization of thousands of workers, leading in many cases to chronic disability. In 1906, 22,000 workers were admitted to hospital for malaria or roughly eight out of ten.[42] In fiscal year 1911, there were nearly 10,000 hospital cases, of which 42 died. Of the total hospitalized, 5,081 were white employees and 4,817 were black.[43] In 1914, malaria was the fifth leading cause of death and contributed to the highest number (2,884 or 65.06 per cent) of hospital admissions.

By 1908, though, the horrors of death by tropical disease were largely a thing of the past. Dr Gorgas and his team so substantially reduced the death rate in the Canal Zone that by 1909 he could claim that these rates were comparable to those of any American city. The sick rates, however, continued to tell a different story, and chronic illnesses, such as malaria and pulmonary infections, continued to plague the workers. Among the white workforce, death from accidents consistently exceeded death from disease. The opposite held true for the black workers.

For the construction years 1904 to 1914, approximately 5,609 workers are recorded as dying on the job. Of these, 4,500 were black employees. However, as Michael Conniff has pointed out, since the majority of West Indians lived outside the Zone, where sanitation and medical treatment were inferior, the total number of deaths among West Indians would have been much higher.[44]

"THE FEVER LASHED GOOD AND PLENTY"

The miracle of cleaning up the Zone and terminal cities created an environment that made it possible for the ICC to embark fully on construction from 1907 onwards. Ironically, 1906 was to prove to be the worst year for deaths on the isthmus, particularly among the black workforce, and sickness and death remained prominent features of the construction years. Silver workers were most strongly affected by typhoid, pneumonia, tuberculosis and respiratory illnesses. Deaths from typhoid and pneumonia occurred almost entirely

Figure 5.18
Drawing of silver men in hospital (by Anne Cordts McKeown in Core, *Maid in Panama*, 185).

among black workers. Tuberculosis was the third highest cause of death among canal employees.

In the early years, pneumonia felled many new arrivals because they had no exposure in their home countries to influenza, then prevalent on the isthmus and an inevitable precursor to pneumonia. Bad living and working conditions combined with undernourishment and the stresses of poverty worsened matters.[45] Many West Indian workers could afford only one set of work clothes. At work they got wet and slept in the same damp clothing. When they did have a change, the perpetual dampness made drying their clothes impossible. "We used a scheme to put on those wet clothes," Aaron Clarke explains, "we took the clothes to the bath room with us and immediately leaving the shower without drying our skin we put the wet clothes on, took our breakfast and was off to work for anoth[er] day of hard toil."[46]

Clothes and shoes disintegrated quickly in the rain and mud. John Prescod at Bas Obispo worked at the steam shovel in mud and water. "One pair boot last me one day. In the afternoon walk to the camp bear foot."[47] Clifford Hunt arrived as a contract labourer in 1906 and "the second week the Red Mud took of my boot sole I wonder what was the meaning of that; I had no money I had to tie my foot with canvas".[48]

The workers also slept in overcrowded tenement rooms in the towns or in the barracks where a single pneumonia victim could rapidly transmit the infection to all. In 1906, in the month of August alone, 145 black workers died, 60 of them from pneumonia, and a total of 479 deaths that year were due to that cause.[49] So serious was the problem that in 1908 the ICC provided all work camps with drying houses, a room fitted with steam to dry clothes quickly and the men were warned of the dangers of sleeping in damp clothes.

Yet of all the illnesses prevailing on the isthmus, it was malaria that the workers most talked about. Unlike yellow fever, where one attack ended in death or conferred immunity on the survivor, malaria attacks recurred. The sickness usually takes the form of violent shivering and chills ("the shakes") followed by a raging fever. After each attack comes a period of physical debility and mental depression. Attacks would recur at various intervals throughout the person's life. The onset of malaria is very sudden and may produce dramatic effects. George Martin would recall, "The fever lashed good and plenty. Sometimes walking on the Monte-Lirio Stretch, you meet men coming and going in each direction, in a sudden you look, a gang together, something happen, what? One or two of the gang on the ground flatten out, before help reaches, one dead long time, no more of him . . . in those days, you watch men shake, gentlemen, you think they would shake to pieces."[50] Another silver worker, Rufus Forde, declared, "you turn to work in the morning with a gang about 125 men and by Eleven oclock you will find about 40 men all the others fall down with Malaria   the jock about it, they spin all round like a top before they fall and that get you so frighten that at some times you dont come back after dinner."[51] No wonder that at the time, the most popular song being sung by the workmen was "Somebody Dying Every Day".[52] Many got so frightened by the fever that each day they took without complaint the bitter quinine which was used both in the treatment of malaria and as a preventative against attack.

The quinine dispenser's job was to induce the workers to take five grams of the bitter medicine every day. He carried with him "quinine tonic", with various ingredients added to make it attractive in taste and appearance, although nothing could disguise the bitterness of the medicine derived from the bark of the cinchona tree, first used by South American Indians as a cure for fever. The dispenser also offered a choice of quinine pills, capsules and tablets. Dr Gorgas claimed that no attempt was ever made to force anyone to take quinine as a preventive, "but explanation and persuasion were used to their fullest extent".[53]

The workers felt that they had little choice. According to Albert Banister,

> a man having a big leather bag full with paper cups and a one gallon bottle full of quinine will call you and give you a paper cup and will pore out for you many will gladly take and many will behave bad then the man will call the police you either drink or go through the gate you lost your job you will have to get a next job where nobody know you and the next bottle man don't know you.[54]

Others, though, attributed their survival to the regular drinking of quinine:

> The authorities did work on the malaria, they sent men around day after day with a colored looking liquid, the men would shout, come on boys, drink it up. Sweet at first, but bitter in the end, many men were afraid to drink, but I drank it with good heart, for the authorities did not mean to kill, their aims were to revive; this liquid was quinine, so they put a pretty color to it as a catch, so it catch me, for it did me good.[55]

Another told how "there are men going around with quinine to every gan[g] and give you to drink it is so bitter, that when the next man come around, the gan[g] say we got already. If six men come around for the day, I take six glass, and that is why the malaria keep off of me."[56]

Many complained the quinine made them deaf. As John Prescod dramatically expressed it, "Malaria fever have me so bad I has to drink plenty of quine tonic tell I heard singing in my ears   murder murder   going to quits drinking quine   was getting me deaf."[57] Albert Banister discovered other surprising side effects: "The first gentleman that learn me to drink is Uncle-Sammy. I left my Homeland at 19 years of age I never know how to drink, drink was introduce to me at Cristóbal boiler shop   when you drink that quinine you feel for 15 minutes you are the sweetest man in the land."[58]

One worker found the conditions in those days so terrible that "it would stagger your imagination". "I don't think I could ever find words to express the true conditions that existed," Alfred Dottin related. "Death was our constant companion. . . . I saw mosquitoes, I say this without fear of exaggerating, by the thousands attack one man. There were days that we could only work a few hours because of the high fever racking our bodies – it was a living hell."[59] Amos Parks claimed "that's the reason we all use to go to church more regular than today, because in those days you see today and tomorrow you are a dead man".[60]

Healing Oil and BushTea

The vast majority of the West Indian workers came from societies unused to formal medical services but schooled in traditional or folk medicine, the use of locally grown bushes and herbs for ailments, and the appeal to spirit powers for help in healing, and many no doubt resorted to these practices on the isthmus.

Practitioners of the healing arts or of the darker powers travelled to Panama to offer their services. The West Indian writer Eric Walrond, who as a child went to live in Panama in 1910, includes several instances of "obeah" or occult practices among West Indians in his stories in *Tropic Death*. Canal workers carried various herbs, mixtures and charms around with them, including small bottles containing a mixture of kerosene and coconut oil which they rubbed on exposed parts of their bodies to keep mosquitoes and sandflies away.

This was also the heyday of patent medicines, travelling medicine shows and extravagant promises of cure-alls. West Indian entrepreneurs were not to be left out of this lucrative market. P.A. Benjamin started his company in 1879 to manufacture proprietary medicines in Jamaica and the sales volume on the isthmus contributed to his initial success.[61] Advertisements in the papers promised wonderful cures from Benjamin's Celebrated Medicines. The men could doctor themselves with Healing Oil at sixty cents a bottle; Herb Tea at twenty-five cents; Kola wine for fifteen dollars a case; and asthma, liver, and kidney "cures" were also available.[62]

Crocodiles and Snakes

There was no preventative, however, against certain perils. Many of the stories told to grandchildren back home featured encounters with crocodiles (which everyone called alligators)[63] or deadly snakes, and would often be regarded as nothing but "tall tales", such as the story one grandfather told his grandchildren of sitting on a log to have his lunch and sticking the fork into the log only to see blood spurting. It was a huge snake.[64]

But the danger from ferocious wild life was real enough. Austin Kavanagh was famous as a hunter and crack shot – his relatives recalled that the skin of a huge snake he had shot ended up in the Smithsonian Institution, and among the relics he brought back to Jamaica was an enormous bag made from the skin of a crocodile he had killed. He told stories back home of how when he catered to work gangs out in the bush he hunted for food, including wild boar ferocious enough to split a man in two.[65] His listeners might have dismissed his stories also as tall tales, except that Wolfred Nelson in the 1880s had noted in Panama that "boars will rip a horse open or attack a man without the slightest provocation".[66] As for the other dangers, on one occasion Joseph Edwin "had to blast a goodsized log out of the Chilibre River". Wading in, he tied dynamite under it, retreated to the shore and set off the blast. When the log blew up, so did an outsize crocodile which must have been lurking near the log all the time.[67]

Constantine Parkinson was unequivocal about his fear. He was, after all, just a youth, age fifteen or thereabouts, and working with a survey gang as a rear flagman, running a trail through the jungle:

Figure 5.19
Crocodiles captured on a Panama river – postcard titled "A good day's hunt" (author's collection).

What They Endured, 1904–1907   **157**

I incounter with plenty of snakes and animals one day running down a steep hill my feet got intangle with a snakes coiled up sleeping. I call out for the machet men to kill the snake, and was found to swallow a young deer the snakes was 15 feet long . . . . a next time while standing with my flag pool [pole] holding a point for my engineer Mr. Betartan at a very good distant alone with knee deep in swamp I heard a heavey walking comming behind where I was standing and when I turn to look I notice a large mountain cow[68] headed towards me I took my flag pool and ran.

His boss "seeing that I was so frighten change me from rear flagman to rear chainman".[69]

George Martin recalled not just snakes but "short jacket, this fellow when he lights on you, don't feel him until he is getting ready to quit and when he do fly off nothing but blood oosing out. The next fellow was the goosyana fly, when he stings, he leaves worms in the flesh."[70]

In the face of such dangers, prudence was the only course to adopt:

One day about mid-day we met a snake about six inches round, and about 15 feet long at a distance, all we had was shovels to make the attack, but he looked more than us, so we bid him good buy in the bush. Another time, I were sent to fetch water for the men to drink, and the same place I go were five snakes at the same place in the water, if they had made an attack on me, they would certainly harm me for I just couldn't move, I was so frighten, so see me; they went their way and so I dip up my water.[71]

And then there were the poisonous spiders:

On our way from Frijoles to Montelirio, placing the new re-location getting away from the place called the Black Swamp, we had to contack much rotten trees and stumps, our white boss would pass and warn, "Heh Boys don't put your hands under those rotten wood, you may find something under there, that if bitten by same, you would live only about 24 hours, they are called Antelopes or Black-spider." So we were very careful, and we did meet with them plentiful.[72]

"A FOWL LIFE WAS MORE VALUABLE"

Accidents on the job and off were an hourly occurrence: "man die get blow up get kill or get drown   during the time someone would asked where is Brown he dide last night and burry   where is Jerry   he dead a little before dinner and burried so and on all the time."[73]

Virtually no worker who came to the Zone had experienced even a fraction of the frenzied industrial activities encountered there, certainly not the many West Indians from rural agricultural backgrounds. The men's ignorance of the industrial dangers that awaited and their inability to cope with the fast pace of life contributed to the frequency of accidents, but many mishaps were simply not preventable. The number of active railroad tracks and trains operating at any one time was enormous, apart from the scheduled transits of passengers and freight. Labour trains moved the army of workmen from place to place, "spoil" trains moved the millions of tons of earth dug from the bottom of the canal and dumped elsewhere. Frequently, a man would step from one line to avoid an oncoming train only to be hit by one coming in the opposite direction.[74] A visiting American noted of the trains that "the worst is when they creep up on you from behind under cover of the noise of a battery of tripod drills".[75]

In Culebra Cut alone at the height of construction, there were over one hundred miles of tracks along its nine-mile length, or nine parallel tracks.[76] In 1908, the total average train movement along the Panama Railroad in an eight-hour period numbered 410 trains with a maximum movement of 574 trains in twenty-four hours. The average trainload was sixteen twenty-yard cars.[77] In 1911 when the central division which encompassed Culebra Cut achieved its highest record for excavation, 33 loaded trains and an equal number of empty trains ran to and from the cut to the dumping grounds in a single day.[78]

The perpetual dust, smoke, and noise (combined with quinine-induced deafness) no doubt contributed to industrial accidents. Rufus Forde recalled that "there are so many engeins at a time in the Cut that most every month, that a man lost his leg or badly damage, when any thing like that happen one engineer will turn to next engineer, one just grease the wheel   in those days a fowl life was more valuable than our lives".[79]

Accidents from dynamite blasts were frequent. Drownings, electrocutions, cave-ins and landslides, falls from great heights also took their toll. Survivors were frequently left crippled and maimed for life, either physically or mentally, or both. In the post-construction years, the Coloured Cripples Association was founded on the isthmus. In 1904, an editorial in the Jamaica *Daily Gleaner* had prophetically foretold, "it is obvious that the digging of this canal will mean an extraordinary waste of human lives . . . and when the weaker of the emigrants fall ill they will be cast aside as so many broken tools, for sentiment has no place in great commercial undertakings".[80]

The workers received no compensation for accidents in the early years; the ICC offered compensation only after 1 August 1908, and such payment was not automatic. Between 1908 and 1912, compensation was paid for 5,000 cases of non-fatal injuries, a fraction of the total injuries recorded. In the same four years, 13,060 accidents were reported, 395 of them fatal. In fiscal year 1912 alone, 5,141 cases of accidents resulted in incapacity exceeding fifteen days and paid for as meritorious sick leave.[81] Other cases went unreported.

While every effort was made to incorporate the most stringent safety features into the structure of the canal itself, workers' safety was ignored. Workers had none of the equipment that is nowadays required in industrial activity – no goggles, safety hats, gloves, shoes, shields, safety belts and harnesses, or life jackets. They constantly swallowed dust from blasting and drilling, and from the millions of tons of cement that was quarried, mixed and poured. They went deaf from the unceasing noise of pneumatic drills. They got the "bends" (decompression sickness) from diving without pressurized suits. They strained their limbs and organs pushing, pulling and carrying inordinately heavy weights. They worked brutally long hours; in torrential rain or in blistering heat.

At the start, they gave their youthful strength; many decades later, illnesses arose to plague the old survivors from damage suffered (and ignored) during construction days. James Williams wrote a postscript to his memories written fifty years after construction saying, "So far I can say of a truth, the terrible effects of that fever is still telling on my nerves."[82] Constantine Parkinson, born 1894, was fitted with an artificial leg in 1914 after losing his right leg and left heel in an accident while working as a brakeman at Toro Point the previous year. "After coming out of the operation in the ward", he recalled, "I notice all kinds of cripples around my bed with out arms foot one eye telling me to cheer up not to fret we all good soldiers."[83]

Not all were "good soldiers" – West Indians filled the hospital for the insane at Corozal, representing 500 out of 550 inmates in 1912 and including what seemed a disproportionate number of women. In the Ancón Insane Asylum in 1909 were 254 inmates, 155 West Indians with Jamaicans the largest single national group: 51 men and 35 women. Although Ancón's inmates came from everywhere, the only other countries with large numbers were Panama (with 56) and Barbados (30). These Ancón inmates (like the majority of those who had flocked to the isthmus) represented people in their prime: 181 were between ten and forty years of age.[84]

Diagnoses of large numbers of West Indians as insane might be attributable to an overzealous and "ambitious young medical establishment eager to analyse and tame the tropics" and which misread symptoms. Cultural ignorance and bias may have had a part. The British consul received many complaints of wrongful institutionalization from West Indians.[85]

"WHAT THEY MEAN BY THIS BED-BATH?"

The ICC provided hospitals and medical treatment, but access to these facilities was not a simple matter for silver workers. Men were paid for work actually done, so only illness serious enough to require hospitalization stopped a man from work. Not surprisingly, the number of working days lost from illness among the black workforce was a fraction of what it was for the gold roll.[86] White workers were allowed paid sick leave, a privilege denied the silver roll. Many silver workers undoubtedly died from lack of medical attention.

During working hours, entry to ICC quarters was prohibited. If a man felt too ill to work and did not want to be hospitalized, his only other choice was to take to the bush, as many did. Barbadian John Garner did so after he had himself discharged from a line hospital – established in the early years for temporary treatment – following an attack of malaria; he was probably luckier than most in having a sympathetic foreman:

> That Quinine had me grogy and I was unable to walk down the stairs alone so I asked a man to help me down the stairs and out into a path which led to the Camp. It was about 9 o'clock in the day and I had to hide around until five o'clock because it was not allowed to be around the Camp during work hours. When I reach the camp it was very near 6 o'clock for the fever had me down and almost out. When the boys at the Camp saw me they came and lifted me up the steps they wanted to give me something to eat but I had no appetite so they drenched me with Bay Rum and had me drink some also. The following day they assisted me to the labor train and put me off where my gang was suppose to work. The Foreman had me sit around until I could join the ranks again. The boys in this gang were very jolly and we got along nicely together.[87]

Dr Gorgas had found that West Indians and their families (especially the women and children) feared hospitals. Part of the reason was undoubtedly economic. Families of employees (most earning one dollar a day) were charged thirty cents a day for hospital treatment (ICC employees were treated free). Ignorance of working hospitals (as well as associations of death) may have added to the West Indians' fear. At the time of the French, the hospitals had a poor reputation for treatment and survival. Between 1883 and 1889, over five thousand deaths had occurred at the French hospital at Ancón (twelve hundred from yellow fever).[88] When the Americans looked into the situation, armed with the latest medical discoveries, they found that these hospitals provided the perfect breeding ground for mosquitoes: the legs of every bed set in a pan of water to discourage crawling insects, and water often surrounded decorative potted plants adorning the grounds.

The average young man coming from the West Indies had little experience of hospitals and to be institutionalized in even a fine American hospital could be a frightening experience. When a Jamaican teenager named James Williams arrived at hospital and the nurse ordered a "bed bath", he immediately became frightened, because he had never been in a hospital. He happened to be turned over to an orderly who came from his home village in Portland, but they did not recognize each other before the bath began: "While I kept wondering in my mind what do they mean by this bedbath when I saw this Mr. Piercy placed a heavy waterproof Blanket in the bed and two buckets full of heavy crushed ice and several buckets of water and not even the courtesy as to consult me but stripped me naked and threw me in that cold deadly water."[89]

The iced bath (to bring down the fever) over, Williams was soon dying of thirst. Then a kind nurse arrived with a glass of what he thought was water and said drink it, "So thirsty for a drink of water, I hurried and as it reached my lips it went down my stomach. I tell you, I never had before tasted anything so terribly bitter." He had been given quinine, and he was dosed with it every two hours day and night. The next indignity occurred when he was

Figures 5.20–5.21
The cost of the canal: cemetery on Ancón hill for "gold" workers (Abbot, *Panama,* 117) and for "silver" (postcard, author's collection).

sitting at the nurses' desk and a basin of clean water was placed on a stand beside him. He promptly drank some of it, only to discover after emergency treatment that he had drunk poisoned water put there to catch flies. The next morning some men came and placed him on a stretcher: "I thought they were going to bury me as I was actually given over as dead." However, the doctors had just discovered that he had typhoid fever and not malaria and were having him transferred to the typhoid ward. Despite all these setbacks, he eventually recovered and was sent home: "the treatment had me so fat and robus that when I went home to San Pablo Aunt surprise to see how good I was looking". Like James Williams, virtually all the survivors who recorded their memories of the hospitals, had nothing but the highest praise for the American doctors and nurses, Williams attesting, "Those American nurses my own dear mother could not be more kind and tender to me."

Nevertheless, American Harry Franck could not help observing the differences in gold and silver at the great hospitals the Americans had built at Ancón and Colón. At the latter, the "white" wards were built over the sea, "and behind them the 'black' where the negroes must be content with second-hand breezes. Some of the costs of the canal are here," he observed, "sturdy black men in a sort of bed-tick pajamas sitting on the verandas or in wheel chairs, some with one leg gone, some with both. One could not but wonder how it feels to be hopelessly ruined in body early in life for helping to dig a ditch for a foreign power that, however well it may treat you materially, cares not a whistle-blast more for you than for its old worn-out locomotives rusting away in the jungle."[90]

MOURNING LETTERS AND ROUGH BROWN COFFINS

For the rest of their lives, the most pervasive memory for many of the old canal workers was the memory of death. The wife of a white worker recalled the view from her house: "the sanitary building with its huge stacks of dull red pine coffins leaning against one side of it was right in my line of vision".[91] West Indian Alfred Dottin wrote that he would never forget "the train loads of dead men being carted away daily, as if they were so much lumber".[92] Reginald Beckford was more explicit:

> It was nothing unusual to be walking on Front Street and suddenly you see a yard engine with one ICC flat car attached with dead men stretched out, whose faces cannot be seen, because a piece of clean white canvas, the length of the car covers their faces, moving slowly towards the old Colon Freight house to the north end where the Washington Hotel and stops. The people in the vicinity gathers, including myself, trying to get a glimpse of their faces. A police man is on duty to prevent the

people from getting too near. Not only once but on several occasions, these dead men on flat cars their faces covered up, were carried to near the end of the Rail Road tracks near the Washington Hotel. Colon Hospital was around the beach in those days.[93]

The dead who entered Colón and Panama in this manner were usually the victims of accidents. Travelling on the train one day, Beckford noted the impact of such accidents on survivors, recalling that passengers, "including myself, get up from their seats when the train is nearing Culebra, Avalanche covering fifty men at Culebra; something more. Bas Obispo had taken the greatest death toll in one dynamite explosion in one day."

An American who first came to the isthmus in 1905 and who was interviewed in 1958 said that his most vivid recollection was of the funeral train. Another recalled that at Colón,

> When I pulled into Colon . . . there was an engine . . . and next to the engine was a car, a coach, baggage coach, marked with large letters about fourteen inches in height, "Funeral Car". The one behind that was the Hospital Car. I often wondered what that meant, until we started down the road, and we would pick up the dead ones as we went along, and the sick would go in the Hospital Car, the dead in the Funeral Car. . . . And that was the regular equipment on the Panama Railroad.
>
> ([Interviewer:] Did they make daily trips that way?)
>
> Daily trips that way.[94]

As Albert Peters recalled of those earlier times, "Every evening around 4:30 PM one could see #5 engine with a box car and the rough brown coffins sta[c]ked one upon the other bound for Mt. Hope which was called Monkey Hill in those days. . . . If you had a friend that you always see and missed him for a week or two, don't wonder, he's either in the hospital or at Monkey Hill resting in peace."[95] Monkey Hill (later Mount Hope) was the huge cemetery outside of Colón dating from Panama Railroad construction days. Soon after the US takeover, cemeteries for workmen were established in each district of the Zone and no burials were allowed outside. After a time, the funeral car was discontinued.

Many workers died out in the bush alone, some washed away in rivers, unremarked and uncounted. Because workers moved from one worksite to another, often changing their names, some were never properly identified. Many were known, even to their mates, by surnames or nicknames only. After some accidents, little remained to make identification possible. Many of the workers simply "disappeared" – from the records, from their families. Yet when there were friends to take note of a man's death, these survivors sent the news back home, as did the British consulate, when notified. At post offices in West

Indian towns or villages, screams and wails announced these faraway deaths. The black-edged envelope of a dreaded "mourning letter" announced the news on sight: even before opening it, the relative understood that the canal had taken another victim.

Nine Nights and Wailing

When possible, the workers held some sort of wake for the dead as they would have done at home. The sounds from such festivities did not sit well with other nationalities, and the "awful noise" coming at night from the native villages and in the terminal cities were recorded in many a Zone memoir of the period.[96] Shortly after taking control of the Zone, the US authorities prohibited the holding of wakes but such practices continued in areas outside of their jurisdiction. Nor could they prevent West Indians from burying their dead on Sundays so that everyone could attend.[97]

Throughout the Caribbean, people of African descent still see death as the most important rite-of-passage. Many immigrants continued their familiar rituals, especially the elaborate wakes lasting eight nights to mourn the deceased and provide safe passage until the ninth night when he crossed to the other side. Nine nights required singing, elaborate speeches, games and merriment, for death rituals also provide entertainment for the bereaved. Heard from afar, without understanding their significance, these noisy wakes appeared barbaric and unseemly to outsiders who shared the disapproval of other West Indians and that of the authorities who passed numerous laws to ban them. Out in the bush, however, the wakes lived on.

As for the elaborate funerals, these attracted much disapproval as they revealed yet another aspect of West Indians' love of showy rituals, the funeral procession often attended by lodge or society brethren in full regalia. Such ceremonies were reserved for the successful element in West Indian society – those who had joined lodges or societies or those who had risen to positions of dignity within the community. For many workers during construction days, funeral rites on the Zone would be of the briefest. Aaron Clarke, a West Indian who worked in the sanitary department, recalled that he "dug ditches, dropped mosquito oil made drains, dug graves acted as pall bearer and sometimes when we could afford the time I performed a short religious ceremony".[98]

PROTEST AND JUSTICE

The ICC recognized many of the difficulties faced by the earliest workers; by 1905 the chief engineer could see steady improvements and noted that more problems could be solved by a "plenitude of laborers, prompt methods of payment, the proper amount of well-cooked food suitable to their needs and desires, and a more careful selection of foremen and superintendents".[99]

The latter remark went straight to an important issue: that the comfort level of the West Indian worker and his willingness to work often depended on his relationship to his white boss. While good relationships on an individual level developed from the start, the early days of construction were marked by many instances of serious physical and mental abuse of silver workers. As a newspaper of the time commented, at the start all labour on the isthmus was inefficient. In 1907 the ICC noted that "better foremen are now being secured than in the past and with more efficient foremen, the labourers themselves will necessarily prove more efficient".[100]

Even as he was at the mercy of the white foremen, the West Indian worker often stood on his dignity, frequently asserting, "I am a British subject, sar", and flooded the British consulate with complaints. He had come to the Zone imbued with clear-cut notions of British traditions, British labour methods and the rights of workers according to British law. It took a long time for him to adjust to the fact that, on the Canal Zone, he was no longer under the protection of "Missis Queen"; or, as Jamaican workers in another part of Central America were once told, "The Queen has no business with Campeachy Laws."[101] It is not surprising, then, that this early period was marked by the only serious labour disturbances during construction days, much of the unrest attributable to racism and misunderstanding.

In 1904, a general strike of silver workers on the Panama Railroad was soon

Figure 5.22 West Indian workmen paving street in Panama City, 1906 (Panama Canal).

settled with the intervention of the police. In 1905, a group arriving from Martinique rioted because of their fear of being vaccinated, and they had to be forcibly removed from the ship. In that same year occurred the most serious incident of the construction years. It involved Jamaican workers who were laying water mains and sewers in the city of Panama. The ICC annual report recorded the incident:

> The negro laborers, always on the alert for causes for complaint, have at times expressed dissatisfaction at the quality of their food and delays in receiving their pay. In April last, on account of some grievance of this nature, a gang of 150 Jamaicans employed in the laying of water mains and sewers in the city of Panama refused to go to work and became turbulent and threatening. The Panama police interfered and the affair developed into a street riot, in which 21 negroes were severely clubbed or wounded by bayonet thrusts. There were no fatalities and no one was seriously hurt.[102]

Reports appearing in the *Star and Herald* asserted, however, that the men's claims were justified. After a morning's work, they had gone to breakfast (supplied by an ICC contractor); breakfast was late and insufficient. Before the men's time was up and while some were waiting to be served, the American boss ordered them back to work. One protested; others joined in. The boss called a Panamanian policeman to compel the speaker to go back to work. The man resisted, taking up a stone and throwing it at the policeman. Several armed policemen then entered the yard and began to club the men with guns. Some of the men defended themselves with sticks and stones but most rushed over to the canal administration building to make a report. In the meantime, a policeman had telephoned police headquarters to say a rising of the labourers had taken place and requested assistance. A strong body of men was despatched to the scene.

The police attacked the unarmed men outside the ICC building, clubbing them with rifle butts. The Jamaicans ran in all directions and were pursued, clubbed and bayoneted. The excitement spread throughout the city; any Jamaican labourer sighted became a target. Several bystanders joined the police in ill-treating the men and others shouted "Kill him, kill him", in support of the police. A citizen knocked a Jamaican on the head with his revolver and arrested him. A native cab driver mistaken for a Jamaican narrowly escaped a clubbing. Two men about to be beaten to the ground were saved by white Americans. The majority of men received bayonet wounds in their backs as they fled.

The *Star and Herald* laid the blame firmly at the door of the Americans, who, the paper said, had not set a good example in their treatment of West Indians. "Americans are loud in their denunciations of the Panama Police

Force," the paper pointed out, "but it is they themselves who are to be blamed for the cause of the disturbance." It added, "Carelessness and utter indifference to the wants of the men who are brought here to do the actual work of digging the canal is silently, but nevertheless surely, breeding trouble for those responsible."[103] The Jamaica *Daily Gleaner* more explicitly placed the blame on the American bosses:

> From nearly every place in Central America one, at the outset, hears similar stories, and it is well known that the troubles in Ecuador, which resulted in the Jamaican government prohibiting the emigration of labourers to that Republic, was in the main caused by the brutality and harshness of American foremen. The moment these were discharged and their places filled by Englishmen and Jamaicans, or by Americans who had had some previous experience and were able to judge the temperament of the men over whom they were placed, the dissatisfaction ceased, and there were no further disturbances.[104]

The Boss, "He Bring a Quart of Rum"

The boss or foreman was indeed a key element in the day-to-day well-being and satisfaction of the worker: fifty years later many of the old construction workers remembered the names of their bosses and recounted pleasant experiences with them. Whether or not the work was bearable frequently depended on the boss's disposition:

> one day we had some rush work to do and the boss had orders to work right through, we work three day and too night in water to our wa[i]st, but the boss was so good that he bring a quart of rum, he will say, boys take a shot before you all goes into the water, and he take a big shot because he had to be into the water, when we finished he said to us boys take the half day off, you all work hard, and see that you all come out in the morning.[105]

Helon Allick arrived from Trinidad and started work as a ten-cents labourer but because his boss liked him, "he asked me to change my name and take me on as a new man at 13 cent, it was so done and . . . I was then Henry Thomas".[106] Alfred Dottin recalled that when he came out of Ancón hospital after nine weeks with typhoid fever "hovering between life and death", "My fore-man, Mr Sneed, treated me like a king while I was recuperating. He saw to it that I got plenty of sleep and food – good food I enjoyed it very much."[107]

Nevertheless, great animosity sometimes arose between the silver worker and the white boss, mainly because of the poor calibre of such men in the early days. Many white Americans were recruited from the Southern states, as they were supposedly experienced in dealing with Negroes.[108] Abuse of workmen by American bosses persisted as one of the degrading aspects of life on the

Canal Zone during early construction days. However, the authorities did their best to discourage the worst types of abuses and the courts began to deal firmly with such bosses brought to them by the workmen on charges of assault. In 1906 the *Colón Starlet* reported the following cases: a boss charged with assault and battery of a St Kitts bricklayer was fined twenty-five dollars gold and costs; the mayor of the municipality of Colón was fined by a Zone judge for striking a Jamaican; a timekeeper who assaulted a workman who had gone to him with a query was fined ten dollars and costs; a boss at Culebra who attempted to kick and shoot a workman was later fined fifteen dollars in Culebra court for hammering another labourer in the face until the blood flowed.[109] These are just a few of the incidents recorded. Yet, an American letter writer claimed in 1907 that there was so much intimidation by whites that "every man who resorts to the courts, or is a witness in any case, is immediately discharged".[110]

Verbal abuse, threats and reprisals were commonplace. Most of the incidents were probably never reported but they became less frequent with the recruitment of better American personnel, and the workmen demonstrated that they were unafraid to resort to the courts. Intimidation, threats and fear still remained as part of the relationship between individual boss and worker, but physical abuse seems to have ceased to be an important factor. Though Eric Walrond, in his short story "Subjection",[111] chillingly captured the spirit of "dread" surrounding the uneasy relationship between a certain type of white American and the black victimized workers.

Fortunately there was so much demand for labour during construction days that a man could (and frequently did) leave an unpleasant job to join another gang elsewhere. There were also cases where a worker and his superior would become so attached they would form a team, the worker following the boss to wherever he was transferred.[112] Quite often, too, the immediate foreman or "straw boss" was of the same nationality as the men, making for easier relationships.

Relationships between worker and boss may have been tempered by the attitude of Colonel Goethals, who became head of the Panama Canal in 1907.[113] Goethals instituted an "open door" at his office every Sunday, where any canal employee wishing to air grievances could do so in person. West Indian men and women took full advantage of the opportunity. Goethals had their confidence because he investigated and acted upon legitimate complaints. Thus even the lowliest worker could feel that he had access to the highest authority on the Zone – if only to express himself.

The change in the relationships was striking enough to be noted by a foreign visitor who first came in 1907 and observed "an antagonism between the American foremen and their gangs of West Indian negroes which was not conducive to progress or efficiency". Visiting three years later he no longer found the same friction, concluding that "they had each in fact learnt something of each other's ways. The foremen had discovered that the West Indian must be 'handled' differently from the American negro."[114]

While bosses in the West Indies were often white, some reciprocity in relationships existed, especially on the plantations, where bosses knew they could push their black labour so far and no further. Even during the brutal days of slavery, black workers resisted intolerable conditions in subtle or not so subtle ways against a disliked "massa" or "busha". In freedom, as we have seen, where there was mountain land to carve out an independent existence, the formerly enslaved Africans abandoned the estates. Even in Barbados, where the workers remained tied to their plantations, reciprocal obligations and informal rights ensured a social contract of sorts that, to some extent, guided mutual behaviour.[115] In Panama, no reciprocity existed.

The many books and newspaper articles written about the greatest news story of its time encouraged a view of West Indian workers as stupid, lazy and infantile, views that foremen and supervisors arriving on the Canal Zone imbibed, especially since many of these articles were written by high-ranking canal executives or with their collaboration. For instance, a book co-authored by the former chief engineer asserted that "they are a childlike race, easy to handle, but as in the case of the average child, sometimes a practical object lesson is far more effective than moral suasion".[116] Another former executive claimed, "These big, strong, black men have to be looked after like so many children."[117]

But just as they had done during plantation slavery, West Indian workers resisted coercion and domination by subtle forms of rebellion: moving from the assigned jobs, changing their names, taking time off from work when it suited them, refusing to stay in ICC barracks, refusing ICC food and resorting to their own catering, or taking advantage of their mobility to find a bit of land to farm. They could also return home or move to another country. The ICC in its wisdom neglected to grant them agency, and it also failed to recognize that different work rhythms and attitudes characterized West Indian culture. Some of the tensions between the two groups arose from mutual ignorance. In looking at the lives of West Indians on the Zone, American Julie Greene, like others, concluded that they "developed a wide range of strategies to shape their personal and working lives, improve their circumstances, and resist attempts by government officials to control them".[118] The West Indian worker could swallow insults or exploitation as long as he was armoured by the vision of what he could become back home once he had earned a little "Panama money".

Policemen and Justice

After 1904, the new Republic of Panama was forced to disband its army and rely on its police force. West Indians became involved in policing both the Canal Zone and the Republic. In 1904 the *Colón Starlet* reported the presence of a newly formed detective or secret service on the isthmus, composed largely of West Indians under the direction of Governor Melendez.[119] Some West Indians served on the regular force among a majority of Spanish-speaking Panamanians.

On the Canal Zone, during construction days policemen were recruited from West Indian islands but were used exclusively to police "silver" workers; in case of a disturbance in which a white American was involved, the silver policeman was not expected to make an arrest but to go and make a report to the chief at the police station. In 1907, of two hundred policemen on the force, one-fifth were white, the rest were mainly Barbadians and Jamaicans who had served in their local police forces or the West India Regiments.[120] As one of the white policemen explained, the unqualified noun implied African ancestry, so white policemen were always referred to as "grade A" or "first class". As he saw it, "To be sure there were also a couple of negro policemen in the smaller room behind the thin wooden partition of our own, but negro policemen scarcely count in Zone Police reckonings."[121]

The official view was more flattering. The ICC said that the Barbadians and Jamaicans who composed the rank and file of the Zone police force "have proved, in certain respects, better adapted to the performance of their duties than an equal number of white Americans would have been". In dealing with

Figure 5.23 Empire police station, 1904 (www.czbrats.com).

Figure 5.24 Panama national police, consisting mainly of Spanish speakers but including some West Indians (Abbot, *Panama*, 236).

the Negroes, the ICC report continued, "the American is apt to be aggressive and overbearing", adding that the coloured police officers have shown "admirable tact and judgement in dealing with their countrymen". The report added, "They are clean and neat in person and take great pride in their duties."[122]

Not all West Indians would have agreed. Proudly dressed in khaki uniforms with brass buttons, khaki helmets, buff leggings and brown boots, these policemen seemed to have swaggered around the Zone in an overbearing manner, and their countrymen and women frequently found them lacking in "admirable tact and judgement".[123] But the police were compelled to enforce Goethal's "benevolent despotism" with numerous bylaws designed to control social behaviour. Initially the ICC deported offenders, but imprisonment became increasingly common, even for relatively mild infractions. Fines (usually between five and twenty-five dollars) were often beyond a worker's means. Misdemeanours that could result in such fines or imprisonment included loitering, vagrancy, begging or any disturbance of the peace. West Indians were also at the mercy of the white policemen who commonly misinterpreted language, gestures and behaviour, perceiving threats where none existed, with sometimes serious results. Harrigan Austin, who came as a young contract worker, found that "life was some sort of semi slavery, and there was none to appeal to, for we were strangers and actually compelled to accept what we got, for in any case of an argument we would have to shut up, right or wrong. And the bosses or policemen or other officials right or wrong could be always winning the game."[124] The ICC records were filled with grievances by West Indians about police mistreatment: unjust arrest and imprisonment, brutal beatings during arrest, and insulting comments by policemen.[125]

Nevertheless, the West Indian of construction days seems to have been a remarkably law-abiding – if not peaceful – citizen. At first glance, the statistics of arrests might challenge this view, but the most frequent causes of arrests for one year (1907) show that the incidence of serious crime (murder, rape, grand larceny), was extremely low and, in fact, had a higher ratio among other nationalities. Disorderly conduct (1,206 cases) scored the highest, followed by intoxication and disturbance (693), disturbing the peace (332), intoxication (164), fighting (155), gambling (112), and obscene language (46). There were 650 arrests for violating sanitary regulations. This pattern of arrests remained constant for the construction years. In 1911, for instance, the Department of Law reported that most criminal cases on the Zone arose among the English-speaking Negroes (the majority of the population) and were for "disorderly conduct". Most of those arrested were labourers.[126]

Serious offences led to the penitentiary, where those incarcerated discovered that there was only one category of prisoner and that "hard labour" meant just that, mainly road construction. Awakened at 5:30 each morning, prisoners had breakfast then each was shackled to a heavy ball and chain, the ball weighing between eighteen and thirty pounds. They were marched to the work site some distance away where they laboured for ten hours in hot sun or torrential rain under armed guards. Prisoners had to maintain absolute silence; they were allowed to talk only between the hours of 6:00 p.m. and 9:00 p.m. and during brief visits from relatives or friends on Sundays and holidays. Prisoners often complained of beatings and whippings by guards. Of 82 prisoners in the penitentiary in 1907, 39 were West Indians: 17 Barbadians, 14 Jamaicans,

Figure 5.25 Canal Zone prisoners wore ball-and-chain and were surrounded by armed guards (Weir, *Conquest of the Isthmus,* 106). Most of the roads in the Canal Zone were built by prisoners.

7 Antiguans, 1 St Lucian. The prisoners were young men – 63 in the fifteen-to-thirty age group. In 1912, the majority of the 150 convicts in the penitentiary at Culebra were West Indians.

Justice on the Canal Zone at that period was swift and predictable. Two municipal judges sitting during the week handled cases with great dispatch; jury trials were introduced only in 1908. To West Indians accustomed to the lengthy process of a British colonial court and all the opportunity afforded for display and oratory, the swift conduct of a Zone court was a shocking affront. As one man grumbled, "who go to Jail petty charge   10 days 10$ step aside said the judge   you get fine and confine".[127] Another explicitly stated the West Indian's principal complaint: "In Jamaica we used to have a barrister and a good long trial. In the Canal Zone you have no barrister. You just come before a judge and he shouts out: 'You're right, you're right, you're wrong, you're wrong' and that is all there is to it."[128] The process of justice was another area of culture shock for the West Indians transplanted to the US Canal Zone.

RACISM AND THE SILVER WORKERS

The fictional Albert in Maryse Condé's *Tree of Life* no doubt echoed the cry that many Panama Canal workers wanted to make but dared not: "Gatun is mud, mud and affliction, mud and sickness. . . . But let me tell you, it's our hands, our gorilla paws they call them, that're doing the work. Doing the digging. Doing the cutting. Doing the hauling. Putting it together piece by piece. Mama, I met Negroes there who talk English, who talk Portuguese, Spanish, who talk Dutch! But the common language, Mama, is poverty!"[129]

Silver worker Albert Banister put it more mildly: "Uncle Sam had to run through the door   left it open and get foreners to do his work."[130] Or as Cespedes Burke later addressed the US president, Senate and Congress in a lengthy poem (forty-eight verses) titled "The Forgotten Silver Workers":

> When the "Gold" men ate turkey or steak,
> The "Silver" men had but "Johnny Cake"
> They changed at times to their home-made bun,
> As they toiled beneath the broiling sun.
>
> When they asked their boss for a higher rate
> The foreman said: "Boy, you have to wait."
> So the job was done at the cheapest price,
> With "aliens" greatest sacrifice.[131]

But even as they were doing the bulk of the work, the United States continued to search – fruitlessly in the long run – for "better" workers to replace them.

The absence of African Americans did not go unnoticed. Silver worker Enrique Plummer claimed that "the coloured Americans did not stay very long . . . they were shipped back home because they were making trouble". Many were employed as teamsters, since horses and mules were the main means of transportation. "The majority of them was employed as team drivers, and when delivering goods would refuse to unload same, claiming they were no labourers, they were team drivers. They were also tutering the other employes to act accordingly."[132] Albert Banister explains: "We had Colored Americans working   good men skilful men but they can't pull with the White Americans   always a fight and trouble   if not West Indians could never be hear because Uncle Sam have plenty Colored Americans to do his work   also they don't like down here   to get away they make plenty trouble."

The census of 1912 lists only 127 African American employees. Their absence arose from personal choice reinforced by the negative experiences of those who did go to Panama and their inability to find a comfortable place in the biracial Zone. Simply put, white Americans did not want African Americans on the Zone because of the economic and social complications they presented.

In a controversial series of articles published in the United States in 1906, a reporter who visited the isthmus asked, "Why are not American negroes secured for this work?" and answered, "Because the wages offered at Panama are too low to tempt an American negro, he can get better pay for less work along the River Hudson than he can get along the Chagres." But, he added, the chief reason is that Panama Canal officials "do not want under them men who are able to evoke the help of a congressman or of an American newspaper".[133]

The official American narrative was that the British West Indian of the era, reared in centuries of colonialism, was far more tractable than the African American, especially those of the north. Harry Franck was moved to note that "there was nothing even faintly resembling insolence, for these were all British West Indians without a corrupting 'States Nigger' among them".[134] Another visitor to the isthmus claimed that "the British Negro is deeply religious and most respectful. He has no dreams of equality. He is polite and deferential and is generally liked. He reminds one of the good old-time 'darky' of the South."[135]

African Americans seeking work on the Zone presented certain dilemmas for the ICC: as American citizens should they be treated as gold or as silver workers? Eventually the ICC compromised by making them silver with special status – but denied them access to the white facilities. The mixing of the races was out of the question. But potential costs were also a significant deterrent. Apart from wages and other considerations, African Americans would have had to be included in the provisions of any applicable US labour laws such as regulated the eight-hour day, overtime pay, annual paid vacations and holidays and gratuities, none of which applied to non-Americans. As an editorial in the New York *Tribune* late in 1906 explained,

> The engineers and clerks are Americans, but the thousands of common laborers are aliens and will always remain aliens. That is so for the simple reason that Americans will not and can not do the work. It would be entirely out of the question to recruit an army of ten thousand American working men to go down there and dig dirt at Culebra and make roads through the swamps at Cristobal. If such an army could be secured, it would prove a failure, for our men could not efficiently adapt themselves to the strange climate and other conditions.

The paper concluded, "We are engaged in a great work in the tropics, which must be done by native tropical labor and under tropical conditions."[136] This opinion reflected what Michael Conniff characterizes as the concept of "third country labour".[137] It was also a clearly accepted notion from the start that men from the tropics would be willing to accept "tropical" – that is, inferior – wages and working conditions. The ICC believed it would be a mistake to handicap construction with any American laws, save those regarding police controls and sanitation, and argued against any laws passed for the benefit of American labour at home. Applying the eight-hour law to the Zone, it argued, would increase labour costs by at least 25 per cent. The Panama Canal became and would remain a symbol of imperialistic double standards: "American" and "tropical".

While West Indian contract labourers were pouring into Panama and it was clear that workers from the nearby countries (including those who came voluntarily) were almost limitless, the US government continued to conduct a worldwide search for "satisfactory" labour, above all to prevent the West Indians believing that they had a labour monopoly. In the long run, the search was futile. West Indians were never less than 60 per cent of the workforce over the ten years of construction. Of the sixty-two thousand residents on the Zone in the 1912 census, more than thirty thousand were West Indians. They provided the back-breaking manual labour on the canal as well as skills that were vital to every other aspect of operations in the Canal Zone and they were significant contributors to the development of the Republic of Panama. Black – and some white – West Indian men and women were to be found in almost every sphere of endeavour. However, because of the tag of "silver worker" that was imposed from the start, and the racial and social denigration implied, their contribution during construction and after was virtually ignored. Indeed, any form of recognition of this labour has only come about through the efforts of West Indian descendants in Panama.[138]

Stereotypes versus Performance

The early ICC complaints about the quality of West Indian labour were forever to be used as a convenient stereotype long after their performance had, over the years, gained equality with the rest of the workforce and they remained the backbone of that force. Perhaps the most realistic assessment of the evolution of canal workers came from Major R.E. Wood, the quartermaster who was in charge of recruitment and the well-being of personnel. He noted that the majority of unskilled labour recruited from the West Indies consisted of agricultural workers who had never been exposed to industrial activity. Many had never seen a railroad; explosives were almost unknown. Outside of the building trades, few had experience as artisans. At the start, their labour was unreliable. Wood estimates that they averaged fifteen working days a month. But, he added,

> The evolution of the unskilled laborer has been as marked as the evolution of the work. The West Indian, while slow, has learned many of the trades, and many of them have developed into first class construction men. The bulk of the building work on the Canal has been done by West Indian Carpenters, Masons and Painters, under the direction of American foremen. The drilling in the cut and the firing of locomotives were all done by West Indians. Particularly in the trades mentioned, the men developed steadiness, and toward the end of the construction period, the West Indian remained on the job as steadily as the Spaniard or even the American.[139]

As we shall later see, this evolution of the labourers left untouched the highly discriminatory wage and working conditions. Racist stereotyping persisted well into the future of the Zone, tainting the attitudes and treatment of workers up to the second and third generation as West Indians continued to be denied opportunities to rise above the most menial and lowest-paying jobs. Not only was the ceiling of opportunity kept deliberately low but official policy denied the existence of personal ability, incentive and initiative.

As David McCullough noted of the silver work force,

> They were marched out by the hundreds to dig ditches, to cut brush, to carry lumber, to unload boxes of dynamite. "I load cement, I unload cement," remembered one of them. "I carry lumber until my shoulder peel." Previous training or trade skills were generally ignored, former schoolteachers, and skilled craftsmen were made messengers and waiters, experienced carpenters were put to work cutting points on the ends of stakes for the engineers. Rarely did a black man ever rise to a supervisory level and never over white men.[140]

West Indians who migrated to other countries after construction ended could not help comparing the attitudes they encountered elsewhere to those on the Canal Zone. From Cuba in 1920, a former canal employee wrote:

In Havana we enjoy all the privileges as mechanics, the name "straw-boss" is foreign to this town, and a foreman carpenter is not treated mean. We have no gold and silver employees; everybody is called daily at one and the same window, and every Saturday afternoon we receive our pay envelopes without police supervision. The blue prints are not sacred volume, and those of us who can read them have not long to wait before we are sent out with them.[141]

The Panama–West Indian newspaper the *Workman* commented in similar vein on the contribution that West Indian builders and contractors had made throughout Latin America, while they were denied the right to exercise their talent and ability on the Canal Zone. "In Cuba and Costa Rica our contractors are using charts and blue-prints, things which they were kept away from under penalty of being fired on the Canal Zone. They are manipulating the forge and lathe in machine shops, plumbing on the streets and in houses, and constructing massive buildings. . . . Yet these very men were deprived of decent employment and ratings on the 'eternal' Canal Zone because they are considered 'unskilled' and 'inefficient'."[142]

Imperialist thinking of the day and contemporary scholarship on race shed a clear light as to the reasons why West Indian workers were seen as an undifferentiated, inferior mass by white Zonians even though West Indians obviously differed in terms of ability, education and skills.[143] By the 1890s, Social Darwinism had propagated the belief in the racial hierarchy of the world's culture and the presumed superiority of Western civilization. Michael Conniff notes that within the United States, "The South enacted Jim Crow laws and the North adopted segregationist practices at the very moment the U.S. engineers were surveying Central America for the best Canal route."[144]

The *Bricklayer and Mason* expressed a commonly held view among whites, one that harkened back to the earlier diatribes of Thomas Carlyle or Anthony Froude:

> The negro of the tropics will not work longer than is necessary to provide himself with sufficient money with which to buy a few gew-gaws and enough rum to supply for a series of carouses. He knows the country and its resources too well to feel any necessity to labor. With a hut of palm leaves, a banana tree, a coffee bush or two, and a few razor backs, he regards labor as something he only needs to stoop to occasionally.[145]

The portrayal in the New York *World* at about the same time was even more animalistic: "even during resting hours they lie around in the sun as any great dog, only they show no evidence of life, allowing the flies and mosquitoes to swarm all over them. They are as a result bitten by the deadly stegomyia mosquitoes and are, of course, attacked by yellow fever. Many die without trying to get medical attention as they are too lazy to go the short distance from their huts to the camp hospitals."[146] (The majority of yellow-fever deaths occurred, in fact, among whites.)

Francis Burton Harrison, a former Democratic congressman,[147] visited the Zone in 1906 and was master of the situation in a week. (To him, as to many other whites, all West Indians were "Jamaicans".)

> I have a very low opinion of the Jamaica negro as labourers. They are coming by the thousand to the Zone . . . do about one-third or one-fourth of an honest laborer's work and are exceedingly difficult to manage. . . . every time one of them complains of a headache he is hurried off in a hospital car to a model hospital and nursed by a white woman nurse. They are so spoiled that it is offensive for a white man to walk on the streets with them. I suppose they are the most vexatious of the problems with which our engineers have to deal.[148]

These ideas fitted neatly in with notions of racial inequality then prevalent in the United States. The white American public also had to be given a reason why, in the first few years of American occupation, the Canal Zone was in such a mess: the common labourer – clothed in the correct skin colour – was offered up as the scapegoat. West Indian labourers were part of far larger problems that first had to be solved so that the workers' efficiency – and that of the entire operations of the Zone – could be improved. These problems included health and sanitation, the provision of adequate food and housing, and the recruitment of better and more efficient American bosses.

Even as the workforce overcame many of the early difficulties, few in authority took the trouble to remark on this fact. By 1908 the Division of Building Construction found that West Indian construction workers (classified as "mechanics") were doing 75 per cent as much work as the average gold mechanic and at one-third to one-half of the latter's salary. Several other examples from the division showed that silver workers equalled the performance of gold.[149]

West Indians also demonstrated that their productivity increased if it were tied to remuneration. When contractors encouraged task work, they were amazed at the workers' performance – as the French had been in their time. For instance, when the Panama Railroad introduced task work in relocating the line, the speed with which the labourers worked invited official comment. The men were paid ten cents for each car-load of material moved (half a cubic yard). Many of the men formed cooperatives, some doing the digging and loading, others the dumping and spreading, working rapidly until their task was done. The company required that at least fifteen cars be loaded for each man. They found that the task was usually finished in six hours and the men on task work often worked two shifts. Working on an hourly basis, one man could hardly move fifteen cars of material in nine hours.[150]

Again, on another piece of task work, moving material in the lake region, the contractors found that at least 100 per cent more energy was displayed than when the men were paid by the hour. The labourers began at 6:00 a.m. and quit as soon as they earned $1.25 to $1.50, that is, about 1:00 p.m. Unfortunately, the incentive of task work was used only rarely during construction years, nor were the incentives of wage increases, promotions, paid vacation leave or paid sick leave ever offered.[151]

The Search for Others

After some years of American ownership of the Zone (and constant disparagement of the West Indians who were actually doing the work), the United States government was still trying to break the West Indian "monopoly" on labour. ICC chairman Theodore Shonts said, "We intend to get the benefit of competition in labor, as well as everything else . . . the negroes we have found to be practically valueless."[152]

They looked towards Asia – the other traditional source of cheap labour, and in 1906 the ICC attempted to recruit Chinese workers. The initiative failed as the US government refused to relax the 1882 Chinese Exclusion Act.[153] The controversial proposal to hire Chinese alarmed powerful interest groups such as the Knights of Labor. Other American interest groups hailed the initiative, one newspaper carrying the headline, "Coolies to be treated just like white men on Panama Canal Zone".[154]

Chinese naturalized in the West Indies were also refused entry to the Zone, although a Chinese presence in Panama dated from the time of the railroad construction in the 1850s, augmented by arrivals during the French era, and Chinese were active in business in the Republic and in market gardening, grocery stores and laundries.[155] Indian labourers were found acceptable and "Hindu gangs" were at work on the canal, including some Indians who had originally come to the West Indian islands and British Guiana as indentured workers and who went on to Panama after serving out their contracts. The Japanese government sent an official team to investigate working and other conditions on the Zone and announced that the isthmus was not a suitable place for Japanese citizens. The ICC also attempted to recruit Cubans, but their government refused to allow it.

In Cuba at this time were immigrants from Galicia in Northern Spain and the ICC recruited a group of "Gallegos" from that island as well as directly from Spain in what, they hoped, would be a decisive break of the West Indian labour monopoly. The ICC report of 1906 showed satisfaction with the Spaniards, noting they kept good health and their efficiency was double that of the West Indians. At least, such was the justification for giving them double

Figure 5.26 Indian workers line up for pay, 1913 (Panama Canal). Referred to throughout as "Hindoos", many were Sikhs who had first come to work on the Panama Railroad. Some later turned to shopkeeping.

the wages (twenty cents an hour) although both groups did the same kind of work. However, under the European labour contract, the worker was expected to refund the cost of passage out of his wages. He had no guarantee of repatriation but, like others, was offered free passage home by the ICC when canal construction ended. Small numbers of labourers were also recruited from Italy, Greece, France and Armenia. Altogether, ninety-seven countries came to be represented in the labour force.[156]

Socially and administratively, European workers came to occupy a category halfway between white Americans and the West Indian workforce, although they were lumped together as "silver workers" because of the metal in which they were paid. The nationals of all the various countries were housed and fed separately but a precise racial hierarchy maintained with white Americans at the top, followed by Europeans and others, and then West Indians, all racial distinctions reflected in the wage structure. The Spaniards chafed under their ambiguous position and took out their displeasure on those below them, the West Indians, leading to racial tensions and outright disturbances.

From the first experiment with Spanish labourers, the chief engineer of the ICC was convinced that "any white man, so-called, under the same conditions will stand the climate on the isthmus very much better than the blacks, who are supposed to be immune from practically everything, but who, as a matter of fact, are subject to almost everything".[157]

It is a fact that Europeans kept much better health than black West Indians – or white Americans. Few Spaniards wished, however, to cross the Atlantic to work under the appalling conditions they had heard about. The ICC recruited only 8,000 Spaniards for the entire construction period. In all, 11,873 Euro-

Figure 5.27 Spanish railroad labourers at lunch break (Panama Canal).

pean labourers came; by the end of 1907, only 5,121 remained. The 1912 census showed 3,500 Spaniards, 1,300 Greeks and 800 Italians. At one time the ICC considered the colonization of these European labourers to provide a steady and permanent supply of what they considered the best available labour for Canal work.[158] Nothing came of this proposal, probably because the efficiency of the European labourers steadily diminished while that of the West Indian had so improved that "at the end of the construction period there was no great difference between the two classes of labour". Inevitably, the change was seen as a result of the proximity of the Spaniards to an "inferior race" and their consequent degradation.[159]

The *Canal Record* (the ICC's official weekly publication) cited complaints in 1909 that the Spanish labourers were deliberately reducing their output so that "all of our superintendents and foremen are unanimously of the opinion that the efficiency of our 20-cent contract labour is much less now than it was a year ago". Several reported incidents supposedly displayed behaviour said to "border on insolence". This and other complaints were listed in a letter from the ICC chairman General Goethals to the chargé d'affaires of the Spanish legation in Panama. Similar letters were sent to the consuls of Italy and Greece.[160]

The Spaniards were generally truculent, far more willing to defend their rights than other nationalities and were disappointed at how the reality of their existence on the Zone so little matched recruiters' promises. They worked mainly in railroad construction and repairs under American foremen who spoke no Spanish. While their living and other conditions were marginally better than those of the West Indians, they were conscious of the gross inequalities existing between them and the white American employees, such as their exclusion from restaurants and clubs and other facilities reserved for US citizens. Many Spaniards quitted the Zone for more accommodating countries in Spanish-speaking America.

SILVER AND GOLD WAGES

In the final analysis, the Panama Canal was built with West Indian labour including the many thousands who came on their own as well as those brought on contract. (See table 5.1.) The most telling commentary on the racist attitude applied to such labour stands out in the scale of wages paid. During construction, the average monthly wage of the West Indian worker was $30, that of the gold employee, $150. Although there was a wide range of educational and skill levels among West Indians, the ICC placed them into one of three categories: labourers, artisans, and the monthly paid. The latter included teachers, policemen, storekeepers and clerical workers, as well as skilled workers such as cooks, waiters, firemen, blacksmiths and so on, and some unskilled workers whose hours of work were irregular.

Not only was the West Indian discriminated against vis-à-vis the white American, he was also relegated to the lowest end of the pay scale for "silver" workers. In many cases, all categories of workers did exactly the same work but the West Indian labourer's wage was set at $0.10 gold per hour (paid at the rate of $0.20 Panamanian silver). Other "silver" labourers were paid more. The $0.13-an-hour rate was reserved for "Panamanians, Colombians and Hindoos", the $0.16- and $0.20-rate for "Europeans, other white and black American labourers only".[161] As one construction worker exclaimed, "Ten

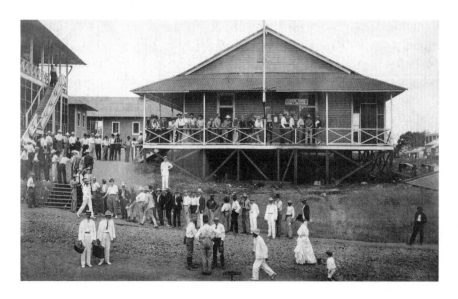

Figure 5.28 Gorgona post office at a busy time, perhaps after payday. (Courtesy of William P. McLaughlin, www.czimages.com)

Table 5.1 Contract Labour Brought to the Isthmus throughout Construction

Country	1904	1905	1906	1907	1908	1909	1910	1911	1912	1913	Total
Spain	–	–	1,174	5,293	1,831	–	–	–	–	–	8,298
*Cuba	–	–	500	–	–	–	–	–	–	–	500
Italy	–	–	909	1,032	–	–	–	–	–	–	1,941
Greece	–	–	–	1,101	–	–	–	–	–	–	1,101
France	–	–	19	–	–	–	–	–	–	–	19
Armenia	–	–	14	–	–	–	–	–	–	–	14
Total European	–	–	2,616	7,426	1,831	–	–	–	–	–	11,873
Fortune Is. (Bahamas)	–	–	361	–	–	–	–	–	–	–	361
Barbados	404	3,019	6,510	3,242	2,592	3,605	–	–	–	528	19,900
Guadeloupe	–	–	–	2,039	–	–	–	–	14	–	2,053
Martinique	–	2,733	585	2,224	–	–	–	–	–	–	5,542
Jamaica	–	47	–	–	–	–	–	–	–	–	47
Trinidad	–	–	1,079	–	–	–	205	–	143	–	1,427
Curaçao	–	–	23	–	–	–	–	–	–	–	23
St Kitts	–	–	933	–	–	–	–	–	9	–	942
St Lucia	–	–	–	–	–	–	–	–	296	–	296
St Vincent	–	–	–	–	–	–	–	–	55	–	55
Grenada	–	–	–	–	–	–	–	–	93	–	93
British Guiana	–	–	–	–	–	–	–	–	332	–	332
Total West Indian	404	5,799	9,491	7,505	2,592	3,605	205	–	942	528	31,071
Costa Rica	–	244	–	–	–	–	–	–	–	–	244
Colombia	–	1,077	416	–	–	–	–	–	–	–	1,493
Panama	–	334	10	13	–	–	–	–	–	–	357
Not Classified	–	–	69	–	–	–	–	–	–	–	69
Total Central America	–	1,655	495	13	–	–	–	–	–	–	2,163
Total All Contract Workers	404	7,454	12,602	14,944	4,423	3,605	205	–	942	528	45,107

*Spanish workers recruited in Cuba
Source: Wood, "Working Force", 198.

Table 5.2 Comparisons of Some Gold and Silver Rates of Pay, Skilled and Unskilled 1909–1910

	White American ("Gold")	West Indian ("Silver")
Foreman	$75.00–$222.00	$37.50
Clerk	$50.00–$200.00	$30.00–$75.00
Druggist	$60.00–$150.00	$40.00–$75.00
Baker	$100.00	$37.00–$75.00
Boatswain	$75.00	$45.00
Compositor	$60.00	$0.20–$0.25 per hour
Hostler	$100.00–140.00	$25.00–$40.00
Laundress	$50.00–$60.00	$15.00–$35.00
Lineman	$125.00–$150.00	$42.50
Painter	$0.32–$0.65	$0.16–$0.25
Wheelwright	$100.00–$125.00	$50.00

Source: Silver rates, *Canal Record,* 28 July 1909; gold rates, *Canal Record,* 5 January 1910.

cents per hour was just like a flie into one of those big American mule nostrill!"[162] Inequity was, however, an institutional structure. Actual payment to West Indians ranged from $0.05 gold per hour for the category "boy", as all messengers of whatever age earning below a certain level were officially rated, to a maximum of $75 per month for the highest category.[163] (See table 5.2.)

The only protest against the ten-cent-an-hour wage was individual withdrawal of labour, an option which West Indians increasingly exercised. For instance, in early 1909 the ICC had to resume recruitment of contract labour in Barbados after a two-year break, as it could not find enough workers, despite a reputed labour surplus on the Zone. The ICC estimated that there were five thousand idle West Indians on the isthmus who had been employed to the commission at one time but were now refusing work at the pay offered.[164]

The position of West Indians did not improve in the post-construction years; in fact, the wage ratio widened. Indeed, West Indians were better off in the early construction years because supervisors had some leeway in hiring at some point within fixed scales and to some extent reward experience and superior ability. This practice was soon dispensed with, however, and the workers became locked into an immutable system of inequality. As the canal neared completion, demand for labourers lessened while need for more skilled workers increased. More than nine thousand skilled West Indians were employed in 1914, classified as "artisans" while Americans doing the same work were classified as "skilled mechanics", reflected in their respective pay. Most artisans were paid between sixteen and twenty cents per hour. In categories of higher paid workers, ceilings were imposed on West Indians that were lower than for all other workers.

In 1907 there were eight hundred white West Indians employed by the canal and the Panama Railroad;[165] they were paid on the gold roll and their children enrolled in white schools. After 1908 they lost this status when employment of skilled persons on the gold roll was restricted to US citizens and citizens of Panama.[166] For some time, labour unions had been campaigning to remove West Indians and Europeans from managerial and skilled posts and they became increasingly successful. For example, after 1909 West Indians could no longer be hired as Panama Railroad engineers. Also coming into force were union regulations restricting the use of certain tools, equipment and machinery, accompanied by demotion of skilled and experienced workers and a purge of West Indians from certain posts.[167] As the position of silver workers continued to erode, designations and pay for many categories of skilled and unskilled West Indians were abolished, and the term "general helper" substituted. Such workers were now all paid at the standard rate of ten cents an hour.[168] The highest rates of pay in the various categories of silver workers were eliminated and as employees earning these rates left the service, no employment or promotions were made at these rates.[169]

Further discrimination arose in the denial or dispensation of benefits: in this case US citizens versus the rest. For instance, hourly paid employees who were US citizens were paid time and a half after eight hours work and on holidays, while citizens of other countries had to work ten hours before receiving overtime and worked at the regular rates on Sundays and holidays. Privileges such as sick leave and vacations were reserved for US citizens. Special medals that were awarded for long service on the canal construction were reserved for white US citizens only.

The reality of Zone life was such that remuneration was tied not to the quantity or quality of a man's work but to the race and geographical origin of the man. In coming to the Zone, the West Indian worker automatically accepted the subordinate status assigned him. But how could he complain when work at home was so difficult to come by and unskilled workers could earn as little as ten pence a day. Living as they did as the "wretched of the earth", many were willing to accept work in this foreign land at any price.

The Pay Car

Payday, of course, was the most important for the men and was monthly after 1907. It took place in a heavily armed setting. A special rail car loaded with cash arrived at each work site and pulled on to a spur track used only for that purpose. No paper money was ever used on the isthmus for the entire construction period – "for sanitary and other reasons" – the men were handed paper rolls of silver or gold coins.[170] At the height of construction when there

Figure 5.29 Payday at Miraflores showing the pay car on a special track. (Courtesy of William P. McLaughlin, www.czimages.com.)

were nearly fifty thousand men on the roll, it took two days to pay off the entire labour force. Payment of the silver employees took $1.6 million of Panama currency monthly and required the services of five men to count and roll the money. Every $1,000 of currency weighed fifty-five pounds, making a requirement of forty-four tons per month.

The designations "silver" and "gold" were first placed by the paymaster on his car to indicate the two sections partitioned off with heavy steel mesh and from there came the euphemisms used throughout for "black" and "white".[171] Outside the car, mounted policemen with carbines guarded the tracks and kept order among the lines of workmen; inside more armed guards protected the paymaster who sat with a revolver on the counter beside each hand. Two guards with guns stood on the steps leading into the car.

Figure 5.30 Silver workers after payday. (Courtesy of William P. McLaughlin, www.czimages.com.)

"Take off your hat and keep moving," the guard ordered as each man started up the steps to get his pay. As the worker moved to the window and showed his identity tag, the paymaster checked to see how much pay was due and ordered, "Hold out your hat." Then he would shove the appropriate roll across the counter and into the hat. A guard at the worker's elbow saw him down the steps. Two guards then fell behind, telling him, "Keep moving. No two men in groups." The men kept moving until well out of sight. Only then would they be able to check to see if they had been given the right pay.[172] For many, the next stop would be the post office to send a postal order to the loved ones waiting at home.

Figure 6.1 Work never stopped for rain or flood (Panama Railroad).

6. THE WORK THEY DID THERE, 1904–1914

The construction of the Panama Canal called together the largest number of men
that were ever employed at one time on any modern or medieval peaceful enterprise.
—W.L. Sibert and J.F. Stevens, *The Construction of the Panama Canal*

WEST INDIAN MEN WERE WILLING to tackle anything, from being lowered
each day into a caisson pit (a concrete cylinder sunk deep into the ground)
seventy-five feet below the murky waters of the harbour, to being suspended
seventy feet in the air, riveting lock gates. Casually, they carried fifty-pound
boxes of dynamite on their heads or worked in small groups to shift three tons
of coal each night to service the big Bucyrus steam shovels. They set fire to
dynamite charges and ran for their lives before the chain of explosions started.
They hunted ferocious wild boar for food when catering to work crews out in
the jungle. Dangers and difficulties surrounded even white-collar workers,
such as the teacher who took a crowded labour train each school day from
Panama City to Matachin and then a canoe three miles on the Chagres River
to his school at Las Cruces.[1]

Of course many found settled or even sedentary work; some held the same
jobs for most of their working lives.[2] Edward Howell was working as a bellhop
at the Marine Hotel in Barbados in 1906 when he decided to go to Panama,
only to meet mudholes and mosquitoes "so big when they stuck you, you saw
blood". After several jobs, the treasurer's office at Cristóbal hired him as a clerk
and money-counter, and he counted money for the next thirty-six years until
his retirement.[3]

Robert J. Atherley was station messenger at the administration building at
Balboa Heights when he was interviewed in 1953.[4] Apprenticed to a tailor in
Barbados, he heard young men were needed to dig the Panama Canal: he
arrived 26 June 1905 to find "rain, mud, steam shovels, drills, dump trains

going up and down . . . digging the canal right where we lived". He mixed concrete for a short time, then started a long period of service as mail messenger until 1930 when he became a distribution messenger in the administration building. At Culebra in 1906, he carried the mailbags on his head and shoulders from the post office to the railroad, spending many a night at the station waiting for delayed trains. Later, he was given a mule and sometimes he and the bags rode the governor's horse. In about 1908 a mail wagon was acquired and in 1915 a Ford automobile. In 1917, the chief clerk taught him to ride a motorcycle and Atherley became the canal's first motorcycle messenger.

Such tasks required individual initiative and effort, but most men were assigned to a work gang the minute they arrived. Dressed in their best clothes for travelling, they were sometimes unprepared. Twenty-one-year-old Albert Peters of Nassau came off the boat in 1906 and found "My nice clothes and shoes that I brought was not for down here in the heavy rain and mud. I was ashamed to go back as I had spent all the money I had so I made up my mind to face it. I sold all my clothes, my black derby, took the money and bought high top boots and blue jungree suits then I started on the job."[5] Barbadian John Garner came on the SS *Solent* in May 1908, and began work as labourer "first class" stationed at Tabernilla: "I set to work with a three piece suit, a pick, shovel, and a claw bar, servicing R.R. tracks for train taking dirt from the Canal to dump area. . . . I worked along with men who had done this work before so I did not take very long to break in."[6]

Soon all were dressed in the standard commissary-bought work clothes: khaki pants or dungarees, blue denim shirts, every man wearing a hat (the Indian gangs wore turbans). Set to work in gangs, the men learned fast: sometimes two or three gangs worked together: "shovel gangs, track gangs, surfacing gangs, dynamite gangs . . . gangs with shovel and pick and crowbar, gangs down on the floor of the canal, gangs far up the steep walls of cut rock, gangs stretching away in either direction till those far off look like upright bands of the leaf-cutting ants of the Panamanian jungles".[7] Gangs might consist of a few men under a straw boss, others totalled in the hundreds. Until a machine was invented to do the job, a gang of up to six hundred men shifted tracks daily for the trains ferrying dirt and rocks from Culebra Cut to the dumps.

Gangs were racially (and ethnically) segregated, even when doing the same work. West Indian "silver men" worked together, with English-speakers and French-speakers from Martinique, Guadeloupe and Haiti or Spanish-speakers from the other islands. For historical reasons, Jamaicans were kept far from coastal Colombians, as were Spaniards from Italians and Greeks.

The mixed nature of West Indian gangs is revealed in accident statistics. In 1913, over twenty-one thousand pounds of dynamite blew up prematurely, killing three and injuring nineteen, with two unaccounted for out of a gang of thirty powder men. The three dead were from Antigua, Jamaica and Martinique. Seven of the injured were from Barbados, three from Antigua, one from Jamaica, four from St Vincent, two from Montserrat, one from St Kitts and one from Cuba.[8] Most accident reports of silver workers showed similar variety of composition.

Men joined gangs with friends or relatives or people from home. Camaraderie continued after work hours as gang members frequently shared housing. Taking a census in the Zone, Harry Franck noted how Americans sharing accommodation almost always knew nothing of their housemates beyond first names while silver workers could always provide information about the other residents.

Individual prejudices were most visible in the social life of West Indians off the Zone, where national and class divisions prevailed. A popular song, "Poor Me One", lampooned Barbadians in verses easily changed to fit other nationalities when the Barbadians sang:

> Nine Barbadians live in a room
> Not enough money to buy a broom
> O poor me one, everybody down on poor me one.[9]

Most personal accounts, however, show West Indians on the job working together and helping one another.

PRIDE IN WORK

While thousands laboured on the actual construction site, another army of workers provided the services necessary to keep the Canal Zone running as smoothly as an American city. In sanitation, stores, police stations, hospitals, schools, hotels and kitchens, thousands laboured, as well as in machine shops, foundries, locomotive pits, boiler shops and carpentry shops so that the Panama Canal became a centre for the best technical training, or for honing skills many had brought from home. Their bosses sometimes recognized both aptitude and skill.

Barbadian John Oswald Butcher recalled that "Mr Walter D. Smith, assistant quartermaster, was a real pusher. He always promised permanent work to the better workmen. Hearing this, I tried my best to work harder and more than anyone else", proudly adding, "of course, as far as plumbers were concerned there were none better than the Nolan-Butcher team".[10] Rufus Forde's boss took note of his skills when working on the locks, and told him, "you have a quick head, you dint spend too years in the foundary [in Trinidad] for nothing, I better make you my straw boss".[11] Barbadian John Garner was promoted to foreman after a year in a new gang where he had to be "broken in to this type of work as I knew nothing about sounding with leadline", having previously worked in preparing the terrain for steam shovels.[12] Barbadian Fitz Thomas worked as a carpenter, helping to build Culebra jail, and he recalled, "My general foreman was Mr Greir, my foreman was a black man, John —— of Jamaica, and the work we performed was so good Mr Grier transferred us to the white quarters, and removed the white gangs as they failed in finish work."[13]

"The Mules Are Trained"

Some jobs were especially memorable. West Indians who worked as teamsters (or who cared for animals in the corrals) recalled sometimes amusing experiences. Heavy draft animals were imported to do all the necessary hauling for the domestic or industrial undertakings of the Zone, and the teamsters included black and white Americans. Albert Banister claimed that "the mules are trained". They knew when the whistle blew to knock off for lunch: "when 11 oclock they stick up their ears straight   if the driver was foolish to call him come on Jacky for a next load he will kick up smash up the cart and put you in jail   they fine you 25$ step aside you are charge for being cruel to dum annimals   better you was charge fighting with someone   never you touch the mule   he will lock you up   he will kick until Police come   many men run away for a mule".[14] Albert Peters was offered work at a corral but resisted at first: "I told him I don't like working around mules. They are bad and can't be trusted." However, he took the job and got so used to the mules he became a driver but left after an accident with his mule and wagon. A friend was not so lucky: "A few weeks later a frien of mine driving 2 mules shied on a bridge at 9th and D Street Colon, everything went over in the muddy water both mules were drowned before they could rescue them."[15]

Figure 6.2 The corral at Cristóbal (Panama Canal). Mule-drawn buckboards and carriages provided transportation across the Canal Zone and employment for many West Indians.

The Labour Train: "Mingling with Cattle on a Drive"

The men themselves worked like mules, a strict ten-hour day, starting work at 7:00 a.m., knocking off for lunch at 11:30 a.m. returning at 1:30 p.m. to work until 5:00 p.m., when the whistle blew for the end of the day shift. Work went on six days a week. Workers rode to and from work on

Figures 6.3–6.4
Labourers rode to
work on flatcars at the
start of construction;
later on the box cars
(shown in figure 6.4)
that replaced them
(Panama Canal).

labour trains on a strict schedule. As with all Zone facilities, the work trains were segregated into cars for white, European and black, with the coaches linked in that order and comfort provided accordingly. Each coach bore its status in large letters but signs were hardly needed: blacks rode open cattle cars (sides boarded up halfway; crude seats placed lengthwise and down the middle). Always dangerously overcrowded, on a day in 1912, a single labour train of fifteen cars carried 2,000 employees. Two-and-a-half cars carried gold employees, 60 to 70 men to a coach, four-and-a half cars Europeans, and eight other cars conveyed black workmen packed up to 160 in a coach.[16]

Alfred Dottin likened going to work on a labour train to "mingling with cattle on a drive". Strict safety rules regulated conduct on these trains: many latecomers who hopped on a train had lost limb or life. "If you were ever seen getting of[f] the trains before they stopped you would be arrested and sentenced to 10 days in jail – it was horrible. There were times when we would get soaked in the rain doing a rush job and then right after have to hustle to catch the train home or you would have [to] sleep on the job site."[17] Because many lived some distance from work, catching the train often meant rising at five o'clock in the morning. And since the canal's construction schedule ran day and night, many had to work double shifts.

The Timekeeper

Once on the job, there were few opportunities for idling. Jeremiah Waisome (who arrived in Panama as an infant in 1895) noted that during the French days timekeeping was so poor, "a man could work on 5 different jobs a day and collect for the 5 on payday".[18] A Jamaican carpenter who had also worked for the French found that with the Americans,

> there are no loafing jobs now such as there used to be. It is like running a race all the time. You don't mind for a day but you can't keep it up. . . . A man must be in his place ready for work the first thing in the morning, tool in hand, and when the whistle blows it is "All right boys" and off it goes. The timekeeper comes round every two hours, making a dot in his little book every time; four dots make a day's work.[19]

Each worker had an assigned number worn on a small brass tag, called a "check", like an army dog-tag. Workers moving around on their own had to change their names and be assigned new numbers so as not to be found out. Timekeepers kept track by suddenly appearing, noting the numbers and recording time and place seen. Thus each man could be located throughout the working day and paid accordingly. To those in charge, a man's only identity was a check number. The metal check had another useful purpose. In serious accidents, particularly explosions, men were so dismembered that the metal tag alone served as identification.

Figure 6.5 The timekeeper at left checks sanitary workers at Culebra (Abbot, *Panama*, 258).

Chanteys and Work Songs

West Indian gangs eased the burden of labour by singing chanteys as they worked, as they had done in their homelands. Sometimes they sang popular current hits, such as "I Love You, Yes I Do", or work chanteys from the United States, such as "Steam Boat Bill from the Mississippi" or "Somebody Dying Every Day" ("Ten Pound

Hammer"). It is possible that these songs were spread by African Americans who worked on the canal from time to time. Others might have been learned from the newly invented phonograph and Edison's records then on sale in both Kingston and Panama ("Won't You Come Home, Bill Bailey" was the hit of 1904).

Most often West Indians sang their own work songs, many of them well known in the islands, others specially composed on the job. Of traditional West Indian songs, "Iron Bar", "Turn the Water Wheel O Matilda", "Hol 'im Joe" and "Monkey Draw Bow So Sweet" were among the most popular. The songs rang out to the rhythm of the work being performed and in call-and-response pattern – a leader singing the first line, the whole group rolling out the chorus with action matching the beat.

George Martin described the action of his railroad track-shifting gang and how songs lightened labour:

> we took the spiking of the rail, to the pulling, like a merry-go-round, this were a sight to watch us work along this line; as I said before, "the work was hard, but we did it cheerful: here is the play, when the rail had been spiked to the pulling, now it has got to be put in place. Every man with an iron-bar about five feet long, one would sing, and while he sings, you watch track line move, "the trang goes, you ball." The white bosses stands off and laugh, the Songster had a song, goes this way, he would sing part one, or first part, and we comes in with the second part, it goes:
>
> > 1st Nattie oh, Nattie O – first
> > 2nd Gone to Colón
> > 1st Nattie O Nattie O
> > 2nd Gone to Colón
> > 1st Nattie buy sweet powder
> > 2nd Powder her ———— – *you know*
> > 1st Nattie buy sweet powder
> > Powder her ———— same
>
> And so he would sing this song over and over, gentlemen watch track line move, the work appeared sweet, the white foremen enjoyed the singing they laugh and did laughed.[20]

Some songs depicted people and local events and, as they were on the islands, might be salacious or filled with double entendre:

> Sally's gone to the mountain
> Hi, Low Jane
> She's gone for the yellow plantain
> Hi, Low Jane

The day-by-day chants on current events served as newspapers and kept the men up with what was happening, an American worker recalled. "If Colonel Goethals had to go to the Pacific end of the line . . . in his yellow motor car, the gangs along the line as he passed chanted to a monotonous tune: 'Colonel's gone – gone to Balboa / Gone – in his – yellow – motorcar'."[21]

Singing and banter bound the men from the islands together in camaraderie and lightened the burden of labour. Railroad workers, for example, made songs to celebrate and characterize their special tasks. Bought out by the US government, the Panama Railroad was relocated and reconstructed along most of its line, proving to be the backbone of canal construction, the means by which material and men travelled. Before the advent of automobiles, virtually everything on the Canal Zone moved by rail; on the 47-mile-long isthmus, the rail network covered 450 miles. In 1913–14, the Panama Railroad employed over forty-five hundred men of whom a large number were West Indians. "John Crow Today" was among their favourite songs, John Crow being the Caribbean scavenger bird[22] and "cochee" the whistle blown to signal work on the sugar plantations:

Come on boys hear the cochee blowing
(*chorus*): John Crow today
Look down the track see the straw boss coming
John Crow today
Pick up your pick and shovels in your hand
We are going to work for Uncle Sam
Through stormy weather rain or shine
We've got to work for that meagre dime
We work in water mud and sand
To build that railroad for Uncle Sam.[23]

Figures 6.6–6.7 It took a gang of 150 to shift track by hand until a machine (figure 6.7) was invented to do the job with minimal manpower (Panama Canal).

"THE BIGGEST, THE GRANDEST, THE GREATEST"

In construction days, working on the canal or even living on the Zone became branded in memory thanks to the continuous action taking place along its entire length. Towns clung to the edge of the cut, and the vast machinery shops and other industrial services added to the dirt and din; the railway line was the main road for everyone, and women and children, like the men, were caught up in the hellish maelstrom of noise, smoke and dust that swirled everywhere, all the time.

All effort focused on three great tasks, their accomplishment signalling America's greatest triumphs: digging down a mountain at Culebra; taming the Chagres River with the erection of Gatún Dam to create Gatún Lake; and constructing the locks and gates to control the flow of water through the canal.

Everything in Panama became superlative – the biggest, the grandest, the greatest – and with good reason, for much ingenuity went into making each task, each machine, as efficient as could be. It is claimed (in the style of Ripley's *Believe It or Not*) that during construction, enough material was moved at Culebra (230 million cubic yards) to fill a tunnel driven through the sea at the equator. If all the railway cars that carried all the material excavated were lined up one behind the other, they would encircle the world three-and-a-half times and need a string of railway engines reaching from New York to Honolulu to move them.[24] Such was the nature of the mathematical speculation the canal inspired during its construction, and it still excites wonder today. At the start, however, serious questions arose as to whether the task could really be accomplished.

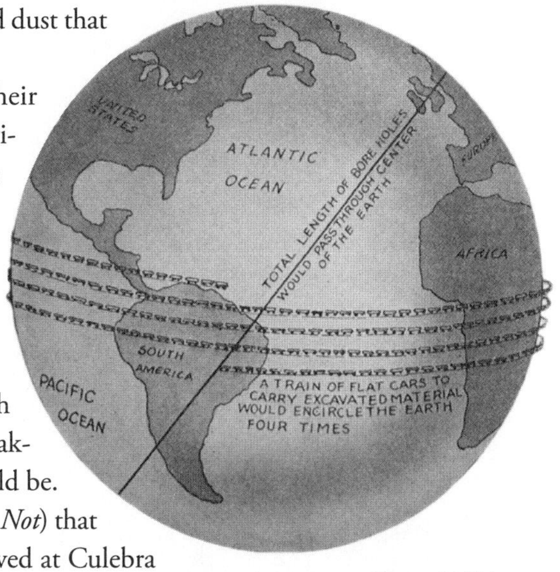

Figure 6.8 This *Scientific American* chart illustrated some of the amazing statistics of the canal construction (Abbot, *Panama*, 135).

"Make the Dirt Fly!"

Impatient with the pace of development, anxious to counter a hostile press and naysayers at home, President Theodore Roosevelt arrived on a whirlwind three-day visit in November 1906 urging the workers to "Make the dirt fly!" The steam shovel men responded with a banner: "WE'LL HELP YOU DIG IT!", echoing the enthusiastic feelings of just about every worker, all energized by Roosevelt's can-do spirit and charisma. Joseph Brewster, recently from Barbados, aged sixteen, proudly recalled that when President Roosevelt came on his inspection of Culebra Cut, "I was one of the workers who operated the pump car, carrying him from Culebra to Empire."[25] The *Colón Starlet* recorded

Figure 6.9 President Theodore Roosevelt (in white) on his tour of inspection of the canal construction in 1906 (Weir, *Conquest of the Isthmus*, 80).

Figure 6.10 President Roosevelt "in command" of a steam shovel became one of the most famous pictures of its times (Panama Canal).

another encounter at Cristóbal when the president was about to take the train: "The watchman at Cristobal, a black Jamaican seeing the President approaching, lifted his hat when the great ruler of the United States of North America stopped, shook hands, and entered into a conversation with him. Some officials of the Zone coming up at the time, the Watchman thought it best to retire, when the President looking around enquired, 'Where is my man?' and encouraged him to walk along with him to the commissary from where he bade him adieu" before taking the train. Unfortunately, we were not given the watchman's name.[26]

Reginald Beckford, on the other hand, witnessed the excitement surrounding Roosevelt's visit to Colón but, as a teenager, he was too young to care. He was taking a walk "on Bottle which has now been named Balboa Ave. and 5 Street. I dont remember the year".

> I saw a man with mustache wearing eye glasses; riding a fine looking black horse. I felt at that time that he is a man of prominence, because their were other men following him on horse back, riding, going towards the Washington Hotel, which in those days was a frame house, nevertheless very imposing. I heard a loud voice from those people who were standing around shouted "Roovelt;" then another voice, Teddy Roovelt. I was not interested, being a teen age boy at the time learning the jewelry trade. I passes that very spot three or four times a day where I saw Roovelt. I was born not very far from where I had seen him.

Despite Beckford's casual tone, he nevertheless rightly concluded that "this man who I saw riding on horse back, was the signal for the building of the Panama Canal".[27]

Once construction proper started in 1907, work along the canal's entire length proceeded at breakneck speed. Work then became the deity, and its pace dominated everyone's life. Competition fostered between the builders on the various sections helped give momentum to the task, and performance figures published in the weekly *Canal Record* fuelled the rivalry between the three geographic divisions: Atlantic, Central and Pacific. Legends grew up around the white steam shovel operators who – in rain or the heat of a hostile tropical sun – drove themselves to drink, madness or suicide in order to top the records.[28]

The Panama Canal: The Plan

The Americans – unlike the French – did not opt for a sea-level canal that would require a waterway flowing from sea to sea. Instead, on the advice of its engineers on the ground, the United States Senate had approved a lock canal. This proposal called for a high-level canal, shaped like a step pyramid. Ships would be lifted up a series of three levels to the waters of Lake Gatún, proceed on the lake for a while and then be lifted down again by three levels to the other side. The transition from one level of water to another would be accomplished by locking the ship in a watertight compartment gated at both ends, letting water into the lock to raise the ship up or down to the next level and once the right level was reached, the gates were opened and the ship would

Figure 6.11 Six submarine chasers being locked through the canal at the same time (postcard, author's collection).

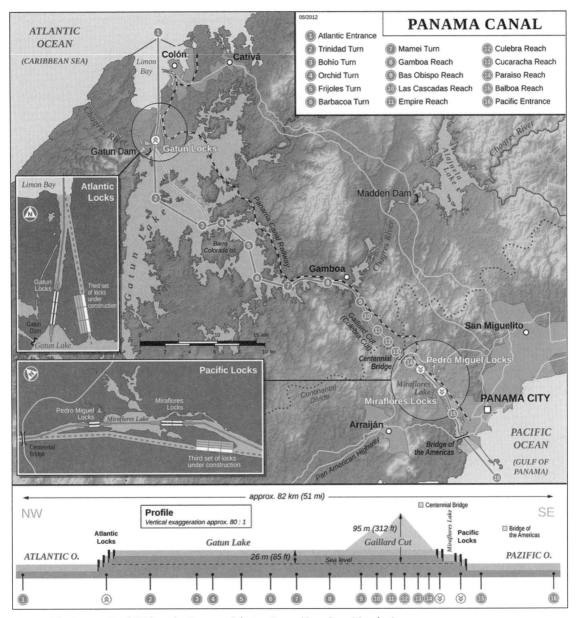

Map 6.1 The Panama Canal (Wikimedia Commons/Thomas Römer/OpenStreetMap data).

proceed until the next lockage. The locks are in pairs so that ships going in opposite directions may be locked through at the same time. Each lock could accommodate one large ship or a number of small ones. At the time of construction, about fifty-two million gallons of fresh water operated the locks and spilled into the ocean for each ship or group of ships passing through, a fact that gave a new appreciation for Panama's high rainfall.

GATÚN DAM

Rain feeds the locks and Gatún Dam, rain such as no worker who came to Panama had ever experienced in his life. Rufus Forde remembered, "In the rainy season when rain start to fall some time you dont see sun for about 2 stright weeks   I had never saw so much rain in all my life as I see in Gatun Cut."[29] For Edgar Young, the rain "did not come down in drops or sheets" but as "avalanches of water hurled from the heavens with force enough to knock a man to his knees".[30] "When you are going to talk about rain," George Martin admonished,

Figure 6.12 Gatún Locks viewed from the end of the approach wall, 1913. In the background can be seen the three pairs of lock gates bridging the ascent of eighty-five feet between waters (Panama Canal).

> please refer back from 1909 & 10 when we worked in rain, just as if it were sun; here is something to note, when we reached the Stretch on the way to Gatun, after leaving Monte-Lirio, it rained for days right through, day and night. We had a white boss whose name were Atkins, a young looking fellow at the time, the rain beat him, it turned us colored people almost white, but our boss, it brought him like white Calico, I mean white, for it was no use stop working, all of us were in the rain, we turned to work in rain, go to lunch in rain, back to work in rain, we used to go to the bathroom in the morning, and put on the same clothes every day[31]

Her husband's damp clothes presented one of the trials for American Rose van Hardeveld when the rainy season started four months after she arrived. "Everything smelled of mold and decay. Water fell from the sky in great, drenching sheets. . . . Jan seldom had a dry shirt or a pair of dry shoes. He would come home with the mud and water squashing in his shoes and his shirt and trousers wringing wet. . . . The small space under the house was the only reasonably dry spot on top of our hill. We dried what clothing we could there."[32] As a West Indian old-timer lamented, "in the morning you had to put your clothes on damp no sun to dry them, what you are going to do, the men that living from that time should praised God morning noon and night".[33] The years 1909 and 1910 were indeed ones of record rainfall. On 1 October 1909, more than eight inches of rain fell between noon and five o'clock in the afternoon. In July 1910, the rainiest month on record, as much as two inches of rain fell in one hour every noontime at Gatún.

Unlike the customary work rules of West Indian plantations, here nothing stopped for the rain and the white bosses found humour in the workers' attempts to improvise shelter. American Frank Rose recalled,

> these black men dreaded a wetting worse than a licking, and we laughed at some of the sights they made trying to keep a dry skin . . . down in the Dry Dock, where a hundred or so might be seen working beneath some boat hauled up for repairs, some with rain coats, some with ear muffs, and some with woollen pull-down caps, some with capes, and others with strips of canvas, burlap or tarpaulin, one with a woman's skirt with holes cut in it for his arms, but the one who took the grand prize, had two pieces of corrugated roofing iron tied so that it hung down front and back, like a sandwich's man advertising something.[34]

Night and day, rain or shine, on went the work of building the canal and relocating the railway: "You had to go through the rain, and work all through rain. I rem[em]ber when I was in the drilling gang, the boss allway say keep the drills agoing, so as to keep your body warm sometimes, you are so could [cold] that your teeth keep nocking together."[35]

A Lake as Large as Barbados

Rain fed the volatile Chagres River and, from the start, one of the greatest natural difficulties in the construction was control of the water's course. A formidable obstacle throughout the history of the isthmus, the 145-mile-long Chagres flows through mountainous country with torrential rainfall. Part of the problem in controlling the river was the variability of the flow, sudden freshets causing it to rise to enormous heights. The solution was to dam the river at an appropriate place, creating an artificial lake that would become the central feature of the waterway and also generate hydroelectricity to operate the locks and provide power to the Canal Zone.

Near the village of Gatún, the river valley reaches its narrowest width of one-and-a-half miles, and it was here that the engineers decided to erect a dam with a spillway to regulate the flow of water. Constructed from rock and earth brought from excavation elsewhere and dumped at the rate of one hundred trainloads per day for several years, this massive bulwark became the largest earth dam in the world (at the time), 115 feet above sea level.

Work on Gatún Dam began in 1907 with the clearing of all organic matter from the six-hundred-acre site. First, machete gangs chopped down all vegetation; another gang then burned the foliage, leaving a desolate blackened wasteland of tree stumps and debris; next, West Indian gangs blasted the trunks out of the ground with dynamite – dirty, dangerous work. Edgar Simmons of Barbados, who was one of the "fire hags", left us a vivid picture of their labour. First, axe-men chopped holes in the trees, up to fifteen holes per tree. The powder gang then placed sticks of dynamite in the holes, and in the evening, after the passenger train had passed, the workers started lighting the charges:

> Some of us has up to 65 or 72 holes to light and find our way out. So . . . when 9 of us start out, each one with two sticks of fire in our hand, running and lighting, at the same time trying to clair ourselves before the first set begin bursting on us. Then its like Hell. Excuse me of this assertion, but its a fact. On one occasion myself and a fellow. . . had to jump in the river that run down to the old Pump Station and hide ourselves under the wild mango roots until all is over. So, it was something to watch and see the pieces of trees flying in the air. They used to call us the fire hags.

After this, the regular gang would pile up the fragmented stumps. "Then days, or a week after, we the same lighters would go around with crude oil and a long brass torch, spilling the oil all over the heap, then apply our torch. Sir, another Hell roar again. Again, you may pardon me. And so, day after day and week after weeks, months after months, we went on piling up and burning up until we had the place where forms the lake now, it were all cleared of trees."[36] As soon as the site was clear, workmen in their thousands swarmed all over the valley. At the height of work on Gatún Dam, over two thousand men worked there daily, men from all parts of the globe, speaking a multitude of languages.

Some workers were putting in spur tracks for the railroad so that waste material from Culebra Cut and other places could be brought to the site and dumped to fill the walls of the dam; others installed steam shovels to excavate hard rocks. Dynamite crews came in to break the rocks into manageable size for the shovels, and suction dredges were at work. While all this went on, work began on the massive job of excavation and construction of the concrete locks and gates at both ends of the lake. There were three pairs of locks at Gatún, one at Pedro Miguel and two at Miraflores. The lock at Gatún would lift the ship to the level of Gatún Lake, 85 feet above sea level, and on the lake it would travel thirty-one miles to Pedro Miguel where another lockage would lower the ship to Miraflores Lake. For part of the transit through Gatún Lake, the canal followed the course of the Chagres River. Then at Gamboa it entered the famous Culebra Cut, a nine-mile passageway with walls towering some 300 feet above it.

Gatún Dam swallowed eleven million cubic yards of earth and rock, and ten million tons of hydraulic fill placed across the river valley where the village of Gatún once stood, the villagers having been moved in 1908 to New Gatún above the lake. To construct the dam, two great ridges of rock and earth were piled across the valley, east to west, parallel to one another and about 600 feet apart at the natural level of the ground. Dry material in these ridges was first deposited from trains run out on long trestles built over the bottomland. Gradually, mounds arose from which earth and rock could be dumped without the use of trestles. The material dumped here was subject to constant packing from the weight of the heavy trains running above, and from the soaking, heavy rains. At the height of this work, one hundred train loads of earth and rock were dumped in a day. Between these two ridges of hard material, an impermeable core of waterborne sand and clay was deposited by the suction dredges. Daily, from one to four twenty-inch suction dredges poured their streams of water heavy with clay over the ridges, the water draining off to leave a heavily packed core as durable as concrete. The core was built from the ground up to a height of 95 feet by the water process, then brought up to 105 feet by the dumping of dense clay found in borrow pits nearby. One of these pits was on

Figure 6.13
Gatún spillway in operation (postcard, author's collection).

the site of a village known as Jamaica Town where foundations of buildings once occupied by the French canal workers could still be seen.

Midway in the dam, a spillway was built that was capable of discharging 154,000 cubic yards of water per second, adequate (it was believed) to take the excess water from the Chagres River. For the locks to work properly, the level of the new river had to be kept at 85 feet, with a deviation of no more than 2 feet. On the side of the spillway rose a hydro-electric plant to provide power for the entire Zone.

To keep the waters of the Chagres River out of the cut while construction was underway, a dike was built at Gamboa. When this dike was finally blown up, the waters of Gatún Lake flowed freely through the cut to Pedro Miguel lock, bringing the level of the cut to that of the lake. When the lake reached its normal height, it permanently submerged 164 square miles, including the bed of the old Panama Railroad and entire villages and farms. Like everything else it was superlative: the largest man-made body of water in the world, larger than many of the islands from which the Silver Men came.

One aspect of the lake struck the workers as supernatural. They left for lunch one day with the lake blue and empty and returned to find it dotted with small green islands. The "islands" turned out to be masses of vegetation loosened from the bottom by the rising water and blowing about by changing winds. George Martin was one of those called on to clear the trees and debris appearing on the surface of the lake the day after water first flowed through the cut.

> the bosses would walk around selecting his men, some of us were placed in death-traps, that is, we were to seize two stumps or bodies of trees that had float on the water and nail them together like rafts, and whether you would swim or not, two of us would have to get on this and go all in the water on the surface and clean it of all the debris . . . for the water brought up everything to top, except stones; you can figure out the job we had to bring all those things to shore and that was how the locks were cleared of its debris; the thing that had me so scared was that I could swim but like lead.[37]

To keep the lake free in future, the vegetation had to be loosened and towed by a launch onto the spillway where it floated over the dam.

The Drowned Villages

As the lake slowly rose, it drowned the villages between Gatún and Matachin, places once vital to the isthmus story. The *Canal Record* noted that "they have never been important in the sense of size . . . they are little more than jungle hamlets, yet they have a distinct place in American history, because they were

Figure 6.14 A sight never to be seen again – washerwomen doing laundry in a river near the old town of Gatún, with a glimpse of the church in the distance to the left. The village was one of those buried under rock and dirt in the creation of Gatún dam. (Courtesy of William P. McLaughlin, www.czimages.com.)

known to European civilization many years before Jamestown was settled or Massachusetts Bay was an English colony". The very names of these vanished villages were evocative of their indigenous or Spanish origins as stopping points on the Chagres River trail – Ahorca Lagarto, Barbacoas, Caimito, Matachin, Bailamonos, Santa Cruz, Cruz de Juan Gallego and Cruces (Venta Cruz). These lake settlements were all under water by August 1912. The more substantial houses were moved and relocated in new villages, the shacks abandoned to the jungle, the villagers dispersed.[38]

Gatún (so prominent during the gold-rush days) was the first village to vanish, entombed under eighty feet of rock and earth beneath Gatún Dam, burying the lusty memories of an old settlement with a fort, pirates, merchants and railroad travellers passing through. Here the *bungo* boats had stopped for refreshments on their way up the Chagres, and their gold-rush passengers bought eggs at four for a dollar and rented hammocks for four dollars a night. Here Mary Seacole had disembarked from the train and hired a boat to take her and her baggage to Cruces. The French used Gatún as a centre for residence and for work. When the Americans arrived in 1904, Gatún formed the centre of a large river trade; boatloads of bananas and other produce from the Gatún, Trinidad and Chagres Rivers arrived here for sale and trans-shipment by rail. By 1908, when the villagers were forced to move, Gatún contained a church, a priest's house, a school, a dozen small shops, and ninety or more small houses of all descriptions, from bamboo huts with palm thatch to the typical sheet-iron–roofed shanty. Most of the buildings were moved to the new site of New Gatún.[39] Other villages and towns immortalized in isthmian history were to disappear until human habitation all along this stretch was erased from sight, if not from record.

THE LOCKS

The locks were all identical: concrete chambers with 1,000-foot-long walls rising to 81 feet, higher than a six-storey building. At 110 feet wide, they were large enough to have housed the *Titanic*. Each lock took more than two million cubic yards of concrete – a mixture of sand, gravel and Portland cement. In constructing them, a vast army of men worked twelve-hour days to feed an endless cycle based on clever mechanization.

The Gatún locks were constructed as gigantic moulds into which the concrete was poured from overhead by means of immense cableways. (At the other locks, giant cantilever cranes were used.) Four towers were erected on either side of the areas excavated for the locks, and from these stretched giant cables spanning some 800 feet. The towers were 85 feet high and mounted on tracks like steam shovels so that they could move forward as work progressed.

Figure 6.15 The sketch shows that the six-storey building to the left could fit into the lock chamber at right (Abbot, *Panama*, 222). Sketches of a wagon and locomotive demonstrate the scale of the conduits through which water flows.

Material for mixing the cement came in barges from along the coast to Cristóbal and up the old French canal to the vicinity of Gatún. The sand came from Nombre de Dios, forty miles from Colón, and the gravel from Portobello, twenty miles away. When the barges with sand and gravel arrived, great buckets from the cableways swept down, taking up two cubic yards of material, lifting it up to the cables and carrying it across to the storage piles to dump it. Then little electric cars that ran without motormen on two small circular railways hauled the material from the storage piles to the concrete mixers. As each car entered a tunnel, it was automatically filled with the proper mixture of sand, cement and gravel to carry to the concrete mixers. Another small railway car operated by a motorman, consisting of two flat cars with two filled buckets of roughly six tons each, took the mixture from the concrete mixer to the cableway. At the cableway the filled buckets rose automatically and replaced two empty buckets, and so the cycle continued.

Figures 6.16–6.17 Much of the construction material for the locks moved overhead (Panama Canal). At Gatún locks, cableways carrying concrete buckets moved on tracks parallel to the locks and had a span of eight hundred feet (figure 6.16); at Miraflores, huge travelling cranes were used (figure 6.17).

Figure 6.18 Concrete mixing plant at Gatún (Panama Canal). Sand, stone and cement used in mixing concrete went on electrical railway cars running on a circular track. The mixing drums emptied the concrete mixture into these big buckets that were transported by railway to the cableway towers.

For the workmen, danger lurked everywhere:

> I left the Cut and got a job in the Cement Mixture my job was at a curb watching three lights, the white light for stone, the blue was for san and the red was for cement, the Automatic Cars, they run with three rails, the too outside rails the cars run on, the centre rail carry the current, it was called the third rail, and when you forgot and stept on it you are a dead man, so many people get kill by it they had to change it and put the current over head.[40]

A report in the *Canal Record* of 8 August 1909 recorded one such accident: "a Barbadian labourer was killed by electricity at Gatun Saturday September 4, on the automatic railway near the south end of the cement tunnel. He was riding on the cars that convey cement to the mixing plant when he slipped and fell, striking the power rail. Death was instantaneous."

Work on constructing the lock chambers as well as the massive lock gates and cableways generally involved workmen in perilous tasks at great heights; falls – usually fatal – often occurred. The West Indian workers song "Money Grows Like Apples" refers to these dangers:

> They puts us off at Balboa, Corozal and Peter Miguel
> There is where the biggest job is done by those men of fate
> McClintock, Marshall and those men who hung the gates.
>
> You gets more money for that job than working in the cut
> But it all depends muh honey on you don't get hurt.
> For if you ever get a drop yuh'll shurely have to die
> For dem gates Lawd Gahd is seventy-five feet high.[41]

Workmen broke their necks falling from trestles; one died after being crushed between a locomotive crane and a staircase in the wall of a lock chamber; another died after being caught between the bed and carriage of a crane.[42] One day, an American, a Barbadian and a Demeraran were killed at Miraflores lock when they fell from a scaffold. They had been riveting the lock gates when one end of the scaffold gave way under the weight of a seven-ton rivet reamer, throwing them to the floor of the lock sixty feet below. A Grenadian fell but was not killed. Another workman saved himself by thrusting a wrench through a hole in the leaf gate and hanging on to it until rescued.[43]

Some men became hardened to witnessing death every day while others broke down when it came too close to them. Lancelot Kavanagh was working at Gatún locks using an air hammer high in the air when an accident hurled men and machines to the ground, killing four and injuring many others. He was so frightened that he "never went back for the 4 days pay I had there".[44] Nehemiah Douglas of Jamaica (who described himself as a "foundationer") was a rigger working on the gates at Miraflores when a cable broke and killed some men. "The amount of blood that flowed gave the appearance of a little gully, and when I saw what appeared an island of blood, I got nervous, I think, because how I got down, I do not know; but I got down and ran like never run a man before, straight home in Paraiso. So fast did I run that when I arrived home I heard the whistle giving the knock off signal."[45]

Work at Both Entrances

As the locks at Gatún were being built, work had also begun at both the Pacific and Atlantic entrances to the canal. Here, ships traverse a man-made channel at sea level before reaching the first set of locks. On approaching the first lock, each ship is run alongside a concrete guide wall where it ties up. From here, using no motive power, the ship is towed and guided through the locks by four very small but powerful locomotives called "mules". The gate of the first lock opens, the ship is guided in, the gate closes and the lock fills with water from Lake Gatún which spills through an intricate network of large and small culverts, raising the water level and lifting the ship to the level of the lock above. A ship entering from the Atlantic side passes Toro Point, an eleven-thousand-foot-long man-made peninsular protecting the canal entrance at Colón. It travels on its own steam the first seven miles of the canal, a sea-level ditch five hundred feet wide and forty-five feet deep.

The French had already dug part of the canal from Colón to Gatún, and this work was continued by the Americans with the use of steam shovels to

Figure 6.19 Gatún Lock gate under construction (Panama Canal).

Figure 6.20 Workmen at the base of Gatún Lock gate shows its scale and the amount of riveting required (Panama Canal).

chop through the rocks of the Mindi Hills. At sea level, dredges sucked up mud from the bottom of the canal to lower it to the proper depth. Similar dredging and blasting was taking place at the Pacific side. Wharves, fortifications and a breakwater were also built at both ends. Men were equally at risk working in water as on land, and the incidence of drowning was high among West Indians.

Out in the harbour, hard rock (first broken by blasting) had to be scraped from the bottom of the canal. A drill barge made holes in the rock bottom for dynamite charges. Then a rock-breaker raised its twenty-ton steam ram to a height of ten feet or more, and let it drop on to the rock. It would repeatedly hammer one spot until it reached the desired depth of forty-five feet below mean tide. Then it moved to another spot nearby and continued. On the sea side, in addition to drill barges and rock-breakers, dipper dredges as well as suction dredges scooped up rock and mud out of the channel. Work in these areas went on twenty-four hours a day, six days a week.

One of the most dangerous and difficult jobs on the canal, and undertaken by West Indians, was constructing the foundations of the quay at Balboa, where men had to work inside caissons sunk deep into the ground. As the caissons frequently became filled with water, pumps had to be kept going to dry the holes. Sometimes the cylinder struck an underground spring. Once, two labourers working seventy feet below inside a caisson had a lucky escape when there was a rush of water and the cylinder began to sink faster than usual. The men in the pit shouted, and the engine hoisted them to the surface, cold and trembling with fear.[46] Others were not so lucky. A Vincentian asphyxiated at the bottom of one of these pits seventy-five feet below the surface. Another Vincentian went down to investigate but he too was overcome. A third man

Figure 6.21 A drill barge at work (Panama Canal).

who went down also became unconscious but was later revived.[47] What permanent mental and physical damage the survivors suffered is not recorded. Apart from the risk to their lives, the men working in the caisson pits deep in the earth had to contend with constant semi-darkness, wetness, mud and foul air. On occasions when conditions were particularly bad, they were paid at the rate of sixteen cents an hour.[48]

As the date for completion of the canal neared, the workers made almost superhuman effort. The *Canal Record* recorded in March 1914 the following performance by a squad of five West Indians who laid the brick floors for a portion of the quay wall of the Balboa terminals. The five masons, working in relays with three men on and two resting at a time, in one day of ten working hours laid a total of 96,000 bricks. The bricks were laid in a width of fifty feet over a distance of more than four hundred feet or approximately twenty thousand square feet. With its passion for statistics, the *Record* informs us that counting five men in the squad, each laid at the rate of 1,920 bricks per hour or 32 per minute. With three men at work at a time, the bricks were laid at the rate of 3,200 per man hour or 53.33 by each man each minute. The entire gang (including the white foreman and men who moved the bricks from the cars, mixed and carried mortar, and so on) consisted of sixty-seven men. The five masons were paid at the rate of $0.13 per hour, or $1.30 each for the day's work.[49]

CULEBRA CUT

To West Indians, Culebra was the most famous place on the canal construction, immortalized in song from the time of the French: "Matilda deh pon dying bed / Seh mi wan'go Colibra".[50] A song during US construction was aimed at the planters back home:

> Before me work fe bit a day
> me would come out America Cut
> Dem a bawl out, "O come out
> America Cut, O come out America Cut."[51]

It was telling them, "rather than work for a pittance here I will go to work on the Panama Canal; they are crying out for workers". (The "bit" was four-and-a-half pence British currency).

From the time of the French, Culebra Cut represented the greatest engineering challenge; the widening and deepening of a nine-mile-long gorge through a mountain 550 feet high. In 1881 the French began excavation, removing 20 million cubic yards to deepen the gorge. Following the failure of the first company, the Compagnie Nouvelle continued work here on a small scale. As soon as the Americans took over in May 1904, they concentrated men and machinery on the site and by the time construction ended, they had moved another 105 million cubic yards, blasting their way through with dynamite, battling the endless landslips that undid the work at every turn.

As Edgar Young (who worked as a crane-man in 1907) later wrote,

> An army of men had fought Culebra. Day by day they had gone out to give battle. And day by day Culebra gave answer. The walls caved in and great cracks in the earth extended back into the hills for miles, the bottom belched up from the weight of earth on the sides, overturning steam-shovels and disrupting tracks; slides came down. Cucaracha dropped four million yards into the cut in one day over and above her regular schedule. . . . An unknown bed of mineral was dug into, which took fire at exposure to the air and smoldered like a volcano for weeks until it was dug up bodily and hauled from the cut.[52]

So frenzied was the activity along its length – with upwards of nine thousand men at a time poured into the battle, Culebra Cut became a "hell's gorge" with towns "hanging by their fingernails all along its edge".[53] The rain or sun beat down on everyone in the gorge day after day and the constant fallout of dust turned all workers the same colour.

Figure 6.22 Slides in Culebra Cut ripped up tracks and wrecked trains (Panama Canal).

Visitors to Culebra – and the tourists came in their thousands – would stand gawking at the dazzling array of colours that shone from the walls of the cut, revealing the violent volcanic convulsions that led to the birth of the Isthmus of Panama, and the interlaying of many types of soil and rock. Red predominated, but there were also blues and yellows: the colours of the clays and rocks exposed by the cuttings.

The greater part of Culebra was hard volcanic rock and it was necessary to drill and blast all the way through, cutting steps down the sides of the canyon. As excavation deepened, the steps stretched wider and wider and, as the sides grew steeper, landslides became more frequent, sweeping down on men, machinery and trains, burying some so deeply they were never seen again.

The predominant volcanic rock sat on softer rock that frequently destabilized when the surface was disturbed. The material did not fall as in a rock-slide, but sideways like the surface ice on a glacier. The dreaded Cucaracha ("Cockroach") slide on the eastern end of the canal first started to move in 1885, slowed, then moved again in 1905 and continued to do so in the wet seasons. Some slides became so bad that they broke back the crests of the hills bordering the cut. The engineers partly solved this problem by pumping water to sluice the material down the hill before it fell, leaving the rest at a stable angle. The problem of the slides, however, remained one of the builders' worst challenges, delaying the opening of the canal for several months.

Men on the job barely had time to appreciate the dramatic spectacle thanks to the frenzied activity that took place on all the steps simultaneously, the steps being connected by ladders. Some evenings, tired workmen in the bottom of the cut had to climb 154 steps to get to the top.

In the cut,

> The different levels varied from ten to twenty feet one above the other, each with a railroad on it, back and forth along which incessantly rumbled and screeched dirt trains full or empty, halting before the steam-shovels, that shivered and spouted thick black smoke as they ate away the rocky hills and cast them in great giant handfuls on the train of one-sided flat-cars that moved forward bit by bit at the flourish of the conductor's yellow flag. Steam-shovels . . . tore up the solid rocks with snorts of rage . . . now and then flinging some troublesome, stubborn boulder angrily upon the cars.[54]

Each step up the side of the canyon was cut wide enough to accommodate two sets of temporary railway tracks – the inner tracks for the huge steam shovels that chewed away at the rock, the outer track for the spoil trains that took away the material to be dumped.

These Bucyrus steam shovels were the workhorses of the excavation. Their operators as well as onlookers were so awed by their enormous size and power that many came to imbue them with both human and animal qualities. Albert Bullard quotes one of the operators as saying, "Why . . . she'll do anything for a man who treats her decent." Bullard described them as "monsters of steel whose food is fire and whose breath is alternate steam and black smoke . . . when the wind dies down . . . the pall of their breath hangs so heavy you can scarce see them. But through all the long day you can hear them roaring and shrieking over their prey."[55] Viewing the cut, Winifred James found "the men had become machines, the machines were uncannily like men". The steam shovel she saw as a prehistoric animal: "on the end of a long neck it craned forth its square head and nibbled away at the sides of the canal. When it opened its great square jaw and spat out the few tons of rock and soil it had so casually bitten off, the likeness was extraordinary."[56]

Figures 6.23–6.24 The 95-ton Bucyrus steam shovel was the wonder of the Culebra dig (Panama Canal). The dipper had room for 8.7 tons of rock or 6.7 tons of earth (figure 6.23). The shovel moved backward and forward on one track and loaded material on to the dump cars on the second track alongside it.

Two Americans operated each shovel – an engineer or driver inside the machine and a craneman on the shovel arm – with a West Indian stoker outside whose job it was to keep shovelling coal into the furnace of its huge red-hot boiler. The temperature was often well over one hundred degrees Fahrenheit and baked the West Indian stoker as well as the engineer under the corrugated iron roof of the shovel. In the rainy season, the stoker, like the rest of the silver gang attached to each shovel, worked exposed to the elements and knee deep in mud all day. The shovel was mounted on four-wheel railway tracks but had slow motive power of its own so that it could move forward or backward along the track or clamp itself when digging. The driver sat on a platform operating the shovel and the crane arm. On the right side of the crane arm was a little enclosed platform for the "craney", who operated the shovel or dipper which scooped up the earth. Like some huge metal beast snuffling around, the shovel ate huge chunks of earth and rocks, including five-ton boulders. When the dipper got its full load, the engineer swung the crane to the left above a spoil car on the railroad track. The craney threw the switch lever, which opened the bottom of the dipper and the load fell on to the rail car. The dipper closed and swung back to the right to get ready for another bite of rock.

Edgar Young later dramatically recalled his days as a craney:

> Perched high on the side of the throbbing boom underneath a piece of corrugated iron, butterfly throttle in left hand, dumping rope in right, swoop, the big five-yard dipper bit into the slate-hard clay. *Chow; chow! Chuff; chuff; chuff!* A shove on the butterfly, *chuck-achuck-chuck!* out go the sticks, a yank on the dumping rope, a thundering of earth on the steel bottom of the Lidgerwood; *clang* goes the dipper door back into place, snap goes the latch and wildly we swing back for another trip. Five yards at a trip and seconds measured the interval between. Hundreds of shovels were beating the world's record for moving earth.[57]

The importance of their task is attested by the fact that the steam shovel operators were the only ones to successfully go on strike for more pay during construction days and the competition among them to be top of the *Canal Record* list each week for the most earth moved meant that some literally worked themselves to madness or death. Young remembered his steely-eyed operator "figuring the swing of the boom, studying the moves forward between trains of empty cars, calculating to the exact fraction of an inch just where we would drop the dipper, watching me and working with me until he and I shovel, dipper, boom and engines were just one huge machine".[58]

Seven or eight dippers filled one dump car and the attendant signalled the engineer to pull the train ahead by one car. The shovel filled the next car, and so it went, the train moving one car ahead at a time. A spoil train hauled twenty-one cars and as each train pulled out another took its place. In an average day at the height of construction, thirty-seven hundred cars were loaded and hauled from the cut. Twenty-five trains worked nonstop in the central division, an area thirty-two miles long. The millions of tons of spoil removed from the bottom of the cut were hauled distances ten to thirty miles away, to the Atlantic or Pacific side, the direction depending on whether it was hard rock to be used on the breakwater or waste for the dump. The first chief engineer, John Stevens, worked out the system whereby each loaded train was positioned to go downhill; empty trains went uphill.

The shovel worked to cut a new step ahead. Two shovels working together could cut a step twenty-eight feet wide, enough for laying double tracks. Then the shovel paused just long enough for the track laying gang to rush in. As soon as they finished, the shovel shifted on to this track and continued working. Once the track was laid, the workers wired the track, putting in switches and other mechanical devices. The track would eventually enter the main track line of the Panama Railroad and head out to the disposal dumps and other places where fill was needed, such as Gatún Dam. At the dump, material was automatically unloaded and spread until it was wide enough to permit the shifting of the track so spoil could be spread over another area.

At first, a gang of six hundred men was required to shift the track until a special machine was invented to do this job with the aid of only a handful of men, all literally up to their knees in mud, the heat intense, no shelter anywhere. The men sang, over and over, "Hard work today, Ba Congreja".

Dynamite and Dobies

Noise, dust and smoke were everywhere: smoke, steam and coal dust barrelling from the roaring steam shovels; black smoke belching from the racing rail engines dragging long flatbeds heaped high with dirt along the maze of tracks; steam popping out in little puffs from the air drills; dust from the constant drilling and blasting of rocks; noise from explosions large and small which shattered the peace of the cut and surrounding areas by day and night. With constant shouts of "Look out!" in many languages, men were barely able to jump out of the paths of trains bearing down on them in all directions. The task of waving signal flags was an essential one, and the casual-seeming West Indian flagmen "lounging at every switch" (one every hundred yards under shelter made of four upright sticks and a sheet of corrugated iron) caught the eye of visitor Arthur Bullard, who was amazed that

Figure 6.25 Artist William Harnden Foster's painting *Premature Explosion*, showing dynamite at Empire, 1910, captures one of the frequent dangers the men faced. (Courtesy of William P. McLaughlin, www.czimages.com.)

suddenly something will galvanize them. They jump up, grab a red or white flag, wave it violently for a moment and stick it in a bracket. Then they return to their cigarette or their self-contemplation. In a few minutes they will have another burst of activity, taking down one flag and waving another. . . . They have no telephones, and do not seem to be watching any set of signals . . . they always wave the right flag at the right moment. These ineffectual-looking, dandified Jamaicans are very important cogs in the vast machine.[59]

Yellow flags were waved for trains to move off; white flags were hoisted to mark a disabled steam shovel; red flags announced the firing of "dobie shots", small charges of dynamite tamped down with adobe clay. They were set off whenever stubborn boulders needed smashing. As the chantey[60] warned:

Tussle and toil, clamor and curse
War is Hell but this is worse;
Those that stay with the cursed ditch
May get a medal or the dhobie itch. A una!

Even small dobie shots were dangerous and sometimes fatal for those who happened to be hit with flying rock. The men in the gangs tried to protect their heads with whatever metal was handy, safety helmets being unknown: "Blasting every minute no shelter in the Cut one has to run for a fair distant every once a while some one will get head injuries no steel hat those days."[61]

Apart from the constant small shots, two huge dynamite blasts using thousands of pounds of explosives were set to go off twice each day and each night. Holes for the charges were bored in the rocks by Star-drills that operated constantly, whole battalions of deafening machines run by compressed air brought along a nine-mile pipeline. There were also gravity drills, all pounding and grinding and jamming holes in the rocks. In all, 377 tripod and well drills were in use simultaneously, contributing to the deafening noise.[62] The favourite

Figure 6.26 Loading with dynamite to blast a slide in Culebra Cut, 1912 (Panama Canal). Up to ninety miles of holes were drilled every month to blast through Culebra rock.

chantey of the drill gangs working with sledgehammers (sung to the up-and-down rhythm of the drills) was:

Ten pound hammer (Uh-huh)
Kill my partner
Somebody dying
Every day

Somebody died almost every day as a result of dynamite blasts, another feature of life on the Canal Zone. Gangs of "powder men" pounded the drill holes full of dynamite then tamped them down ready to "blow" at 11:30 a.m. when the men left for lunch and at 5:30 p.m. when they had gone home. Huge blasts were also set to go at midnight and daybreak. Six million pounds of dynamite were used each year and nearly one thousand miles of holes drilled annually, some six hundred blasts being fired every workday.

The continuous explosions set porch chairs rocking in the villages clinging to the edge of the cut and were heard far out to sea. Buildings shook and earth, rock fragments and mud spattered the roofs. Zone workers and residents knew when to run for cover from falling rocks and debris. Reed E. Hopkins worked as a railroad conductor from 1907 and remembered that "there was many a blast shot off without warning; you would always hear a blast, then duck under a car or something to get out of the way of the rocks that were falling. There weren't many safety devices in those days."[63] Teacher Gertrude B. Hoffman's most vivid memory was of the "premature blast at Bas Obispo. . . . The father of one of my scholars was able to get into the dipper of a steam shovel . . . and his steam shovel was completely covered with broken rocks. I used that as an illustration of quick action when I wanted to hurry the youngsters along."[64]

Figure 6.27 Steam drills at work at Bas Obispo (Weir, *Conquest of the Isthmus*, 98). These and other types of drills were all powered by compressed air brought into Culebra Cut through some thirty miles of pipe from big compressors at three locations.

The effects of the blasts were far reaching. American Mrs Bruce Sanders (who came in 1910 to join her husband and lived for a while in a small tin-roofed house) remembered that "blasting on the canal played havoc with cake-baking, because the blasts shook the whole house. A cake would either fall flat or spill out into the bottom of the oven."[65]

While the overall loss of life from dynamite explosions might have been lower than expected, the spectacular blasts caused much damage to workers. On 8 October 1908 a steam shovel struck an unexploded cap in the cut near Empire, the explosion killing five workmen and injuring eight, all except two being West Indians.[66] An entire gang was almost wiped out in April 1913 when twenty-one thousand pounds of 60 per cent dynamite exploded prematurely in the canal prism opposite Corozal. Three were killed and nineteen seriously injured. The report five days later added that "two men are still missing and although a crew of labourers has been at work digging over the ground in or near the site of the explosion, no trace of them has ever been found". The gang consisted of thirty men, of whom twenty-seven were powder men.[67] In July 1914, less than a month before the opening of the canal to commercial traffic, a premature explosion of dynamite at the base of Cucaracha slide caused the drill barge *Teredo* to sink in thirty feet of water. Three workers on the barge died in the explosion, two were missing and fourteen injured.[68] This accident occurred just a week after the powder and dynamite magazine at Mindi blew up, destroying over 450,000 pounds of explosives. The day watchman – a West Indian – was killed instantly, his body found in the bush some distance away. The family of the West Indian night watchman, consisting of himself, his wife and seven children who lived in a small house about three hundred yards south of the magazine, escaped with slight injuries.[69]

These were only a few of the accidents caused by dynamite. By far the most serious accident during construction occurred 12 December 1908 at Bas Obispo when an explosion left at least seventy killed or injured. A newspaper reporter visited the scene the next day and found

> fully 600 feet by about 300 feet of the Cut one complete mass of huge loose rock and debris with a 91 ton steam shovel no. 262 smashed to atoms and imbedded by the fallen rocks with only the crane and the dipper still standing. Men were at work laying the fuses for charges of dynamite set around the rocks for the purpose of clearing the track in the cut, as also to get at any bodies which may be covered under.[70]

He added that bits of human bodies were still scattered around, or as one construction worker Amos Clarke many years later recalled the horror of that scene, "their instral and flesh could be seen hanging from trees".[71] Reginald Beckford was travelling past on a train. "Passengers, including myself, get up from their seats when the train is nearing Culebra. Avalanche covering fifty men at Culebra; something more. Bas Obispo had taken the greatest death toll in one dynamite explosion in one day."[72] Twenty-six persons were confirmed dead and forty injured and a number reported missing. Many of them were so fragmented that identification was impossible. Also lost, presumably, were the money bags all the men wore tied around their waists.

Occasionally, a gang escaped by a hair's breadth – in the Bas Obispo case, an explosion as the last of fifty-three holes was being tamped down set off all the fuses. George Hodges recalled his role in saving a number of gangs from almost certain death when, one Saturday, the gangs and their bosses were preparing to "make a shot", that is, lay dynamite charges at Culebra.

> my boss called to me, Hodges come here; he ask me as you all the time been going to the powder house, please let me know what kind of powder do you have up there; I intern said to him that I have key-stone, du-pont and Trojan. He again ask me Hodges, what kind of powder do you think best to used to shoot these holes today? I immediately told him to take my advise and use the Trojan powder.
>
> He said to me, why should you choose Trojan powder, and leave out Key-stone and du-pont the best? I told him that I know that they are the best but I prefer Trojan powder, because you have a better chance with Trojan than the other two powders. In case of danger, Trojan powder will give you a sign. He ask me what do you mean by a sign? I told him that the sign is that when the Trojan powder gets into the hole, that it boils like a pot because you can naturally hear it. But not key stone and du-pont. When ever they get hot, they fired off right away. . . . And they all had come to an agreement, to use Trojan powder.

One hundred and seventy-five boxes of dynamite were brought, each containing fifty pounds.

> Now the loading started . . . some of the holes were 30 ft vertical, and some were less. The toe holes . . . some were 10 ft to 12 ft deep. . . . About 5 minutes after they had started loading these holes, I heard Sandyford shouted out, "look out fellows!" And when we did look we saw the holes started to discharge one by one without any electrical wire attached to them. . . . And what did really happen, the bosses and all of the men had to run to save their lives.

The men were so grateful that they all took up a collection for him next payday.[73]

On occasion, a steam shovel would strike a dynamite charge set long before but which had failed to explode. In one such case, five were killed and eight injured.[74] Sometimes the explosions were caused by inexperience or carelessness. For instance, two West Indians were sent to get a piece of pipe through which to load the dynamite. Finding one that had explosives at the end of it, they attempted to dislodge this by pounding the iron on a rail. Both were

Figure 6.28
Dynamite gangs
carry the volatile
material on their
heads (Panama
Canal).

killed in the resulting explosion. The report of the accident stated that both
had worked on dynamite gangs for several years and were experienced in han-
dling explosives.[75] In another case, three labourers were carrying fifty-pound
boxes of dynamite to a work site. The first man stopped to rest and placed his
box on a pile of old railway ties. The second man did likewise, at which point
the dynamite exploded and killed them both, injuring four others.[76]

The insouciance of the men who handled the dynamite also struck Bullard,
who viewed the dynamite boxes – "they look as innocuous as soap boxes" –
with considerable awe. "Each stick of dynamite is done up in brown wrapping
paper . . . it certainly looks like an insecure, not to say undignified way, to treat
dynamite. The men, with the lack of respect bred of familiarity, chuck the
sticks about nonchalantly, poke them down into the hole, and ram the earth
down on top of them with a cynicism that knocks the bottom out of one's
stomach."[77]

Night Crews

At five in the afternoon when the whistles blew, the shovels ceased work, the
trains were laid up, the noise of the drills stopped, and men who had been
working since seven in the morning started up the steep banks to their homes
in the villages overlooking the cut, or gathered in groups to await the labour
train travelling along the bottom of the cut. Those who lived at the very top
climbed their weary way up the ladder staircase of 154 stairs.

But activity never ceased in the cut, for the night crews would be setting
out. The coal trains would start down the incline into the cut, and the repair
trains left the workshop at Empire. The repair men immediately set to work
on whatever piece of machinery needed their services and the coal men – all

West Indians – began the arduous task (called "spotting") of filling the bins of the steam shovels. A train ran alongside each shovel dropping off a carload of coal. The spotters' task was to shovel the coal from train to steam shovel either directly or by wheelbarrow. Labourers moved two or three tons of coal this way. Six nights a week, rain or shine, for fifty-two weeks each year, the coal gang worked, for the shovels had to be ready to work nonstop during the day. In good times the gangs finished at midnight, but sometimes morning would find them still shovelling coal.[78]

A night in the cut was as awesome as daytime. The constant dynamite blasts in the lonely nights created a strange sensation:

Figure 6.29 After a ten-hour workday, the stairway had to be climbed from the bottom of Culebra Cut to get to the village above (Panama Canal).

> At the point where the crest of the Continental divide is pierced all the sounds of the night work seem to focus. The whistle of a locomotive at Bas Obispo, the chug-chug of churn drills at Empire, the tapping of a pneumatic hammer on the iron boom of a shovel, and the roar of a dynamite blast all travel along the chasm until they strike the rock sides of Gold and Contractors Hills towering 400 feet above the bottom of the trench. There they ricochet from wall to wall, and when many of them meet, they make a bewildering uproar.[79]

Also in the cut at night one could see the movement of lanterns here and there and the brighter glare of the electric headlights of the locomotives. This was possible on clear nights. But on many nights in the cut, "blinding rain arrests the rays even of the searchlights and the rush of water adds to or drowns the sound of labour. And there are nights when a heavy mist settles on the Cut, when the opposite bank is visible, but in the trench below one can see only a white river of fog so dense that it looks like water."[80] A river of fog in which men worked unceasingly.

Breakthrough

Work on Culebra Cut had been tackled simultaneously at both ends and, on 20 May 1913 at 4:30 p.m., two steam shovels met dramatically in the centre of the cut, forty feet above sea level. Workers threw their hats in the air and

Figure 6.30 September 1913, workmen remove ties and rails in Culebra Cut in preparation for water flowing through (Panama Canal).

Figure 6.31 Labourers dig a ditch around the toe of Cucaracha slide 11 October 1913. The railroad network had already been moved so the slide had to be excavated by hand (Panama Canal).

cheered. The end of the work was near. On 10 September, excavation by steam shovel at Culebra finally ceased. Any clearing thereafter had to be done by hand, including clearing the landslides. The locks were all finished; final touches had been put on the dam and water had already begun to flow into Gatún Lake. On 16 September, the tug *Gatún* made the first trial lockage – from the Atlantic to the lake at the summit. It demonstrated that everything was working perfectly.

The dike (which kept the lake water from flowing into the cut) was still in place, but from 5 October 1913 water had been allowed to pass through pipes. On 10 October in Washington, President Woodrow Wilson pushed the button to send the telegraphic signal to Panama and trigger the dynamite blast which blew up the dike. The pent-up waters of the Chagres rushed through the cut, and for the first time water flowed freely through the waterway that now joined the Atlantic and Pacific Oceans.

Figure 6.32 The Panama–California exposition in San Diego in 1915 celebrated the completion of the canal (Wikipedia).

This act, however, was not really the end, for the endless mudslides into the cut continued and had to be cleared. The work was accomplished at breakneck speed and, on 15 August 1914, the SS *Ancon*, a ship which had been a cement carrier during construction, made the first official ocean-to-ocean transit of the Panama Canal. In 1915 Culebra Cut was renamed Gaillard Cut in honour of Colonel David DuBose Gaillard, the engineer in charge of the central division, whose fortitude had emboldened the diggers but he was one of the estimated twenty-five thousand workers[81] thrown into the struggle of man versus nature who did not live to see man triumphant and water passing through the cut; he died of a brain tumour in New York on 5 December 1913.[82]

Figure 7.1 The stark inequalities on the Canal Zone were revealed in housing. In time, gold workers were provided with spacious, comfortable dwellings, like these screened two-family houses at Cristóbal in 1915. (Courtesy of William P. McLaughlin, www.czimages.com.)

7. THE LIVES THEY LIVED, 1904–1914

"Ef I did hear what me Mammee did say
I would't be in dis wort'less Colón"
. . . it seemed to her that, despite the words, the singer's voice was cheerful.
—H.G de Lisser, *Susan Proudleigh*

FOR A FEW OF THE SILVER workers on the labour train, going home meant a wife, family and a good meal. But they were the exceptions. Most had no homes, wives or sweethearts. As Philip McDonald put it, "women were scares as hen's teeth",[1] especially in the early years. For many, home was a harsh, restrictive, labour camp where new labourers stayed on arrival. But many left these barracks as soon as they could, to share rooms in the terminal cities and "native" sections of Zone towns; to slap up a shanty of their own on the fringes, or start a small cultivation out in the bush. In the camps, every aspect of life was regulated. Watchmen and police enforced the rules: women, gambling and drinking were prohibited; only lawfully married couples could live in family quarters. At nine o'clock every night, the watchman knocked on a piece of angle bar kept hanging in the kitchen to signal lights out. One worker found that "the camp life was so rought, that I had to go in a place call now Gatun paying five dollars for a room, the hard part of it, when you come from work and take you supper, and resting off, and nine oclock pass and your light is still burning, a Police Officer will come up an say cut off that light, and go to bed". He added: "it is not so much care they want to take of you, they want you to be able to go to be[d] soon, so you will be able to get up soon to go to work".[2]

It was precisely for this reason that the health and well-being of the workers was such a preoccupation of the Isthmian Canal Commission (ICC). Labour was viewed strictly as another unit of production and healthy, well-fed, well-rested workmen would give of their best on the job.

Figure 7.2 Silver families lived in unscreened barracks with primitive sanitary arrangements (Weir, *Conquest of the Isthmus,* 40).

LIVING CONDITIONS

The earliest workers – gold or silver pioneers – were housed in tents, railway boxcars and the old French barracks reclaimed from the jungle until better housing was built, for bachelors first, later for married quarters. In 1905 the ICC decided to build barracks to house the men on the silver roll and camps soon arose along the line of works from Panama City to Colón, the men travelling to work sites on the labour trains.

The camps were usually near to or part of a Zone town sprawled on the bank of the canal. Each American-built town eventually had a church or two, a commissary, separate schools for black and white, and fire, police and sanitation services. Workshops, stables and railway yards jostled side by side with places of business. Major industrial and engineering works required for the canal expanded towns such as Empire, which, at its height, had a population of seven thousand. Main streets were eventually paved.

A glance around swiftly revealed a town's social, racial and industrial divisions. The gold workers' district in time consisted of detached one- or two-family bungalows fully screened to keep out mosquitoes and set on manicured lawns. Gold housing would eventually be allotted to families in strict accordance to salary levels. White servants were allocated half of family-assigned spaces; "native or colored servants" had to live in "such excluded space as might be available".[3] The US government provided gold workers on the Zone with free housing, furniture, light, water, fuel, ice and garbage disposal service.

On the outskirts was the silver district: barracks for bachelors or family apartment blocks (without screening or amenities) adjoining the "native section", the original hamlet or stopping place on the trail or railroad that, over time, had become a helter-skelter collection of houses occupied by Panamanians, West Indians and others of long-standing residence on the Zone. Here could be found the American saloons, the Spanish cantinas and restaurants, Chinese shops, East Indian fancy-work shops, and Negro tailors and shoemakers.[4] Married quarters provided for silver workers were always inadequate to meet their needs, and many silver workers and their families rented accommodation in the towns. Others squatted on the margins, erecting huts, two-room cottages or well-built bungalows, and raising chickens and vegetables as they would have done at home.

This informal way of life might have seemed squalid to American and European visitors, especially when contrasted to the measured and manicured gold section, but those who lived there remembered it as offering spaces for warmth and freedom, where they might recreate the lives they had left behind. As one French islander recalled, "these little improvised villages were the theatre of a rustic but warm existence with women using river water for clothes washing and men working their bit of land for food and occasional barter".[5] An English visitor noted the contrast when he encountered on the outskirts of one village "the huts of the labourers who prefer the half-jungle life with its freedom; and here with discomfort and squalor and liberty, is the only picturesque part of the settlement; all else is orderly, of one pattern, almost smug".[6]

Figure 7.3 Village of Cruces during construction years showing, in the background, typical thatch-roofed housing of rural Panama (postcard, author's collection). These so-called native towns of earlier times came to house a mixture of native Panamanians, immigrant workers of long standing from the railroad and French canal construction, and the newcomers attracted by the construction of the US canal.

Harry Franck, working as a census taker in 1911, recorded only the worst aspects of such settlements. In the native town at Empire he entered "tenements and wobbly-kneed shanties" filled with people. "Day after blazing day I sat on rickety chairs, wash-tubs, ironing-boards, veranda railings, climbing creaking stairways . . . burrowing into blind but inhabited cubby-holes, hunting out squatters' nests of tin cans and dry-goods boxes hidden away behind the legitimate buildings." The living quarters he described as chiefly

> windowless, six-by-eight rooms, always a cheap, dirty calico curtain dividing the three-foot parlor in front from the five-foot bedroom behind, the former cluttered with junk . . . a black baby squirming naked in a basket of rags with an Episcopal prayerbook under its pillow. . . . Every inch of the walls was "decorated" . . . with pages of illustrated magazines or newspapers . . . the muscular imbruted likeness of a certain black champion rarely missing, frequently with a Bible laid reverently beneath it. Outside, before each room, a tin fireplace for cooking precariously bestrided the veranda rail.[7]

Sometimes he entered a "tumble-down hovel where three would seem a crowd", yielding up more than a dozen occupants.[8]

The Barracks

Each silver camp eventually consisted of bachelors' quarters (barracks), married quarters, labourers kitchens (for West Indians) or mess halls (for Europeans), separate bathhouses, toilets, and dry and wash rooms. Black labourers' latrines were outhouses, often located hundreds of yards away from the camps. Completely separate facilities were provided for black and European employees[9] and the various national groups were, as far as possible, housed separately.

The silver bachelors' barracks housed either forty or eighty men and measured thirty-five by fifty feet with flanking verandas. Instead of windows, the upper portions of the walls were left open for ventilation and the openings screened to keep mosquitoes out. Just below the sheet-iron roof ran a wooden platform or shelf reached by a ladder and stacked high with tin trunks, bundles and pressed-paper suitcases containing the worldly possessions of the men. Most men carried their money in leather belts worn around their waists next to their skin.

Camp life could get crowded and was entirely lacking in privacy. The men slept on cots hung in threes, one above the other, hanging on both sides of iron frames about seven feet high. Later covered with canvas, in the early days the cots were made of latticed metal work without bedding:[10] "we sleep on chain bunks   a pease of canvas tie with rope no mattress blanket sheet or piller jhus the cold cain bunk".[11] Fortunately barracks occupancy frequently fell below capacity.

Although some found camaraderie in camp life, one worker reflected what was, no doubt, the feeling of many: "There is no privacy or quiet in the old bachelor buildings, thirty or forty to a room. Some of the men are noisy at night and have no sense of decency. There ought to be cots instead of bunks on the sides where men have to sleep on top of each other." He added, "there is no sense in putting so many different races together – Jamaicans and Bims [Barbadians] and Martiniques in the same room. It is not right."[12]

Certain workers, however, did prefer the stability of the camps. In 1911, the subsistence officer noted that those remaining "are not 'floaters' or people who work irregularly or new arrivals . . . they are in fact old employees and men generally who work every day; generally speaking the most reliable and most industrious of the negro workmen".[13]

One night in 1906, H.G. de Lisser (editor of the Jamaica *Gleaner*) visited a camp and found in the darkness outside the long

Figure 7.4 Sleeping quarters for silver workers in barracks for seventy-two men (Panama Canal).

Figure 7.5 Cots hung one above the other on which the men slept, their personal belongings stored on shelves under the roof (Abbot, *Panama*, 344).

rows of houses scores of little fires where the men were cooking dinner: "here one is frying an egg; further on something in the nature of a stew is simmering in a pot". Inside the houses themselves, some were already in bed but others were engaged in other activities: one group of men sat around a box playing cards; one was playing softly on a flute.[14] Playing, that is, until the watchman knocked to signal lights out.

"THEY COOK THE LIFE OUT OF IT"

In the beginning, workmen were expected to prepare their own meals but many failed to do so, too tired out after a ten-hour working day and supplies were not easily obtained. The men's low efficiency was (according to the 1905 annual report) "attributed by the chief engineer in large part to the lack of proper nourishment".[15] Consequently, in 1907 the ICC began to provide meals for labourers in the camps, deducting thirty cents (gold) daily for three meals; confident that this food would enhance the worker's "efficiency as a productive unit".[16] The results were not quite as expected. In the first three months after camp kitchens were established, up to 7,000 were fed daily, but the number soon dwindled to 3,000 (out of 8,578 bachelor employees at the time).[17]

In a further effort to ensure a captive, reliable, and compliant workforce, the ICC issued a new order in June 1908 tying meal tickets to accommodation.[18] Employees reporting for the evening meals received camp checks enabling them to bunk in the barracks.[19] Police and watchmen checked every night. Workmen found without lodging checks were arrested and charged with loitering: the sentence was thirty days. Unsurprisingly, the labourers voted with their feet: sixteen hundred left ICC quarters immediately. The ICC complained that at the end of 1908, some thirty-three hundred more lived in the "bush" than in the previous year; in 1909 barrack occupancy fell by 40 per

Figures 7.6–7.7
Silver workers eating at ICC kitchens lined up for food, then had to find some place to eat as no provision was made for seating (Panama Canal).

Figure 7.8 Interior of the gold workers' mess house at Culebra, circa 1910 (Weir, *Conquest of the Isthmus*, 124).

cent. As the ICC was to discover, West Indians improvised ways of improving their lives, even within the confines of the Zone.

ICC planning for black workers' meals, for example, involved no seating. While Europeans had a "mess hall" and Americans a "dining room", the black workers' "kitchen" consisted of a long shed-like building open on one side with a counter running down its length. The labourers lined up, each clutching a tin mug, plate and cutlery purchased from the commissary. At the counter, he handed over his meal ticket (which varied in colour according to his department), and passed down the counter to have his plate filled. Unlike American and European workers, he was expected to eat wherever he could – along the side of a road, underneath a building or tree. The difficulties of finding a dry spot to sit and eat a meal during the rainy season can only be imagined and many options were downright dangerous: "I recall one workday two brothers by surname, Phillips were sitting under a dump truck train having lunch, after lunch they fell asleep and the engine coupled up and moved, that was the end of their lives."[20] At Culebra lumber yard, a similar accident involved three workmen who sat under a boxcar to eat lunch and then fell asleep during the two-hour break. An engineer moved the car, killing all three men. In another incident, the victim, a Chinese man, heard the engine start up and attempted to escape but his body was mangled in the wheels of the train. According to witness John Butcher, "His head was severed and I actually heard his voice cry out 'ya ya'."[21]

Other dangers lay in the quality of the meals. Food suppliers contracted by the ICC provided the cheapest possible meals prepared under the most careless conditions. Responding to a US Senate investigation of conditions in Panama, an American food supplier for 1905 and 1906 described how the cooks for the West Indians threw everything into one big kettle and boiled it. "Just the same as we do for our hogs out on the farm", he admitted. "The only difference I could see between the way they fed those negroes and the way I feed my hogs is that the food was put on a tin plate instead of in a trough."[22]

After endless complaints and discontent, the ICC established the kitchens with its own caterers in 1907. But food remained a problem. Menus followed standard US Army rations:

Breakfast: 5–5.30 a.m. Bread, cornmeal porridge, coffee
Lunch: 11.30–12.00 p.m. Bread, beef stew with vegetables, beans and rice, potatoes, tea, dessert
Dinner: 5–6 p.m. Bread, bean soup with doughboys, potatoes, roast beef, rice and beans, coffee and dessert.

Although these meals met nutritional requirements beyond what the workers consumed in their homeland, and no one complained about quantity, they did not satisfy men who believed from childhood that a real meal was "hard food" – yams, dasheen, sweet potatoes, breadfruit and other starches, perhaps with some fish or meat in a spicy sauce. When John Butcher first arrived from Barbados in 1906, he found the rice "hard enough to shoot deers", sauce spread over the rice and "a slab of meat which many men spent either an hour trying to chew or eventually threw away because it was too hard". The only satisfying items seem to have been bread and coffee.[23] In 1908, Grenadian Philip McDonald found garbanzo beans "like bullets", rice and kidney beans half cooked, and the water so bad "when you take a drink it was like a banana stain in your mouth".[24] Even when the ICC hired West Indian cooks, the men complained: "things don't taste right; they cook the life out of it. Some . . . don't like rice and won't eat potatoes."[25] Nevertheless, one worker described the food as "rough and regular". That, he said, "was the chief piece of tool which we use to dig Uncle Sam Canal   Uncl knows what he was doing he both kill Malaria and open up our appetite and get the work done."[26]

By 1911 the price of the meals fell to twenty-seven cents[27] and the common labourers' kitchens were abolished.[28] Food for the Europeans and the West Indians was prepared in the same kitchen and passed out to the West Indians from a service window on the side opposite to the Spaniards' mess hall. Such racial segregation at mealtimes – as at other times – was maintained even when a work crew was off in the jungle.[29]

As time passed, workers living outside of the camp could easily find locally grown yams, sweet potatoes and other foods of the island diet as well as supplies imported by the commissaries from Jamaica and Barbados.[30] West Indian women continued to offer cooked meals, as did the Chinese.

One increasingly popular solution to the food problem was to get a West Indian woman to keep house: "You pay her $10 to $12 when the pay car comes round every fortnight and buy her dresses and things", one worker narrated. But, he added, "some of the women don't know how to cook. They just fix up some little foolishness – fish balls and the like of that. A man can't work on such stuff."[31]

Some women made a living from cooking and washing for a number of bachelors. Undoubtedly some took advantage of their scarcity value, like the woman celebrated in the song called "No Man fuh Bounce pon Muh":

> I'm a gal who believe in sporting
> So uh must have lots of everything
> When the whistle blow fuh the first book issue
> No gal reach them locks before me
> Uh gets me books from John and Harry
> But Joe Jim and Jack
> Bring them home and gimme.[32]

The book referred to in the song was the coupon book which ICC and railroad workers used for purchases in the commissaries and the desirability of a man with such a book obviously persisted long after construction days.[33]

The Commissaries

The Panama Railroad Company had established a commissary at Colón, somewhat in the nature of a general store, some time before the American canal effort. In taking over the railroad, the ICC expanded the operation and by 1905 established commissaries all along the line. These department stores were eventually stocked with everything that the Zone dweller could possibly need; items were sold at a much lower price than at the stores in the Panamanian cities and, as the system of bulk buying became more efficient, than on the US mainland. The commissaries, after all, had a huge pool of captive purchasers.

Figure 7.9 Interior of a well-stocked commissary (Weir, *Conquest of the Isthmus*, 116).

In 1914, Canal Zone dwellers could purchase working trousers at $0.85 each, shoes at $2.50, sheets at $0.60 and bedspreads at $1.00. Salt pork could be had at $0.14 per pound, butter for $0.32 and oranges from Jamaica at $0.16 per dozen. Flour was $0.3 per pound, codfish $0.08 per pound, washing soap was $0.01. An iron double-bed could be had for $3.35.

No cash changed hands in the commissary. Workers purchased books of commissary tickets in various denominations, the money being deducted from their pay. A limit was placed on the number that could be bought at a time by each category of worker, the West Indians at the start being limited to books of $2.50. The "book" was at first a continuous length of paper accordion folded and marked off in coupons of various denominations. At the commissary, coupons would be torn off to cover purchases. George Martin described the novelty of having his first commissary book when he landed as a contract worker.[34]

> This gentleman said to us, "Boys," I am going to put you on your own . . . I am going to give you a $2.50 book where you will take to the Commissary and purchase what you want, every man in the gang were given a book for $2.50 so from there we started on our own . . . $2.50 book had been plenty in those days, they were in five cents bretts, to 2.50, it was called the tango . . . our lunch mostly in those days were bread, sardine, and ice cream, and at times for a change, we would have bread, corn-beef-hash, and never forget our ice cream.

For long afterwards the construction workers talked about the cheapness of things in those pre-war days. Despite the low salary, a man could easily feel like a king – or a big spender:

> If we order a $5.00 book, and in a day or two and that book does not show up, you are told to order again   Sometimes both orders would meet, and we would have two $5.00 book, $10.00   what to do with $10.00 in those days? Here is a story, it caught me once. I bought some of everything, shoes also, to do away with it, $10.00 would not finish. I bought a ham, at that time it look as big as I were, I paid $2.21, talking about ham, real lean, I took ham to work every day in order to have it finish, my associate and I ate ham for days.

Many years later, at an age when most things are dimmed by memory, this worker was still able to recall prices of items in the commissary some fifty years earlier:

> in I.C.C. days bought flour by the gallon, not the pound . . . the soap was only 4 cents a bar, but it would take a woman hand like Goliath to hold it, it was so big, not like today. The bread 3 to 4c each. Cod fish 4 to 8c per pound, the best; sugar by the 25 lbs bag, I try to remember the price, it had been 95c to $1.00 only. . . I bought Quaker Oats at 13c the tin, now it is over 29c; corn meal, 3c the pound, corn beef, 10 to 11c the tin, matches 5c the pack this was called Parrott matches

. . . Something to wear, in those days we bought pants as low as $1.00, silk shirts, the popular wear, we took advantage of this item, in those days we paid as high as 2.75, we could buy a two-piece suit for as high as $3.00 & change . . . construction days were better days, never to be seen again, the money was paid small, but we live big.

It was no wonder that many workers appeared so dandified on their days off and especially when they returned home to the West Indies, wearing three-piece suits, with walking canes and umbrellas, rings and gold watches on chains, their mouths gleaming with fresh gold teeth put in by the ICC dentists. Again, another generation back home in Jamaica could keep alive the old folk song which had been first sung about the French canal workers:

One two three four
Colón man a come
With him watch chain
A knock him belly
bam bam bam

Although "Panama Money" brought women flocking to the men on the isthmus as well as those who returned to the islands, not all women were seduced by the show. In Eric Walrond's short story "Panama Gold", Ella, the Barbadian countrywoman, weighs up her substance against that of shopkeeping Mr Poyer, the "Panama Man", who attempts to court her, and finds him wanting: "All dem bag o' flour yo' 'a' got, an' dem silk shut, an' dem gold teets, an' dem Palama hats, yo'a spote round heah wid – dem don't frighten me. I is a woman what is usta t'ings. I got me hogs an' me fowls an' me potatoes. No wooden foot neygah man can frighten me wit' he clothes or he barrels o' cologne."[35]

Yet so ingrained in West Indian culture was the iconic image of the flashy returnee that there were also songs mocking those who returned without Panama Money.

Come from Colón wid him big empty trunk,
Not a boot to him foot, not a ting to him front,
Rub him dung, in him Santampee
Give him a rum, can't even buy cawfee[36]

"Panama Man" from Barbados spelled it out in full:

Oh de Panama man 'ent got no money
Still de Panama man want love,
Wen de Panama man come back from sea
An' de Panama canal

Chorus
But 'e cahn get me
Widout de money
To buy me a taffeta dress!
If de Panama man gwine court wid me,
He gwine treat me like a queen. (*Rep.*)

Look de Panama man come home from sea
As skinny as a Church rat,
An' all he had in his grip fo' me
Was a wide-brim Panama hat.

When de Curacao man come back to Bim
He bring me a calico dress
When de Panama man come back to Bim
All he bring is de Spanish caress![37]

WOMEN ON THE ZONE

"It wouldn't be a feather weight of worth without a woman in it", said silver worker Reginald Beckford as he approvingly noted the arrival of West Indian women during construction days.[38]

The ICC's policy at the start held that the Canal Zone was no place for women. American nurses alone were encouraged to come, presumably hardened since many early recruits had served in far-flung places during the Spanish-American war. This official stance crumbled as, in the first few years, most American men refused to stay. West Indian workers allegedly threatened to quit if deprived of their women. The ICC began to encourage men on the gold roll to bring their wives, but the Zone was to remain a hyper-masculine world, all activities subordinated to the work of construction. Red-light districts flourished in the Republic.

By the time the Zone became fully organized, ICC-sponsored clubhouses and social organizations provided alternative entertainment for white workers. However, a separation clearly remained between college-educated, white-collar Americans in jobs as engineers, timekeepers or foremen, and the adventurers known as "huskies", "tropical tramps" or "roughnecks" who took on the rougher jobs on the gold roll and lived outside of American social conventions. In order to build a more settled community of men, the ICC encouraged wives and offered inducements to bachelors to marry. The policy of hiring women relaxed somewhat over time, and the census of 1912 showed 321 women employed by the ICC and Panama Railroad, of whom 251 were Americans. These women included nurses, teachers, stenographers and clerks. West Indian

Figures 7.10–7.13 (*Clockwise from top left*) "Making do" was the lot of poor working women in Panama as it was on the islands. Many West Indians in the Republic of Panama and the Canal Zone worked as washerwomen (7.10, Panama Canal; 7.11, Weir, *Conquest*, 48), as itinerant vendors (7.12, Panama Canal) and as bakers (7.13, colour painting by F.E. Wright, 1913, in Abbot, *Panama*, 177).

women teachers were hired from the start and were, like their men, among the elite of the silver workforce.

Little inducement existed for other West Indian women but significant numbers made their way to Colón as wives, relatives and other dependents of male workers. A great many single women arrived on their own. As Elizabeth Thomas-Hope points out, while upper-class migrations usually involve a family unit, the prevalence of household headship among lower-class West Indian women contributes to their independence, one which includes seeking migration opportunities. And – as we shall see from the Panama experience – it is frequently the woman who "spearheads the subsequent migration of other family members".[39]

Figure 7.14 West Indian and Panamanian washerwomen were regarded as "exotic" by visitors and many, such as this one, featured in the books and postcards of the era (Weir, *Conquest of the Isthmus*, 184).

While we do not know their marital status, West Indian women in Panama included teachers, midwives, hoteliers, businesswomen, secretaries and clerks. Patrick Bryan notes that in Jamaica by the end of the nineteenth century there was an increase in literacy among women, and women were dominating jobs requiring skills such as shorthand, typing and telegraph operation.[40] Some emigrant women would have brought such skills with them to Panama. The non-working wives of elite men such as doctors have left little trace of their lives in contemporary accounts. More note continued to be taken of women who were highly visible and ubiquitous, such as market and food vendors, and we know that other women worked as seamstresses, cooks, laundresses and in the sexual services.

However, we have no direct evidence of this latter activity except for the existence of red-light districts that flourished in Colón, Panama City and elsewhere attracting multiethnic women and clientele. Laura Putnam noted of Costa Rica (where many West Indian men and women had migrated from the 1870s during railway construction and the banana plantation boom) that "every evidence is that men preferred to pay women to do their laundry when they could afford it – and that they preferred to pay for more intimate comforts as well, rather than improvise on their own or with each other. Hot meals, sliced fruit, a close dance, and sex were just some of the goods and services that female migrants might profitably offer for sale in Limón." She pointed out that "in years when male laborers were earning 1.50 to 2.15 *colones* a day ($0.70 to $1.00) and skilled male artisans five *colones* at most, a washerwoman or cook earned up to two *colones* a day in Port Limón. Women who worked as prostitutes earned a good deal more, between one and five *colones* for a single sexual encounter at the turn of the century."[41]

The ICC records offer little information on women, and newspapers of the time ignored them, unless to note their transgressions. On the Zone, women appeared in judicial records if they landed in court and some were punished equally with their men, facing fines or imprisonment for offences ranging from domestic issues, flouting sanitary regulations, fighting, to using "indecent language". Women could also face arrest or deportation for suspected prostitution.

We do not often hear women's voices at any level, and few names of West Indian females during the construction era on the Zone have come down to us. Of the 112 entrants in the contest for best true stories during construction days, only two names are identifiably female. Louise Cramer (who collected "Songs of West Indian Negroes" in the 1940s) listed among her informants Mrs Sarah Humphrey, aged fifty, who recorded several songs which she had learned in Jamaica before coming to the Zone in 1910. During construction she lived in the old town of Empire. Cramer added in a footnote: "Mrs Humphrey described for us the thrilling moment when she stood on the bridge at Empire and watched the green water come swirling into the great cut." Also living at Empire was Mrs Viola Brathwaite, born in Barbados in 1896. She sang songs she learned in Barbados before coming to the Zone in 1909. A record of the Chinese in Panama[42] also takes note of "Miss Potts from St Thomas", a famous midwife of Colón.

Fictional women do appear: in Maryse Condé's novel *Tree of Life* (though subordinate to the male protagonist in Panama), and in Eric Walrond's short stories, including the abominable brown brothel keeper Miss Buckner in "The Palm Porch". Her clientele "from Colón to Cocoa Grove the pale faced folk who drank sumptuously in the bowl of life churned by her. . . . Machinists at Balboa, engineers at Miraflores, sun-burned sea folk. . . . All had words of beauty for the ardor of Miss Buckner's salon."[43] Her own light-skinned daughters of dubious ancestry cater to her white clientele, but she bemoans the fact that one of them has taken up with a "young mulatto, a Christian in the Moravian Church. He was an able young man, strong and honest, and wore shoes, but Miss Buckner almost went mad" because "he was but a clerk in the cold storage; sixty dollars a month – wages of an accursed silver employee. . . . Why, roared Miss Buckner, stockings could not be bought with that, much more take care of a woman accustomed to 'foxy clothes an such'."[44]

And the first novel written about West Indians in Panama – by Jamaican journalist and novelist H.G. de Lisser – has a woman protagonist, Susan Proudleigh, who emigrates with one man to try her luck in Colón during construction days (for whom she "keeps house") and ends up marrying another who dies in an accident, enabling her to return to Jamaica a well-off woman. Susan's sojourn reveals what life was like for poor women who aspired to "respectability" and how this was linked to male attachment, although her sister and aunt do keep their independence by running a laundry service, hiring someone to do the pickup and delivery in order to protect their status.[45]

Many West Indian women worked as maids for white women on the Zone and many a memoir of Zone life is littered with anecdotes of these maids who, like some of their male counterparts, were at first completely lacking in skills or training and unfamiliar with even the most elementary appliance in the

American-style kitchens. It was in the domestic environment that the clash of cultures, of colour, of class, probably became most pronounced. If the American boss was amused or exasperated by the accents and customs of his West Indian workmen, his wife at home was finding it equally difficult to comprehend the accent, inflection, or placement of "h's" in the speech of the black woman who toiled in her kitchen or minded her children. And the black woman in her turn seemed to have found the accents of Louisiana or Kentucky as incomprehensible as the appliances in the kitchen. Maids on the Zone earned $12.00 to $15.00 per month, though some might work for $10.00 and a good cook could get $20.00. Payment to maids in the Republic was about $2.50 per month.[46] "Good cooks" in Jamaica at the time were earning twenty-four shillings a month, or $6.00.

Some maids worked for years with the same families and sometimes bossed their employers around, especially young brides who themselves were new to everything. Zone memoirs by women are often condescending as they complain about their domestics. Sue Core at least demonstrated some humour in her *Maid in Panama*, a collection of anecdotes on the subject. While the jokes were mainly at the expense of West Indian women and their ignorance of American ways, dietary requirements or kitchen equipment (and, above all by their island tongues), some stories also demonstrate that these women possessed a strong sense of their own self and knew their value in the smooth running of the Zonian home. Their insights were far more astute than their employers realized. Sue Core recounts how two maids met, one boasting of a grand dinner party held at her employers' house on the previous night.

"The governor and his laidy wuz there, and a ambassador and some gin'rals and adm'rals and other fine laidies and gentl'men."

The other enviously asked, "Jus' whut does fine peoples . . . talk about when them gits together like that?"

"Us!" the other replied.[47]

Equally self-assured was the maid's response to her white employer, who pointed out that her housecleaning did not keep pace with her culinary prowess: "I specks you right, Madam," she said cheerfully, "but you cyan't have everyt'ing, you know. You never gits good biscuits and clean corners from the same maid!"[48]

The first American women were daughters or wives of canal workers, nurses for the hospital and teachers. They, too, experienced the hardships of the early days before the Zone was organized into a comfortable white enclave. Some of them shared their memories of early life on the Zone in a 1976 article titled "Men Dug the Canal . . . but Women Played a Vital Role".[49] When they first came, "Anything with four walls, a roof and a floor was considered living quarters." Even as late as 1910, "home" was uncertain and precarious as the construction overwhelmed town after town. Mrs Bruce Sanders came as a bride in 1910: she and her husband moved thirteen times the first year. While living at Gorgona they were notified on a Monday morning that they must be out of the house by one o'clock: the next time she saw the house it was halfway down the banks of the excavation. "If you didn't have the pioneer spirit," Mrs Sanders concluded, "you just left."

She has never had a complex;
Inhibitions? Not a chance!
She's serenely set the tempo
Of her life to circumstance.

Figure 7.16 Sue Core put the strong black woman on the cover of her book *Maid in Panama*. While the anecdotes inside reflected the mockery and exasperation of their gold employers and patrons, the book's frontispiece acknowledged the strength of these women with the lines below the image (Sue Core, *Maid in Panama*, frontispiece).

She it was who noted how the dynamite blasts shook the whole house and made her cakes fall. "A cake would either fall flat or spill out into the bottom of the oven." So she baked "upside down biscuits".[50] Others found housekeeping in the early years "almost as much an adventure as digging the canal", a constant battle with ants, roaches, and spiders, with mud, rain, fevers, and foraging for food.[51] Like all Zone dwellers, living as they did in the towns along its edge, they could not escape the overwhelming presence of the "big ditch", from the constant dynamite blasts resounding everywhere, the rain and the mud in the wet season, the constant dust in the dry. A favourite pastime for women and children was walking to the edge of the cut to witness the pace of construction, running the risk of being hit by trains or spattered with missiles from a "dobie" shot.

Figure 7.17 West Indian women on the Zone kept families together, stretched the husband's paycheque and groomed the children, imparting values and setting high standards for education and deportment. Mrs Georgina Harry, pictured with her daughters Elvira and Sara, might have been typical of educated West Indians on the Zone. A schoolteacher like her husband, Gervaise Verner Harry, she travelled with him to Panama in 1907 and spent the rest of her life there. Mr Harry worked in various capacities for the ICC and from 1922 was a teacher in the Canal Zone coloured school system, becoming in 1931, shortly before his death, inspector of schools. The Harrys, like many others in Panama, sent their son back home to Jamaica to be educated at Calabar College. Gervaise Valentine (Val) Harry had an outstanding academic career and went on to become a leading doctor in Jamaica. (Courtesy of Dr Elizabeth Harry.)

Sometimes seemingly small things could prove extremely trying. For one teacher it was the changing of shoes several times a day during the rainy season. "Teachers would board the train and before reaching Gatun would change to boots to walk through the mud to the schoolhouse, then change to shoes and then back to boots when it was time to go home. It was a bothersome chore considering the high buttoned shoes of the day." But, as the chief nurse noted, after the first two years of hardships, "we were surrounded by all the modern comforts and conveniences. Telephones buzzed, electric lights were flashed on, and we recognised ourselves as only a part of an ideal community."[52]

We can only infer from these accounts what life might have been like for West Indian women, coping with greatly inferior living conditions and wages. Although life improved for everyone as the Zone became sanitized and organized and the white families were provided with comfortable homes and opportunities for socializing, life never became "ideal" for the silver workers. Nevertheless, it was the women of the silver workers who held their families together, stretched the fathers' salaries to make ends meet, inculcated in their children the values they brought from home, and groomed them for a better life.

Zone Families

By 1908 the number of women on the Zone had increased, though the proportion was still far less than two to one. There were 24,717 black males and 10,068 black females in the census of that year. As silver worker Jules LeCurrieux admonishes us many years later,

> Just recant and think of the life of pioneers of this Big Ditch . . . the 1903 to 1908 gang   Now here comes a little improvement   the West Indian Negro women began to immigrate here, then the poor old bastards found themselves wives of their tribes and began to live like human beings and not beasts, or slaves, they found someone to cook them a decent meal, to wash their clothes, some one to be a companion, and then to find a clean and decent place to sleep, and started a new generation of West Indian Panamanians.[53]

But the sexual imbalance continued throughout construction years. By 1912, the number of women on the Zone had dropped to 8,521 against 22,427 males, a fall probably due to the depopulation of Zone towns as the canal construction encroached. (See table 7.2.) In Colón, however, the ratio was similar: 22,946 black males to 8,579 females. Among the white population, the male-female ratio was even greater, 4,175 white females to 14,387 white males on the Zone.

One aspect of West Indian life that foreigners often disparagingly noted was

Table 7.1 West Indian Population by Nationality on the Canal Zone, 1908

Total population of the Zone	50,000	
Total employed by ICC and PRR	24,963	
Total white	14,635	
Black	34,785	
Chinese	583	
West Indies Origin	**Total on Zone**	**Employed by ICC and PRR**
Antigua	634	533
Barbados	6,483	5,625
Bermuda	7	6
British Guiana	147	91
British Honduras	6	5
Dominica	65	40
Grenada	561	344
Jamaica	8,418	3,535
Montserrat	314	254
Nevis	20	16
St Kitts	81	70
St Lucia	1,273	452
St Vincent	181	150
Tobago	6	3
Tortola	1	1
Trinidad	410	246

Source: Canal Record, 26 August 1908.

what they considered the loose morals of West Indians who cohabited and had children without benefit of marriage. On the Zone itself, cohabitation without marriage was forbidden. While most West Indian men tried to escape communal living in the bachelor camps, there was a great demand for married quarters on the Zone and an almost continuous shortage of such housing. Only a small percentage of married West Indians were accommodated, as shown in table 7.3.

The small number of children can be attributed to the fact that the married population of the Zone consisted mainly of newlyweds,[54] as inducements were offered to white bachelors to marry and contribute to the stability of the white Zone community. On marriage, the gold roll bachelor was immediately provided with attractive, spacious furnished quarters.

Blacks, on the other hand, were forced into marriage if they got caught cohabiting, but marriage was not otherwise encouraged since the labourers were regarded as essentially transient; low priority was given to the provision of married quarters for them and when these were made available, they were little better than the barracks. Life here was also precarious as when silver men lost their jobs on the Zone, they and their families had to immediately vacate

Table 7.2 West Indians on the Canal Zone by Country of Birth, 1912

Country	Total	Male	Female
British West Indies			
Anguilla	1	1	–
Antigua	879	706	173
Bahamas			
Acklin Is.	4	4	–
Cat Is.	9	9	–
Andros Is.	6	6	–
Exuma	1	1	–
(Long Cay) Fortune Is.	277	275	2
Inagua	5	5	–
New Providence	147	133	14
Watling	11	11	–
Total Bahamas	460	444	16
Barbados	9,699	7,955	1,744
Bermuda	17	17	–
British Guiana	454	359	95
British Honduras	18	14	4
Caicos	1	1	–
Dominica	106	83	23
Grand Cayman	23	19	4
Grenada	1,056	818	238
Jamaica	12,204	8,132	4,072
Montserrat	493	378	115
Nevis	136	124	12
St Croix	1	1	–
St Kitts	158	139	19
St Lucia	1,080	635	445
St Thomas	54	35	19
St Vincent	469	421	48
Tobago	9	9	–
Tortola	5	4	1
Trinidad	601	449	152
Turks Islands	34	33	1
Total BWI	**27,958**	**20,777**	**7,181**
Dutch			
Curaçao	14	14	–
Dutch Guiana	3	3	–
St Marten	4	4	–
Saba	1	1	–
Total Dutch	**22**	**22**	**–**

Table 7.2 continues

Table 7.2 West Indians on the Canal Zone by Country of Birth, 1912 (cont'd)

Country	Total	Male	Female
French			
French Guiana	7	6	1
St Martin	5	5	–
Guadeloupe	552	465	87
Martinique	1,840	1,515	325
Total French	**2,404**	**1,991**	413
Panama*	6,850	3,430	3,420
Canal Zone*	4,615	2,315	2,300

*Would have included children born to West Indians after 1904
Source: *Census of the Canal Zone*, 1 February 1912 (Mount Hope: ICC Press, 1912).
Note: The census distinguished between those born on the Canal Zone before 26 February 1904 when the treaty between Panama and the United States was ratified and those born after. These numbers for most West Indians were small and are included in the aggregate figures above. The only significant numbers of West Indian born on the Canal Zone prior to 1904, were as follows:
    Jamaica: 1,338 males and 579 females
    St Lucia: 194 males and 105 females
    Barbados: 62 males and 5 females

Table 7.3 A Canal Zone Family 1909 (Occupancy of Married Quarters)

	Men	Women	Children	Total
American	1,416	1,458	1,398	4,272
European	317	333	397	1,047
Negro	1,018	1,024	1,014	3,056
Total	2,751	2,815	2,809	8,375

Source: *Canal Record*, 27 January 1909.

the premises. Thousands were increasingly forced out of their homes as the canal neared completion and the entire west bank was cleared; Panamanians and West Indian settlers were also forced off large tracts of land for military reasons.

Married quarters in the "coloured" section resembled the barracks, a set of long narrow buildings up to three stories high, with railed verandas in front and rear running the full length of each building. Each family was assigned an apartment of two rooms. The toilet was in a separate building. Cooking was done on the communal veranda.[55] These kitchens were a striking feature of the Zone: "Perched on the rails of the balustrades, at intervals of 20 feet, and usually facing a door leading into the building are boxes of corrugated iron

Figures 7.18–7.19 Quarters for the silver workers at Cristóbal circa 1906 (Panama Canal).

about 3 feet high, the top sloping upward like one side of a roof and the inner side open. These are the kitchens – one to each family. Within is room for a smouldering fire of soft coal, or charcoal, and a few pots or frying pans. Here the family meal is prepared."[56] This type of living arrangement was also copied in the terminal cities, except that the buildings there were usually several stories higher. Traveller Winifred James[57] remarked that the train leaving Colón ran through "the negro settlement" where the houses ranged up on the left side of the railway line. On the verandas and balconies,

Figure 7.20 Silver housing by the railroad track in Colón (Abbot, *Panama*, 343).

"everything happens", the domestic lives of those living in these buildings laid open to the passengers, though, from the dwellings, only the children seemed to take notice of the trains.

The law that only legally married couples could cohabit on the Zone was rigidly enforced. Unmarried couples found together were taken off to jail and fined. "Lewd and lascivious behaviour" was the charge. In one sample year (1908) there were 131 arrests on this charge. A worker amusingly describes one such incident:

> One of the men leave the camp go the bush in Mandinga to sleep   12 o'clock midnight police knock at the room door   open the door   go in   you married no   come out put yer shoes un to go jail   in the morning   court house at Empire judge say you married   no sir   12 midnight too late to go   Sir I live in the camp

judge say dont say camp say quarters   I go for my pot   The court laught   too late for that $10 and the woman $10.[58]

When the law was first passed in 1906, in three months 110 West Indian couples rushed to get married. On one occasion, at Empire, eleven couples were hauled off to jail for living together without benefit of marriage. A total of 264 marriage licences were issued in five days and 223 marriages performed; at one stage the municipal judge performed forty-six marriages in forty-five minutes.[59]

A worker who didn't think much of these marriages complained, "you get fine and confine   that was the law   men and women would run for their lives through the bush   if caught go jail pay a fine and get married   many people get married for six months but it did not last for their was no love they just went for a short time but bad luck catch them so marriage did not last but it was the law of the Canal Zone dont stand for bad life."[60]

Some of these workers had wives and children back home. One murder case involving a West Indian was over this cause and led to a Barbadian sentenced to death by hanging. He had lived for two years with a woman on the isthmus when his wife from the island suddenly arrived. He moved in with his wife but was subsequently convicted of killing her with arsenic. The first execution in the Zone in 1903 was also of a Barbadian man for the murder of a woman, and later there were several such domestic cases involving West Indians.[61]

Wives coming in search of errant husbands seem not to have been uncommon; the mother of writer Eric Walrond is one who had done so, and his story, "Tropic Death", also deals with the subject.[62] Nor was the incidence of double families in Panama and back home so unusual. Such duplicity took its toll on all sides. A Jamaican family memoir recalls an uncle absent for twenty years without supporting his family. On his return (amid rumours of another family in Colón), he was rejected not only by his wife but by the extended family. He went off to live by himself and remained a lonely outsider until he died.[63] One can only speculate on how frequently such situations might have arisen, especially for those who returned without "Panama gold". Sometimes the reverse happened. Men with new wealth could now acquire mates of a much higher social standing or desirability, effectively rejecting the women and children they had left behind.[64]

The Martinique Women

Perhaps the strictness with which the marriage rule was enforced reflected not simply Anglo-Saxon norms but arose from an incident in early construction days when the ICC attempted to lessen the sexual imbalance among its black

Figure 7.21 A Martinique woman on the Canal Zone. (Courtesy of William P. McLaughlin, www.czimages.com.)

Figure 7.22 The French islanders were also favourites of photographers, such as this lady wearing her traditional dress; a postcard titled "Canal laborer's wife" (postcard, author's collection).

workers and triggered off a scandal in Washington. This was "the case of the Martinique women" which Jamaican governor Alexander Swettenham had thrown in the face of the canal emissary seeking to recruit Jamaicans.

In December 1905, a US senator charged in the Senate that women were being imported into the Zone from the island of Martinique for "immoral" purposes. The charges were based on correspondence in the New York *Herald* that a "cargo" of women had been brought to Colón on one of the ICC vessels to be distributed up and down the Zone among the labourers. A furore ensued, in which the morals of black West Indians as a whole were freely discussed, or "Jamaicans" as the *Herald* and most other people chose to call them all. The *Herald* claimed that its correspondents had interviewed heads of the various churches in Panama, and that the churchmen collectively deplored the bringing of these women to the Canal Zone and demanded that they be deported forthwith.[65]

The scandals that had overtaken the French haunted the ICC and the American government; it was believed that somehow high living and licentiousness had contributed to their disaster. Consequently, avoiding scandal became an unwritten rule for the ICC, especially with the attention of the world's press focused on the canal. The explanation for the debacle about the "cargo" made it all the way to the Oval Office. The ICC claimed that it had brought 283 women from Martinique following promises to the labourers to have their wives join them. Most were wives, they said, "a majority . . . beyond the age of thirty. This was done for the purpose of getting elderly settled women who would be, or likely to be, good and reliable servants on reaching the Isthmus."[66] Alarmed, members of the Senate continued to investigate, acquiring affidavits from more than 150 of the women who were forced to swear before a duly appointed ICC official as to their marital status, employment and moral behaviour. These responses were sent to the appropriate congressional committee. The issue was eventually forgotten.

One of the Martinique women interviewed by newspapermen in 1906 said that many had been leaving Martinique because they were afraid "since the great mountain burst", a reference to the eruption of Mount Pelée in 1902 which had completely destroyed the town of St Pierre and killed 29,933 persons. "So when an American came and told us that we girls could all get good wages in Panama, and that he would take us for nothing, a lot of us wanted to go." The women travelled as deck passengers. Some were married and most were her age (twenty-five). "I only saw three or four over thirty, but you can't always tell, can you? We were five days on the ship and we all had to be vaccinated before we landed at Colón. We got to Colón in the morning and in half an hour we were off the ship and on the train. They put us off at different places and gave us board for a few days." Ninety of the women got off at her stop (Bas Obispo) but there were jobs for only sixteen. She could not say what became of the rest. She, like many others, at first made her living as a washerwoman, sharing with her brother a six-by-ten-foot room at Chagres. Then she worked as a maid in a doctor's house, earning ten dollars a month.[67]

Whatever were the motives of the ICC in bringing these women to the Zone, they survived the slur on their characters and remained a picturesque addition to the Panama scene. Women from the French islands of Martinique and Guadeloupe attracted notice not only because of their language but also for their dress. Thousands of men and women from these islands had gone to the isthmus from the time of the French canal construction, and several thousand more came during the US era. The women – at least the older ones – maintained their creole manner of dress, which made them an exotic addition to the Zone landscape, especially those who perambulated as higglers. One American woman noticed

> a picturesque woman approaching. She was tall and stately. Her stiffly starched skirt was long and full. The train was daintily tucked up at her waist, showing an immaculate white petticoat with a wide ruffle of embroidery and high-button shoes with pointed toes. The basque was tight-fitting and round her neck she wore a gay kerchief. Another was perched on her proud head, intricately folded – its ends

standing up like two little birds about to fly from their nest. She carried a basket on her arm and, on her head, she nonchalantly balanced a set of rusty scales.

"Bonjour, Madame," she greeted me.[68]

Winifred James recorded an unforgettable scene the day after the canal opened in 1914, shortly after the declaration of war in Europe. With the tricolour waving and the Marseillaise playing, uniformed former canal workers from Martinique and Guadeloupe were boarding the train in Panama City for Colón where they would embark to fight for France.

> Beside them walked their women, the older ones wearing the gaudy bandana of the Martinique woman, which is the gayest of all the turbans. They were, men and women alike, smiling a little in a hypnotized way, caught up in the trance of the music and the flying colours. . . . Every now and then the band would strike up, and from the station came the sound of singing, for whenever they played the *Marseillaise* or *Rentrons a la Patrie* all the people sang.[69]

French islanders also added to the creation of multinational, multicultural West Indian families on the isthmus where the meeting and mingling was not just of the waters but of people from the hemisphere whose descendants became a "pepperpot" or "sancocho" of those who came (to name two popular dishes that are a melange of many ingredients). West Indians from all over were to bond in friendship and kinship networks that would reach back to the islands and also to other places to which emigrants went. Citing the case of Costa Rica, Laura Putnam notes that "it was not unusual for a family to include relatives in Kingston, Cuba, Bocas del Toro, Colón and Limón. A man from Nicaragua might run into a sister in Limón, an uncle on Costa Rica's Pacific Coast, and a former lover in Sixaola, and he would certainly find former work companions at all those sites."[70] This situation would be replicated in other places, including the United States to which many later travelled.

At times, however, such multinational mixing created problems for children and grandchildren of these unions, especially when Panama later refused them citizenship. Some of the French islanders lacked birth certificates and were unable to claim French citizenship, such as the Laval family from Martinique, born in Trinidad, where their family had emigrated before going on to Panama, but whose births were not registered.[71]

Simon Clarke, who became a noted educator in Jamaica, provides other examples of citizenship problems. His father was a Jamaican who worked on the Panama Canal, as was his maternal grandfather, who met his Martiniquan grandmother in St Lucia and brought her to Panama. Although his parents met and married in Panama and he was born there, Clarke was denied Panamanian citizenship, like other first- and second-generation West Indian children. His entire family eventually moved to Jamaica, where they would be visited by immigration authorities who warned them their status was not legal; their claim to Jamaican citizenship was confirmed only by the new constitution of 1962 at Jamaica's independence due to their father having been born there.[72] Despite such complications, it was in the migrant communities in places such as Panama that true West Indian bonds were forged.

EDUCATION AND THE EXPERIENCE OF CHILDREN

West Indian children brought to Panama or born there were to experience other difficulties, not least the effect on their sense of identity and notions of "home". Some were put to work at an early age. Even those men and women who were in steady employment seemed to have found it hard to make ends meet and child labour was a feature of life, with children as young as five or six working as household helpers. On the canal, many youngsters were employed as "water boys". Jeremiah Waisome was twelve or thirteen when he first started working; another was fourteen-year-old Alfred Mitchell, whose mother brought him to Panama in 1904. "Mother was working and fortunately I got a job as a water-boy on the Panama Rail Road docks, the same year Mother took me on the lines, to a place called Bas-Obispo Canal Zone. I worked there carrying water for a drilling gang."[73]

Edward Howell (who was to work for the Panama Canal for forty-seven years) also started out as a water boy "lugging big buckets equipped with drinking dippers to and from the spring in Paraiso, up hill and down hill, over the railroad tracks in the canal prism and on slippery boardwalk streets in the towns. The boards were equipped with wooden cleats to make them a little less slippery after the tropical rains." One compensation was that the foreman liked him and paid him to bring Scotch as well as water on his rounds.[74] Cecil

Figure 7.23 Childhood on the Canal Zone for gold workers was an idyllic time. This 1915 photo shows children at play in Balboa. (Photo contributed by Ron Armstrong, courtesy of William P. McLaughlin, www.czimages.com.)

Haynes decided on his own to seek a job at age fourteen to help out his family (and was to continue working for the next "71 years, six months and 30 days", as he explained to an interviewer). Asked about his childhood and his fondest memories, Haynes recalled going to meet the fishing boats and bringing back fish for his family, but there was little more to say. Since he began working as a child, "my mind and everything was more intent in doing something to help myself and to help my father to raise us . . . going out to work at an early age was like an institution for me", he said, referring to adults in the workplace ready to teach him and his willingness to learn.[75] This might well have been the case for many others, since fourteen was the age at which most children in the islands and in Panama left school in those days, the boys to seek employment or an apprenticeship. Even when their labour might not have been necessary for the family, some youngsters were dazzled by the fact of their companions earning money and dropped out of school to seek employment. In any case, the Canal Zone school could take these children only so far.

Education

Canal Zone schools for the children of silver workers could not have been attractive. A survey as late as the 1940s found "the coloured schools", as they were called, to consist of dark one-room buildings, poorly ventilated and lacking adequate sanitary facilities. During construction, children made their way to school early in the morning and returned late afternoon on crowded labour trains. Teachers from the West Indies tried their best under conditions of extreme overcrowding (an average of 115 students in classes up to 1909), and impoverishment of both curriculum and facilities. Students used cast-off books from the white schools. While American children were offered the equivalent

Figure 7.24
Children of silver workers at school in Culebra, 1905 (Panama Canal).

Figure 7.25 Children work in the school garden at Empire, Canal Zone, 1910 (Panama Canal).

of a US stateside education up to high school, black children were offered elementary schooling only, with no vocational training; the curriculum was limited to reading, writing, spelling, the fundamentals of arithmetic, hygiene and language.

When the United States took over in 1904, a census of school-age children showed 1,936 children in the villages within a radius of one and a half miles of the railroad. The majority – 1,045 – were between the ages of six and ten and the rest eleven to fifteen. Less than half of the children (898) could read and write. Many of them were of Jamaican parentage.[76] The lack of literacy was not surprising since all official and some private schools in Panama were closed down during the almost continuous civil wars of 1899 to 1903.[77]

By act number 8, September 1904, the ICC established a school system on the Canal Zone, and in December 1905 appointed a director of schools. On 1 February of the following year, the ICC formally assumed responsibility for education in the Zone, including seven schools conducted by Panamanian municipalities. The ICC immediately instituted separate schools for black and white children. Of thirty schools established, four were reserved for white children only. Eighteen hundred children were enrolled, of whom 10 per cent were white. According to Michael Conniff, "Few people at the time realized that West Indians and Panamanians, but not Americans, paid the taxes that sustained all of the Zone schools. In other words, the nonwhites paid for the whites' quality education while their own children got inferior schooling. One could never point to the early Canal Zone schools as an example of the civilizing influence of American imperialism. They were merely an instrument of social control paid for by the controlled."[78] Thirty-four teachers were employed: fourteen from the United States, one from Panama and nineteen from Jamaica. Teachers were assigned exclusively to children of their own race. The labels "white" and "coloured" would continue to be applied to the schools in the Zone until 1954 when, following the schools desegregation decision of the US Supreme Court, the euphemisms "American" and "Latin American" were substituted.

The first "coloured" school under the new system opened at Corozal on 2 January 1906, but was closed in a little over four months due to inadequate preparation, supplies and enrolment, although schools in other villages opened in the meantime.[79] After 1906, school enrolment climbed, but poor attendance continued to be a problem, partly stemming from the shifting labour on the construction site and the frequently uncertain location of home.[80] By 1909, West Indian children enrolled at Canal Zone schools were from Jamaica (415), St Lucia (73), Barbados (61), Grenada (24), Trinidad (9), Demerara (5), Antigua (5), St Vincent (2), and British Honduras (1). By 1911 there were fifteen schools for coloured children with a total enrolment of fifteen hundred and a staff of teachers who were regarded as "first class" by the canal authorities.[81]

Teachers from Jamaica, Barbados and Antigua provided the backbone of the Zone system, and they tried to improve the lives of their students by augmenting the curriculum with vocational training and extra-curricular activities. George Westerman, a notable son of construction era immigrants,[82] recorded the names and activities of many of those who were dedicated pioneers in every sense of the word. Most were graduates of Mico Teacher Training Colleges.[83] Arthur B. Kinnimouth, assigned to Las Cruces school in 1906, had to travel by train then by boat to reach his classroom. John A. Parchment, another Mico graduate, rose early each school day to catch the six o'clock labour train at Colón, the only way to get to his school at Gatún, where he spent the next hour and a half in the schoolyard until the janitor arrived to open the door. Like other teachers on the silver roll, he was paid for only nine months of the year[84] and had to find other ways of "making do" in the summer months. Some teachers worked on their cultivations, others went back to the islands; in the summer of 1913 Parchment worked for the construction company that was building the lock gates.

Alfred Osborne went on to become a notable educator and community leader in the post-construction years, but his own early schooldays with his father Reverend David Osborne, who had come from Antigua as a teacher in 1912, were trying times. "I used to accompany my father on those daily rides on the labour train," he recalled.

Figure 7.26 Alfred Osborne, one of the second generation of teachers of West Indian background. Educated in America, he became a significant force in improving educational opportunities for descendants of silver workers in Panama.

The Lives They Lived, 1904–1914   **257**

Father was up at 4.00 a.m.; my mother woke me or tried to wake me fifteen minutes later. It was a difficult job for her to dress a six year old boy who was fast asleep. By 4.50 father and I had breakfasted and we were soon on our precarious way through the dangerous Culebra Cut, where we boarded the labour train for a rough ride to Balboa. We invariably arrived at La Boca at 6 o'clock long before the town was up. At 5 p.m. we made the return trip to Culebra.[85]

Other notable construction-era teachers remembered in a tribute organized by Westerman included James C. Webster, who came in 1910 armed with rubber boots, umbrella and a stock of home remedies. In 1936 he was awarded the Centennial Gold Medal by the Miconian Association for Meritorious Service, the first to someone whose achievement lay outside Jamaica. His two sisters also taught in Canal Zone schools, Mrs A.B. Kipling, the first female West Indian teacher, and Miss Hannah Webster, who came later. George B. Parker, another Mico graduate from Jamaica, became principal of Cristóbal School. He sent his five children back to Jamaica for high school, and his eldest son returned as a teacher in Silver City. Several of the men who came as teachers were to be later ordained as ministers in the Anglican and other churches.

From the French era, teachers had also come from the West Indies to run private schools, and such schools continued to provide an alternative to the segregated schools, offering post-primary education for the Zone as well as the Republic of Panama. Parents who could manage to do so also sent their children back home for their schooling. Calabar College in Kingston had been advertising for students since the French canal era, and like Catholic schools such as St George's College and the Convent of the Immaculate Conception, offered boarding facilities. For several generations, these Jamaican schools also attracted Spanish-speaking students who wanted to learn English from all over Latin America.

As in the West Indies, churches were involved in education in Panama. In 1904, the Wesleyan Church School was the main private school for English-speaking children, having been established in 1883. By August 1904, several Mico College graduates (including L. Horatio Barclay and J.T. and C.J. Barton) had opened schools.[86] Between 1904 and 1907 there was also in Colón a private academy, managed by a graduate of the "Scots Academy" of Montego Bay, which provided not only a "thorough English education" but also elements of Greek, Latin, Euclidian geometry and algebra. There were as well the Colón English School, the Bethel Private School, the Baptist Church School and the Colón Commercial High School, among others. It was hard to keep track of these schools both on the Zone and in the Republic since they seemed to have changed names and ownership with some frequency.[87]

On the Zone itself, private schools were allowed to continue until 1914. The Zonian superintendent of schools was critical of them, alleging poor discipline. In 1910 he claimed that "the lack of proper administrative measures in the private schools for colored children has greatly hampered the successful operation of the colored public schools on the Zone. In a number of instances, pupils have left the Zone public schools to go over to the private schools, solely to secure freedom from disciplinary restraint."[88]

Private schools seem to have been of varied quality. In 1919, the Panama Health Office made a survey of all schools in Panama City. The majority were found to be overcrowded, especially the West Indian schools.[89] As late as 1938, the inspector of primary education spoke of children in schools who could not write because they had neither paper nor pencil, and who could not read because they had no books.[90]

Although the private schools made a valiant effort to provide West Indian children with an education, they were certainly not preparing them to be citizens of the Republic. A survey of West Indian schools in Panama as late as 1948 regarded the West Indians in private schools as special pupils because "they do not know the language, the history, and the geography of . . . [Panama]".[91] In short, the West Indian schools – like the churches – remained the principal media through which British West Indian culture was focused and transmitted. With the rising tide of Panamanian nationalism in the 1920s, increasing pressure was brought to bear on private schools to make the Spanish language an integral part of the curriculum. It should be noted that, at the same time, there was severe discrimination against allowing West Indians to enter the Panamanian public schools. The children, like their parents, were caught up in the problems of third-country labour. The private schools nevertheless provided a bridge between the children and the culture of their parents and were the centres of artistic and cultural activities for the communities as well as agents for social control. At times, the teacher might overextend his authority, as the writer of a letter carried in the *Colón Starlet* in 1905 believed. It was from "one who had been on the Isthmus 18 years" and commented on a recent "educational entertainment" offered at the Culebra schoolhouse. The writer praised the chairman's "elegant" speech at the close of the entertainment, "relative to the incentives which he hoped this will give the interested parents". This was highly appreciated, said the writer, "but his reference to their drinking less rum was unnecessary".[92]

The role played by West Indian teachers in Panama was similar to that played by teachers back home in inculcating manners and values to those in their charge, along with the three Rs. Their manner was strict and sometimes authoritarian, but they nevertheless left countless adults acknowledging the profound influence of these early role models in shaping them for life. Where the teacher was the parent, the strictness also permeated the home, as Cecil Haynes recalled with fondness his schoolteacher mother's high standards and the lessons he retained all his life: "she's always insisted that she wanted me to be a gentleman". She herself set the tone, he recalled: "she had . . . the old English customs in her, she dressed well and when she's going to church with her prayerbook and whatnot and her hat and so . . . and her gloves, very, very stately . . . even in her coffin when she died it portrayed, you could see it, that's a fact".[93]

LIFE IN THE REPUBLIC

The popular image of Panama in the Caribbean is still that of "Colón Man", and Panama of construction days a place where "money grew on trees". While the move to Panama contributed greatly to the development of the islands and to those individuals who managed to better themselves, the reality for many in Panama was to be poverty, ill-health and destitution.

At the start of construction, the society was composed mainly of young men and the way the new arrival conducted himself often determined his future success or failure. The minute the young worker arrived, he became prey to rapacious landlords, speculators and con-men who were prepared to accommodate him in every way. Those who were brought on contracts were immediately whisked off to the Zone's bachelor camps, but many soon chafed under rules there and left to live in the Zone towns and the terminal cities where speculators hurriedly threw up huge frame tenements.

Within a few months in 1906, the *Colón Starlet* reported that "a dozen large three-story buildings have been erected and each one of them has a saloon on the ground floor . . . about 60 or 80 men board and live on the upper floors of the houses. The saloons below have a sufficient number of patrons to furnish a living from the sale of liquors for the men who rent the buildings."[94] The men crowded together to save money, and one of these tenements was soon so overcrowded it became known as the "Ants Nest". These Panama tenements consisted of buildings of several stories that might sometimes occupy a whole city block. In 1907 construction of new frame buildings or remodelling of old ones of more than two stories was prohibited and the larger buildings were built of masonry, but fire remained a hazard. Smaller buildings had an average of thirty-eight rooms, the larger ones had seventy-five.[95] Each apartment was one room off a dingy corridor. Each was equipped with a balcony of sorts and a veranda running the length of the buildings, and it is here that the life of the tenement dwellers was centred. On the balconies they cooked, washed and hung their clothes to dry, dined, chatted to neighbours or shared in the life of the street below and at night found extra sleeping accommodation.

Until West Indians themselves organized social activities, there was nowhere for the men to meet socially outside of their rooms – or the bars. A visiting American was moved to comment in 1906 that "the negro needs recreation when his day's work is done – cricket, football, music, dancing and the society of women. Twenty thousand normal men will not stay contented forever without their wives or sweethearts. We have grossly exaggerated the lack of orthodox morality among the negroes, but have done nothing to improve the condition of those who are working on our canal, under our laws. While I was there, cock-fights, prize-fights, saloons and worse offered entertainment for our employees."[96]

Many soon fell into a life of dissipation and it took considerable strength of character to evade the temptations in the way. Coming from rural based economies where nothing much happened, the men were suddenly thrust into a dynamic frontier society where their ability to earn what was to them real money coincided with a total freedom from the restraints of home. So it had been at the time of the Panama Railroad and the French canal and so it continued now. While many undoubtedly settled down to a life of sobriety and hard work, and set goals which included the improvement of their own lives and those of their families back home, a large number were unable to handle the transition. Frail family ties were quickly severed, women and children waiting back home in Bridgetown or Castries or Kingston were forever abandoned, and freedom became licence to patronize the endless bars, cockfights, bullfights, gambling dens and whorehouses. By 1914 venereal disease became the leading cause of admission to hospital, and the rising incidence of this disease was a cause of concern back in the West Indies.[97]

As the young men acquired families, "poor me one" might indeed have been the cry of many. The flashy returnee to the islands or the natty Zone worker on his day off masked the condition of a significant portion of those West Indians who – like those fifty years earlier – continued to live in poverty and squalor. Taking a room in the Republic was preferred by many for the freedom it offered, though by going outside the Zone they exposed themselves to greater risk. The standard of living and accommodation and sanitation were higher on the Zone and mortality rates were always lower, but it was in the Republic that the majority of West Indians chose to live. Those employed by the ICC travelled to the Zone each day, some provided services for Zone dwellers, many earned a living in the Republic as self-employed tradesmen, artisans or professionals; still others provided managerial, secretarial or clerical services in Panamanian stores or offices where ability to speak English was considered an asset. There is also no doubt that many of the West Indians continued to "scuffle" to make a living.

The 1906 Census of Panama (excluding the Canal Zone) showed 3,127 West Indians, of whom 1,877 were Jamaicans living outside the Zone. By 1911 the total population of the Republic had more than doubled, to 55,113. Just under 11,000 in Panama City and 10,000 in Colón were classified as "negroes". By the 1914 census, when a great many construction workers had left (but when many people from the abandoned Zone towns were pouring into the Republic), persons listed as "black" were now the overwhelming majority in both cities – 33,691 of 56,106 persons in Panama City and 21,679 of 27,831 in Colón. Presumably the blacks were West Indians as there were separate entries for "white", "Panamanian" and "yellow".

In the back streets of Colón known as "Jamaica Town" or "Coolie Town" and in sections of Panama City known as Calidonia and Guatachapali, huge and notorious West Indian slums emerged. As more people poured into the cities, the condition of the tenement dwellers worsened. In 1911 when a public health campaign began after a disastrous fire which wiped out over ten city blocks in Colón, that city was estimated to have a population of ten to fifteen thousand persons. The health authorities estimated that some 90 per cent of this population was "floating", more than half of the "unstable portion" composed of West Indians who had come to Panama in search of work.[98] By 1914 the infantile death rate among blacks was regarded as "enormous". In the Zone and Republic, the birth rate in the last nine months of the year was 19 per thousand, while for the same period the infant mortality for black children under one year old was 347 per thousand (compared to 29 per thousand for white children). The death rate for children under five was 42 per thousand. In Panama itself, the birth rate was 54.52 while the infant mortality in the same period was 272. Half of these deaths were of children under five and gastrointestinal illnesses the principal cause.[99] But, as West Indians were to discover, their situation after construction ended was to grow progressively worse.

A PIECE OF GROUND

Many immigrant workers chose life outside of towns and villages. Those who abandoned Zone housing or construction jobs were often described as "going to the bush". The ICC disapproved: what they hoped would be a pool of surplus labour simply disappeared, causing continuous recruitment. The term was also used to suggest a shiftless sort of life, frequently cited as evidence of the West Indian's racial inferiority. The West Indian, the argument went, was indolent enough to be "scratching around in the bush" and fulfilling his most elementary needs rather than applying himself to "honest labour", that is, wage labour. This conflict stood at the heart of the West Indian's relationship to the plantations at home. There, the worker who chose to sell his labour seasonally

Figures 7.27–7.28 Many West Indians in Panama simply replicated life from back home as they tried to earn a living outside of canal construction. Some set up little sugar mills (7.27, courtesy of the National Library of Jamaica) or burned charcoal (7.28, Abbot, *Panama*, 198).

or as it suited him was also condemned. The equation of labour exclusively with wage labour remained as central to the thinking of the Canal Zone enterprise as it was to the West Indian plantation.

The West Indian's idea of labour also included working for him or herself, finding ways of "making do". Gardening or cultivating the soil was in the lifeblood of many and where land was available, as in Panama, they cultivated it. Farming became a lifelong vocation for some; and for others it opened a way to augment wages or as a means of survival.

Farming, in fact, had been part of the islanders' strategy from their earliest arrivals in continental America. On the Talamanca coast of Costa Rica, and the Atlantic coasts of Mexico and Honduras especially, they were the first to

Figure 7.29
The riverside market at Matachin (Abbot, *Panama*, 191).

put forks to virgin soil or machetes to the vegetation. On the Isthmus of Panama itself, West Indians were responsible for the settlement of many areas, including Bocas del Toro in the north and Rio Abajo and Pablo Nuevo, now suburbs of Panama City. They also introduced flora and livestock to these areas: "The Jamaicans brought over fruits, vegetables and flowers with them; and the virgin lands that were awaiting exploitation . . . began to bloom."[100]

On the Zone, "bush living" was not necessarily the same as farming since spaces beyond those cleared by canal authorities were simply the preferred place of residence for many canal workers who wanted to avoid the ever-present surveillance of Uncle Sam in the camps and villages. It was also a way to save money, to prepare food that was satisfying and to have some autonomy in one's personal life. But kitchen gardens, bush living or farming – any escape to more natural surroundings – was also of profound psychological significance. The majority of West Indians on the Zone were of rural origin and for people suddenly exposed to such a high level of urban industrialization, the bush provided a breathing space, the soil a kind of touchstone to remind of another life outside the frantic and sometimes unbearable pace of construction. A cultivated plot could be an anchor, something over which he or she had some control. In conditions of uncertainty and transience, a piece of ground provided not just food but spiritual nourishment. It also provided a space apart from prying eyes in which men and women could worship as they pleased, summoning the deities or the ancestors to intercede in times of affliction, offering spirit protection otherwise, a space for ritual worship and healing. All these were important elements of the West Indian cosmos, the touchstone of belief systems partly derived from Africa, which required not a church building but a ritually prepared space in which one's feet could touch bare earth and the gods and ancestors could be summoned.

Throughout construction years and long after, West Indians on the Panama Canal lived precariously. Work fluctuated with no assurance of permanence or stability. Workers endured sudden and arbitrary transfers, layoffs or termination, at the mercy of capricious bosses with no security of tenure. Their lives and health were constantly at risk, but without promise of compensation in case of injury, dismemberment, or death. Wages could not stretch to fill the need, especially for those with families. Many workers had cultivations and garden plots simply to feed themselves and their families, and to provide a buffer against a fragile future. Others wanted the freedom to have a family life without overseers and regulators. And many were simply full-time farmers, supplying foodstuff so desperately needed in the Zone and terminal cities.

Early Farmers

In the early years in Panama, vast tracts of virgin land were available to anyone willing to clear the jungle and make a start. Many West Indians did so, but such cultivators were technically squatters, farming near village settlements and along the line of the railroad and later the canal works. They employed simple tools – the fork, hoe and machete – clearing the land by slash-and-burn methods, as they did at home. In time, large farming settlements had grown, starting with a nucleus of people from the days of railroad construction, augmented by many who had not returned home when the French canal failed (among whom were a number of Chinese who engaged in market gardening). By US construction years, there was, for instance, near the village of Empire, a settlement of West Indian cultivators in the vicinity of the Masambi River, producing sugar, bananas and fruit for sale at Empire and Culebra, the nearest markets. Pack animals brought the produce to the towns, crossing Culebra Cut on a suspension bridge at Empire. So great was this kind of traffic that in one weekday morning, twenty-nine pack animals were counted crossing the bridge in one hour. Settlers moved west of Empire during this time, facilitated by the cutting of a road from Panama City to Corozal. The occasional Spanish labourer also settled down to farming but the majority were from Jamaica, Barbados and Martinique. Similar developments lay along the road from Mount Hope to Gatún.[101]

When the United States acquired the Canal Zone, it included within its boundaries much of the area under cultivation with the old railroad line providing the chief means of travel for men and pack animals. The few trails leading from the railroad to the interior villages were used only in the dry season. The ICC constructed a trunk line of roads parallel to the canal with branches into the fertile hinterland.[102] This road network facilitated agricultural settlement and the squatter movement into the bush.

The Zone authorities imposed a rent of three dollars per hectare per year for agricultural land. In 1907, 83 persons had rented a total of 344 hectares and by 1910, these numbers had climbed to 1,261 persons renting 1,430 hectares.[103] It is obvious, however, that many people simply remained squatters, since it was frequently reported that labourers numbering in their thousands had left the canal works for the bush. The men took with them empty dynamite boxes and packing cases to erect their shanties. In 1911, the *Canal Record* commented on the increase in squatting and its undesirability. A notice was posted throughout the Zone: "Every person who wilfully commits any trespass by cutting down, destroying, or injuring any kind of wood or timber standing or growing upon the lands of another, or upon public lands, is guilty of a misdemeanour and will be prosecuted accordingly. Permission to occupy public lands or lands of the Panama Railroad Company, must be obtained from the land agent, Ancon, Canal Zone."[104]

Squatting continued: in 1913 the chief of police was ordered to maintain a patrol by land and water of all trails and navigable waters to prevent the movement of people from one part of the Zone to another. As the completion of the canal neared, the entire west bank was cleared of dwellings. On 9 June 1913, all squatters were ordered to move. Entire Zone villages were relocated, and many small settlers were forced to give up their livelihoods. By the time the canal opened in 1914, the only housing remaining in the Zone was US-owned housing in US-created towns. The vast majority of West Indians and their families were forced to move into the already overcrowded terminal cities, construction workers and farmers alike. Many West Indians had settled outside the jurisdiction of the Canal Zone, located mainly in the Chagres area, Gatún Valley, Cano Quebrado and Trinidad, and this process continued as land in the Republic opened up for settlement.

The ICC itself understood the role the small farms and rural settlements had played in relieving some of the pressure on the West Indian population. At a time of severe labour unrest on the Zone and the start of the economic depression, the 1920 report referred to the past, noting that "between ten and fifteen thousand men and their families, accustomed to country life and to raising a part at least of their food, are unable to assist themselves by gardening, and at the same time feel forced to accept the city standards of dress and entertainment".[105] The ICC later opened up idle lands to farming again but, to a very limited extent. Interestingly enough, the ICC itself began to establish large agricultural plantations to supply the Zone with food and meat in the post-construction years, but found that one of the severest drawbacks was the shortage of silver labourers.

Although life in construction years was "ruff and tuff", West Indians were to look at those years as the best of times for many reasons, not least of which was having their own piece of ground.

8. HOW THEY LOVED, LAUGHED AND PRAYED

"West Indians may not have been pious and hell-fearing Christians, but they were devout, sociable and hard-toiling workers to whom the divine gifts of song and laughter made their community human and livable, despite all its physical pains and social deficiencies."

—George Westerman, "Historical Notes on West Indians in the Isthmus of Panama"

"COLÓN MAN" MIGHT HAVE BEEN born in Panama but only became an icon back home in the West Indies when he returned with new styles and clothing far beyond what the stay-at-homes wore or could afford, leading to admiration, parody or ridicule.

In Panama, stylish dress was important at all levels and – unless outrageous – seems to have been taken for granted. There were, of course, differences based on nationality, colour, class, occupation and personal preferences, with behaviour modified accordingly. But to outsiders, all West Indians were the same, and what struck observers most was the silver workers' love of dress and lavish display.[1] The pomp and formality of West Indian funerals became legendary; huge lodge processions with members in full regalia were common; weddings were sometimes occasions for great ostentation. It was as if, with their newly acquired money, some West Indians on the Zone not only transplanted but elaborated on the styles and customs of their homelands. Dress has always been of great symbolic value to Afro-Antilleans, even during slavery, and continued to be expressive not only of individual personality but also of group affiliation, occupational status and class.[2] Those who had imbibed British values adopted the sober dress of what was imagined to be the English middle class. For example, young Gerald's sleepy recollections of church (in "Tropic Death") ended on the note, "All in black – veil, hat, gloves, shoes,

Figures 8.1–8.3 Elaborate weddings were part of the West Indian image in Panama during construction days (8.1, Panama Canal; 8.2, Abbot, *Panama*, 235). Figure 8.3, by contrast, shows a much more sober gathering in rural Jamaica in a photograph titled "native wedding party". (Courtesy of the National Library of Jamaica.)

dress."³ Even the children were not spared English style. Among Cecil Haynes's recollections are those of his school teacher mother taking him and his brother to St Peter's Episcopalian Church in La Boca from an early age, and how she dressed them up in the style of English boys in knickerbockers, long stockings and Eton collars, leading to the agony of discomfort but worse, teasing on the way from other little boys "who weren't like that".⁴ Of course, those with middle-class aspirations in the West Indies were dressing themselves and their children in similar ways.

While dress was significant for all, what stood out then in contrast to the sober middle class, was the more flamboyant style of the working class. Jamaican Clifford Allen recalled of his Panamanian childhood, "When deh have a dance yu know, the man have di scissor tail coat. . . . An' him have him dancing slippers an' him have him glove on – don't dance without the glove."⁵ Later observers noted that labourers and artisans owned frock coats and top hats, derbies, tweeds and blue serge suits.⁶ The more modern in outlook were increasingly influenced by American styles, leading to the widespread adoption of African American "zoot-suit" styles during the 1920s.

The "dandified" way some West Indians dressed for work at times drew unfavourable comment from white Americans who themselves tended to "dress down". Harry Franck might have been exaggerating somewhat when he observed during construction days that "on the tail of every train lounged an

American conductor, dressed more like a miner, though his 'front' and 'hind' negro brakemen were as apt to be in silk ties and patent-leathers".[7] Winifred James bewailed the informality of Americans: "Why, oh, why does the United States as a nation come to the table in its shirt-sleeves?"[8] Panamanians seemed to have been, on the whole, sober and formal in their dress.

In their use of leisure time, West Indians appeared to put themselves on display. By their dress, by expressing themselves through their religion and their social and cultural activities, they magnified the differences between them and the host societies. West Indian institutions – churches, schools, benevolent associations – served to reinforce their separateness. But given the nature of the society in which they found themselves and the dehumanizing experiences of life on the Zone, only by asserting familiar values and customs could they affirm their humanity and – in the process – enjoy themselves.

Figure 8.4
Knickerbocker suits of the era (Wikipedia).

SILVER WORKERS' DAY OFF

Sunday was the worker's only day off – and the silver worker made the most of it. During the week he was constantly herded and driven – in the camps to form a line for breakfast at 5:30; the mad rush to catch the labour train in the morning and again at 11:00 a.m. to be dropped off at his camp for lunch. He lined up for a quick meal before rushing to catch the train back to work. In the evening, it was another rush to catch the train home. There he joined a stampede to the commissary to purchase the necessaries in the few hours it remained open or rushed to the mess kitchen where he again lined up for food. Afterwards, there was hardly time for anything else – a chat with comrades perhaps, a Bible lesson or a moment's reflection before the "watchie" banged on the iron bar to signal lights out. For six days of the week, it was "nosuh", "yessuh" to the boss all day long. Only on Sunday was the worker his own man. For many, it was the day to complete personal chores such as washing clothes, to get a haircut, and to go to the post office to send off the precious letter or postal order to loved ones at home. A few chose to spend all day in the camp.

After their chores, the vast majority would bathe and put on their finest clothes if only to indulge in two simple but popular pastimes: riding on the passenger trains and eating ice cream. Sunday was also a day for going to church, for sporting, for funerals, for lodge processions and meetings, for concerts, for sea bathing, and for picnics. While the gold workers were provided with their Isthmian Canal Commission (ICC) clubhouses as the centre of social activities, West Indians were left to themselves to create their own amusement. And whatever it was they chose to do, they did it with a dash and style that became legendary. Sunday was the day when canal workers partied or worshipped, according to preference, and socialized with their compatriots who lived in the Republic. There, if the canal worker had the money, his friends no doubt were willing to help him to find pleasing ways to both spend

Figures 8.5–8.6 West Indians enjoyed themselves as best they could, whether boxing on the beach or roller-skating (Abbot, *Panama*, 236, 240).

it and pass the time. For those who lived on the Canal Zone, passage into the Republic must have seemed like a breath of fresh air, a transition into freedom – if only for a day. As time went on, "Uncle Sam" on the Zone must have seemed more like a strict, spoil-sport auntie as Zone camps and towns became circumscribed by rules and restrictions with the force of law behind them. Gambling and drinking were among the early prohibitions, with drinking on the Zone limited to strictly licensed and supervised bars. Both laws were the subject of verses which the labourers incorporated into their work songs and chanteys, though the punishment meted out for transgressions was no laughing matter. One version of "Poor Me One" advised that

> To gamble in the street won't do us any harm
> When the police come he'll grab us by the arm
> *O poor me one, all a dem pon poor me one.*

> Roll yuh dice and have you fun
> You gotta run like hell when the police come
> *O poor me one, all a dem pon poor me one.*[9]

And the popular chantey "John Crow today" included the verse:

> When we get pay we gwine drink gin
> *John Crow today, today.*
> If it don't make us fat, it won't make us thin.
> *John Crow today, today.*[10]

Drinking

Zone villages were full of bars and cantinas at the start. In the first year of US control, the most frequent cause of arrest was drunkenness and disorderly conduct,[11] but these infractions decreased rapidly once Zone drinking laws clamped down. The government quickly imposed an annual licence fee of six hundred dollars gold per annum on drinking places that once paid a liquor tax of from one to five dollars, immediately reducing the number of bars from 327 to 60. Only 56 bars remained open after the licence fee was doubled in 1907.[12] Of course, these fees affected white as well as black workers though the bars remained segregated. The bars were also made deliberately unattractive, and they could have neither chairs nor tables: the rule was perpendicular drinking in full view of passers-by. Drinking outside of these licensed premises was strictly forbidden, although a great many of the workers seemed to have been armed with a flask of rum or whisky for "medicinal" purposes. As work on the canal progressed, more and more Zone towns disappeared, and by 1913 bars were permitted in only five settlements, two of which were about to be abandoned. In early 1913 the ICC decided to extend Prohibition, that is, a ban on the sale, manufacture and transportation of alcohol, to the entire Zone starting 1 July that year.

This meant that the official opening of the canal on 14 August 1914 was "dry", a fact that did not sit well with some of the passengers invited on the boat that made the first formal transit from sea to sea. The event was meant to be low-key in any event, in view of the fact that a world war had broken out in Europe only two weeks earlier. But as Winifred James lamented: "It was a long day and a hot day. . . . There was nothing to drink on the ship. . . . From four in the morning till five in the evening is a long time for men of generous temperament, making holiday to last on cold tea and water. . . . As the hours went by and the heat grew, the *fiesta* spirit wilted and wilted."[13]

Gambling

Gambling was also prohibited on the Zone, though games such as poker seemed to have been prevalent among white bachelors. In the Republic, gambling was a ceaseless attraction for Latins, Americans and West Indians who all seemed to have devised their own methods for working out the numbers that were "certain" to win. But one system mentioned by Harry Franck was special to the Zone – based as it was on the numbers of Panama Railroad engines and cars. He claimed that more than one Zone housewife "has slipped into the kitchen to find the roast burning and her West Indian cook hiding hastily behind her ample skirt a long list of the figures on every freight car that passed that morning . . . from which she was to find the magic number".[14]

The national lottery was drawn every Sunday before a huge crowd at Cathedral Plaza in Panama City, where the lottery office was located on the ground floor of the Bishop's Palace, the Catholic Church being a beneficiary. Even today, people still talk of West Indian "fortunes" founded on lottery winnings while an equal number attribute the destitute condition of many to lottery losses. In George Lamming's *In the Castle of My Skin,* Pa has a special place in his Panama memories of "Duckey" money, referring to the Duque family who controlled the lottery: "An' once I come as near as any man to winnin' the Duckey. . . . But they always say that if you come so near to winnin' the Duckey an' you ain't win, there be bad times for you 'head."[15] One recorded winning was during the French canal construction by "an industrious young Jamaican", William Josephs, who was employed as a storeman to A.N. Henriques. The *Star and Herald* in its report (19 January 1884) noted approvingly that the young man had converted his windfall into a draft to send to his mother in Jamaica to enable her to buy a house.

In addition to the lottery, West Indians played a numbers game based on the winning ticket. There were also gambling-related sports such as horseracing and cockfights. West Indians had a long history of organized horseracing in their homelands, going back to the earliest days of English settlements in the seventeenth and eighteenth centuries, and they brought this interest to Panama, including the importation of racehorses from Jamaica. West Indians took the lead in staging race meets in the line towns as well as in Panama City and Colón[16] until racing in time became big business at the modern Juan Franco track.

Although cockfighting, like horseracing, was a sport brought to the West Indies by the early English planters, its popularity on the islands had faded over time. The workers' interest was rekindled by their contact with Latin America, where cockfighting was widespread and legal. A visitor described a Sunday cockpit where "money is bet freely on the birds, and men, whose demeanor is usually dignified and self-possessed abandon themselves to wild excitement. The choicest seats are occupied by persons prominent in the community. I have seen the Chief of Police holding a watch on the game cocks and a Legislator acting as referee."[17] Another visitor during construction days claimed that "the Jamaicans particularly have their favourite cocks and will wager a week's pay on their favourites and all of their wives' laundry earnings they can lay hands upon as well. One or two gamecocks tethered by the leg" are a common sight about a Jamaican's hut.[18] From his cockfighting activities in Panama, Ecuador or Cuba, the Jamaican brought home the word "mampala", from the word *mampolon*, which meant a common as opposed to a fighting cock – and contributed to a clandestine revival of the sport in his native land up to the 1920s and 1930s. Panamanian bullfighting seemed not to have been a big attraction for the islanders.

Figure 8.7
The cockpit was a popular attraction in the Republic (postcard, author's collection).

Other Sports

Of course the workers brought their favourite sports with them, and on Sundays many dressed in their white flannels and congregated around the nearest flat area they could call a cricket pitch. From the start, cricket was taken seriously. In 1882, the Panama Cricket and Baseball Club formed; in 1904 Colón boasted four cricket teams. They competed for a cup presented by Frederick Martinez, the Barbados-based "Prince of Commercial Travellers". Under the leadership of Dr A.M. Fyfe, the Panama Cricket Club acquired its own land,

Figures 8.8–8.9
George Headley,
immortalized in
Jamaica by a statue
and stamps.

stand and grounds in 1919. Up to the early 1920s there were many cricket teams on the isthmus, with six teams in Panama City alone.[19] In later years, however, the Americanization of the West Indians eroded interest in cricket, and those born in Panama increasingly turned to baseball as their favourite game. But this was not before the birth in Colón (to Jamaican parents, in 1909) of George Headley, widely regarded as one of the greatest cricketers of all time.

West Indians also introduced to Panama competitive events such as cycling and track and field, frequently bringing teams from the West Indies to compete. Jamaican Dr F.B. Lowe, who practised for a long time on the isthmus, was the first person to organize inter-schools track and field athletics in Panama.[20] Panama's foremost athlete, Lloyd La Beach, was born in 1922 to Jamaican immigrants who took him back to Jamaica where he was schooled. Later, as a student at the University of Wisconsin, he ran for Panama in the 1948 summer Olympics, winning bronze medals in both the 100 metres and 200 metres, Panama's first Olympic medals.[21]

All of these activities show an overlay of West Indian cultural life on the isthmian matrix. But it is in terms of religion and social organization that we see most clearly how, although life in Panama had its novel dimensions, it was really an extension of Caribbean island life.

Figure 8.10 Lloyd La Beach (University of Wisconsin).

SOCIAL ACTIVITIES

West Indians were well aware of the dangers awaiting them in a strange and sometimes hostile land, and they clung to their countrymen and -women for support. Social and cultural events went hand in hand with entrepreneurial activities catering to their compatriots. Thus was born transportation services – taxi companies and the colourful Panama buses called "chivas" first operated by two West Indians. Other entrepreneurs catered to the taste for ice cream and aerated water. Philip McDonald from Grenada was delighted to find at Empire a soda shop called Swains Ice House operated by a Trinidad man. "He had the same kind of soda we had in our homes ie the patent bottles with the marble inside, we were delighted to meet that kind of drink so we gave justice to ourselves."[22] Another Grenadian, E.W. Martineau, arrived in Panama in 1912 "not in search of work, but to find a better field of endeavour. I brought with me an airated water equipment which is commonly called soda factory. After I paid duty for same, I applied for permission to operate in the Canal Zone, and authority obtained, I was established at High Street, Gatun." Later, when the Zone became depopulated, like others Martineau went into the taxi and bus business.[23]

Women made and sold island drinks such as sorrel, ginger beer, mauby and Irish moss; Christmas was celebrated with plum pudding West Indian–style,

Figures 8.11–8.12 The way urban vendors in Panama carried objects on their heads fascinated visitors. (Courtesy of William P. McLaughlin, www.czimages.com.)

weddings with genuine rum-soaked "wedding cake", and no Easter was complete without Easter bun and cheese – all treats that are still available to West Indian Panamanians today. There were West Indian drugstores[24] and bookstores, seamstresses, tailors and jewellers, funeral directors to see them off, and ministers of religion to bless, christen, marry and bury them.

As the Canal Zone became organized and Panama acquired a healthier reputation, larger numbers of emigrants, and especially women, began to arrive and there was no lack of effort to organize social and cultural activities for the "upliftment" of the community. Many of these organizations were short-lived and reflect the social divisions that existed among the various classes and also among the different nationalities. Between 1906 and 1911, for instance, there were, among others, an International Social and Literary Association (formed in Panama in 1905), a Men's Social League (active in Colón), a West Indian Protective League, a Culebra Coloured Association, and the Intercolonial Club.

The Protective League was formed in the Canal Zone mainly to represent the legal interests of its members and other West Indians on the isthmus. The organization held monthly meetings and distributed literature. Its membership in 1910 consisted of 150 persons, including children over twelve.[25] The Intercolonial Club, formed in 1910, consisted of "American, West Indian and African Negro men". The club was organized specifically to meet the needs of the "educated class of negroes" on the isthmus and Canal Zone. Its members included lawyers, ministers, doctors, and other professionals, merchants and businessmen, including some residents of Kingston, Jamaica. The club rooms situated on Bolivar Street in Colón had a library, billiard room, reception room, club bar, and reading room furnished with newspapers from New York and London, "the better class English and American magazines and such publications as deal with the affairs of the negro race".[26] The club concerned itself with all matters affecting the race and worked in conjunction with the Pan African Club of London and the National Club of Kingston (this latter was a reformist political organization led by S.A.G. Cox, with Marcus Garvey and W.A. Domingo among its members).

The Culebra Colored Association was housed in what was formerly the Young Men's Colored Institute. The ICC had constructed the building in 1909 and provided it with a reading room and reading material as well as games.[27] While dominoes, checkers and billiard-playing were allowed, the "playing of cards, dancing, and the use of liquor and profane language in the building was forbidden".[28] With Uncle Sam watching so hard, the total that ever joined was fifty-eight or 2 per cent of the available males in the vicinity. When this fell to only seven men on the roll, the institute was closed on the recommendation of the Zone chaplain under whose charge it was. The building was then rented to the Culebra Colored Association, a social club which held regular dances and charged a monthly fee.[29]

Concerts formed an important part of social lives, as they did back home in the West Indies. Frequently there were visiting performers from the islands to augment local talent. Note was taken in 1919 alone of an Isthmian Dramatic Association, a Colón Negro Glee Club and a Colón Coloured Comedy Company. School concerts and church harvest exhibitions also took place regularly as did the most popular social event, the "picnic". This was usually a large excursion by train to some open area where people enjoyed the day with food, music and games. A public holiday never passed without huge picnics. Music and dances with their own musicians, bands and orchestras were also important components of West Indian cultural life.

Fraternal Organizations

Joining a lodge or secret society was one way of affirming one's place in an in-group. Nearly everyone in Panama seemed to have been a member of a fraternal or benevolent association. It was in these mutual aid societies that the yearning for comradeship found its fullest expression. But they were also a form of insurance. Far from home, the only way the emigrant could guarantee help in sickness, a good funeral, and some aid and comfort to his family left behind was by joining a society. Generally, a member subscribed seventy-five cents to a dollar a month. In sickness, the society would provide some funds for the worker to live on until he was well again. The societies also paid death and burial benefits.

The whole notion of secret societies with their regalia, their ritual, their titles, their sense of mystery and the opportunity they presented for elaborate ceremony was attractive to West Indians. Besides, the development of an officer caste provided a social structure within which many could find validation and fulfilment denied them elsewhere.

Many of the early lodges founded in Panama were at first under the jurisdiction of lodges back home. Among organizations listed in the *Handbook of Jamaica* for 1904, the Imperial Order of Good Samaritans and Daughters of Samaria (established in Kingston in 1882) had lodges in Panama and Central America under its jurisdiction. The Independent Order of Odd Fellows (Jamaica District established in 1885); St Charles, Colón, established the same year; and the Loyal Order of Ancient Shepherds Ashton Unity (founded in Kingston 1885) also had lodges in Kingston and Costa Rica under its jurisdiction. Lodges from other islands were also represented. The French islanders had their own Fraternité de Panamá, a mutual aid society created in 1917.[30]

When there was an Empire Day demonstration of friendly societies in

Colón in 1908, members from twenty different lodges arrived by train from all along the line for an elaborate procession that included riders and bands. The governor of the province had an official reception for them. The Union of Friendly Societies obtained a concession for a burial plot at Mount Hope cemetery for their use. A sixty-foot square plot – God's Acre – was consecrated there in 1908. In 1932 it was claimed that there were at least three hundred lodges on the isthmus with an aggregate membership of 60 per cent of the adult males, 25 per cent of the females, and 5 per cent of West Indian children. They had a total of bank deposits of $1.5 million.

Mutual aid societies and lodges were flourishing in the West Indies when the emigrants left and they simply took their organizations with them. By the same token, some returning emigrants took their fraternal interests back home.[31] For many years the societies had remained lodges or friendly societies coming via the colonies but having headquarters in England and the United States. However, around the 1920s the West Indians began to establish purely local lodges in their own countries and some of these became dominant. They were known as "colonial lodges", of which the largest and most successful was the Jamaica Provident and Benevolent Society established in 1927. Barbados and Grenada also had national benevolent societies. The Jamaica Provident was in the first year of its existence able to purchase land and erect its own building.[32] The Silver Employees Association was also a benevolent society though it was better known as a West Indian pressure group on the isthmus. In the 1960s, George Westerman noted that a number of these lodges had continued to function for over fifty years, and a few had made substantial investments in real estate and in local commerce. He claimed that "over the years of their existence these societies have paid out in claims for sickness, death and the like, benefits exceeding more than half the cost of the Panama Canal construction".[33]

During the First World War, the Friendly Societies War Contingent was mobilized from Bocas del Toro and Colón and it contributed 650 of the 3,000 men who joined the West Indies Regiments from Panama.

Connections with Home

The eagerness to be part of what was happening at "home" continued until well into the twentieth century, facilitated by the ease of communications back and forth. West Indians were able to maintain close contact with their homelands in other ways as they were served by English-language newspapers that regularly carried news of the islands.[34] As they had done from the days of the French, the people on the isthmus continued to respond to events on the islands. Victims of disasters often benefited from relief funds they organized.

Sometimes the connection was almost psychic. When downtown Kingston was destroyed by the earthquake and fire of 1907, the hysteria from Jamaica quickly communicated itself to the expatriates and Colón was immediately swept by rumours and prophesies of similar disasters about to occur there.[35] Panamanians also maintained an active interest in political developments in their homelands. Such interest was to be transferred in person as the emigrants increasingly returned home to the islands and became the spark that would ignite the fires of rebellion against the colonial order.

THE ISTHMIAN CHURCH

Religion provided another rock of stability to the strangers in a strange land. During construction days, the most popular book in the work camps was the Bible followed by Ira D. Sankey's *Songs and Solos,* as both books probably were in many an island home. The American Bible Society and the British and Foreign Bible Society were active from the start. A West Indian colporteur followed the pay car each month (as did every kind of huckster) and as the men got paid he would persuade them to buy a Bible. He also visited outlying settlements where workers resided and by 1910 had sold over four thousand Bibles this way.[36]

Religion had played a key role in the transformation of the lives of black West Indians from slavery to freedom, and in the early twentieth century the church – of one sort or another – continued to be a powerful force in the islands. While from the seventeenth century the Anglican Church had been, as in England, the state church, it was the nonconformist churches that led the fight against slavery both in the Mother Country and in the colonies. The Wesleyans, Methodists, Baptists and Quakers were the ones to minister to the enslaved Africans, assist them in freedom to establish their own villages and set up the first schools. In the process they gave the enslaved Africans an Old Testament narrative that matched their own – the stories of David versus Goliath, Moses and the dream of a Promised Land, and so forth. These same stories and heroes were incorporated by African Americans into their freedom songs and Spirituals. The Bible, even for those who could not read, became a talismanic object, a source of consolation, the touchstone of Hope and Salvation. For the canal workers, it also served as a reminder of home.

In the islands, in the absence of state support, it was the church to which one turned for schooling, legal assistance and advice, social services, and activities. The church, in turn, functioned as the spiritual guardian and demanding moral arbiter for much of the population. Church membership equated with "respectability", or the expression of what essentially were Victorian values.

Figure 8.13
Salvation Army band
in Panama (Abbot,
Panama, 250).

The isthmian church came to play the same roles for the emigrants. Here, more than ever, in this foreign land, they needed the safe haven their church provided. George Westerman asserted that the "West Indian Isthmian 'old timer' supported the church not only because he was brought up under its spiritual influence but also because there was no other agencies to fill its place. The church served as a channel for various kinds of expressions and met the needs, stimulated the pride and preserved the self-respect of these workers who might otherwise have been submerged in despair and futility."[37]

Many of the emigrant workers were Roman Catholic – especially those from the French and Spanish islands – and they augmented the dominant faith of the host country, with Catholic priests arriving from the islands to serve them. But the vast majority of the emigrants were Protestants and they brought that faith to the isthmus. Because of the early close connections in the islands between church and school, the churches were also pioneers in education in Panama.

The isthmian church embraced the entire range of religious activities, from the orthodox churches first organized in the late nineteenth century to all the various creeds, sects and cult groups. With the West Indians of English, French, Spanish and Dutch ancestry bringing their own forms of worship with them, new hybrids undoubtedly developed. Even today in downtown Panama or remote farms in Bocas del Toro, voodoo, revivalism and balmyards still persist, and West Indian forms of witchcraft still flourish in a society where the *bruja* (witch) has been a long standing phenomenon. Eric Walrond elaborates on both the pull of obeah and the powerful religious spirit that sustained the emigrants in his story "The Wharf Rats".[38] In his story "Tropic Death", the young boy, Gerald, is taken by his mother to a branch of the Plymouth Brethren:

By way of the Sixth Street Mission, his mother rooted religion into his soul. Every night he was marched off to meeting. There, he'd meet the dredge-digging, Zone-building, Lord-loving peasants of the West Indies on sore knees of atonement asking the Lord to bring salvation to their perfidious souls. . . .

. . . . His mother had become of one them. He was one of them now. He'd go on Thursday evenings to prayer meetings. The evenings were long and hot. He would go to sleep in the midst of some drowsy exhaustless prayer. All would be silent. Hours of silence to God . . . His mother'd pinch him, quietly, but he'd be as stiff as a log till the service was over.[39]

The Protestant churches in the West Indies were supportive of the emigrant populations from the start. They sent over ministers to undertake missionary work, establish congregations along the line and set up schools. Their activities also embraced non-West Indians. Where the Catholic Church was absent (as in Bocas del Toro), they attracted Latins as well. One Methodist minister from Jamaica, the Reverend Clifford Surgeon, is noted for his pioneering work among the Valiente or Guaymí Indians of Bocas, a work later carried on by Bishop Ephraim Alphonse.[40]

Figures 8.14–8.15 Guaymí children, like those pictured in figure 8.14 (Abbot, *Panama*, 374), were the beneficiaries of the astonishing work done by Bishop Ephraim S. Alphonse (1896–1995) (shown in figure 8.15) in his thirty-seven years among the Guaymí or Valiente Indians of Bocas del Toro, Panama, including conversion of their language into written text. Born in Bocas del Toro and educated in Jamaica at Calabar Theological College, he became a Methodist minister and combined his missionary work among the Valiente with his linguistic feats. Working on his own, his achievements includes reducing the Valiente Indian language to writing; the writing of the first grammar in Guaymí and grammar and vocabulary in Hindustani, Spanish and English. His translation of the four gospels into the Guaymí tongue was published by the American Bible Society, and his translation of the psalms and some 150 hymns were published by the Methodist Missionary Society. He was also the author of many books, a composer of church music, a playwright, and in his retirement he became professor of Guaymí languages at the University of Panama. In his early years in Jamaica, he served at Methodist churches in Spanish Town and Yallahs and at Coke Memorial in Kingston. Among his many honours was an honorary doctorate from the University of the West Indies, Mona, Jamaica, in 1982, which cited his contributions as "evangelist, humanist and linguist extra-ordinaire".

The oldest established Protestant church for the immigrant workers was Anglican and the politics that came to surround the mother church in Colón reflected the racial prejudice and racial segregation which the Americans imposed. Christ Church, Colón, was built by the Panama Railroad Company for its workers in 1865.[41] At first, it was under the auspices of the Episcopal (Anglican) Church of America. With the influx of West Indians at the time of the French, in 1883 it was leased to the Church of England, and the Anglican Church in Panama then came under the auspices of the Synod of the West Indies. In 1906 the synod took a decision to hand the church in Panama back to the Episcopalians since the United States now had territorial rights. The *Colón Telegram*, no doubt reflecting West Indian public opinion, commented adversely on this move, charging that the change would bring "difficulty and trouble" as "American prejudices have to be taken into account as against the fact that in the British West Indies all races and colours are to be found worshipping together and that freedom has been enjoyed here up to the present".[42]

Indeed, in the agreement between the British and American church it was clearly recognized that the need for segregated communities would arise. The agreement, signed by the archbishop of the West Indies, clearly set out how this fact was to be accomplished for each congregation:

> (The churches at Panama and the Mission House on the route of the canal have been erected by the Church of England for ALL the people, and the spiritual requirements of ALL shall, in accordance with the methods employed ever since the Mission was established continue to be provided for them without race or colour distinction and special efforts shall be made therein to provide regular ministration in a manner acceptable to the coloured people) . . .
>
> . . . Christ Church Colón is the property of the American Railway, but has been leased to the Church of England, at a nominal rent. If it should be found necessary or advisable to have a separate church for the white people in Colón, the Protestant Episcopal Church of America will arrange to use Christ Church for that purpose, and provide a separate and convenient building for the coloured people.
>
> In the case of Panama [City] if a separate church building be required for the use of the white people, then the American church will provide it, and the coloured congregation shall retain the use of the present Church, built by their own money assisted by funds from English societies and from Jamaica.
>
> . . . In any case where it may be found necessary or advisable, separate churches shall be provided for the white people, or separate services shall be arranged in the same buildings.[43]

As soon as the Episcopal Church took over, separate services for black and white were instituted. Sunday schools in these congregations also became segregated, separate schools being established for white children. Despite any resentment among West Indians that these arrangements might have caused, the church continued to have a strong following among the workers with, in 1912, thirteen congregations of black people and five of white, and some fifteen thousand members.[44]

The Wesleyan-Methodist Church was also a powerful force on the isthmus. Methodist activity had started in the 1820s when a pioneering missionary, Mother Abel, went from Jamaica to Bocas del Toro,[45] where there was already a settlement of Jamaicans. The church in Panama City was started at the time of a powerful earthquake in 1882 when panic gripped the population. A Jamaican threw open his house for prayer and this was the start of the Methodist Mission, which came under the direct supervision of the church in Jamaica.[46] The Methodists opened missions along the line of canal construction and also at Bocas del Toro and at Darién, where West Indians had gone to work in the gold mines. They also operated a number of day schools, the Wesleyan Day School in Colón being one of the best on the isthmus.

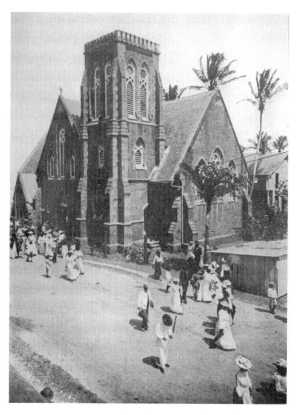

Figure 8.16 Christ Church, Colón (Abbot, *Panama*, 28).

The Salvation Army, Baptists and Seventh-Day Adventists also sent missionaries from Jamaica. In 1904 a Salvation Army superintendent came to explore the possibility of starting activities there, and in January 1905 officers began work. The Salvation Army held meetings and helped the men during their off hours, especially in the important job of writing letters home. In 1909 the Salvation Army was undertaking evangelistic work in Panama and the Zone as well as institutional work, with a rest home established in Colón. This home provided shelter for men who were temporarily out of work and supplied them with meals and lodgings. During self-denial week of 1909, offerings from the Isthmus of Panama exceeded those of any of the West Indian islands.[47] In 1921, the Seventh-Day Adventists established an academy in Las Cascadas for natives and West Indians. The Jamaican Missionary Society of the Baptist Church maintained a clergyman at Culebra. The Southern Baptist Convention of the United States was also represented on the Zone as was the Barbados-based Christian Mission,[48] the church that Eric Walrond's fictional mother joined.

While the ICC was unwilling to provide recreational facilities for the silver workers, they actively encouraged church work because they considered it a strong influence "making for the stability of the work force and the good order of canal villages". They granted free land and provided building materials at cost for the construction of churches.[49] They also paid a number of priests and ministers and provided them with housing. In 1908 the *Canal Record* reported that the ICC maintained thirteen chaplains.[50] In 1910 there were thirty-nine church buildings on the Zone, twenty-six owned by the ICC.

Around 1919, at a time of intense racial ferment on the Zone, as elsewhere, many of these established churches came under attack for their failure to "uplift the Negro". White ministers were accused of being impolite and insulting to coloured members.[51] Certainly many of the ministers of religion at the time interpreted their role as preservers of the status quo and were actively hostile to dissension among their congregations, openly preaching, for instance, against the widespread attempts at unionization that took place in 1919–20.

Nevertheless, the churches in Panama provided significant spiritual and social supports for the men away from home, especially in the early construction days when they were without other organized recreational or social activity. They also provided guidance in the material sphere by founding "dime banks" and other savings institutions, for example. Some of the ministers, such as those from the Salvation Army, materially aided the workers when they were homeless and destitute. During construction days and after, the churches were significant in providing the workers with a sense of stability and continuity and forging a valuable link with their homelands. They were also viewed with satisfaction by the canal authorities as a form of social control.

There are no statistics of what percentage of the emigrants were church supporters, though a large number professed religion. Nor do we have information on those who participated in "spiritual" activities that were off the official radar – the many who attended small revivalist "clap-hand" churches like those on the islands, or new and obscure religions, or who supported obeah and witchcraft or spiritual healing such as Myal. Many of these activities were subterranean, as they were at home where such practices were lumped under the rubric of obeah. But for many, the approach might have been the same as at home: to attend one of the established churches on Sunday to appear respectable; to attend the less-dry spiritual and revivalist churches as well, and to resort to African-derived practices for mental and physical healing as the case demanded. Since the isthmian residents seemed to have replicated all other aspects of West Indian life in their new homes, there is no reason to think otherwise.

One new religious element was to arise, however. Increasingly, as demonstrated by the emigrants who returned home, isthmian residents were to become involved in the new revival and fundamentalist Pentecostal movements born in the United States and brought to Panama. As we shall see, these movements – whether coming directly from the United States or brought via Panama – were to find fertile ground on the islands.

"OUR GLORIOUS EMPIRE"

One remarkable aspect of life on the isthmus was the patriotic fervour. An American woman living on the Zone during construction days claimed that the straw-boss of a West Indian gang used to have his men "stand the colours" every morning before work. "It is something like the flag salute at the beginning of a school day and the men like it. They always sing 'God Save the King' and then reach for their picks and shovels."[52] The community was lavish in its celebration of Empire Day and the Queen's Birthday, for which labour was usually given time off.

British subjects in Panama subscribed a fund of thirty-five hundred dollars for a memorial to mark the Coronation of King George V in 1911. It was planned to send a cable message to the king and queen and as a souvenir of the day each subscriber would receive a King George button and a lithograph copy of the cable message.[53]

Tumultuous welcomes were given by these homesick exiles to royal visitors. These included the Prince of Wales in 1920 and the Duke and Duchess of York in 1927. On this latter occasion, the West Indian newspaper, the *Workman*, commented that "nobody seems to have remained on his job and nobody seems to have stayed at home. It was a jubilant manifestation by the colony of British West Indians on the isthmus which drew them all to the capital to do honour to members of the Royal Household."[54] The address given by the West Indians was far more fulsome than those given by the British expatriates, East Indians or the British Chinese.[55]

It is perhaps not so remarkable after all that the "colony" of West Indians in the Republic of Panama could publicly express such sentiments about an empire that was largely indifferent to their existence. Such patriotic emotions were not extraordinary among West Indians at home. After all, when in 1919 two thousand dock workers in Kingston decided to go on strike, they first gave three cheers for the British governor Sir Leslie Probyn – "the worker's friend" – before they downed their tools.[56]

Part of the patriotic impulse was no doubt derived from the nostalgia that grips people away from home. It was as if West Indians in Panama gained collective strength by emphasizing their differences from the Panamanians and the Americans. In the face of widespread and persistent attempts to belittle their race, their culture, even their humanness, they could proudly and

Figure 8.17
Eric Walrond
(Wikipedia).

defiantly claim association with, and protection of, an empire with a royal family at its head.

As Eric Walrond wrote in 1935, reflecting on the consciousness of those earlier times, "As a West Indian Negro, I was reared on the belief that England was the one country where the black man was sure of getting a square deal. . . . We were made to believe that in none of the other colonies were the blacks treated as nicely as we were. We developed an excessive regard for the English. . . . It was to us a source of pride and conceit to be attached to England."[57] Nevertheless, the claim of neglect on the part of local consular officers and the imperial government in the post-construction period was to be made later, documented in a report submitted to the Colonial Office in 1943 on the subject. It called West Indians in Panama "the forgotten people".[58]

Inter-Island Rivalry

Despite the elements that bound them together – common traditions, language and race – and the many individual friendships and liaisons that were formed, West Indians on the isthmus were sometimes motivated by a petty nationalism that engendered deep divisions among them. Many of these divisions – translated to a wider arena – were the same ones that contributed to the break-up of the West Indies federation many years later. The West Indian character in the Republic of Panama expressed itself first in "Britishness" and second in insularity. And even though some of the more progressive elements tried to foster a community spirit, the concept remained elusive.[59] It was only under the racial banner of Marcus Garvey's Universal Negro Improvement Association (UNIA) or the economic banner of union organization that West Indians were able to come together as a group, though both efforts at organization, in their different ways, would fail to last.

Aside from inter-island rivalry, there were also as strong racial and class divisions as there were at home. Finally, there was division between the canal workers and others, although this was less visible during construction years. In the post-construction years, as the pay rates on the Zone declined relative to other sectors and opportunities for non-labouring jobs were increasingly denied to West Indians, Panama Canal workers came to occupy a lower status vis-à-vis those other Antilleans who were doing better economically.

In the 1920s, during a time of social ferment, the *Workman* newspaper repeatedly berated West Indians for their failure to follow intelligent leadership or support efforts promoted by their countrymen. In 1924, the paper claimed that "no where is the intercolonial antipathy so strongly fostered as on the Isthmus of Panama".[60] The divisions were visible to outsiders in many ways. To an American woman living on the Zone during construction days, it was apparent, for instance, that there existed a "not too deeply veiled antagonism" between Barbadians and Jamaicans. She thought the antipathy was "somewhat like the disdain existing between two dowagers heading separate and rival social sets. They may buddy up together in individual and isolated cases, but on the whole they don't like one another too well."[61]

The popular song "Poor Me One" had several verses directed at the Barbadians:

> What the Bajan people call a spree
> Is a pint of sody divide in three
> O poor me one, everybody down on poor me one.[62]

Songs like these in fact might have been saying a great deal more about national character in relation to issues such as thrift and the differing approaches to life among the islanders than at first appears. Some of these differences prevail to the present. It was only to outsiders that the West Indians appeared an undifferentiated, homogenous mass. Nevertheless, love certainly crossed national and other boundaries as the numerous intermarriages among different islanders proved. Many of the new generations would have no discernible island pedigree, with grandparents sometimes from four different countries who met at a place that would be portrayed in posters celebrating the opening of the Panama Canal as "the kiss of the oceans".

Figure 8.18 A blended Panamanian family: Mr Isidore (first name unknown) from Grace in Vieux-Fort, St Lucia, with his Guatemalan wife and daughters. (Courtesy of his grand-niece Emelda Brathwaite.)

Figure 8.19 Love trumps poverty in this colourised postcard from Panama of "Honeymooners" on a bicycle. (Postcard courtesy of Tricia Spencer at www.thebridalmuseum.com)

PART 4

THE
POST-CONSTRUCTION
YEARS AND
THE RETURN HOME

Figures 9.1–9.2 First-day cover (figure 9.1, author's collection) and stamp (figure 9.2, Wikipedia) honouring West Indian builders of the Panama Canal. This is one of the few signs of the recognition of the contribution of so-called silver workers; it came about only through the efforts of their descendants in Panama.

9. LIFE IN PANAMA AFTER CONSTRUCTION ENDED

> Evidently the governments of the United States, Great Britain and Panama either failed, neglected, or did not care to consider the West Indian worker as a human factor in the new social and cultural environment in which he would be projected as a consequence of his relation to the Panama Canal enterprise.
>
> —George Westerman, "Towards a Better Understanding"

PANAMANIANS OF WEST INDIAN ANCESTRY would eventually find their place as full-fledged citizens of the Republic. The journey to acceptance would be, however, a long and painful one.[1] Many of those who stayed behind when construction ended were to find themselves worse off than those who returned home. As long as the West Indian returnee brought back a bit of Panama money, his position and status improved; his peers looked up to him as someone who had made it. And even if he had not, he could have the satisfaction of knowing he was back in his own "yard", a man of experience.

Those who remained were to look back on construction days as the best of times for them on the Zone. No one questioned their place in society then: they were the workers. Both the United States and the Panamanian governments operated on the notion – perhaps – that as soon as their services were no longer required, West Indians would magically disappear. The fact that repatriation was provided for in the agreement with contract workers and was offered to others after construction ended underscored this notion. But seemingly mobile and transient labourers were not the only ones who had come to Panama. From the nineteenth century, West Indians had been establishing permanent settlements in Colón, Panama City, Bocas del Toro and elsewhere, and there were about forty to fifty thousand of them living on the isthmus.

During construction, there was a great deal of money in circulation and business flourished in the Republic. In the post-construction years, work on the canal fluctuated and with depression in the terminal cities, there was no alternative employment. Opportunities in the Zone itself became extremely limited and West Indians, including those who had been there from the nineteenth century, were to receive little or no compensation for their homes and farms along the canal route that they were forced to abandon.

REPATRIATION

As the ending of construction neared, many West Indians did in fact leave, either for home or for other jobs that were opening up around them. In 1912–19 the United Fruit Company recruited between five and six thousand men from Panama for work in the banana plantations of Bocas del Toro, Costa Rica and Honduras. On the outbreak of war in 1914, three thousand joined the British West Indies Regiment and the French islanders joined the French forces. Thousands of others headed out on their own and restless, ambitious bands of West Indian nomads continued for decades to roam over the Americas in a pattern of circular migration – from one country to another, back to home or to the United States, in search of jobs and opportunity.

Although the Panama Canal was obliged only to repatriate contract workers who had completed five hundred days of work, after construction ended, it offered to repatriate any former worker who wished to return home. By 1921, some thirteen thousand West Indians had been repatriated but people from the islands still kept coming, so the net outflow was only four thousand. In the late 1920s and early 1930s the Panama Canal again made funds available for the repatriation of workers who had given at least three years' service, an offer that included their families. This offer was made was during the Great Depression. Allowances were granted "in meritorious cases" of $25 for a single man and $50 for men with families, with $10 for each minor child up to a maximum of $100. On the whole, this repatriation was a failure. The Panama Canal authorities noted that, for the most part, those repatriated were older persons whose usefulness had ended. Very few family members accompanied them. For instance, in 1937, seventy-eight employees leaving were accompanied by only thirty-eight family members.[2] Thus it was mostly the old worn-out workers who were dumped on their home countries, often with nothing to show but a broken body or missing limbs.

The Panama Canal personnel officer John Collins aptly summed up the situation of those who refused to return home, as being "too proud to return as poor as when they left".[3] Construction worker Albert Banister, who had come from St Lucia, expanded on that: "why you did not go home Bannister

Table 9.1. Repatriation of Workers to the West Indies by the Panama Canal, 1914–1953

Country	1914–1950	1951–1953	Total
Jamaica	10,400	41	10,441
Barbados	6,800	46	6,846
Trinidad	950	–	950
St Lucia	450	–	450
St Kitts	325	–	325
Montserrat	90	1	91
Grenada	100	2	102
St Vincent	110	1	111
Antigua	75	–	75
Bahamas	275	–	275
Virgin Islands	25	–	25
British Guiana	275	1	276
Guadeloupe	950	2	952
Martinique	1,300	1	1,301
Others	575	6	582
Total	**22,700**	**101**	**22,801**

Source: Omar Jaen Suarez, *La Poblacion del Istmo de Panamá* (Panama: Impresora Nacional, 1979), quoted in Jos, *Guadeloupéens*, 183.

respectful I answered   Mam I would like to go home but I cant go home empty handed first all of my relative is dead   nobody know me at home I am a perfect stranger no friends no family   they all dead out   I have all my people down here whom I accustom to."[4]

But what of those who had established families in Panama and had "all my people down here"? Some, no doubt, were doing well and there was a growing middle class. Although there were no large West Indian businesses, small businesses thrived in Colón especially, such as barber shops, photo studios, furniture stores, shoe stores, tailoring and dressmaking establishments, pharmacies, and taxi and transportation services. The three most prominent Panamanian businessmen of West Indian origin – Stirling, De Veaux and Omphroy – had started in Colón and later made their fortunes in automotive dealerships and garages.[5]

A significant number, however, were to find themselves getting poorer, and as the years went by and economic depression hit, they were to be increasingly assailed on every side. The position of the West Indian versus the Panamanian became openly conflict-ridden and West Indians had to fight overt racism on three fronts – in the Republic, on the Zone, and against the powerful union-backed lobbies organized in the United States against their continued employment on the Zone. The history of the Panama Canal in the post-construction years is the history of the "whitening" of the Zone.

LABOUR AND HOUSING

The wages earned by Canal Zone workers fuelled West Indian prosperity in Panama but there was to be a dramatic fall in earnings and status in the post-construction years. Silver workers' power as a group declined as the workforce was drastically reduced and wages failed to keep pace with the cost of living. Silver workers earned a combined $10 million annually in the peak construction years; by 1916 this had fallen to $6.8 million.[6] The workforce continued to fall, too, to an average of 7,623 in 1920 following a disastrous strike, the lowest in the history of the canal. Thereafter, the average was 9,000 to 10,000 silver workers. But even the employed were plagued by job insecurity, the workforce in any given year fluctuating by as much as 20 per cent. Many were laid off and others were employed for short periods only. The turnover rate among silver employees in 1933 was almost 50 per cent.[7] The worker invariably lost his rating if he lost his job or sought a transfer, and in a new job he would be forced to start again at a lower rating. Until January 1928 the maximum that any silver worker on the Zone could earn was $0.40 an hour or $80.00 a month. In January 1928, after repeated representations, this ceiling was raised to $102.50 but was limited to one hundred silver employees at a time.[8] Even teachers, the elite of the silver workers, were hardly better off. Up to 1927, teachers on the silver roll were paid for only nine months of the year and had to find other ways of "making do" and supporting their families during the enforced vacation; their pay was $60.00 a month.

Until 1930, West Indian workers received no fully paid sick leave, until 1945 no paid vacation, and until 1937 no pension for either old age or disability. In 1928 the Panama Railroad had started to pay a retirement benefit of $15.00 to $20.00 a month, a boon especially to those who had returned home. In 1937 after repeated representations, disability relief for the silver workers received congressional approval (with a ceiling of $25.00) but the men (most now in their sixties and over) were compelled to go through a demeaning and time-consuming process to verify their eligibility since no records of the silver employees after 1908 were maintained. Many old workers kept on toiling as long as possible. A worker earning $0.40 an hour had to pay $3.00 daily for a family member in Canal Zone hospitals. Many a worker endured years of pain and illness so as not to have his pay cheque docked for time off.

Worn-out black workers were forced to shift for themselves. American resident Sue Core noted one such grandfather who walked up and down the

Zone trying to sell a few fruits or whatever he could get to survive, and commented, "During his days of exuberant vitality, he donated his physical strength, his only capital, in answer to the world's insistent demand for brawn. Now, his strength gone . . . he is left stranded . . . tossed carelessly upon the world's economic beaches."[9]

Those who remained behind in Panama were to form a large pool of surplus labour in the terminal cities. The canal policy favoured the development of such pools from which it could draw to meet fluctuating demands. During labour disturbances in 1919–20, the governor of the Canal Zone recognized these seasonally employed pools as being at the heart of the unrest and spoke of the need to provide alternative means of employment for the workers during slack times on the canal: "It will never be practicable to operate without a fluctuation of several thousand men throughout the year."[10]

Other means of making a living (such as farming) had been destroyed when the canal opened, as were other opportunities in the Zone towns. During construction days,

> there was no commercial stagnation; no curbing of privileges. Every employee, both white and coloured, could invest his savings, in some way or other, in order to add to his income. Permits were given to build houses, to peddle, to operate stores, coaches, automobiles, farms etc. . . . when they were out of work with the government they could rent a private house without having to resort to the terminal cities; they could find among themselves anything which would keep them until other work was procured. . . .
>
> Here is where the happiness of the West Indians lay. They are accustomed to own their houses large or small, they are accustomed to cultivate gardens, raise chickens, keep a horse, a cow, pigs, sheep, goats, keep a shop or store, and follow many other ways of making a livelihood which is denied them on the Zone.[11]

Although the Americans later raised restrictions on farming and made some land available for cultivation, for many it was too late.

While they were being squeezed in the matter of wages and employment, the workers were also being squeezed in the matter of housing since only employees could live on the Zone once the canal opened. In 1930 only four thousand employees were in silver quarters, a falling away from over twelve thousand workers and families in 1913.[12] After January 1915, unlike gold workers, silver workers were charged rental for quarters and for electricity and fuel, though the quarters remained third-rate and were improperly maintained. For example, at Red Tank there were thirty twelve-family barracks with approximately sixty persons to a building. There were only four toilets, two on each floor, two sinks and two baths for each building.[13] Workers who did not live on the Zone had to pay school fees for their children. Since occupancy of

Zone quarters was tied to employment, workers who lost their jobs had to immediately leave the Zone, becoming jobless and homeless at once.

The displaced workers were forced to crowd into the terminal cities. In the same tenements that were jerry-built at the start of construction by Panamanian speculators, the West Indians still huddled, this time paying rent that had sharply escalated in the post-war years. The health statistics continued to tell their story. Tuberculosis was now the main cause of death and the leading cause of admission to hospital. Enormous fires continued to roar through the brittle wooden tenements of Colón: in April 1915, 430 buildings in twenty-three blocks – or one-third of Colón – were consumed (leaving seventy-five hundred homeless); in 1916, 19 buildings in fourteen blocks went; and in 1917, so did 13 buildings on nine lots.[14]

WHITE SUPREMACY AND BLACK ACTIVISM

Once construction ended, gold workers conducted a relentless campaign to oust silver workers from all skilled jobs on the Zone, wanting them to be employed as janitors and messengers only. The gold employees and their families had become entrenched, enjoying status and living conditions far beyond what they would have enjoyed at home. They were "a close-knit, defensive, inbred, status-conscious, white supremacist society"[15] that was prepared to defend its interests at all costs. These interests included pay and working conditions matched to American rates plus perks such as free housing, free schooling, paid home leave, free health care, commissaries and recreational facilities, and high status versus West Indians and Panamanians.

Gold workers were represented by a number of unions, of which the Metal Trades Council was the most powerful, and they were to use their influence with politicians and political parties back home to jealously preserve the workers' privileges. Many of the policies pursued by the canal administration – such as the wage ceiling for black workers and the refusal to provide higher educational opportunities – merely reflected the positions taken by the white workforce and their powerful union and legislative supporters in the United States. Through these powerful lobbies it was fixed that black workers could not be employed beyond a certain level, could not earn more than a fixed maximum, and could not be promoted save in exceptional cases. The Metal Trades Council repeatedly advocated the ousting of all silver workers from the Zone. Around 1931 the American Legion joined in the battle to evict them and was instrumental in getting such a bill introduced into Congress. As Michael Conniff points out, "Gold employees and their families constituted a local oligarchy, supervising a mass of destitute blacks. Blacks should not even compete with whites and their status should indicate that clearly." Conniff quotes a union leader testifying before Congress in 1913: "We do not feel inclined to work on a level basis with a Negro. . . . We are willing to use the Negro as a helper, but [not] as far as 'Mr Negro' being on the job with me, as my equal."[16] Canal administrators of the time shared such sentiments and colluded with white workers to make it as unpleasant as possible for their black workers.[17]

Black Activism

Later generations would come along and accuse the construction workers from the islands of not being assertive about race and playing the role of "Uncle Tom". But overt acknowledgement of racism seems only to have come about in the post-war years. While old construction workers mentioned treatment that was clearly racist, they infrequently cited racism as such during their recollections about those days,[18] and when asked about the subject those interviewed refused to be drawn. "I have nothing to say against working in the Canal Zone", one retired worker explained. "I work with men who always treated me well, the bosses that I work with I always do my duty and they treated me alright. I never absent from work or neglect my duties and by that I have men who always appreciated my work and treated me well. Mind you," he added, "many of those old ones are gone away now."[19] Cecil Haynes, who worked on the canal for over seventy-one years, put the attitude of older workers into some perspective when he said, "You know in many of the interviews I have been having people would ask me of this discrimination that existed on the canal at the time. Well, it is something very ugly . . . and I have decided of myself it serves no purpose or any point for me to mention of the hardships that we went through . . . to mention it in these interviews but I would admit it really existed and it wasn't pleasant."[20] Haynes had made a much stronger point at the ceremony on 31 December 1999, which marked the handing over of the canal from America to Panama. Seated as an honoured guest among the VIPs, he asserted that "he was doing so as a living representative of the true VIPs, what he called the 'Very Invisible People', those like his father and thousands of other West Indians who built the canal".[21]

When construction ended, the changes on the Canal Zone were to be of both the black and the white workforce. Construction workers took pride in their jobs and the contribution they were making to a great undertaking, and this attitude might have somewhat modified the effects of racism. It is also likely that those who felt keenly about the racial situation on the Zone simply left to seek work elsewhere. One informant explained that since segregation applied only to the worker on the Zone, he could spend his spare time off the Zone and away from racially aggravating factors.

During construction the races seem to have worked out some accommodation within the system. Only toward the end of construction did a few cracks appear. In 1913 at Miraflores, some black workers attempted to board a car on a labour train reserved for white silver workers but were prevented from doing so by the men inside. Some of the blacks then began to throw stones, one of which hit a Peruvian labourer, killing him. The identity of the person who threw the rock was never established, but five of the West Indians were arrested, tried and each sentenced to five months in the penitentiary.[22] Later that same year, eight to ten West Indians boarded a European car in a labour train, "causing the Europeans to remonstrate". When the car reached a stop, a few of the black workers left and on reaching the ground, one of them picked up a rock and threw it, killing an Italian labourer, whom it struck on the head. A reward of fifty dollars was offered for the person causing his death.[23] On the whole, clashes seemed to have been avoided on the Zone, though in the Republic, clashes between the West Indians and Panamanian police as well as US servicemen seemed to have been fairly frequent.

Once the canal opened and the European labourers left, the starkness of the division between black and white was to be fully revealed.

The "New Negro" and Labour Organization

During construction, community cohesion was forged through churches, schools, social organizations and mutual aid societies based heavily on West Indian models. In the post-construction years, cohesion also came to be expressed through labour solidarity and Garveyism, and a greater awareness of international events and ideologies. From their wartime experiences, an assertive "New Negro" was to arise among African Americans in the United States and race became a prominent part of the international discourse, affecting the attitudes and behaviour of many in Panama as well as back home on the islands. The "New Negro" perceived the betterment of his economic position as a key to the development of the race and saw organization in trade unions as a means of achieving this goal. Throughout the world, industrial action was soon bound up with the racial question, fostered by large-scale migrations within the United States itself and abroad.

Many of the ideas relating to race and economic organization were given impetus by the teachings of Marcus Garvey and the dissemination of such ideas through Garvey's paper, the *Negro World*, founded in 1918. From 1919 Garvey's Universal Negro Improvement Association (UNIA) was to become a powerful force among West Indians in Panama, as elsewhere, and it coincided with the rise of a militant labour group among Zone workers. In many cases, labour leaders were also active in the UNIA. The *Workman*, a weekly

Figure 9.3 March of silver workers through Colón, during the famous 1920s strike (Wikipedia).

founded in 1912 by H.N. Walrond, a Barbadian, was another vehicle for the spread of progressive ideas and racial assertiveness. During fervent union organization in 1919, under a heading "Of Course Be Manly", the *Workman* told its readers that "the kind of Negro that doesn't talk back . . . is the old school kind who was taught to quiver 'when backra massa a tawk'. There are very few of that class on the Isthmus now; those who were here are either dead, or gone back home as superannuated worn-outs with their knees bent and their shoulders stooping from too much curtseying and bowing and scraping in their days."[24] The silver workers were now demanding not just better treatment at the workplace but respect all round. It is against the backdrop of these developments that West Indians on the Canal Zone attempted to challenge the US government.

The first challenge had been made in September 1916, when Latins on the dredging division at Paraiso struck and turned to the West Indians for support. Some three thousand silver workers failed to turn up for work but the strike fizzled out although it did result in a small wage increase. On 29 September 1917 a thirty-nine-year-old Jamaican policeman on the Zone force, Samuel Horatio Whyte, founded the Silver Employees Association following the demise of an earlier group, the Isthmian League of British West Indians. Though the Silver Employees Association attracted only limited membership

Whyte submitted the first petition to the governor of the Canal Zone covering wages, living and working conditions, sick and rest leave, schooling, railroad transportation, hospitalization, and commissary privileges. No reply was forthcoming and the organization staged a demonstration on Labour Day, marching from La Boca to Balboa Heights and back. The district judge of the Canal Zone objected to some of the placards displayed and these were seized by the police. Some of the slogans read "We seek not citizens rights but ask for a square deal", "Make the world safe for democracy and some part of it for the Negro", and "Labourer, learn or perish".

For all of this, Whyte's organization was essentially a conservative one, though their demonstration was apparently successful. On 24 October the silver employees were granted an increase of $0.23, or $7.50 a month, and were allowed sick leave of thirty days per year at the rate of 50 per cent of pay for married men with families and 25 per cent for others. This success attracted new members to the Silver Employees Association and at the end of the year it stood at seventy-five hundred silver employees, the largest the organization would ever have.[25] Around this time there was labour unrest in Costa Rica, where a strike by West Indian banana workers against the United Fruit Company was violently put down with reports of even more brutal repression of workers elsewhere.[26] The response of the company and local authorities must have influenced the Panama Canal workers to organize to defend their interests. Because of the extensive support workers from the banana belt were able to drum up outside, United Fruit Company was forced to ameliorate some of the worst conditions complained of since they were finding it difficult to recruit labour.

At the same time, the illegal arrests and evictions from United Fruit Company housing should also have alerted the workers as to what was in store for them in their own test of strength against the Panama Canal. Adding to the discontent in Panama and Costa Rica were demobilized soldiers of the British West Indies Regiment who were returned to these countries after the war, many of them destitute; the fact that many of the United Fruit Company managers in the banana belt were Germans did not help matters.

In April 1919 two white Americans, J.L. Allen and C.B. Seavers, arrived on the isthmus from the United States and began to organize silver workers. They claimed to be accredited representatives of the United Brotherhood of Maintenance of Way Employees and Railroad Shop Laborers based in Detroit, Michigan, a subgroup of the American Federation of Labor, representing black workers.[27] The Brotherhood met with phenomenal success. A local governing body was established in which William Stoute, a Canal Zone schoolteacher from Barbados, was to play a leading role. With the advent of the Brotherhood, dissatisfaction set in with the Silver Employees Association and its lack of militancy. Whyte resigned as president and the organization went out of existence.

What followed was to be a time of exhilaration, of "organization fever" on the Zone, though events would prove that local leaders were inexperienced and essentially naïve about their US connections, although they had the support of the elite among silver workers.[28] When the governor of the Canal Zone refused to enter into any agreement with the workers after they had submitted a number of claims, the Brotherhood called for strike action, having enrolled some thirteen thousand silver workers. For the first time since the start of construction, on 24 February 1920 the labour trains left Colón and Panama City with no silver workers on board. In all, fifteen to seventeen thousand silver workers walked off the job. That evening the governor issued an ultimatum. All employees who did not return to work on 26 February would be fired and deprived of living quarters. The gold workers, aided by some two thousand silver workers, were able to keep the canal going. Advance information on the strike had enabled the commissary division to ship large stocks of food from the Balboa warehouse to the line commissaries. On the Zone there was no shortage of food, electricity or water; the residents were totally self-sufficient.[29]

When the ultimatum expired without work resumption, Canal Zone police and soldiers began to eject the black families from their homes and from the Zone. At La Boca, the largest of the silver settlements, the ejections were carried out shortly before daybreak. By that evening, not more than four families and a handful of bachelors were left in the "silver" town and 391 families were evicted, along with their furniture and belongings.

The workers held out for nine days but by 3 March the strike was over, defeated by a number of circumstances, including the fact that there was no strike pay forthcoming from the estimated $150,000 in dues the workers had contributed to the North American coffers. The American organizers were no longer in Panama and communications between the strikers and the Brotherhood in the United States were mysteriously cut off. The strikers were left without support and had no option but to return to work. Some got their old jobs back but were re-employed at lower ratings; others failed to regain employment. While in February there were 18,231 silver workers, by March this had dropped to 6,770. In 1920, the gold roll increased by 1,318 employees, partly due to the employment of gold roll employees to replace silver workers. By 1921–22, not only had the silver workforce shrunk by two-thirds, but wages were reduced from twenty-three to twenty cents. The strike leaders never regained their jobs and several were arrested, many tainted by the "red scare" of communist affiliation. Strike leader Stoute, who had been a respected head teacher living in Panama for many years, was arrested and deported, sailing for Cuba.

The slim resources of the terminal cities were taxed by thousands of poor and homeless people thrown out of the Zone. The misery of the tenements was compounded by an influenza epidemic, part of the worldwide pandemic. Thousands of cases were reported between March and June, and 133 persons died.[30] Infant mortality soared and malnutrition increased among children of destitute families.[31] Hunger became widespread; from a US inspection of 179 families, 156 were found to have little or no food and 174 had no cash in hand. From the exhilaration of the pre-strike organizational fever, the community was plunged into the greatest despair. "We gaze in the faces of those around us", said the *Workman* in an editorial, "and the look of furtive fear is there. We have been unnerved, unmanned and we are in bad shape".[32] Those who could got on to boats leaving for the West Indies, Cuba, Bocas del Toro and Nicaragua (where banana fields were opening up) or the United States. Thousands did. Those left behind kept body and soul together by attending the soup kitchens that had been set up in Panama City and Colón. Some of the jobless were at this time repatriated by the Panama Canal. Conditions improved somewhat in 1924 with the development of farm settlements and road construction in the Republic, which made work available and contributed to an economic upsurge. But it was at this time that Panamanian–West Indian relations began to seriously unravel.

PANAMANIAN–WEST INDIAN RELATIONS

During construction, the West Indian presence was regarded as good for business. The workers were big spenders and kept the slum landlords happy by occupying their tenements. While Panamanians and West Indians scoffed at each other's ways and culture, there was usually an air of tolerance. With the growth of the Republic, a nationalist outlook developed, and increasingly the West Indians were seen as aliens.[33] Few Panamanians had sought work on the Zone during construction years. West Indians were, on the whole, better educated, acquired skill and long service in large numbers, and had a command of English, the language of the Zone. As an increasing number of Panamanians sought work in the Zone after the canal's opening, the West Indian presence was seen as a stumbling block to their own employment or advancement.

As the new Republic entered its second decade, it must have become apparent to Panamanians that the West Indians had become a strong and ubiquitous presence. Because of their skills and superior education, West Indians were also commanding better jobs in the Republic and were visible at many levels; construction workers had used their money to acquire their own businesses,

Figures 9.4–9.5 West Indians also contributed a great deal to the development of the Republic of Panama. From laying streetcar tracks (figure 9.4, postcard, author's collection) to starting the now popular bus service "chivas" (figure 9.5, courtesy of the Sandero Company).

controlling the bus services, taxicabs and garages. They were shop owners, and providers of services. West Indians educated in their homelands and in foreign universities were providing many of the professional services.

Apart from highlighting their differences of language, religion and lifestyle, Panamanians also believed the West Indians were reproducing at an alarming rate (although the West Indian birth rate was substantially below that of Panamanians) and perceived this as a further threat.[34] Through their labour unions and newspapers, the Panamanians began to mount an overt campaign. Simultaneously, a campaign to evict West Indians from the Zone, or at least reduce the range of jobs to which they could have access, was underway, backed by powerful Knights of Labor.[35]

Blatant discrimination became evident on all fronts, but reached its zenith in the administration of justice on the Zone. West Indians, for instance, could not serve on Zone juries, though they were frequently the defendants. The

"Feuille case" in 1920 publicly served notice to all West Indians that the Zone system of justice was no longer prepared to treat them impartially. Feuille was the son of the Panama Railroad attorney and head of the depot at Cristóbal docks. He masterminded a robbery at the depot with West Indian employees there as his accomplices. On being arrested, Feuille was immediately granted bail but this was refused the West Indians. At the jury trial, Feuille admitted responsibility, describing the other defendants as his tools. All were found guilty and sentenced to a year's imprisonment. However, Feuille was immediately released on a pardon from the governor of the Canal Zone. A petition by the West Indian community for a pardon for the other defendants was rejected and they served out their time.[36]

While the West Indian community was at its lowest ebb following the strike, the anti-West Indian campaign got into full swing in the newspapers such as *La Estrella de Panama*. With reduced money in circulation, competition between groups increased as everyone began to feel the pinch and cultural and racial differences began to be emphasized. In June 1921, the semi-official *La Defensa* published articles criticizing West Indian labourers as part of a campaign to deny them road construction jobs in the Republic. The first article was headed "The Chombo Competition" and the other "Chinks and Chombos", using the worst possible epithets in referring to Chinese and West Indians. Referring to the arrival of West Indians for canal construction work and the "competition" this presented, the paper concluded that "our laborers are anything but subservient and prefer starvation with all its horrors, to submitting themselves to the insolent ways and abusive manners of employers, our laborers have consequently placed themselves on an inferior level before the capitalists".[37] Not surprisingly, West Indians were unable to obtain employment on the road construction. In the editorial headed "Chinks and Chombos" the newspaper favourably contrasted the Chinese to the "Chombo", who was seen as "a true social plague". Reflecting the views of the Metal Trades Council on the Zone, the paper reiterated that the West Indian "has been born specially to wear uniform, the uniform of a porter and servant".[38] In March 1922 the Panamanian government passed a measure providing for the employment of West Indians on the new roads in the interior, but the opposition to them continued. In certain sections they were not permitted to visit native villages and were confined to work camps.[39] The anti-alien campaign, which had begun around 1915, continued intermittently in the 1920s and accelerated towards the end of the decade, when West Indians were threatened with wholesale expulsion.

West Indian Attitudes

There is no doubt that the attitude of West Indians themselves contributed to the perception of them as outsiders. Most had come to Panama with the intention of working to make some money and return home. Over time, however, many found themselves transformed from migrant workers into immigrant settlers. They acquired spouses and children, land and cultivation, a home and roots. Soon, there were so many West Indians in Panama that the lives they lived there became replicas of their lives back home, and they formed self-supporting enclaves, enjoying a social life and acquiring social status within tightly locked circles of compatriots. In short, the West Indian during construction days continued to be unequivocally West Indian. Even those who took the decision to settle in Panama showed little inclination to learn about the host culture. While there were of course individual exceptions, most proudly retained their British ways, were scornful of Latin culture, refused to learn Spanish and were adamantly Protestant. If they assimilated anything of the experience of being in Panama it was American mores and the American way of life on the Zone that they copied. West Indians made no attempt to legalize or clarify their status. And it was as aliens that the Panamanians and Americans began to view them – even those who had residence of many decades or had been born there. In the 1920s this meant a quarter of the non-white population on the Zone.[40] Ultimately, it was their value as consumers that prevented their wholesale expulsion when exclusion laws were passed.

Figure 9.6 Street scene in Panama City, post-construction years (Wikipedia).

Anti-alien Laws

With the rise of Panamanian nationalism, there was increasing pressure on West Indians to adopt Latin practice and usage, especially in the use of Spanish in their daily lives. Various measures were passed requiring a knowledge of Spanish as essential in order to operate a business in the Republic. For instance, in 1924 the Municipality of Colón issued a decree requiring knowledge of Spanish for all chauffeurs, motorists and operators of vehicles before licences could be issued. The majority of the owners of cabs and motor vehicles at the time were West Indians. There was also increasing pressure for the use of Spanish as the language of instruction in all schools, with English taught only as a second language.

An anti-alien bill placed before the Panama National Assembly in 1926 listed as undesirable the following: Chinese, Japanese, Syrians, Turks, East Indians and West Indians of the black race. Passage of the legislation would have meant that all black West Indians would have been considered aliens, and further immigration of the nationalities listed would be prohibited. The Chambers of Commerce of Panama and Colón immediately petitioned the government to exclude West Indians from the bill on the grounds that there were fifty thousand them in Panama and they were essential for the functioning of business. If they were forced to leave they would take 90 per cent of business with them.[41] The United Fruit Company as a large employer of labour also protested.

Some of the offending clauses of the bill were eventually removed after extensive protest, including by the British minister. But the assembly did pass a constitutional amendment to Law 13, withholding citizenship to children of prohibited foreigners until their twenty-first birthday. Since the amendment was not retroactive it affected only those born after 1928, throwing them into a kind of limbo. Previously Panamanian citizenship was granted to anyone born in the national territory. Birth in the Canal Zone did not confer American citizenship, and the British admitted to citizenship only children of married parents, at least one of whom was a British subject registered at a consulate.[42]

The bill was eventually vetoed by the president and returned to the assembly, and the law was amended to exclude foreigners already on the isthmus. However, with the passage of Law 13 in October 1926, further entry into the country of black English-speaking Antilleans and Guyanese was restricted.

In January 1927 a discriminatory labour law was passed that severely limited the participation of West Indians (and other ethnic minorities) in the workforce. The amendment to Law 6 originally provided that Panamanians should provide 75 per cent of total employees of all firms doing business in the Republic. Again, there was strong protest from large concerns such as the United Fruit Company and the Chambers of Commerce. The law was eventually amended to introduce the measures gradually: all companies were required to have at least 30 per cent of Panamanians on the payroll within the first two years, 50 per cent during the next three years, and the full 75 per cent five years after the law had been in effect.

The psychological impact of these measures on the West Indian community was incalculable. Many who operated on a small scale went out of business. But it also awakened West Indians to their situation. By now there was a first generation of Panamanian-born whose attachment to the islands was loosening. Some sought quick assimilation through rejection of their Antillean background as a way of dealing with their status. Overnight, they became hispanicized, changing their names, their religion, "forgetting" English and generally attempting to transform themselves into Panamanians as quickly as possible. The discrimination against anglophone blacks did not extend to native black Panamanians. "Henry" immediately became "Enrique" and "Charles" became "Carlos". Surnames were also, where possible, transformed to sound more Spanish. For many, turning one's back on one's roots, and uncertain status, was a small price to pay for the possibilities of assimilation and certainty. Still, the Panamanians remained dubious, charging that West Indians were "British by loyalty, American by economic necessity, and Panamanians for expediency".[43]

By 1931 the American Legion was waging a campaign on the United States mainland for the ouster of all aliens from the Panama Canal Zone, particularly West Indians. Such a bill was introduced into the US Congress and was accompanied by a press campaign. In 1932 there were huge demonstrations in Panama demanding repatriation of West Indians as part of the "Panama for Panamanian" movement.

Following a new influx of West Indians in the late 1930s to construct a third set of locks on the canal, the short-lived regime of President Arnulfo Arias in 1941 passed measures that further alienated West Indians. The first was a clause in the new constitution which denied citizenship to children of "prohibited immigrants" born in Panama after 1928. Second were bills nationalizing merchandising which prohibited West Indians and other immigrants from participation at a certain level in economic life. But the boom years provided by the Second World War eased some of the pressures against the West Indians and their rights were restored by a more liberal constitution of 1946. Today, many Panamanian-born who were young at the time still claim that the legacy and uncertainty of these years will remain with them forever.

SPEAKING UP: THE PANAMA CANAL WEST INDIAN
EMPLOYEES ASSOCIATION

The 1920s continued to be the heyday of lodges and benevolent societies, but only one labour organization remained, the Panama Canal West Indian Employees Association (PCWIEA), founded by Samuel Horatio Whyte of the short-lived Silver Employees Association. In 1924 Whyte formed the PCWIEA at a meeting at LaBoca attended by thirty-six persons; membership was restricted to persons of West Indian descent. The association functioned as a lobby group and benevolent society, operating sickness and death benefit funds for its members. The PCWIEA never had more than eighteen hundred members at any one time and came to be regarded as a "one man band" due to the personality and organizational style of the leader. Nevertheless, Whyte, through the PCWIEA, became the de facto spokesman for the black workers for the next twenty years until he retired from the office in 1945. He was awarded the MBE by the British government for his services.

The PCWIEA never relented in its lobbying of both the Canal Zone governor and the relevant Panamanian and other authorities in the interest of West Indians. Though the organization's impact is hard to assess, many of the concessions granted to wage labour on the canal only came about after many years of representation by the association.

Whyte was able to secure an annual meeting of PCWIEA representatives with the governor of the Canal Zone to discuss matters relevant to West Indian interests. Whyte, it was said, was known for his meticulous written presentations and polite manner of address and "believed that confrontation must fail, so he perfected a style of deferential petitioning that never challenged but had a touch of controlled anger".[44] A good sample of his style appears in this report of an exchange with the Panama Canal governor, Colonel Walker, in 1927 in a discussion about wages. To show their condition was "not so bad" the governor said the manager of one of the banks in Panama told him the savings of "coloured people" in the bank was one-and-a-half million dollars. Whyte pointed out that in aggregate the sum represented the savings of twenty to thirty thousand persons. The dialogue continued as follows:

> **Governor**: Speaking of conditions, I think you men can do a great deal of good if you lecture your people on their gambling habit. They are the same as the colored people of my home State, and I daresay of the United States generally. Your people waste a great deal of their money here at the Race Track at Juan Franco and at the Dog Races when they are here, and in gambling chances on the lottery. Little boys can be seen gambling. I have seen them at the Golf Club, for instance. I give a boy a half-a-dollar to pick up golf balls, and before long he is off gambling with some other boy with that half-a-dollar. . . .

Whyte: It is appreciated, Sir, that our people gamble and spend money in a foolish way. . . . Far be it from us to plead any justification for any kind of spending, but the people believe they are doing something to help themselves. They see all around them the happy and contented faces of the gold employees in their automobiles, in their comfortable and well-appointed homes, and they make an effort to get some of this contentment and comfort they see around them by taking chances in the hope of placing themselves in a better condition.

Ignoring the irony, the governor reiterated that the gambling habit was the principal cause of "your people's condition".[45]

Education as Racial Policy

While it might be argued that black workers in the early years were regarded as a temporary part of Zone life and therefore did not warrant the investment of large sums in the education of their children, after the Panama Canal opened, the role of education as part of a racial policy was fully revealed. Black schools were always inferior in facilities; were inadequate for the number of children needing schooling; and the level of education provided was deliberately kept low. Although high schooling for white children was introduced as soon as there were American children on the Zone of this age, up until 1931 "coloured" schools on the Zone only went as far as elementary grade eight; junior high was not introduced until 1931, and senior high grades introduced gradually between 1946 and 1948. Kindergarten was introduced in 1941 and occupational high schools in 1946.

With the depopulation of the Zone following the opening of the canal, the number of black schools was drastically reduced and located only in La Boca, Paraiso, Gatún and Cristóbal, places where black populations had become concentrated. Eleven white schools were in operation. The ratio of white to black schools was now the opposite of the situation during construction days. While attendance of white children was stable, average daily attendance of coloured children dropped from 1,762 to 436, partly reflecting the continuing job instability of their fathers. By 1923, the structure and conditions of coloured schools, always second rate, had been allowed to deteriorate even further. The Panama Canal annual report noted that "the buildings are overcrowded, and there is a waiting list of children who cannot be admitted; the equipment is inadequate; and teachers are required to take care of more children than they can properly instruct".[46] In some coloured schools the pupil-teacher ratio was 1 to 50. In 1928, despite provision of additional schoolrooms and employment of an extra thirteen teachers, there were still on the Zone 1,278 black children between the ages of six and sixteen for whom there were no school places.[47] Between 1927 and 1930 the enrolment in coloured schools increased from

2,332 to 4,080, and teachers increased from forty-seven to eighty-five.[48] However, these times were a far cry from the pioneering days when in the canal administration's own words "first class" teachers were being attracted from the West Indies. In 1930, among coloured teachers on the Zone, seventeen had no training beyond primary school.[49]

In the post-construction years, agitation increased for the provision of high schools and vocational training for children of silver workers. However, it was no accident that children could go only as far as grade eight in primary school and that when manual training was first introduced (1927) the PCWIEA could complain that such training consisted of simple carpentry, which left much to be desired from the standpoint of utility. Parents, however, tried to fill the gap as best they could, including private education. As Simon Clarke recalled, they also placed emphasis on providing their children with vocational training and instruction in instrumental and vocal music as well as cultural enrichment through music, drama and dance: "The feeling was that one had to have a marketable skill, not academic training alone. Shorthand and typing, dressmaking and tailoring, radio repair, playing a musical instrument, were all popular activities." Many parents continued to send their children back to their country of origin for their education.[50]

The Metal Trades Council, the lobby of white Zonian workers, reflected the thinking which influenced educational policy on the Zone when it wrote to the PCWIEA in 1930 that it would not interfere in the association's endeavours to obtain higher wages and working conditions, so long as it was satisfied that silver workers would be employed in no capacity higher than a janitor or messenger. It is not surprising that the council was also opposed to education higher than primary for silver employees.[51]

In 1930 an educational survey committee on the Canal Zone arrived from Columbia University and noted that the coloured schools "offer no more than a bare academic training, with no opportunities for self-expression, appreciation, or training for the task of earning a livelihood".[52] It was not until 1946–48 that the US government provided academic and vocational training for students up to grade twelve. The Zone schools continued to be labelled white and coloured until 1954 when, following desegregation legislation in the United States, they were classified according to American or Latin American citizenship. This policy managed to preserve *de jure* segregation. It also represented a further blow for children of West Indian origin, though in the long run it helped to facilitate their integration into Panamanian life. By a new ruling, almost overnight, classes in the former "coloured" schools, now converted to "Latin American", had to be conducted in Spanish rather than English.

Thus it was that through an inadequate educational system in the post-construction years, no outlets or opportunities were provided for the children and grandchildren of construction workers to better themselves or express themselves creatively. These generations became alienated both from their fore-bears and from the government which oppressed them, and from the country in which they were born but in which they did not feel at home. They did not share with the older generation the escapism provided by the notion of a home overseas or a heavenly home above. Many became, as they were frequently referred to in Panama, "men without a country".

THE UNIVERSAL NEGRO IMPROVEMENT ASSOCIATION

In this environment of psychological distress, there was one agency that did help to provide younger generations as well as adults with a sense of self-worth. It was Marcus Garvey's Universal Negro Improvement Association (UNIA) and for many, its effects were incalculable. Although membership and interest in the UNIA fell over time, the movement remained a strong one in Panama at least until the 1940s. The Colón branch in particular continued to attract young people because of the educational programme it offered. The UNIA high school, which flourished in Colón for some time in the 1920s, was the only school providing a secondary education for black students and boasted outstanding teachers such as James Smellie, Cyril Thomas and Franklyn Hector-Connor.[53] As a former member of that time explained, the UNIA offered all forms of educational advantages which attracted younger people:

Figure 9.7
Marcus Garvey.

> I don't think we were very much keen on the going back to Africa business but we were keen on the programme they had outlined. They would train us to be secretaries and hold meetings . . . part one would be religious and part two would be secular where the younger people would recite, they would have debates conducted and things of that sort. So that they had a terrific hold on the younger people. But it wasn't because of ideology it was because of opportunities.[54]

Simon Clarke's father, Frederick Alanzo Clarke, a commissary worker, was president of the UNIA (Colón Division) for several years. Simon and all his brothers and sisters were members of the Youth Division which met every Sunday afternoon, and he too noted the psychological benefits provided through its cultural and educational programmes.[55]

The organization also provided its members with security. Through a health and death-benefit scheme, the UNIA tried to give members some economic organization and imbued them with a sense of community and race pride. The particular appeal that held primacy varied with each individual. But its lasting intensity is attested to by the fact that old Garveyites in Panama interviewed in the 1970s still regarded their days of membership in the UNIA as the high

point of their lives. In the Bocas area, one member who lived on an island in the lagoons rowed a boat twenty miles each way to attended meetings of his UNIA chapter in the town.[56] There are also former Garvey supporters who cite the vast financial contributions that Garveyites made to the movement as being responsible for the destitute condition of such people today. What is not in doubt is the tremendous impact the movement created on the West Indian communities in Panama as it did in Costa Rica.

On 24 November 1918, shortly after Garvey established the UNIA in the United States, the first UNIA branch was organized on the isthmus, in Panama City with J.H. Seymour and S.P. Radway among its founders. Both men were regarded as "agitators" by the British authorities there, as was Garvey.[57] By 1919 there were branches all over Panama; in all there would be thirty-nine divisions. The cause was boosted when the SS *Frederick Douglass*, flagship of

Figures 9.8–9.9 UNIA march in New York City at the height of the movement (Wikimedia Commons); UNIA members in front of the office in Harlem (courtesy of the National Library of Jamaica).

the Black Star Line, docked at Cristóbal in late December 1919. Captain Cockburn was given a tumultuous welcome and travelled to Panama City, where he met prominent West Indians. As he came off the train, the huge crowd that had gathered outside pushed and craned their necks to get a glimpse of "the first Negro captain to navigate a ship across the Atlantic". The captain and party had difficulty in getting through the masses waiting to see their hero when the train stopped. He was again besieged by admirers when he spoke at a meeting at the West Indies Red Cross hall. Henrietta Vinton Davis, international organizer of the UNIA, also visited Panama on the SS *Yarmouth* late in 1919 and spoke to large and receptive gatherings.[58]

The charter of the Panama branch was unveiled in January 1920. In September of that year the Colón Liberty Hall was opened. The building which was located on Eighth Street cost six thousand dollars.[59]

Garveyites were active in the events leading up to a strike of silver workers in February 1920. They had a forum for their views in the West Indian newspaper the *Workman* and in Garvey's *Negro World*, and Garveyism and union fervour found a marriage in the call for racial upliftment and economic unity among black people. By the time of the strike, in a situation of mounting unrest among West Indian workers in Central America, Garvey was regarded as a distinct threat by the Panama Canal authorities. When it was announced that he planned to visit Central America and Panama in early 1921, he was banned from landing in the Canal Zone. By this time Garvey had received tumultuous welcomes from West Indians in Port Limón, Costa Rica and Bocas del Toro.

At Bocas, he boarded an auxiliary schooner *Linda S*, and landed at Colón, evading the US authorities who were watching at the port. Garvey's one-upmanship boosted his popularity. He spoke first at Colón Liberty Hall then travelled by train to Panama City, where a dense crowd of supporters awaited him, some even climbing into the windows of his compartment to see and touch the great man.

The refusal of the Panama secretary of the treasury to allow Garvey to speak at the national theatre showed up some of the class divisions in the West Indian community, for prominent West Indians were accused of using their influence to deny Garvey the theatre. This they refuted, pointing out that they had nothing to do with the theatre but that the regulations governing its use provided only for artistic events. Garvey went on to speak from the tent of a circus then in town, from the bullring and from another theatre. The venues were all packed with people wanting to see and hear him (at one dollar per head admission) and hundreds had to be turned away.

On Garvey's return to Colón, crowds followed him from the train station up the street to the headquarters of the UNIA, where a reception was to be held. The reception had to be called off because of the crush of people and the car carrying Garvey drove away. The crowd did not realize he had left and people hung around in the pouring rain hoping to catch a glimpse of their hero. Handbills were eventually thrown down from the balcony of the building giving times and details of the meetings.

In his farewell speech, Garvey told his followers in Colón, that he had studied their lives there. "Politically," he said, "I find you are drifters, drifting to the land of nowhere. Because I am interested, I desire to see the good ship strike a port. I am endeavouring to point you to a haven of peace and safety – to the haven of Africa."[60]

Yet with the economic depression that followed – and the lost money which had been invested by thousands in the Black Star Line – the faith in the movement, though not apparently in Garvey – was severely tested. The *Workman,* usually staunchly supportive of black nationalism and the Garvey movement, in March 1922 carried an editorial headed "More Bubbles in Harlem" in which it hit out at the loss of the investments of poor black people in the Black Star Line. The vanished subscriptions, said the paper, "came from people, many of whom are paupers today. Speaking for Panama, it is no exaggeration to state that 90 per cent of the shareholders are now reduced to the state of abject impecuniosity; and those who still cling to the organization do so on account of the benevolent feature which characterizes one of its subsidiary departments." The paper added: "The Panama Canal is repatriating hundreds of West Indian paupers every month. . . . Where do the delegates [from Panama] of the Universal Negro Improvement Association get their inspiration from when they pledge unbounded support and financial backing to the impossible Black Star Line business?"[61]

The personal support for Garvey continued. His last direct contact with Panama was in 1927, after he had been released from Atlanta Penitentiary. He travelled on board the SS *Saramaca* en route to Jamaica, changing to the *Santa Marta* at Panama. Garvey was not allowed to leave the ship but well-wishers secured permission to visit him on board. The delegation read an address of welcome and pledged allegiance to the movement and faith in Garvey's leadership. They presented him with a purse subscribed to by members of the local UNIA.[62]

The Colón membership was at one time well over one thousand strong, and the institution operated business interests, including a bakery, restaurants and stores. But mainly because of lack of organizational ability and knowhow, and some dishonesty, none of these businesses prospered for any length of time. A former member of the Colón organization said that nobody left the group because of Garvey's personal problems. Eventually, however, they began to question the usefulness of sending subscriptions abroad, and there was a split from headquarters. Although the Colón group continued to support the tenets of the Garvey movement, they operated autonomously. They retained the letters UNIA but, for legal reasons, the word "united" was substituted for "universal". With the continued failure of the business ventures, however, the local UNIA eventually foundered.[63] In Bocas del Toro province, where at one time over thirty branches of the UNIA existed, a former branch secretary recalled that the UNIA stopped functioning in this area in 1936.[64]

While no visible trace of Garveyism and the UNIA remain in the Republic of Panama today, the beliefs and doctrines of the organization were, for a while, a profound influence in shaping isthmian–West Indies life and thought. More than anything else, it provided a glimpse of the opportunities that were possible for black people in a place where these were for many years deliberately denied.

With the passage of time, new generations shifted their loyalty to Panama and the story became one of "becoming Panamanian". Those who returned to the West Indies, meanwhile, would become engaged in trimming old growth and putting down new roots.

Figure 10.1 The Panama Canal – built with West Indian blood, sweat and pride (Wikimedia Commons).

10. WHAT THEY BROUGHT BACK HOME

Above all things . . . to which the comparative contentment of the past half century can be attributed was the outlet to the energies of the people provided by the emigration.

—*Report of the Commission Appointed to Enquire into the Disturbances which Took Place in Barbados on the 27th July 1937 and Subsequent Days*

JAMAICAN LOUISE BENNETT CAPTURES in her poem "Amy Son"[1] the popular idea of the transformation wrought by a sojourn overseas, as well as the emigrant's capacity to influence those who had remained at home:

> Him bring back walkin'-stick an watch
> Wid gole chain bout soh long;
> Him bring back bed, him bring gole-teet,
> Him bring back Spanish twang
> . . . .
> As him always drive in Spanish
> Jamaica drive feel strange
> So him say to me, "Chikita,
> Wat muchos grandos change?"

Not only has Amy's son been changed by the experience of travel – his clothes, his speech, his looks and his entire perception of things around him, but as Louise Bennett clearly brings out, the transformation also attracts admiration and, as a natural progression, the flattery of imitation. In the final stanza, the narrator has quickly learned to "cut language" herself:

> Doah me and him noh fambily
> Me proud o'him soh tell
> Me please fe se him get awn soh
> Muy exibonos well.

In material ways as well as in speech, manners, and more subtle cultural behaviours, the complicated influence of returning migrants often provoked satire, enshrining forever the stereotype of the "Colón Man" or "Panama Man". But the overall impact on their homelands was to be far more complex and far-reaching. The effects were to be felt economically, socially and politically.

AGENTS OF CHANGE

What the emigrants brought back to their homelands depended on when they returned. The years up to the 1920s were relatively prosperous ones for the West Indies, aided by the flow of money into the islands from wage earners abroad. Some 45,000 Barbadians had emigrated to Panama in the first two decades of the twentieth century,[2] and almost 90,000 departures were recorded from Jamaica between 1905 and 1915. Panama continued to attract the majority of travellers, though some of them later left for other countries such as Costa Rica, Cuba and the United States. In addition to "Panama money" flowing into the islands, the war years 1914 to 1918 brought prosperity in the form of higher prices for sugar, the economic mainstay. But as American investment poured into Cuba, it supplanted the British West Indies as the world's leading sugar producer and became a magnet for British West Indian workers. Some 140,000 of them flocked into Cuba between 1898 and 1930, more than half (75,871) arriving in the four years from 1916 to 1920 during the period known as the Dance of the Millions,[3] when sugar prices skyrocketed.

This rosy scenario changed dramatically and with bruising effect as the 1920s came to a close. By the end of the decade, more people were returning to the islands than were leaving.[4] In 1924 the United States enacted immigration laws that made entry difficult.[5] The Wall Street crash of 1929 and the worldwide economic depression closed more borders. Cuba and other Latin American countries introduced restrictive legislation against black English-speaking West Indians. As economic and political instability increased, the emigrants' position became precarious; public opinion turned against them since they were increasingly perceived as "aliens" and "cheap labour". In 1928 British West Indians in Panama were threatened with wholesale expulsion. Though this did not occur, further immigration to that country of Afro-Antilleans was prohibited. In times of greatest depression in the 1920s and 1930s, thousands were repatriated by the Panama Canal Company. Thousands were also sent home from Cuba in the 1930s. They were returning at the worst possible time:

> Things get tough in Cuba,
> Not a work to do,

All the people coming back
Have to start life all anew.

Some folks pay their passage,
Some repatriate,
Some can't even find a cent,
To buy a grater-cake.

Going back to Jamaica where I'm from (repeat)
Not a furniture, not a thing,
One machete that's all I bring.
Coming back to Jamaica where I'm from.[6]

What emigrants brought back to their homelands changed dramatically over the years. At first, their contribution was tangible and visible in the form of money, goods and skills. In the post-Depression years, their contribution was more weighted to intangibles in the form of ideas and influences that would radically alter the social, spiritual and political landscape in the decades to come. Much of the leadership at various levels in the social ferment of the 1920s and 1930s in all the islands came from men and women who had travelled. They brought home not just "gold chain and watch" but ideas, influences and a changed psychology that created entirely new mental maps on these islands. As an emigration cycle lasting some eight decades came to a close,[7] those returnees who had been fired in the crucible of foreign experience (including soldiers returning from the First World War) and those now penned in at home were to prove an explosive combination. Bonham Richardson noted that "the era of Panama money represented a turning point in Barbados history". And so it was for the other islands and territories.

ECONOMIC EFFECTS

The most striking effect of emigration was economic, one that had an impact over the whole period as the emigrants travelled back and forth. The point at which they returned home depended on personal factors, such as whether or not they had acquired enough of a nest egg. Once they returned, some stayed for longer or shorter periods and then left again for work overseas while others settled back home. A returning migrant could bring enough money to start building a house, run out of money, and then return to the isthmus for another spell of work so he could finish it, a phenomenon that is still visible among emigrants from the islands today. Some return home and start a small business or purchase land and livestock and leave these in the care of relatives while they leave again to continue to earn while family networks absorb children left behind. Because of the reciprocal system of obligations among poorer families,[8] "Panama money" could also be used to finance a trip overseas by another family member.

In her memoir *Triangular Road*, writer Paule Marshall describes her own family's experience of emigration to the United States: "The West Indian wing of black America's Great Migration North [more than three hundred thousand West Indians between 1900 and 1925] could not have taken place without Panama Money." Emigrants needed to show fifty dollars on arrival, called "show money", and in the case of Paule Marshall's mother, the show money, "as well as the much larger sum that had paid her passage north had come from a single source: Panama Money from an older brother she had never really known". He had gone to work on the canal when she was an infant. He died of illness in Panama but not before he had "sent home the better part of his pay during his years there". In the Clement family, Panama money was used to purchase small plots – cane pieces – which were rented out until one of the children or, later, grandchildren was of an age to travel, and the land would be sold to pay for his or her passage. The person in charge of the entire operation was a stay-at-home woman in Barbados, Paule Marshall's grandmother.[9]

Because of the continued close contact that was possible between home and work overseas, virtually all the possibilities and consequences linking "home" and "away" were explored, not all of them successfully. In another classic pattern in West Indian culture, stories abound of money sent home being stolen, diverted or frittered away and not used for the purpose intended, leading to anger, family divisions and even madness of the broken-hearted.

Business Skills and Know-how

The earthquake and fire that devastated the city of Kingston in 1907 was one of those seminal events that influenced people both to leave and to return. One example of returnees who saw this as opportunity and engaged in the rebuilding of the city were five brothers of an impoverished Jewish family called Henriques. They had gone abroad to try their luck and ended up in Panama as Isthmian Canal Commission (ICC) and Panama Railroad employees on the gold roll. Vernon worked as an engineer for the ICC and Panama Railroad until August 1907; Rudolph went to Panama in 1906 and worked as a topographical draughtsman in the Colón Municipal Division of the engineering works; Emanuel ("Manny") first went to Ecuador in 1901 and worked on the engineering staff of the Guayaquil–Quito Railroad company and later in Panama for three years as an inspector of machinery for the ICC; Horace was employed in the office of the Panama Railroad as an accountant; and Owen

Figure 10.2 Kingston devastated after earthquake and fire, 1907. (Courtesy of the National Library of Jamaica.)

("OK") joined the office staff of the Panama Railroad as a teenager and two years later was made secretary to the company's auditor, a position he held for three years. On their return to Jamaica after the earthquake, they were joined by the sixth brother, Fabian, a structural engineer. The sons of an engineer, the brothers had all left school in their early teens and the practical professions they chose and the experiences they gained overseas provided them with the combined skills needed to form their successful enterprises, Henriques Brothers Construction Company and Kingston Industrial Works, an iron foundry,[10] and a dynasty which continues to this day. The Ward Theatre is now the best known of the iconic buildings they designed and constructed in downtown Kingston after the earthquake. They also established Kingston Industrial Garage to import Ford motor cars only four years after Henry Ford established his American company in 1903. Kingston Industrial Garage became the first Ford dealership to be established outside of the United States and remains today the world's oldest Ford dealership in continuous existence.[11]

While the story of the Henriques brothers is extraordinary and unique, many thousands of others throughout the islands were also to make their mark in business large and small as a result of "Panama money". Returning emigrants augmented the pool of skills and technical knowledge, ignited the entrepreneurial spirit and gave impetus to the concept of the self-made man. Modern modes of transportation seem to have been an attraction, and many West Indians started taxi and bus services both in Panama and when they

Figure 10.3 The success of the Henriques brothers in early-twentieth-century Kingston is attested by the picture of the staff of their main company, Kingston Industrial Works (*Planters Punch*).

£180 at our Garage.

5 Passenger, Model T Touring Car.
4 Cyl : 4 Cycle. 22½ Horse Power.
5,000 Miles on 1 set tyres (over any road in Jamaica.)
20 to 25 Miles to a gallon of gasolene.

No other car manufactured can approach them as a hill climber. They say of the Model T "good for any climb in any clime, any time." All cars are fully equipped: Top Windshield, Gas Lamp, Generator, Side Oil Lamp, Tail Lamp, Horn and Tools.

Look Out for Next Saturday's Issue of the "Gleaner".

KINGSTON INDUSTRIAL GARAGE.

Sole Agents : FORD MOTOR COY.

17 West Street & 4 Pechon Street, Kingston.

Figure 10.4 The Henriques brothers also founded Kingston Industrial Garage in 1907 to import Ford motorcars. (Courtesy of the National Library of Jamaica.)

returned home. The manufacture of aerated water was another popular choice, requiring little outlay. The returnees also opened shops and pharmacies, became small- or large-scale contractors and builders, set up as carpenters and cabinetmakers, tailors, dressmakers, shoemakers and so on, their "foreign" air and exposure no doubt giving them cachet.

One example of individual success was Wilfred John Fenton, from a rural parish of Westmoreland in Jamaica, who was forced to leave school at fourteen and learn the trade of cabinetmaking. At the age of nineteen he emigrated to Costa Rica, where he practised his craft, then left for Panama in 1904. He was first employed as a carpenter by the ICC, then as a foreman carpenter for fourteen years. He returned to Jamaica in 1919 and started with a small cabinetmaking shop in Kingston which was to grow into Fenton's Hardware and Cabinet Making Establishment, which became a byword for fine furniture in Jamaica.[12] Not all returnees established themselves in the towns. The Kavanagh brothers Lancelot and Austin went back to their rural parish. Lancelot used earnings from his

Figure 10.5 Wilfred J. Fenton (*Who's Who*, 27–28).

Figure 10.6 Lancelot Kavanagh. (Courtesy of Rosemary Kavanagh.)

Figure 10.7 Austin Kavanagh, with his wife, Marjorie. (Courtesy of Rosemary Kavanagh.)

years in Panama (1905–12) to establish a successful grocery, haberdashery and bakery in Malvern, St Elizabeth, before settling on a property in the parish, where he built a fine house and farmed on a large scale.[13] Austin also owned a haberdashery and grocery store and a more modest farm in the same area. These experiences were not isolated cases of how "Panama money" was used; many families could tell similar stories of the elevation of their forefathers to the rural mercantile and land-owning class.

Cash Contribution

Money earned abroad had a tremendous impact on island economies. The overall contribution would have been much greater than officially noted, since only cash that passed through banks and via registered letters, postal money orders and what returning emigrants disclosed on arrival was recorded. We have little information regarding the Panama Railroad workers, but we do know that the inflow to Jamaica during the French canal effort was considerable. St Lucia sent about 10 per cent of its entire population to Panama at this time, and the island treasurer was happy to record that between 1885 and 1890 £66,337 representing the American gold received in the island from Colón was re-exported, and large sums were also received in drafts.[14]

Usurious exchange rates had made it difficult and costly to send money home until the US government established a postal money order facility on the Zone in 1906. Even though workers still had to pay to convert their silver dollars to gold, the post offices were swamped after each payday. In the first six months of operations, $295,842 worth of postal orders destined for the West Indies were sold, and by 1907 a regular increase in the monthly totals was noted.[15]

The governor of Barbados in 1909 stated that workers on the Panama Canal had so far contributed $425,000 to their island (£62,210 in money orders and £21,844 brought back).[16] Jamaican emigrants (to all destinations) were said to have contributed an average of £125,000 a year to theirs.[17] In examining the economic contribution to Barbados, George Roberts commented that "emigration appears as a valuable foreign investment rather than as a loss to the island . . . it has been estimated that during the zenith of the movement 1904–1920, these remittances were sufficient to pay for between one-tenth and one-fifth of the annual imports of the island".[18]

The Export Trade

Island exports provided another promising source of income. Precise figures are not available and the trade might have been considerably undervalued because a great deal of "invisible" exports took place. Goods for trade carried by migrants as personal baggage on steamships would not be shown on the ship's manifest or be officially recorded. Many migrants – and goods – also slipped away from the islands and evaded official notice. Rum and tobacco products were among the main exports but surprising items were shipped such as these three in 1905–6: bricks from Jamaica to build the municipal buildings on Bolívar Street, Colón, in 1905;[19] cattle for General Huertas, former commander in chief of the Panama army for his farm at Agua Dulce;[20] and horses for commercial stables in Panama.[21] A great deal of food, fruit and livestock came via Barbados and Jamaica. Big companies were involved but so were individuals at all levels, from the itinerant vendor who travelled back and forth with supplies, to the small farmer, such as those from the parish of Hanover in Jamaica who grew the famous Lucea yam, to the middleman who shipped it. In the good times, money truly flowed.

This flow of money was a major factor in the growth of government institutions such as the Government Savings Banks and the post office. Commercial banking also thrived. During the height of the emigration to Cuba in the first two decades of the twentieth century, the Royal Bank of Canada, which opened a branch in Kingston in 1911, had to employ three extra staff to handle remittances from Cuba alone.[22]

Employment of Capital

What the emigrants did with their money helped to transform the physical landscape. They invested mainly in housing, land and livestock, the latter two especially by the growing small settler class.[23] In Jamaica, attractive new houses sprang up all over the island, and new suburbs developed in Kingston. The

Figures 10.8–10.10 Emigration played a role in the education of successive generations of Jamaicans, an example of which is the Harry family of Kingston. Dr Archippus Harry (figure 10.8) was the son of Thomas Harry, who was implicated in the Morant Bay Rebellion and served a five-year prison sentence in England as a result. On his return to the island, he set up a successful tailoring business known as "The Knickerbocker" and sent his son to medical school. Dr Archippus Harry's son Gervaise Verner Harry (figure 10.9) was a Mico College graduate who migrated to Panama and worked there until his death in 1931; his son, Gervaise ("Val") Harry (figure 10.10). was sent back to Jamaica for his education at Calabar College and became a prominent doctor, practising mainly in the parish of St Mary. Two of the three children of Val Harry and his wife, Grace, Gervaise and Philip, are also medical doctors and Elizabeth, PhD, is a university professor. (Courtesy of Elizabeth Harry.)

investment in land might have reflected cultural values placed on land ownership,[24] but it was also strategic. Referring to the water metaphor for money as something flowing freely, Bonham Richardson noted that this "liquid quality" probably inspired Barbadians to invest it in a fixed asset like land, in order to keep their money from flowing to friends, kinsmen and others.[25]

Jamaica's peasantry expanded and prospered in the late nineteenth and early twentieth century, thanks to the greater availability of both land and money to buy land. As the *Daily Gleaner* commented in 1905, "It is a well known fact that the opening of the canal works over 20 years ago by the French Canal Company gave an impetus to the growth of the Jamaican peasant proprietary, and helped to put the peasants in a more secure position than they had formerly occupied."[26] Nevertheless, most plots remained small, and big property owners controlled the best land for producing export crops such as bananas: the land issue continued to be a source of contention. As Ken Post points out, "In 1890 cultivators with less than twenty acres were producing about 39 per cent of the island's agricultural exports. In 1930, although their actual numbers had considerably increased, they were producing about 41 per cent – almost the same proportion as forty years before."[27]

Figure 10.11 A group of middle-class Jamaicans, early twentieth century (author's collection). The woman at left is Isoline Hilton whose father, Edward Rupert Peart, worked in Panama for many years, then emigrated to New York, a path taken by many West Indians of the time. On his return to Jamaica he established himself as a successful pen keeper at Haddo, Westmoreland.

Other forms of investment cannot be easily quantified although they touched everyone. Such was the investment in education that enabled emigrants and their children to acquire professional and other training, adding to the pool of skills and technical knowledge in their homelands. This enrichment contrasts with recent and current emigration from the Caribbean which is regarded as a drain of human capital, especially of professional skills frequently acquired at taxpayer expense through scholarships or student loans. For the earlier emigrants, the opposite held true. Although skilled and trained persons did emigrate, in the long run the societies recovered a great deal more than they lost. Foreign travel was not only the university but the technical school of our forebears. Even those who did not acquire specific skills abroad usually learned from the foreign exposure the discipline of work, and it was frequently commented that employers found those who had gone away and returned to be much better workers.

Consumers and Creators

Returning emigrants added to their countries' stock in other ways. They brought in a great deal of personal goods – including household articles, appliances and tools – which they would not otherwise have been able to acquire. Their modernizing influence helped to alter standards of behaviour, of dress, housing and modes of living. Part of their style derived from the American influence. The women working in institutions and homes overseas acquired knowledge of sophisticated kitchen equipment and appliances; of diet, food preparation and presentation; and an associated vocabulary. Household articles and appliances were available in the commissaries at affordable prices. Items such as drapes, bedspreads, household linen, furniture, clothing and personal adornment would all have been brought back by the émigrés and were usually of styles and quality beyond the means of all but the very rich at home. When the emigrants returned, they not only acted differently, they looked different, and many set up housekeeping in ways that were different from prevailing standards.

As creators they also brought back new styles, influences and trends. Thus the tailor or dressmaker who had travelled introduced new ways of constructing clothes, cabinetmakers new styles of furniture, and hairdressers and barbers new ways of treating hair. Even the houses that some of the returning emigrants built displayed a difference in styles and led to an increase in importation of construction material such as wooden roofing shingles. West Indian carpenters were, after all, the ones who constructed the buildings on the Canal Zone, and they no doubt learned from the American architects even as they introduced their own touches. Many wooden houses constructed in Jamaica from around the turn of the century with foreign money would not be out of place in those areas of Panama developed by silver workers.[28]

Figure 10.12 An example of a West Indian house in Panama. (Courtesy of the National Library of Jamaica.)

One aspect of a modern lifestyle that had a negative effect was the importation of foreign foods, especially processed foods which affected nutritional levels. Bonham Richardson shows for Barbados that returning emigrants might have been investing in land and the building of houses thereon, but this practice did not represent "a return to or a yearning by black Barbadians for more agrarian, traditional, subsistence, or more rustic modes of livelihood".[29] Many used their land to plant sugar cane as a cash crop and there was growing dependency on imported staples such as rice and the growing propensity to buy food from country shops. The rising prices of imported food stuff would lead to growing nutritional deficiencies.[30]

SOCIAL EFFECTS

Although the successful emigrants came home to be seen and admired, and although their financial contributions were regarded with approval by the authorities, there was also the underside, the dark side of the story – those who returned home, sick, maimed, damaged and often with nothing to show from the experience but a broken body or mind. Many became charges on their poverty-stricken families or, worse, outcasts and beggars. Still others brought back some cash or valuables only to throw it all away in foolish displays of wealth so that they too ended up paupers. Stories of such "characters" seem to exist in all the islands. But perhaps the most telling effect on those left behind came from those emigrants who – for whatever reason – never returned home and were never heard from again. The missing ones left a profound impact on the West Indian psyche lasting for generations and leaving gaps in the family circle still requiring closure and wounds of abandonment that have never fully healed.[31] Many who left their homelands were in fact to remain abroad forever: about one-third of all emigrants from St Lucia in the nineteenth century,[32] more than one-half of Barbadians,[33] and an estimated 146,000 Jamaicans between 1881 and 1921.[34] Many were joined by partners and children overseas and remained there, but too many simply vanished.

Demographic Changes

So many men sailing away from home was bound to affect social and family life, the most obvious being the gender imbalance it created. Women did travel to join their men, and increasingly travelled on their own, especially in the later years to Cuba. In Barbados between 1911 and 1921, 44 per cent of population loss was due to the emigration of females.[35] But the vast majority of the emigrants were young men in their prime. Their going affected population growth and composition, the age structure, the composition of the labour force, sickness and death rates, marriage and divorce rates, and the breakup and insecurity of families and the abandonment of children. It also reinforced the role of Caribbean women not only as child-bearers but as family heads.

The greatest impact of migration was on birth rates. Emigration was the most effective birth control device of its time, each period contributing to very marked declines in the birth rate, the rate soaring when large numbers of emigrants returned. In nineteenth-century Jamaica, for instance, the first three years of emigration up to 1884 attracted one-fifth of the male population of reproductive age,[36] and a similarly high outflow of males continued until the end of the decade. As a result, the years 1881 to 1889 saw a birth rate under 1 per cent per year, lower than the rates experienced over the preceding twenty years.[37] Similar falls in the birth rate were recorded for later episodes; up to 1921 emigration was a powerful factor in controlling population growth, especially in rural areas where the outflow of males was greatest. Once emigration ceased, the annual addition to the rural population in Jamaica from 1921 to 1943 was about five times greater than when emigration was highest.[38] The effects were even more remarkable in the case of Barbados, where fully 70 per cent of the total net emigration of 1861 to 1921 was of males.[39] Here, "births dropped from more than 7,000 a year in 1895–1904 to less than 6,000 in 1911–15, and continued to fall for another twenty years".[40]

Populations swelled with the return of the emigrants after 1920. The male population in Jamaica increased by 68 per cent (114,200 to 191,300) between 1921 and 1943, while the increase for females was 50 per cent. Particularly striking was the increase of males in the working group aged thirty to sixty-four.[41] In conditions of shrinking employment, this rise had serious social and political implications.

The effects of the migrations could also be seen in the balance between the sexes. In Jamaica the male-to-female ratio started to fall in the 1880s and reached its lowest point in 1921 of 881 males to every 1,000 females,[42] becoming equally balanced again only after 1921. The case of Barbados was extreme. During the years 1911 to 1921, there were twice as many females of marriage age as males, a gap that was reduced by the time of the 1946 census.

The departure of so many breadwinners affected women and children in numerous ways. While many of the men supported those back home or sent for them, many were never heard from again or their deaths left their families destitute. The smallness of the average sums left behind by emigrants attests to this.[43] In societies where even then the norm was for working-class women to singlehandedly fend for children,[44] desertion of families and consequent destitution was sufficiently serious to come under official notice. In Jamaica, more and more children were forced to forage for food on other people's property, and an increase in praedial larceny was attributed to this. Infanticide and concealment of births also increased, some of these cases occurring while the husband was away. Infant mortality (regarded as a reflection of the mother's inability to care for the child) also increased.[45] The number of popular songs that touched on the effects of so many males leaving suggests widespread consciousness of the situation it created. One which is still known in Jamaica and elsewhere has the chorus sarcastically declaring, "it's nobody's business but his own":

> Solomon Grandpa gone a Ecuador
> Lef him wife and pickni outa door
> Nobody's business but his own
>
> Solomon Grandma swear she na go beg
> Tief weh all Bra' Sammy fowl and egg
> Nobody's business but her own.

Abandonment of women and children as a consequence of migration was frequently noted by observers, and emerged as a theme in literature.[46] In many cases, males returned home with other women acquired abroad or, with their new-found wealth and glamour, found themselves the centre of competing sweethearts, distributing, as a former governor noted, cash and venereal disease with equal abandon.[47] Desertion and its consequences were not lost on the wider society, as in the reference in "Nobody's Business". The more poignant "Dallas Gone a Cuba" – described in collections as a "love song" – sets out the problem in one stanza and solves it in a practical way, in another:

> Dallas gone a Cuba
> Left Francella one fe wanda
> Mamie wai o, me faint weh! . . .
>
> Po Miss Mary daughrer
> Po Francella left fe wanda
> Johnny round the corner
> Him naw left you one fe wanda

Even the children's ring game "My Lover Gone a Colón Bay" adds a pragmatic touch to the situation:

> My lover gone a Colón Bay
> With a handsome concertina
>
> Gal, who going to marry to you
> For kisses go by favour.

A shortage of men also meant a change in the composition of the labour force as, for a while at least, women and children had to undertake many jobs hitherto the preserve of males; many references throughout the period emphasize such a shift. With the absence of men, there was an increase of women employed in the agricultural sector as well. Payment to women in the labour force was considerably below that of males, so even working women found it difficult to provide for themselves and families.

While some of the changes to which emigration gave rise were irreversible, many of the effects were temporary and were turned around by the return of males in the 1920s.

Difficulties of Adjustment

Even when men and women kept their families together overseas, there were often difficulties of readjustment for those returning to their islands. Unless the emigrants had earned enough to set themselves up and create homes for their families, emigration to other places of the primary breadwinner, male or female, sometimes continued with consequent separation and instability. An older migrant who contributed to the Jamaican Memory Bank project[48] revealed one side to this story. Mrs W. Robertson was born in Panama. As a child, she was about to be taken by her mother to join her father, who had left Panama for Cuba. Before they set out, news came that he had died there suddenly, and they returned to Jamaica instead. They lived with her mother's sister for three years before the sister left for Cuba, leaving her own children behind to be cared for by the others. Mrs Robertson recalled that she was told nothing about Panama although her birth certificate was in Spanish. She was later naturalized in Jamaica.[49] As it was to be for many, once the contact with

Figure 10.13 The dress and appearance of the two boys in Panama no doubt reflect their parents' differing status. (Courtesy of William P. McLaughlin, www.czimages.com.)

Panama was broken, it was never revived, and the experience of travel faded. In other cases, returnees were rejected by their families, especially those who had not kept in touch, and some returned to their adopted country.

For years afterwards and for various reasons, many of those who had gone away and returned were set apart from their peers who had not travelled; they would be "marked" for good or ill. For children, initial problems of adjustment were sometimes acute. Their differences in speech and dress made them, for a while at least, objects of both fascination and derision among their peers.

Cleveland Stanhope was born in 1911 in Panama, where his father worked on the canal as a carpenter. When Mr Stanhope returned to Jamaica with his children, he bought a property of about 150 acres and planted sugar cane and acquired mules and drays to transport the canes. Cleveland Stanhope was himself trained as a sugar boiler and became a master at his craft. He recalled that when he and his siblings returned on visits to Jamaica as a child, his relatives used to take them around the village: "our dress was different our speech was different the people would come to see us and talk to us". Difference was magnified when he returned permanently and went to school: "it was foreign to me, the life style and the bushes around the trees". Going to school in the rural parish of Westmoreland, he had problems with the children because of his mode of dress and speech. "I was talking like an American and we could speak Spanish too. . . . So we were kind of isolated. . . . We would not walk with the other children because they would laugh and we don't understand what they are saying" – because they were talking Jamaican patois.[50]

Dress also set apart even those children who had not travelled but received gifts of clothing from abroad. In Barbados, a retired schoolmaster remembered that, "as a schoolchild himself, his classmates who had relatives in Panama or the United States always looked different from everyone else because of their distinctive clothing sent from abroad or purchased with money sent home to Barbados".[51]

Similarly, Clifford Allen left Panama in 1911 and returned to rural Jamaica when he was about twelve years old and found that "when I come from Panama yah now, a little boy – I come in my three piece [suit] yuh know . . . an' when di other children dem come round an' de look. . . . A have a little touch of Spanish yuh know – an' de come an' seh, Allen, tell us a Spanish word. . . . Yu come from Panama."[52] He remembers everyone being poor and living in thatched huts with wattle-and-daub walls. Back in Jamaica, his father earned only three shillings a day, and he sent his son to learn the trade of boat building.

One Jamaican whose father returned to become headmaster of a school in a rural parish was to recall somewhat different experiences. He and his brother derived status as children of the headmaster, but they nevertheless felt the strangeness of life in a completely new environment. Dudley H. Thompson went on to have a celebrated career as a Rhodes scholar, lawyer, pan-Africanist, politician and diplomat. He recalled that although his father had a job in the Canal Zone system, teaching at Red Bank School, he chose to return to Jamaica even though he "never earned half as much as he earned in Panama", and when he was settled he sent for Dudley and his brother who had been left behind in Panama. His father, Thompson explained, "had never felt himself a second class citizen in his own land". And he did not want his children growing up in an atmosphere where racial discrimination was accepted. Even here, far into rural Jamaica, where people were poor, his parents "preferred to stay

Figures 10.14–10.15 Ambassador Dudley Thompson (figure 10.14, in Royal Air Force uniform), born in Panama where his father taught, recipient of the Order of Balboa, Grand Cross (figure 10.15), the second highest order awarded by Panama, "for distinguished diplomatic services and contribution to international relations between Panama and other states". (Courtesy of Margaret Cezaire-Thompson and Cecile Eistrup.)

where they could enjoy the overriding feeling of ownership and equality, a sense of dignity that even their colonial status had not denied them".[53]

This sense of dignity was no doubt a motivating factor for many who returned, especially in the post-construction years. The foreign-born children could also enjoy what had so far been only spoken about by their parents, for instance devouring for the first time a Jamaican patty, as Thompson and his brother did as soon as they arrived. They would also enjoy the pleasures and freedom of running wild in a well-fruited place after their initial culture shock, coming as they did from the "urban" Canal Zone. Thompson recalls: "The next few days found us trying to adjust to the new surroundings. The people we met were very kind and respectful to 'teacher's' two young boys. It was nice to see so much vegetation growing around. There was so much to learn from an outdoor life. Carl kept pointing out the differences." Soon, "I learned to ride horses and climb trees. I learned to distinguish the sounds of birds, the leaves of trees, the seasons when fruits like guinep, mangoes, or star apples ripened. It was a new world unto itself."[54]

THE COLÓN MAN MYSTIQUE

Some returnees chose to be highly visible, flaunting their difference. Every village or district the length and breadth of the islands would end up with at least one "Colón Man", "Panama Man" or "Cuban grandee". He had a style of

Figure 10.16
"Colón Man"? The
unidentified man
in this Jamaican
postcard might well
have been a Colón
man (author's
collection).

walking (the Yankee strut), of talking (the Yankee twang salted with Spanish words and phrases), of dressing and, more important, of behaviour. After the war he was joined by the former soldier, who had also travelled overseas. It was the romance of being a travelled man that set them apart and gave them heroic status in their own eyes and among some of their peers. But attitudes to their presence were mixed, and very much in the eye of the beholder.

Because Colón Man was no longer servile or subservient in his manner, he represented a challenge to existing social mores and to imperial authority, an authority that rested on subordination and repression. It is perhaps most in this respect that Colón Man might be described as subversive.

Yet his subversive nature should not be exaggerated. In terms of the future development of these societies, Colón Man was the precursor of change, rather than the revolutionary. Although his time was spent in Latin America – seedbed of revolutions – socially he emerged as an agent of US cultural imperialism. The enterprises for which he was engaged were undertaken with US capital and dominated by US personnel. Socially, it was the American rather than the Latin style that prevailed. Although many salted their speech with Spanish words and assumed a kind of Latin pseudo gentility in dress and manner, it was American behaviour that most influenced the emigrant, who admired and emulated it. As Jamaican Cleveland Stanhope recalled many years later, "My father used to talk about the Americans. He never talked about Panamanians so much. Americans, Americans, Americans."[55] The ubiquitous commissary system, with its proliferation of mass-produced consumer goods, helped him to easily acquire the trappings of the "Yankee" lifestyle, which he not only imitated but elaborated.[56]

The "subversion" of which we speak was a subtle and elusive concept that has been scarcely documented, and it is perhaps in literature that we can best pin it down, exaggerated though some of it might be. Maryse Condé in her novel *Tree of Life* described the return of her hero Albert to the French island of Guadeloupe after making his fortune in Panama and the United States. From the start, Albert makes it clear that his struggle as a migrant worker is to enact a kind of social revenge, to enhance his status and that of his family in his native island. This goal might not have been so unusual for many emigrants; his single-minded pursuit of it, however, is unusual. He begins to adopt the American lifestyle from the very start, and sets himself apart, criticized by his fellow blacks who continue to live as they had done in the island. For his first wife he builds a bungalow "modeled on those of the Canal's American workers", takes Lisa to a hospital to give birth under the care of American doctors and refuses folk medicine. Later, he takes his son back to the island and leaves him with his own mother with the warning that he is to learn to speak French, not Creole. "I want him to go to the best school, to have the most beautiful clothes, to wear patent-leather shoes on his feet and speak French-French like a white man – you hear me?"[57]

Nevertheless, Albert takes Marcus Garvey's teachings of race pride and black economic independence to heart. When he finally returns home, he creates shock, awe and consternation in his native land by his transgression of centuries of racial and class boundaries. "People say that when Albert Louis returned from his ten-year stay overseas, he deposited so many American dollars in the bank that the white manager came out of his office himself to stare at that river of green."[58] Albert also bought land and established a lakou (a tenement yard), and then he "purchased an import-export store that had belonged to a white from Saint Martin. . . . A Negro in the import-export trade!" Finally, he bought a seafront property and erected a large "high-class" house. "When Albert planted pots of bougainvillea and poinsettia on the balconies, the townspeople's fury rose and overflowed."[59] The narrator (one of his descendants) feels the need to add: "Certainly there was no lack of Negroes in La Pointe who belonged to the upper classes and ruled the roost in politics. But they were doctors, lawyers, even teachers – that is to say, people who had risen to where they were by dint of education. Who was Albert Louis? A former sugarcane cutter whose mother, a former cane bundler, still wore the Creole dress called a *matador* and did not know how to read."[60]

Throughout the West Indies were many actual men (and women) like Albert Louis who returned home with some money and used it to rise in society. The most outstanding example was George Stiebel of Jamaica: he left home a lowly carpenter and emerged from gold-mining in South America as the hemisphere's "first black millionaire". Devon House, the lovely home Stiebel built himself in 1881 in Kingston's most exclusive suburb, is now a government-owned national monument and tourist attraction. The brown-skinned Stiebel himself enjoyed high status among Kingston's population, becoming custos of the parish, officially the leading citizen.[61]

There were many sober returnees who inserted themselves back home quietly, without fuss, and those whose presence "added to the local reservoir of wisdom and knowledge of the world outside". Throughout the Caribbean they

Figure 10.17 Devon House, Jamaica, built by George Stiebel with money earned abroad – in this case "Ecuador gold". (Courtesy of Dennis Ranston.)

Figure 10.18 Claude McKay (Wikiepdia).

became "the village elders, older and experienced men and women to whom everyone else in the community would take their problems as well as appeals for advice".[62] Men such as Pa in George Lamming's *In the Castle of My Skin* were among them. Others used their new wealth to snobbishly mask their lowly origins or hide the type of labour they had undertaken abroad, and many were enabled by their new-found wealth to marry up.[63]

In Claude McKay's works set at the time of the Panama exodus, we perhaps find most fully revealed the impact of the Panama experience on a typical village such as the one where McKay grew up, especially in the semi-autobiographical *My Green Hills of Jamaica* and the documentary novel *Banana Bottom,* written after McKay himself had emigrated to the United States in 1912.

Mr Andry of "Naseberry Park" spends thirty years in Panama and Costa Rica and returns with a wife, two exotic daughters, money, but little social pretention or polish (though his wife and daughters take full advantage of their status). He seems to be the exception to the typical returnee described by McKay and other contemporaries.[64] The schoolmaster in "Crazy Mary" who ran away to Panama to avoid an awkward social situation returned "a little dapper with a gait the islanders called 'the Yankee strut' ". He was married "to a girl he met over there, a saucy brown dressed in an extreme mode of the Boston dip of the day".[65] The story "Crazy Mary" also exposed the social phenomenon of the travelling men deserting their women at home and finding new women overseas. In "The Strange Burial of Sue", Johnny Cross, the new romantic rival for Sue, came from Panama with "eye-catching American-style suits and a gold watch and chain and rings of Spanish gold". At the village fete,

"Johnny Cross was fixed with more money than the village bucks could muster for a year".[66]

But McKay's personification of the Panama experience is most fully developed in the character of Tack Tally in his novel *Banana Bottom*. In his dress, Tack Tally is the epitome of the Colón Man,

> proudly wearing his decorations from Panama: gold watch and chain of three strands, and a foreign gold coin attached to it as large as a florin, a gold stick-pin with a huge blue stone, and five gold rings flashing from his fingers. He had on a fine bottle-green tweed suit with the well-creased and deep-turned pantaloons called peg-top, the coat of long points and lapels known as American style. And wherever he went he was accompanied by an admiring gang.[67]

Tack Tally was, a few decades removed, the "big swell" described by a planter in the 1870s, who swaggered in with "a watch and gold chain, a revolver pistol, red sash, big boots up to his knees".[68]

Tack Tally also embodied the seamier side of the migration experience, the one that the authority figures complained about. Even his *compadres* of the village secretly resented – and were perhaps fearful of – his ways ("his Panama ways which were equivalent to bad manners"), which threatened the established order laid down by centuries of British colonialism: "his bold and forward talk about the finest type of village folk as if everybody could be cooked together in the same Panama pot".[69]

People like Tack Tally both represented and contributed to a process then taking place – a loosening of the social structure and the conflict that this elicited in the minds of the more timid stay-at-homes. McKay reflects the middle-class values of the time in presenting Tack Tally in a most unsympathetic, even melodramatic, light and ends up with a distillation of all that the society saw as wrong with the Panama experience. The varying points of view are presented by McKay in a discussion between Priscilla, the white English missionary's wife, and Bita, the black heroine of *Banana Bottom*. When Priscilla first settles in the area, the natives are contented with mild drinks like orange wine and ginger beer. But now so many of them are getting the habit of the hot Jamaica rum, the parsons and all the pious people, she claims, are alarmed at the change.

> "It's the Panama Canal", said Priscilla. "Our Negroes are not the same after contact with the Americans. They come back ruder."
>
> Bita replied, "But they make more money there, though. The least two dollars a day, they say. And here they get only a shilling. Eight times more gain over there."
>
> "And a loss of eight times eighty in native worth. They come back hard-drinking and strutting with bad manners, loud clothes and louder jewellery."
>
> "I don't like it," continued Priscilla. "Times may be hard here and our black folk

Figure 10.19 *Banana Plantation* by Jamaican barber-painter John Dunkley, who spent his early years in Panama and whose work is believed to reflect the world he experienced there. (Courtesy of the National Gallery of Jamaica.)

terribly poor. But I like them better so than when they come back peacocks from Panama."[70]

Priscilla's attitude is the same as that of visiting travel writers of the day who freely attributed lack of "manners" on the part of any Jamaican they met to the influence of the Panama experience.[71] After all, the Jamaican peasant had continued to be viewed and portrayed by local and visiting whites alike as the stereotyped smiling "Quashee". Bessie Pullen-Burry claims that the "happy irresponsible character of the Jamaican negro, together with his docility and politeness to strangers, produces favourable impressions upon visitors to the colony".[72]

The impact of the social repercussions of the emigrant experience depends on the perception of the society from which one starts. Certainly to this day, the myth of the suave, Latinized Alexander Bustamante, say, is as pervasive as that of the boorish Colón Man, Tack Tally.

Scapegoats

There is little doubt, however, of the émigrés' influence in another respect. The emigrants to Latin America brought back to their Caribbean societies notions of overt violence, of violent rhetoric, and new symbols and instruments of violence. Part of the change had to do with availability: sticks, stones and machetes were the weapons of even the most threatening mob in former times. Although he undoubtedly towered over his contemporaries in many ways, Jamaican prime minister Alexander Bustamante in his years as populist leader, with his ever-present six-shooter, chest bared dramatically to the police guns, his sheathed dagger brandished on public platforms, was perhaps representative of that change brought about by travel. Such symbols were clearly not reflections of Anglo-Saxon attitudes.[73]

Tack Tally embodies the most vulgar expression of Colón Man with regard to violence. "He boasted two notches in his stick for two hearts that he had shot out in Panama",[74] and his favourite cry when roused was, "If it wasn't foh the law I'd shot him down like a dog."[75] The only difference between this manifestation of Colón Man and that other creature of myth-making, the Wild West outlaw, is that the outlaw usually dispensed with the excuse, a notion which suggests that the British West Indian rebel or "bad man" of the times was as torn with contradictions as his more law-abiding compatriots, a tribute to the thoroughness of the colonial indoctrination.[76]

West Indians in nineteenth-century Panama lived amid forms and levels of violence that in the twentieth were curtailed by strict governance of the Canal Zone, by the formation of an organized police force in the Republic of Panama, and the cessation there of revolutionary activities. In the twentieth century, violence against West Indians reached great heights in Nicaragua, Honduras and Cuba especially. From the time of the French canal, police reports in Jamaica began attributing certain forms of antisocial behaviour to the Panama experience, particularly an increase in crimes of violence. The police report for 1885–86, for instance, noted an increase in cutting and wounding and commented that "the resort of large numbers of labourers to Colón and other portions of Central America from time to time to work on the canal and elsewhere and the bad habits they acquire, has, no doubt, much to do with the increase". The next year's report specifically stated that "the offence rapidly increased on the cessation of work on the Panama Canal in 1887–8, and the repatriation of several thousands of able-bodied men, who had acquired the habit of using the knife on the Isthmus when excited by drink, jealousy, etc.".[77]

Gun ownership, carrying a gun, or having some other weapon such as a dagger, became the hallmark of a sojourn in Latin America. Along with boastful and exaggerated language and behaviour, these habits became markers for the whole new culture derived from the foreign experience.[78] The return of "hooligans" was also noted in Barbados and officials here, as in the rest of the Caribbean, assumed relationships between rates of robbery and returned migrants.[79]

However, the overall impact of this aspect of the migration experience should not be exaggerated because Colón Man, the man who had gone away and separated himself from society, had also become its scapegoat. All civic and social evils in the society were soon his fault. Crimes and other antisocial behaviour were attributed to returnees from Colón even when no evidence existed to support such notions.[80] These widely held and hostile beliefs reinforced antipathy, nourished by the stay-at-homes, against those who had gone away. Part of it was undoubtedly jealousy that the men and women who had gone away had returned changed and in some ways superior folk. Local envy and mistrust, however, ran parallel to official attitudes.

Increasingly, the governing authorities in the West Indies saw these returning emigrants as a threat to the good order of society, and the Colonial Office in London was kept busy giving advice to island governors on the subject. Various strategies were used to keep dissenters in check or muzzle them: outright condemnation, false charges, arrest, imprisonment, confinement in mental asylums, intimidation, and the use of police and military force often resulting in injury or death. Colonial authorities of the time offered nothing in the way of dialogue or compromise with those who dared to challenge them. Yet they could not halt the whirlwinds of change sweeping across the Caribbean Sea, shifting the balance of power from European control to American hegemony.

The neglect handed down over centuries of colonial rule was starkly revealed when those who had gone away and secured the means to better themselves came home. Their visibly improved standard of living produced what was called the "demonstration effect" fuelling discontent. The West India Royal Commission investigated the causes of the disturbances of 1937–38 and observed of the man who had stayed at home that

> what would have seemed to him years ago to be luxuries quite beyond the means of all but the rich have become the necessities of to-day. Many of his people, leaving the West Indian colonies to work in Panama, Cuba and the United States of America, have returned with accounts of higher wages and better conditions in other countries. The British West Indian, from his insanitary or inadequate home, has seen beside him the building of good houses out of their savings by these returning friends. . . . Everywhere the urge is being felt for better housing, better education and other amenities normally associated with modern civilization.[81]

The nineteenth-century emigrants left behind a land of tiny rural settlements where ideas circulated slowly and innovation was rare. These stagnant conditions changed, especially in larger islands such as Jamaica. The banana trade had begun on that island and spread to Central America, leading to expansion of transport and tourism; some seventeen steamship lines sailing between Jamaica and the eastern seaboard ports of America contributed to the circulation of both people and ideas. Internal roads and communications were vastly improved as post offices, new schools, and both rail and bus services began to appear. At the same time, an educated and articulate middle class arose from the peasantry, a class which contributed not just teachers, doctors, ministers of religion and other professionals to their own and to foreign lands but one that evolved a cadre of nation-building leaders at home: men and women who wanted a say in how their countries were run. Only 7 per cent of the population of Jamaica could vote before the widening of the franchise in 1944. But it was the consequences of dramatic urban growth in the years after the First World War that provided the tipping point for social and political upheaval.

POLITICAL EFFECTS

The vast majority of people leaving the islands came from rural areas: they included 88 per cent of Jamaican male migrants between 1911 and 1921. Most of the other islands were agricultural with a small urban area, the capital city. While in the early years many emigrants returned to their original homes, most of those who returned after the 1920s chose not to go back to the countryside. In Jamaica, they disembarked in Kingston and remained there. At the same time, people from the rural areas were pouring into the city in search of work. Overcrowding was swift and overwhelming. The population of Kingston more than doubled between 1921 and 1943,[82] much of it from the swelling tide of poorly fed, housed, unemployed yard dwellers. Lord Olivier, a former governor, described the city of Kingston as "the sink of the landless, casual labouring folk of most of the island".[83] These migrants from internal and external sources concentrating in the capital, many unemployed and without means of support, were to become bitter and militant, a combustible, urban proletariat waiting to join with the exploited working class to seek betterment of their condition.

The trek to the city of the rural poor reflected the inability of small farmers to provide for growing families on their small plots with no wage work to be had. Modernization in the sugar industry had reduced the demand for rural labour. And the new growth industry – bananas – was much less labour intensive. There was a dramatic shift of female employment from agriculture to domestic service which meant, essentially, seeking a job in the town. Even those emigrants who had invested in land were finding it hard to make a living in the post-war years. The prices for major crops fell and, at the same time, most of these crops were attacked by serious diseases. As Major Orde-Browne, who investigated labour conditions in the West Indies, noted, "sugar cane suffered from mosaic disease, bananas from Panama disease and leaf spot, cocoa from witch broom, and limes from redroot and withertip, each of these causing widespread havoc; coffee, citrus and coconuts had their troubles, while even Jamaica's special product, pimento, was almost wiped out by rust".[84]

"Banana wars" between the large growers were helping to shut small growers out of this profitable market, and week after week many small farmers watched their fruit rotting at railway stations for lack of buyers,[85] one fact which gave impetus to the formation of the All Island Banana Growers Association in which returning émigrés were to play a role.[86]

Hardly any jobs were to be had in the capital city. In the Depression years, the Kingston Charity Organization Society opened a soup kitchen to ease some of the distress, providing for many their only meal of the day. Where in 1931 a little over thirteen thousand were assisted, the figure climbed to over forty-four thousand by 1936. Because job opportunities vanished, wages remained low, a shilling a day still being the norm. The maximum for rural labourers was three shillings and sixpence per day. But as an alderman, Dr O.E. Anderson argued, the man who had to work for the private company from 6 a.m. to 5 p.m. or along the public highway for 2/6 to 3/- per day could not feed himself properly[87] (a US dollar was then four shillings). The situation was exaggerated by the extraordinary rise in the cost of living in 1920, shown in a

45 per cent increase in the cost of food, 100 per cent increase in the cost of clothing and over 100 per cent in the cost of furniture.[88]

In some of the smaller islands heavily dependent on sugar, the situation was worse. The price of sugar, like other exports, had almost halved between 1929 and 1933, and workers faced drastic wage cuts, increased taxation, under-employment and unemployment. Totally dependent on sugar, St Kitts was the most extreme case: workers had experienced wage reductions, leading to an offer of work cutting cane at eight pence per ton (sixteen cents);[89] the workers' refusal led to the first of a series of strikes leading to the labour rebellions that rocked the region in the 1930s. A close connection existed between local misery, the rise of working-class militancy and the circulation of radical ideas from overseas, much of it brought back by those who had travelled.

Challenges to Authority

While for decades the impact of emigration affected mainly economic and social life, the influence would become increasingly political, as both workers and the unemployed challenged the status quo, starting in the years after the First World War. The emigrants were the catalysts. As participant observer of the events of these times Frank Hill said of those returning, "If their fellows who stayed at home were the dough, they were the leaven to give vigor and shape and process to the end result."[90] Consciousness that was defused through emigration would now become concentrated at home.[91] The emigrants' influence might be seen in the cry of "a dollar a day" – the standard wage in most foreign enterprises but still beyond the basic wage at home – and in their agitation for fringe benefits such as better working conditions and better housing. Hill noted that "these were a new breed of Jamaican workers. Many of them had recently returned home from Cuba and Panama and Colombia and Costa Rica where they had drunk deeply at the well of Republicanism."[92] They were sufficiently disciplined from their foreign sojourn to understand and respond to calls for solidarity and united action. Like the African American radicals, they no longer believed in the monolithic power of the white race. They were frequently the people who incited others to actively defend their interests as workers. They were the ones who stood to defy the police and the guards. Some lost their lives in the process. Returning emigrants were in the forefront of the social ferment that was taking place throughout the Caribbean at this time and were regarded as the leaders in the riots in St Vincent and St Kitts, among others.

Many of the challenges to authority were filtered through the prism of growing race consciousness now woven through a number of strands: black nationalism, pan-Africanism, Socialism[93] and anti-imperialism, all bound together by the influence of new ideologies and ideologues, such as Marcus Garvey. These influences were to lead to the emergence of a labour movement, the rise of trade unions and nationalist political parties. But religion was also to play a leading role in challenging the status quo by people in search of a more acceptable path to salvation.

RACE AND RADICALISM

Not all the returnees had left home as wage-seekers. Among those transformed by their sojourn overseas were former soldiers of the British West Indies Regiment who had served in the First World War. Conscription had been unnecessary as some sixteen thousand men (eleven battalions) from the islands, including three thousand via Panama, had volunteered to fight for "king and country". But on arrival in England they were not treated as the equals of British troops, although on enlistment they were promised such treatment. The British War Office simply did not want black men to fight white Europeans, and black soldiers were to experience segregation and humiliation both during and after the war. On their return to the West Indies, they did not receive their promised pay and were unable to find jobs.[94] Those from Panama who had joined the regiments were sent back to Panama, whether or not this was their desire, and many also arrived destitute.[95]

Figure 10.20
The sailing of the Jamaican contingent to the First World War. Returning ex-soldiers were to be in the forefront of the post-war political ferment. (Courtesy of the National Library of Jamaica.)

West Indian soldiers returned home in 1918 exploding with anger and ideas. Their wartime experiences were as transformative as those of African Americans who had hitherto been excluded from many areas of mainstream life. Service overseas had brought African Americans "into contacts that widened both their perceptions and their perspectives, broadened them, gave them new angles on life, on government, and on race".[96] In 1919, the "New Negro" emerged to challenge the status quo, and the United States was torn by race riots – twenty-two in the "Red Summer" of 1919 alone. West Indian former servicemen were affected by their wartime experiences too, but in different ways. Racial clashes in Britain, especially London, Liverpool and Cardiff, involved black former servicemen in the British West Indies Regiment and black sailors who found themselves jobless and destitute on demobilization and frustrated by racial discrimination. The soldiers had experienced so much anger and frustration that even before the war ended, a group had begun an organization named the Caribbean League, with the aim of changing the status of black men on their return home. In the West Indies, these former soldiers were regarded as a threat to the peace and good order of the colonies, and they received no sympathetic treatment from local authorities. They were among the radical elements testing authority in the coming decades, beginning with their central role in uprisings in 1919 in British Honduras and Trinidad.[97]

Garvey and the Universal Negro Improvement Association

The war veterans were, like so many others, no doubt influenced by the teachings of Marcus Garvey, founder of what by now had become "the largest pan-African movement in history". Founded in Jamaica in 1914, Garvey's UNIA had not really taken off until he established it in the United States in 1917. By the mid-1920s, the UNIA had approximately eleven hundred branches in over forty countries and millions of followers, and Garvey's message of black self-reliance and racial pride crossed cultural and linguistic barriers. His strongest support came from expatriate West Indians in places like Panama and Costa Rica, and, later, in Cuba (where there were fifty-two branches), as well as throughout the West Indies. Membership in the UNIA would be responsible for forging many of the links between leaders of the budding labour movement in the Caribbean itself and would foster solidarity among nationals of the different islands, both in their homelands and abroad. Tony Martin could state that "by 1919 the UNIA in the West Indies was firmly entrenched enough to figure prominently in the labour riots and racial unrest that swept the area", and "by the 1920s the UNIA had become, in several greater Caribbean territories, the virtual representatives of the black population. At a time when most black people in the area were denied the right to vote, and in an age mostly predating mass political parties, the UNIA often performed the function of quasi-political party as well as mutual aid organization."[98]

From 1918 onwards, Garvey's ideas were channelled through his newspaper, the New York–based *Negro World*. The fact that it was declared banned literature by many of the colonial governments did not prevent its widespread circulation in the islands, carried there by black seamen. Garvey himself had begun his journey to political consciousness as an emigrant in Costa Rica between 1910 and 1912, working as a timekeeper for the United Fruit Company, and he would later return to Central America to empower the workers in these places with his ideas of racial pride. Garveyites at home and those returning, including Garvey himself (forcibly repatriated by United States authorities to Jamaica in 1926), contributed the yeast to the political ferment of the times and helped to unite regional and diasporic consciousness. Garvey started the *Black Man* newspaper and launched the Peoples Political Party in Jamaica in 1928. He failed to gain a seat in the election of 1930, and the party went out of existence but not the ideas he had set in motion.

Anti-Chinese Riots

Some returnees were to find fertile ground for expressing their discontent, including xenophobia. Finding that while they were away, conditions had worsened in their homelands, some blamed the addition of new groups of migrants consisting of Chinese,[99] "Syrians"[100] and Indian "Bombay merchants",[101] who were prospering, it appeared, at the expense of the nationals. As James Carnegie expressed it in discussing the politics of those times, "for Jamaicans in Latin America the island apparently represented the *ideal* haven. The first attitude that *they* had *had* to go abroad to *fight* for a living also clarifies others such as why they were so hostile to non-indigenous groups in Jamaica like the Chinese. . . . They resented how the Chinese had made Jamaica their oyster (and found 'pearls') while natives like themselves had to leave to survive."[102] It is not surprising that at this time the "aliens" in Jamaica, particularly the Chinese, became targets for attack, especially by one group, the Native Defenders Committee. One of its leaders, Leonard Waison, was born in Panama to Jamaican parents, and the group apparently appealed "specifically to men returning from Latin America with 'republican' ideas". The committee's verbal attacks on aliens were followed by physical attacks: arson, violence and murder; a link between the work of returning emigrants and the attacks was suggested.

Writing about the politics of the period, Carnegie came to the conclusion that "their overseas experiences often shaped the thinking of some Jamaicans, who in turn, considerably influenced others without such experience".[103] Indeed, it may be argued that the labour riots of 1937–38 represented the fortuitous marriage between charismatic leaders and workers who gained experience of labour organization overseas, who had been exposed to extreme racism and confrontation with white society. Their experiences with a violent way of life overseas also helped to stiffen their resistance. Carnegie comments that "when the mob 'ruled' Kingston in late May and early June 1938, it seemed that some people were emulating Latin examples".[104] To those who occupied the seats of power and authority, those who had travelled overseas were now definitely a threat to the good order of the society.

RELIGION

Religion was one area in which growing discontent against the established churches was expressed as a more rebellious African-centred world view emerged. Religion had a political component from the start of the enslaved Africans' arrival in the New World, with African priests in the service of violent uprisings throughout the Caribbean.[105] In the British territories, those who operated the slave societies were members of the official church, the Church of England, but the enslaved populations were excluded. The introduction of evangelical Christianity to the enslaved began in the eighteenth century with the arrival of Moravians, followed by Methodists, Baptists and others. But as has happened to so many foreign imports, black West Indians were to hijack Christianity to their own purposes, giving rise to a plethora of "native" churches such as the Black Baptist and indigenous Revivalists. Shirley C. Gordon described the progression for Jamaica in this way:

> The varying fortunes of ex-slaves and their children were reflected in their religious life. The moderately successful added to their growing status by accepting the European Protestant standards of respectability and moral rectitude in the missionary chapels. Those who looked for the means of dealing with the evils they found in their situation developed native forms of Christian observance drawing on their Afro-Jamaican preferences in worship and in forms of personal participation very different from those sanctioned in the mission chapels.[106]

People supported one or both of these models, and changed their allegiance according to circumstances. Those who aspired to "respectability" supported formal religious institutions, even as they preached deference to white authority, since they were also the providers of education and forms of social welfare.

Revival and Pentecostalism

Rising race consciousness in the twentieth century led to an increasing perception of European-based churches as bastions of the white and brown elites. A "religious upheaval" in which returning emigrants played a role, though Garvey himself was to decry some religious manifestations as "ignorance and superstition", was underway. Some of this new religious influence came from the United States, in the rise of Pentecostalism and Revivalism, and in the influence of such phenomena as Father Divine, brought to the islands from Panama as well as from the United States directly.[107]

The turning away from the established churches seems to have been widespread. Bonham Richardson was to note of Barbados that in a sea of social change brought about by the migration, thousands of black Barbadians "turned to the revivalist churches as lifeboats of stability and group identity".[108] Preachers and missionaries came usually from the United States, some by way of Panama. The revivalist churches attracted mainly poor black people and – listed as "Other Denominations" – by the 1911 census showed the largest growth, with substantial losses to the traditional Anglican, Wesleyan and Moravian churches. More than that,

> fundamentalist church sermons were providing not only escape and identity but also taking on quasi-political tones. Although most black Barbadians were better off than in the pre-Panama era, they had improved just enough to see how little they had in comparison with whites. More and more black congregations were challenged by their own preachers to contemplate the basis for black-white inequities. Colonial authorities were aware of the inherent dangers. In particular, they worried about instigators and agitators from abroad coming to Barbados in religious disguise.[109]

One potential agitator identified as such was "Bishop Jack" of St Vincent, suggesting that similar developments were taking place on the other islands. In Jamaica, American Pentecostalism was introduced in the second decade of the twentieth century by both black and white missionaries from America, and has continued to flourish to the point where it is today the most popular religious movement,[110] through a variety of churches known as "Church of God", "Pentecostal", "Apostolic" and the like.[111] Pentecostalism, like the indigenous Revivalist churches of Pukumina and Revival Zion, found fertile ground in the new urban slums and poverty-stricken hill communities.

Bedwardism

In Jamaica, though, it was the religions springing directly from island roots that posed the greatest challenges to authority through Bedwardism and Rasta-fari. Alexander Bedward reigned from the 1890s to 1921 as the messianic leader of his church at August Town, on the bank of the Hope River in Kingston. Tens of thousands of pilgrims from all over Jamaica as well as from Panama, Costa Rica, Cuba and other places came to be dipped in the "healing stream" and carry sanctified water from the Hope River home in bottles. Alexander Bedward himself had emigrated to Colón during the French construction and it was there that he had his visionary experience, which led him to return to Jamaica, found his church and challenge the social order, leading to the suggestion that "his labour in Colon seemed to make him bold before Jamaican officials".[112] Perhaps this was the case with other messianic preachers who had also travelled and become popular figures in Kingston of the times: Solomon Hewitt of Smith Village ("Brother Sal"), who had also gone to Panama, or "Father Higgins", a notable street preacher who had spent some time in England. None was to have Bedward's type of following, although many of these preachers attracted the attention of the British authorities, some were imprisoned, sedition being the usual charge.

Bedward's enormous popularity and his use of analogy in his preaching of a growing "black wall that will push against the white wall" and knock it down alarmed the authorities enough to have him charged with "seditious speech and discourse", and eventually to have him judged mentally incompetent and

Figures 10.21–10.22 Regarded by many as a "madman", Alexander Bedward nevertheless commanded an enormous following in the first two decades of the twentieth century to the consternation of the authorities who frequently arrested him (*centre*, in figure 10.21) and his followers (figure 10.22). (Courtesy of the National Library of Jamaica.)

lodged in the asylum.[113] Bedward's authority faded with time, but the thirst among the poor and dispossessed to worship on their own terms did not. The upsurge of religious revivalism in the 1930s led the authorities to contemplate legislative action against "these curious religious cults".[114]

Rastafari

It was also among the poor and dispossessed that another major African-centred fundamentalist religion was to spring: Rastafari. The aura gained from the experience of travel perhaps helped to endorse the legitimacy of the three men who are acknowledged as the main founders of the millennial movement originally dubbed a "cult of outcasts" but which has become universally known: Leonard Howell, who had travelled as a seaman and also lived in the United States; Joseph Hibbert who had lived in Costa Rica and established the King of Kings Mission; and Henry Dunkley, who travelled as a seaman on banana boats and established the Ethiopian Coptic Faith. They were influenced by biblical teachings, by Garvey's ideas, as well as by growing Ethiopianism brought about by the coronation of a "black king", Ras Tafari, as the Emperor Haile Selassie in 1930, and his perceived divinity by those who were later called Rastafari.[115] The invasion of Abyssinia by Mussolini's fascist Italian forces in 1935–36 roused people of African descent everywhere, especially in America, and deepened the ideology of "Ethiopianism" in Jamaica.[116] Many observers of the time agreed that this event

Figure 10.23 Haile Selassie whose coronation as Emporer of Ethiopia in 1930 gave the incipient Jamaican religion of Rastafari a black divinity (Wikipedia).

increased political and race consciousness and destroyed black faith in white government, especially as it was felt that Britain had failed Ethiopia. Rastafari, Bedwardism and other cults and fundamentalist churches that were born of discontent were questioning colonial legitimacy just as the European churches continued to encourage deference and support for the social order. Perhaps it was not incidental that 1938 was the centenary of the emancipation of the enslaved Africans in the British territories.

THE RISE OF ORGANIZED LABOUR

In 1937–38, the poverty-stricken proletariat and starving workers of the islands of the West Indies exploded in a series of strikes, riots and violent demonstrations.[117] Discontent had been simmering from the immediate post-war years with unemployment, low wages, rising prices and other factors which bore heavily on the working class, but this discontent began to gather steam in 1935. That year, a strike of agricultural labourers in St Kitts (population twenty thousand) was followed by strikes and disturbances in the oilfields of Trinidad, in British Guiana, St Vincent and St Lucia. In 1937 there were upheavals in Trinidad, Barbados, British Guiana, St Lucia and Jamaica. All of these were put down or suppressed by force by the British authorities. In outlining these events, Arthur Lewis was to note, "it was the general strike in Jamaica in the following year, immediately succeeded by further strikes in British Guiana which really roused the public mind. By that time at least 46 persons had been killed in the course of suppressing these upheavals, 429 injured, and thousands arrested and prosecuted."[118]

Although many local factors contributed to the unrest, much of the discontent was officially attributed to the ending of emigration outlets. The late 1920s marked the end of a vital freedom which Caribbean peoples for the previous seventy years had enjoyed: the freedom of movement.

As a commission of enquiry into disturbances in Barbados would observe after the fact, "above all things . . . to which the comparative contentment of the past half century can be attributed was the outlet to the energies of the people provided by the emigration".[119] The West India Royal Commission which investigated the causes of the unrest throughout the West Indies similarly commented:

> The average West Indian labourer is indeed more strictly confined to his own island, which may be no larger than an average British county, than the English labourer was tied to his parish in the most rigid phase of the Settlement Laws. We have indications that this extreme difficulty of movement, which is as we have seen an essentially modern phenomenon, creates a sense of being shut in, of being denied opportunity and choice, and of consequent frustration in the minds of many young men of adventurous disposition, particularly in the smaller islands. It may be a more important element than appears at first in the psychology of discontent.[120]

Or, as a letter writer to a local newspaper in Jamaica more succinctly observed, "Why we are like a horse that is tied and where we are tethered we must feed."[121] The problem is that there was now not much feeding to be had.

Leadership

Those who had travelled were to provide leadership at all levels throughout the region.

The influence of a foreign sojourn on their ideological development is probably most marked in the case of those who became prominent such as Marcus Garvey, Alexander Bustamante, Hugh Buchanan, G.S. Coombs, St William

Grant and Norman Manley from Jamaica; T.A. Marryshow from Grenada; Captain Arthur Cipriani, Albert Gomes and Uriah Butler of Trinidad; and Grantley Adams of Barbados, to name a few.

We may ask ourselves, would Bustamante have acquired from staying at home the altered perspective, the economic base, or the confidence to challenge authority and provide leadership for the masses? Or, staying home, would he have become another rum shop ne'er-do-well of frustrated energy and blighted hopes? Indeed, had he not acquired a certain style and glamour as a result of his travels, would he have gained the admiration and trust of the masses? Would Marcus Garvey have developed his key internationalist perspective had he remained in Jamaica, or been able to build a mass following at all? How far did their wartime experiences and exposure to racism in Europe move Norman Manley or Arthur Cipriani to return home and defend the rights of the poor and downtrodden?

We are conscious of the ways in which foreign experiences influenced the lives of certain key individuals, because their lives have been written about and examined. It is perhaps correct to assume that the foreign experience affected in no less measure the lives of even the humblest of emigrants. Indeed, there is evidence of a second-tier leadership cadre, functioning at the community level that came out of the foreign experience. Although largely unsung and unnamed, these people added to the intellectual stock of their country, providing direct contact and leadership at a critical time.

The evidence we have to go on is fragmentary but persuasive. Carnegie, for instance, notes that the returnees were active in community organizations which showed an upsurge in the 1930s.[122] Olivier suggests that they played leadership roles in organizations such as the All Island Banana Growers Association and, more than likely, in existing groups such as the Jamaica Teachers Association and the Jamaica Agricultural Society.[123] Carnegie has also shown the role played by émigrés in many politico-social organizations in the 1920s and 1930s, many of them short-lived. In examining the politics of protest in the 1930s, Ken Post noted that "the 1930s witnessed the emergence of numerous organizations, in which it would seem that returning emigrants from the United States, Cuba and Central America often played an important leadership role". He cites the National Reform Association and the Federation of Citizens Associations, the Workers and Tradesmen Union, the UNIA, the first Jamaica Labour Party (founded April 1937), the Jamaica Protective League, the Artisans Federated Union, Social Reconstruction League, and the Jamaica Permanent Development Convention. In analysing their role, Post commented that their "emergence in the 1930's is a sign that at some lower level of the class hierarchy a consciousness was beginning to emerge which could only in the end find itself opposed to existing power structures".[124]

George Eaton describes the return of the emigrants thus: "To the many thousands who had worked in Latin American Republics, whose governments were toppled and changed frequently by palace revolutions, the British monarchy and imperial power, as well as the local Governor and administration were no longer sacrosanct persons and institutions, insulated against criticism. The inarticulate black masses were being provided with spokesmen of their own, who would hold forth at street corners and under shop piazzas and within the bars, espousing their cause."[125] Allied to this ferment would be the increasing interest of the middle classes in effecting change by constitutional means.

Such political and constitutional changes in the West Indies would only come about later, as the start of the Second World War in 1939 curtailed all forms of protest in the islands and led to the imprisonment of several of the prominent leaders under wartime regulations. But the social ferment of the 1920s and 1930s would definitely lead to the development of trade union organization, which in turn would lead to the formation of nationalist political parties and the eventual broadening of the franchise to include all adult West Indians, change coming at different times in each island. Eventually, these changes led to political independence for virtually all the former British islands and territories. Such fundamental changes should be seen as part of the legacy of Panama men and women: of those who had travelled elsewhere and of all that they brought back to their homelands.

NOTES

Chapter 1

1. All figures in US dollars unless otherwise specified. The cost included forty million dollars paid to the French company and ten million dollars paid to the new Republic of Panama.

2. Arthur Bullard, *Panama: The Canal, the Country and the People*, rev. ed. (New York: Macmillan, 1914).

3. Michael L. Conniff, *Black Labor on a White Canal: Panama, 1904–1981* (Pittsburgh: University of Pittsburgh Press, 1985), estimates the total number of deaths in the West Indian community during construction as approaching fifteen thousand, or one in ten immigrants.

4. Between January and June 1913, twenty thousand visitors were counted, according to the official *Canal Record*.

5. Edgar Young, "A Few Will Remember", *Excavating Engineer*, August 1921. http://www.czbrats.com/Builders/afew.htm.

6. Daniel T. Lawson, Isthmian Historical Society, "Letters in a Competition for the Best True Stories of Life and Work on the Isthmus of Panama during Construction of the Canal" (manuscript, Balboa, Canal Zone, 1963). Hereafter cited as "True Stories". The quotations are reproduced exactly as they were from the letters typed by Ruth Stuhl, who organized the contest on behalf of the Isthmian Historical Society. Spaces were often used in place of punctuation and have been retained here. For a discussion of the letters and their significance see Rhonda D. Frederick, *"Colón Man a Come": Mythographies of Panama Canal Migration* (Lanham, MD: Lexington, 2005).

7. Charles Booth, "True Stories".

8. Wesley Clarke, "True Stories".

9. Albert Banister, "True Stories".

10. George H. Martin, "True Stories".

11. John F. Prescod, "True Stories".

12. W.L. Sibert and J.F. Stevens, *The Construction of the Panama Canal* (New York: Appleton, 1915).

13. *Canal Record*, 6 December 1911.

14. Mrs Mary Couloote, "True Stories".

15. Z.H. McKenzie, "True Stories".

16. Prince George Green, "True Stories".

17. Albert Banister, "True Stories". Regarding the "disability relief retiree", Ruth C. Stuhl, the competition organizer and editor, noted that most of the non-US citizens who worked during the construction years were not eligible for US government pensions. The US Congress would not appropriate funds for this purpose but eventually did provide for a system of relief payments for those disabled while employed. Old workers not eligible for a regular pension became eligible for disability relief by signing a statement at the time of their retirement saying they had become disabled. At June 1964, the maximum monthly payment was fifty-five dollars, and many received less.

18. Clifford Hunt, "True Stories".

19. The mythical El Dorado ("the golden one") was an Amerindian king of a city on the Amazon River who was fabulously wealthy. Historic expeditions – including two led by Sir Walter Raleigh – failed to locate El Dorado and the term has come to represent the fruitless search for quick riches.

20. Quoted in "Spirit of Good Old Days Preserved in Chanteys of West Indian Workers", *Panama American*, 15 August 1939, http://cbrats.com/Builders/chantey.htm.

21. Conniff, *Black Labor*, 29.

22. The population of the British West Indian islands and the mainland territories of British Guiana and British Honduras (Belize) was 1,607,218 in 1891 and 1,951,327 in 1911. George W. Roberts, *The Population of Jamaica* (Cambridge: Cambridge University Press, 1957), 330–31.

23. The Panama narrative continues in the contemporary song "Panama", by noted Trinidad calypsonian David Rudder (on the album *Haiti* [1988]), representing Panama as a location where dishonest politicians go to hide their "gold". A stronger link was forged by the Jamaican female traders called "higglers", who when hard times hit in 1979 instituted the "skellion run", taking products such as escallion, thyme and other island produce to sell in Panama, buying in the free-trade zone manufactured items for sale at home.

24. Josephus Acosta, *Natural and Moral History of the Indies* (1625), quoted in Ira E. Bennett, *History of the Panama Canal: Its Construction and Builders* (Washington, DC: Historical Publishing Company, 1915), 120.

25. www.thefullwiki.org/Isthmus_of_Panama.

26. Beckford in "True Stories" also noted special gemstone rocks thrown up during construction that were sent to the United States, cut and polished and returned as "Canal stones", including moss agates, moonstones and bloodstones that were not seen elsewhere. He also mounted extraordinary shells that were thrown up in dredging from the harbour.

27. Francisco Watlington, "The Physical Environment: Biogeographical Teleconnections in Caribbean Prehistory", in *UNESCO General History of the Caribbean,* vol. 1, *Autochthonous Societies*, ed. Jalil Sued-Badillo (London and Paris: Macmillan and UNESCO, 2003), 30.

28. Slavery ended in the United States in 1865, Brazil in 1888 and Cuba in 1890.

29. Franklin W. Knight, "Migration and the American Experience", in *Regional Footprints: The Travels and Travails of Early Caribbean Migrants*, ed. Annette Insanally, Mark Clifford and Sean Sheriff (Kingston: Latin America–Caribbean Centre, University of the West Indies, 2006), 8.

30. Ernesto J. Castillero, in the history of Colón, *La isla que se transformó en cuidad: Historia de un siglo de la ciudad de Colón* (Panama: Imprenta Nacional, 1962), states that the first effort to establish a railroad across the isthmus was by Wolwood Hislop, a businessman of Jamaica in 1828, but he did not secure a concession from the government of New Granada (48). Hislop was an agent for plantation owners and an associate of Bolívar.

31. Willis J. Abbot, *Panama and the Canal in Picture and Prose* (London: Syndicate, 1913), 9.

32. Sylvia Wynter, "Bernardo de Balbuena: Epic Poet and Abbot of Jamaica, 1562–1627", part 2 of 4, *Jamaica Journal* 3, no. 4 (1969): 24.

33. Verene A. Shepherd, "Roots of Routes: Intra-Caribbean Trade Links since the Fifteenth Century", in *Regional Footprints: The Travels and Travails of Early Caribbean Migrants*, ed. Annette Insanally, Mark Clifford and Sean Sheriff (Kingston: Latin American–Caribbean Centre, University of the West Indies, 2006), 25.

34. Alexandre-Olivier Exquemelin, *The History of the Buccaneers of America* (1698; repr., Boston, 1853).

35. John Prebble, *The Darien Disaster* (London: Secker and Warburg, 1968) is one of several books on the settlement, which is also the subject of the BBC film *Disaster in Paradise* (2003).

36. Paula Palmer, *"What Happen?" A Folk History of Costa Rica's Talamanca Coast* (San Jose: Ecodesarrollos, 1979).

37. F.U. Adams, *Conquest of the Tropics: The Story of the Creative Enterprises Conducted by the United Fruit Company* (New York: Doubleday Page, 1914); Palmer, *"What Happen?"*.

38. For example, Adams, *Conquest.* An authenticated case of a slave ship wrecked off these coasts and the enslaved Africans settling in a life of freedom occurred on the Miskito Coast (Cabo Gracias a Dios) in 1641. See Julian H. Steward, ed., *Handbook of South American Indians,* Bulletin 143, Bureau of American Ethnology, vol. 4 (Washington, DC: Smithsonian Institution, 1948); Exquemelin, *Buccaneers,* 220.

39. Frances Armytage, *The Free Port System in the British West Indies* (London: Longman, 1953).

40. Aims McGuinness, *Path of Empire: Panama and the California Gold Rush* (Ithaca: Cornell University Press, 2008), 20.

41. An account of a voyage to Panama is given in the nineteenth-century novel *Tom Cringle's Log* (London, 1834) by sailor-author Michael Scott.

Chapter 2

1. The confederation included what are now the republics of Venezuela, Ecuador and Colombia.

2. Ovidio Diaz Espino, *How Wall Street Created a Nation: J.P. Morgan, Teddy Roosevelt, and the Panama Canal* (New York: Four Walls Eight Windows, 2001), 37.

3. Philippe Bunau-Varilla, *Panama: The Creation, Destruction, and Resurrection* (New York: McBride, Nast, 1914), 263.

4. British statesman George Canning had written of the independence of the Spanish

colonies in 1824, "The deed is done, the nail is driven, Spanish America is free; and if we do not mismanage our affairs sadly, she is *English*." Letter from Canning to Lord Grenville, quoted in William W. Kaufmann, *British Policy and Independence of Latin America* (New Haven: Yale University Press, 1951), 178.

5. The Monroe Doctrine, proclaimed in 1823 by President James Monroe, was the US policy that opposed the interference of outside powers in the Americas.

6. Richard Henry Dana Jr's account of a voyage around Cape Horn, *Two Years before the Mast* (1840), became a best seller.

7. Aspinwall, described as "an unusually honest, pious man", was a founder of the Society for the Prevention of Cruelty to Animals and the Metropolitan Museum of Art. http://www.panamarailroad.org/aspinwall.html.

8. Quoted in Joseph L. Schott, *Rails across Panama: The Story of the Building of the Panama Railroad, 1849–1855* (Indianapolis: Bobbs-Merrill, 1967), 10.

9. Known later as the Panama Railway or Panama Rail Road and then as the Panama Canal Railway.

10. Stephens must have recovered, for on his way home he stopped off in Jamaica, toured the island, and was "so struck with its natural beauties" and the "moral and social conditions" growing out of the abolition of slavery that it is believed he made considerable notes of incidents with a view to a future publication. But on his return to New York he assumed duties as president of the Panama Railroad Company, which seemed to have consumed his interests until his death. www.panamarail road.org/stephens/html.

11. Robert Tomes, *Panama in 1855* (New York: Harper Brothers, 1855), 23.

12. http://www.panamarailroad.org/history.

13. The gold seekers were in fact representative of virtually all humanity, women among them, and some men arrived in top hats and three-piece-suits.

14. From *silla*, a kind of chair lashed to the backs of human carriers (see figure 2.18). Wolfred Nelson, *Five Years at Panama: The Trans-Isthmian Canal* (New York: Belford, 1889), 188.

15. Schott, *Rails across Panama*, 17.

16. Errol Hill, *The Jamaican Stage 1655–1900: Profile of a Colonial Theatre* (Amherst: University of Massachusetts Press, 1992), 255.

17. F.N. Otis, *Illustrated History of the Panama Railroad*, 2nd ed. (New York: Harper and Bros., 1862), 26. The "cocoa" was more likely a coconut palm.

18. Tomes's trip across the isthmus by rail (*Panama in 1855*) captures the rich, changing scenery.

19. The tree (*Hippomane mancinella*) is a member of the Euphorbia family and its toxicity depends on both the sensitivity of the individual and the location of the tree. Different island populations have varying toxicity.

20. Tomes, *Panama in 1855*.

21. Gerstle Mack, *The Land Divided* (New York: Octagon Books, 1944), 156.

22. Otis, *Illustrated History*.

23. http://www.panamarailroad.org/history.

24. Ibid.

25. *Star and Herald*, quoted in http://www.panamarailroad.org chinesetragedy.html, from which most of this account is taken.

26. They might have been new to this part of the world, but small groups of Chinese were recorded in the Americas from as early as the sixteenth century. See Walton Look Lai, *The Chinese in the West Indies, 1806–1995* (Kingston: University of the West Indies Press, 1998), 6–7. News of the California gold strike had reached the Far East long before it reached America's east coast, and Chinese gold seekers began to arrive in California from 1849.

27. Organized Chinese migrations began in the aftermath of the Opium Wars (1839–42, 1858–60), which led to greater exposure to Western labour demands in general, particularly in the Americas. Ibid., 9.

28. For example, McGuinness, *Path of Empire*.

29. I have been unable to find an exact date for this event but it probably occurred between July and September.

30. Schott, *Rails across Panama*, 181.

31. "The Chinese Character", *Star and Herald*, 20 July 1854; other articles in the *Star and Herald* on Chinese runaways in Panama: 19 August, 23 August, 29 August, 3 September, 18 September 1854.

32. *Star and Herald*, 3 September 1854. The Chinese gentleman was Wang-te-Chang, Chinese interpreter, who arrived with Mr Wortley (emigration agent) and Mr Harrison from Jamaica. His journal entry is a harrowing account of the conditions he found there and of the surviving Chinese whom he arranged to be sent to Jamaica. He makes no mention of dramatic mass suicide but he does record that only about 400 Chinese remained in Panama, of whom half were ill. Of the rest, he estimated some 500 had died by disease, 30 or 40 committed suicide, and more than 30 were believed to have gone to California. The remaining workers he found "sick in their appearance, with pale and thin faces", some with sores and swollen legs and feet. They complained, among other things, of the perpetual rain and wet clothes, lack of adequate food and fresh vegetables, and of severe floggings by the company "headman" who could not understand them. He found more than 150 in the company hospital, in the most appalling conditions, and also recorded encountering seriously ill or dead Chinese on the wayside. Those in the seaside hospital complained of lack and food and drinking water, and many were drinking salt water to quench their thirst. Most appalling to the Chinese was the way the dead on the Panama works were treated, dumped into a hole without coffin or funeral ceremony. "Those who are dead in the hospital, they Company's people carry them out, each one with two ropes fastened on legs and arms to some wild place, and heap them up in some number to be buried into one hole of the ground without coffin, and with nothing wrap of only naked against cold and wet ground," Wang-te-Chang recorded. All the Chinese he asked whether they wanted to go to Jamaica agreed that they would "go anywhere" to get away. Copy of translation of "Journal of the Chinese Interpreter, Wang-te-Chang, Reporting State of Chinese Immigrants at Panama". I am grateful to Dr Keith Lowe for bringing this manuscript to my attention, too late to be included in the main text.

33. See *Star and Herald*, above.

34. Otis, *Illustrated History*, 27.

35. *Morning Journal*, quoted in *Falmouth Post*, 28 May 1850.

36. http://en.wikipedia.org/wiki/Panama_Canal_Railway.

37. Quoted in Wikipedia.org/wiki/Panama_Canal_Railway. It was Balboa, of course, who sighted the Pacific for the first time and not Cortez, the writer replicating the error John Keats made in his poem "On First Looking into Chapman's Homer".

38. *Morning Journal,* quoted in *Falmouth Post,* 28 May 1850.

39. See Velma Newton, *The Silver Men: West Indian Labour Migration to Panama 1850–1914* (Kingston: Institute of Social and Economic Research, University of the West Indies, 1984), for a discussion of the reliability of migration figures.

40. The name was changed to the Cunard Steamship Company Limited in 1878, shortened to Cunard Line.

41. T.A. Bushell, *"Royal Mail": A Centenary History of the Royal Mail Line, 1839–1939* (London: Trade and Travel Publications, 1939), 34.

42. *Daily Advertiser,* 18 April 1854.

43. Tomes, *Panama in 1855.*

44. *Daily Advertiser,* 14 February 1853; *Falmouth Post,* 23 July 1850. See also Barry Higman, "Jamaicans in the Australian Gold Rushes", *Jamaica Journal* 10, no. 2 (1976).

45. *Daily Advertiser,* 14 February 1853.

46. *Morning Journal,* quoted in *Falmouth Post,* 28 May 1850.

47. *Report of the Commissioners of Inquiry upon the Condition of the Juvenile Population of Jamaica with the evidence taken and an appendix* (Kingston: Government Printer, 1879), 52.

48. Roberts, *Population of Jamaica, 177.*

49. The governor's estimate at the end of 1851 was twenty to thirty thousand.

50. Mary Seacole, *Wonderful Adventures of Mrs Seacole in Many Lands*, 2nd ed., ed. and intr. Ziggy Alexander and Audrey Dewjee (orig. pub. London: James Blackwood, 1857; repr., Bristol: Falling Wall, 1984); George W. Groh, *Gold Fever: Being a True Account . . . of the Art of Healing . . . during the California Gold Rush* (New York: William Morrow, 1963), 34.

51. See, for example, Nadine Wilkins, "The Medical Profession in Jamaica in the Post-Emancipation Period", *Jamaica Journal* 21, no. 4 (1989). The most famous "doctoress" was Couba Cornwallis of Port Royal who nursed and, it is claimed, saved the lives of the future British hero Lord Horatio Nelson and the future King of England, William IV, in their youthful naval days at Port Royal. Mary Seacole's mother was also a practitioner of "creole medical arts" based on traditional African medicine evolved in the Caribbean as well as observations of the practices of medical men trained in Europe who were often welcoming to these local women and also learned from them. Mary's mother operated a boarding house in Kingston which served as a guest house and, in the absence of hospitals, as a treatment centre for Europeans, especially British officers and their families stationed in the island. Mary learned from her and carried on the practice as healer and boarding-house keeper.

52. See Ziggy Alexander and Audrey Dewjee, introduction to Seacole, *Wonderful Adventures*, 16. For recent re-evaluations of Mary Seacole see Alan Eyre, "Dusky Doctress: A Jamaican Perspective on Mary Grant-Seacole", *Jamaica Journal* 30, nos. 1–2 (2006); Helen Rappaport, "The Lost Portrait", *Jamaica Journal* 30, nos. 1–2 (2006); Jane Robinson*, Mary Seacole: The Most Famous Black Woman of the Victorian Age* (New York: Carroll and Graff, 2004).

53. Although she gives no date in her book, it would have been after 1 October when the first trains landed at Gatún.

54. Seacole, *Wonderful Adventures*, 66.

55. In 2004, Mary Seacole was named number one in a poll in the United Kingdom to identify One Hundred Great Black Britons; her newly discovered portrait in oils is on loan to England's National Portrait Gallery.

56. Seacole, *Wonderful Adventures*, 64.

57. Groh, *Gold Fever*, 24.

58. Seacole, *Wonderful Adventures*, 77.

59. But Seacole failed in her attempt to join the nurses Florence Nightingale was assembling to go to the Crimea.

60. Seacole, *Wonderful Adventures*, 77.

61. It is claimed that Mary Seacole's techniques for treatment of cholera as described in her autobiography (which included fresh air, cleanliness and isolation of patients) were "based on the same principles as 20th century treatments before the successful introduction of antibiotics in the 1940s". Alexander and Dewjee, introduction to *Wonderful Adventures*, 16. See Groh, *Gold Fever*, for the status of medicine at the time.

62. Groh, *Gold Fever*, 28.

63. Schott, *Rails across Panama*.

64. The deadly nature of Central American "fevers" was well known to the British public. During the well-publicized War of Jenkins' Ear in the mid-eighteenth century, thirteen thousand troops sailed from Jamaica to take Cartagena, Colombia, then a Spanish stronghold. There were six hundred war casualties but most of the troops died on board ships from the "fevers"; by the end of the year, only three hundred men were left fit for duty.

65. Groh, *Gold Fever*, 302n.

66. Tracy Robinson, *Panama: A Personal Record of Forty-six years, 1861–1907* (New York and Panama: Star and Herald, 1907), 1–2. A more loving version of the life of an elite family in colonial Panama is presented by Matilde Obarrio Mallet in her *Sketches of Spanish-colonial Life in Panama* (New York: Sturgis and Walton, 1915). Her book deals with the period that ended in 1821 when Panama became independent. The author was the wife of Sir Claude Coventry Mallet, who served as a British diplomat in Panama for many years and was well known to the West Indian community there.

67. Schott, *Rails across Panama*, 2.

68. Seacole, *Wonderful Adventures*, 64.

69. Tomes, *Panama in 1855*, 63–64.

70. Ibid., 116–17.

71. Schott, *Rails across Panama*.

72. Ibid., 68. The company doctor was the brother of Colonel Totten, the chief engineer.

73. Otis, *Illustrated History*.

74. *Panama Star*, 28 January 1851.

75. *Morning Journal*, quoted in *Falmouth Post*, 28 May 1850.

76. Ibid.

77. Seacole, *Wonderful Adventures*, 71–73.

78. "Respectable" women changed to trousers for this leg of the journey, being unable to sit astride the mules in their long skirts, or they walked. Women not so respectable scandalized everyone by wearing trousers for the entire journey. Some of the perils on the road for female travellers were noted by Bayard Taylor, who crossed the isthmus in 1850. After heavy rain which made the trail perilous, "A lady from Maine, who made the journey alone, was obliged to ford a torrent of water above her waist, with a native on each side to prevent her being washed away." And a Frenchwoman who had been washed from her mule "only got over by the united exertions of seven men". Quoted in John Easter Minter, *The Chagres: River of Westward Passage* (New York: Rinehart, 1948), 235.

79. Quoted in Schott, *Rails across Panama*, 57.

80. Seacole, *Wonderful Adventures*, 74.

81. Otis, *Illustrated History*; Tomes, *Panama in 1855*; Seacole, *Wonderful Adventures*.

82. Minter, *Chagres*, 269.

83. Otis, *Illustrated History*, 104.

84. Tomes, *Panama in 1855*, 24.

85. A modern revival of Jamaican "higglers" to Panama was the "skellion run" in the 1970s and 1980s. See note 23 to chapter 1.

86. Tomes, *Panama in 1855*, 204.

87. Jamaica, Departmental Reports, Police Department, 1886–87.

88. W.P. Livingstone, *Black Jamaica* (London: Sampson, Low, Marston, 1900) 183.

89. Ibid., 186.

90. McGuinness, *Path of Empire*; and John Lindsay-Poland, *Emperors in the Jungle: The Hidden History of the U.S. in Panama* (Durham: Duke University Press, 2003), deal with this event.

91. Schott, *Rails across Panama*, 42.

92. Seacole, *Wonderful Adventures*, 41.

93. Bayard Taylor quoted in Schott, *Rails across Panama*, 52.

94. Seaman Michael Scott, in *Tom Cringle's Log*, 459, presents a more dramatic and amusing description.

95. *Panama Star*, 17 October, 28 October, 31 October 1851.

96. C.T. Bidwell, *The Isthmus of Panama* (London: Chapman and Hall, 1865), 181. Some of these blacks were no doubt natives of Panama. Enslaved people in Panama were officially freed in 1852 but most blacks by that time had secured their freedom by various means, including marronage, so there was already a large population of freed blacks and mixed-race people, some occupying important positions. Bidwell confirmed that public offices were almost all filled by Negro or coloured men.

97. Cited in Shirley C. Gordon, *Our Cause for His Glory: Christianisation and Emancipation in Jamaica* (Kingston: University of the West Indies Press, 1998), 6

98. For example, Bidwell, *Isthmus of Panama*.

99. Seacole, *Wonderful Adventures*, 94.

100. *Panama Herald*, 6 August 1852.

101. *Panama Star*, 24 September 1853.

102. See Olive Senior, "The Panama Railway", *Jamaica Journal*, no. 44 (1980) for details.

103. Schott, *Rails across Panama,* 98.

104. See ibid. for an account of Runnels's life.

105. For example, three Jamaicans of forty-seven in August 1854. *Star and Herald,* 30 August 1854.

106. Tomes, *Panama in 1855*, 58–59.

107. H.P Jacobs, *Sixty Years of Change, 1806–1866: Progress and Reaction in Jamaica and the Countryside* (Kingston: Institute of Jamaica, 1973), 83.

108. Tomes (*Panama in 1855*) described the steward of the Panama Railroad Mess House as a "little brisk white man from Jamaica", 46.

109. "Pardner", or "partner", is a widespread and informal method of saving known throughout the Caribbean under different names. It is also known as "susu" from the Yorbua origin *esusu.* "Societies" refer to friendly or secret societies or lodges.

Chapter 3

1. The Jamaican population in 1891 was estimated at 639,500. Gisella Eisner, *Jamaica, 1830–1930* (Manchester: University of Manchester Press, 1961), 147; M. Proudfoot, *Population Movements in the Caribbean* (Port of Spain: Caribbean Commission, 1950).

2. In these countries Jamaicans were recruited mainly to establish banana plantations for American companies and to build railroads.

3. Among those leaving Jamaica were time-expired East Indian indentured workers; some 485 left for Colón in 1885. St John Robinson, "East Indians from Jamaica to Belize", in *Regional Footprints: The Travels and Travails of Early Caribbean Migrants,* ed. Annette Insanally, Mark Clifford and Sean Sheriff (Kingston: Latin American–Caribbean Centre, University of the West Indies, 2006). Other East Indians and Chinese who had not served out their contracts were often taken off ships bound for Colón and sent to jail (for example, *Star and Herald,* 8 September 1882), but many of them went legitimately to Panama and elsewhere in Central America. Although the reports of Indians on the Panama Railroad and later Canal construction referred to them all as "Hindoos", many of the Indians who were brought to Panama as contract workers from the subcontinent were Sikhs. See www.sikhnet .com//sikhs-panama.

4. Jamaica, Reports on the Blue Books.

5. Laura Putnam, *The Company They Kept: Migrants and the Politics of Gender in Caribbean Costa Rica, 1870–1960.* (Chapel Hill: University of North Carolina Press, 2002).

6. See, for instance, the three-part series "Jamaican Labourers Abroad", dealing mainly with the situation in Ecuador. *Daily Gleaner,* 30 July, 1 August, 7 August 1903.

7. *Star and Herald,* 2 June 1884.

8. *Star and Herald,* 1 November 1883. While the population along the line and terminal cities was estimated at fifteen thousand in 1863 (Commander Bedford Pim, *Gates of the* Pacific [London: Lovel Reeve, 1863], 208), in 1883 it had grown to thirty-six thousand, of which half was of British nationality, the majority Jamaican.

9. *Star and Herald*, 13 October 1886.

10. Cannabis was among the exports. Marijuana or "ganja" (*Cannabis sativa*) at the time was used mainly for medicinal purposes, as it continues to be used by some Jamaicans today, and probably travelled to the emigrants along with other medicinal bush such as cerasee (*Momordica charantia*). Ganja tea in rural Jamaican was believed to be efficacious in the treatment of malaria (among other illnesses). Possession of ganja was not illegal in Jamaica before 1913.

11. *Daily Gleaner*, 28 March 1883. Murray, his father and his brother, William Coleman Murray, were professional storytellers, black or coloured men who employed Jamaican creole in their monologues, only a few of which were written down. Their satirical descriptions, especially of working-class Jamaicans, elicited both amusement and criticism at home, and Andrew Murray's return performance in Panama at the Teatro Quevado in 1886 seems to have offended sections of the audience. While the reporter for the *Star and Herald* found his imitations of the peculiar words and accents of the Jamaican Negro "very lifelike and amusing", part of the audience "annoyed the lecturer and audience by rude and very ungentlemanly conduct during the entertainment", causing some of the "respectable" ladies and gentlemen to leave (*Star and Herald*, 10 February 1886). Panama seemed not to have been kind to the Murrays. The older Murray died in Kingston in January 1877 following an extended illness which began with fever contracted in Panama (*Daily Gleaner*, obituary, 30 January 1877). Shortly after the report of Andrew Murray's performance in February, there was the bald announcement in the *Star and Herald* on 13 March that Andrew C. "Funny Murray" had died in Colón.

12. Reports in *Star and Herald*, 18 December 1882; 15 December 1883; 17 November 1885; 13 March 1886.

13. *Daily Gleaner*, 22 March 1883.

14. *Star and Herald,* 10 January 1884.

15. *Star and Herald*, 25 January 1882.

16. *Gall's News Letter*, quoted in *Star and Herald*, 11 October 1883.

17. *Gall's News Letter,* quoted in *Star and Herald*, 26 January 1884.

18. Report on the Blue Book, 1881–82, xvi.

19. Report on the Blue Book, 1884, xi.

20. Quoted in Mack, *Land Divided*, 339–40.

21. Report on the Blue Book, 1884, 107.

22. *Gall's News Letter*, quoted in *Star and Herald*, 23 March 1885.

23. *Report on the Condition of the Juvenile Population*, 96.

24. *Daily Gleaner*, 7 May 1883.

25. Roberts, *Population of Jamaica*.

26. Report on the Blue Book, 1884.

27. Report on the Blue Book, 1883, 83.

28. Ibid., xviii.

29. *Report on the Condition of the Juvenile Population*, especially Notes of Evidence, 5.

30. Ibid., appendix B, 41.

31. Ibid., appendix B, 9.

32. Conditions in Jamaica are discussed in more detail in Olive Senior, "The Colón People", *Jamaica Journal* 11, no. 3, and 12, no. 4 (1978).

33. Isaac Ford, *Tropical America* (London: Edward Stanford, 1893), 214.

34. Bunau-Varilla, *Panama*, 430.

35. William Crawford Gorgas, *Sanitation in Panama* (New York: D. Appleton, 1916).

36. For a detailed account see David McCullough, *The Path between the Seas* (New York: Simon and Schuster, 1977).

37. Maron J. Simon, *The Panama Affair* (New York: Charles Scribner's Sons, 1971).

38. Robinson, *Panama*, 146.

39. See, among others, Espino, *How Wall Street*.

40. For an account of this company see James M. Skinner, *France and Panama: The Unknown Years, 1894–1908* (New York: Peter Lang, 1989). In 1897, the Compagnie Nouvelle imported 1,022 Jamaicans through its agent Charles Malabre (Newton, *Silver Men*, 87).

41. Simon, *Panama Affair*, 44

42. Dorsenne, *La vie sentimentale de Paul Gauguin*, quoted in Mack, *Land Divided*, 341.

43. Joseph Jos, *Guadeloupéens et Martiniquais au Canal de Panamá* (Paris: L'Harmattan, 2004), 38. All quotes from Jos have been translated from the French by Margot Gibb-Clarke.

44. Jolien Harmsen, Guy Ellis and Robert Devaux, *A History of St Lucia* (Vieux Fort, St Lucia: Lighthouse Road, 2012).

45. *Star and Herald*, 29 January 1884.

46. W.W. Kimball, *Special Intelligence Report on the Progress of the Work on the Panama Canal during the Year 1885* (Washington, DC: Government Printing Office, 1886), 21.

47. Nelson, *Five Years at Panama*, 170.

48. *Star and Herald*, 26 March, 27 March, 28 March, 31 March, 4 April, 7 April, 13 April 1883.

49. *Star and Herald*, 17 July 1882.

50. Ibid.; *Star and Herald,* 30 April 1887; T.P. Porter, *The Railroad Handbook and Guide to the Isthmus 1888–89* (London: Travel and Trade Publications).

51. McCullough, *Path between the Seas, 147.*

52. *Star and Herald*, 5 May 1884.

53. *Star and Herald*, 23 March 1885.

54. For example, *Report on the Condition of the Juvenile Population.*

55. Quoted in Simon, *Panama Affair*, 66–67.

56. *Star and Herald,* 17 September 1883; Kimball, *Intelligence Report,* 22.

57. Consul Claude Mallet quoted in Matthew Parker, *Panama Fever: The Building of the Panama Canal* (New York: Doubleday, 2007), 167.

58. Kimball, *Intelligence Report.*

59. *Star and Herald*, 4 February 1884.

60. Simon, *Panama Affair,* 83.

61. Matthew Parker recounts that Madame Dingler used to ride two beautiful white horses that had been a gift from Gadpaille, the French recruitment agent in Jamaica. On her death, Dingler ordered the horses put down so he would not encounter anyone else riding them. *Panama Fever*, 143.

62. Aizpuru's fate would be very different from Prestán's. He was taken to Bogotá, tried by court martial, and sentenced to ten years' exile.

63. The Colombian government at first believed that Prestán had fled to Jamaica and asked for his extradition. In the letter making the request addressed to Her Majesty's government minister in Bogotá, an alliance of the labourers and the "gang of malefactors" that took up arms was implied. *Star and Herald*, 10 July 1884.

64. In which case his father's anglophone name was most likely Preston. Indeed, in a dramatized version by Andrew Parkin, *Flames of Panama: The True Story of a Forgotten Hero, Pedro Prestan* (London: Matador, 2006), the Jamaican Cocobolo always speaks of his mentor as "Señor Preston".

65. *Star and Herald*, June 1885; Despatches, Governor to Secretary of State, IB/5/18/42, Norman to Derby, 7 April, 17 April 1885.

66. The *New York Times* report of the court martial of Aizpuru also noted that "J.M. Grant, a colored Jamaican, and another foreigner named Gustavo Guerra, accomplices of the rebel Prestan" were also tried and convicted by court martial and sentenced to imprisonment, the former for five and the latter for three years. The court expressed the opinion that the offences of these two men were aggravated by the fact that they were foreigners. "The Colombian Revolutionists", *New York Times*, 25 December 1885.

67. Quoted in Parker, *Panama Fever*, 156.

68. Ibid., 157.

69. Ibid.

70. Ibid., 158.

71. *Star and Herald*, 8 June 1887.

72. *Star and Herald*, 5 May, 6 May 1885; Despatches, Governor to Secretary of State, IB/5/18/42, Norman to Derby, 7 April 1885; IB/5/18/43, Norman to Knutsford, 31 July 1888; *Jamaica Gazette*, 19 November 1885.

73. *Star and Herald*, 4 November 1885.

74. *Star and Herald*, 18 March 1885.

75. Despatches, IB/5/18/43, Norman to Derby, 4 April 1884, 19 April 1884.

76. Walter Jekyll, ed., *Jamaican Song and Story* (New York: Dover, 1904), 246.

77. *Daily Gleaner*, 11 April 1883.

78. *Star and Herald*, 2 June 1884.

79. *Star and Herald*, 24 July 1885.

80. Rogers, *Intelligence Report*, 42.

81. Report on the Blue Book, 1887–88; Livingstone, *Black Jamaica*, 52, 183.

82. Reports on the Blue Books.

83. *Star and Herald*, 25 October 1887; Porter, *Railroad Handbook*.

84. *Star and Herald*, 2 February 1886, 23 November 1882. The relevant laws were law 27 of 1873, "A Law to prohibit in certain cases the holding of wakes and other Assemblages of a similar nature", and law 3 of 1874, an amending law.

85. *Star and Herald*, 13 September 1886.

86. *Star and Herald*, 6 August 1886.

87. *Star and Herald*, 29 May 1884.

88. Examples in the *Star and Herald*, 25 May 1883; 19 January, 29 January, 31 January, 2 February, 28 April, 11 August, 10 September, 15 September, 19 November 1884; 20 August, 27 October 1885; 20 March 1889. Details given in Senior, "Colón People".

89. *Star and Herald*, 12 April 1883; 3 June, 17 July, 25 October 1884.

90. *Star and Herald*, 16 June 1883.

91. Nelson, *Five Years at Panama*, 164.

92. *Star and Herald*, 29 January, 13 February 1889.

93. *Star and Herald*, 14 September 1888.

94. Report on the Blue Book, 1881–82, xxii.

95. Report on the Blue Book, 1883, xvi.

96. *Star and Herald*, 29 May 1884.

97. *Star and Herald*, 10 July 1883.

98. *Report on the Condition of the Juvenile Population*.

99. Law 10 of 1885. See *Jamaica Gazette*, 14 May 1885.

100. Quoted in Simon, *Panama Affair*, 54.

101. Next to de Lesseps, Buneau-Varilla would become the most famous Frenchman associated with the canal. He would remain at the centre of Panama affairs and become part of America's machinations to gain control of the isthmus.

102. *Jamaica Gazette*, 29 March 1886.

103. Reports in the *Star and Herald*, 11 May, 16 May 1888; 18 February, 19 March, 30 March 1889.

104. Governor to Secretary of State IB/5/18/41, Justice to Knutsford, 29 January 1889; 6A, Blake to Knutsford, 25 February 1889

105. *Star and Herald*, various issues March–May 1899; Reports on the Blue Book, 1888–89.

106. Governor to Secretary of State, IB/5/18/41, Blake to Knutsford, 8 April 1889.

107. *Star and Herald*, 6 April 1889, 15 April 1889.

108. Governor to Secretary of State, IB/5/18/41, Blake to Knutsford, 10 April 1889.

109. Blake to Knutsford, 24 April 1889; *Star and Herald*, 17 April 1889; Blake to Knutsford, 6 May 1889.

110. *Star and Herald*, 15 May 1889.

111. Computed from *Star and Herald*, March–May 1889; Reports on the Blue Book, 1888–89; Despatches, Blake to Knutsford.

112. Report on the Blue Book, 1888–89.

113. Robinson, *Panama*, 200.

114. Report on the Blue Book, 1888–89.

115. *Star and Herald*, 30 April 1889.

116. Annual Report, Island Medical Department. Bound with Report on the Blue Book, 1888–89.

117. *Daily Gleaner*, 19 March 1904; 17 February 1905.

118. A type of pungent tobacco produced on small farms and rolled into rope-like lengths and smoked in the small clay and chalk pipes popular with working-class men and women at the time.

119. Report on the Blue Book, 1888–89, 87.

120. Report on the Blue Book, 1885–86.

121. Legislative Council Minutes, 1904.

122. Kimball, *Intelligence Report*; Despatches, IB/5/18/41, Musgrave to Derby, 24 November 1883.

123. Annual Departmental Reports.

124. *Star and Herald*, 29 April 1889.

125. Jamaican carpenter, in Edwin Slosson and Gardner Richardson, "Two Panama Life Stories", *Independent*, 19 April 1906.

126. Jeremiah Waisome, "True Stories".

Chapter 4

1. George Lamming, *In the Castle of My Skin* (London: Longman Caribbean, 1970), 85.

2. *Colón Starlet*, 19 June 1906.

3. Samuel White, interview by the author, Almirante, Panama, July 1976.

4. Albert Peters, "True Stories". Peters's entry won first prize in the competition.

5. *Colón Starlet*, 2 March 1907. ("This seems to be a very funny place. They call two shillings a dollar, they call rum *seco*, and when the steamer was coming alongside the wharf they said we were going to the dock".)

6. Sue Core, *Maid in Panama* (New York: Clermont Press, 1938).

7. Jeremiah Waisome, "True Stories".

8. Harry Franck, *Zone Policeman 88* (New York: Century Company, 1913), provides many examples in his own speech.

9. Numerous accounts of the machinations of the United States to secure Panama for their own interests can be found. See, for example, McCullough, *Path between the Seas*; Espino, *How Wall Street*.

10. The Hay–Bunau-Varilla treaty between the two countries was concluded with terms much less favourable than the Bidlack treaty negotiated with Colombia in 1846 where land on the isthmus had first been leased to the United States in exchange for its defence of the territory. Hereafter, the "Republic" refers to the country of Panama that was distinct from the US-controlled Canal Zone.

11. The Isthmian Canal Commission ceased to exist 1 April 1914 and was succeeded by a new organization, the Panama Canal Company.

12. For some of the difficulties that would result see, for example, John Biesanz and Mavis Biesanz, *The People of Panama* (New York: Columbia University Press, 1955), and Conniff, *Black Labor*.

13. Franck, *Zone Policeman*, 114.

14. Ibid., 115–16.

15. *Spotlight* newsmagazine (Jamaica) March 1946 where the poem appeared, described Roberts as a "Pan-West Indian". The poem was first published in the political weekly newspaper *La Opinion*.

16. *Canal Record*, 1 July 1914.

17. Franck, *Zone Policeman,* 42. Franck worked on the Zone as both census taker and policeman.

18. Abbot, *Panama*, 266–67.

19. See, for example Julie Greene, *The Canal Builders: Making America's Empire at the Panama Canal* (New York: Penguin, 2009), 248.

20. *Colón Starlet*, 5 June 1906.

21. *Colón Starlet*, 10 August 1907.

22. Roberts, *Population of Jamaica*.

23. David Lowenthal, "The Population of Barbados", *Social and Economic Studies* 6, no. 4 (December 1957).

24. Edward (Kamau) Brathwaite, "The Journeys", in *Rights of Passage* (Oxford: Oxford University Press, 1967), 40.

25. Winston A. James, *Holding Aloft the Banner of Ethiopia: Caribbean Radicalism in Early Twentieth-Century America* (London: Verso, 1998), 14–17.

26. Ibid., 15.

27. Harmsen, Ellis and Devaux, *History of St Lucia*.

28. *Daily Gleaner*, 17 and 18 July 1903.

29. James, *Holding Aloft the Banner*, 21

30. *Daily Gleaner,* 12 January 1904.

31. Claude McKay, *Banana Bottom* (1933; repr., New York: Harcourt Brace Jovanovich, 1961), 293. McKay was himself briefly a policeman before migrating to the United States.

32. Despatches, Governor to Secretary of State, IB/5/18/63, Bourne to Crewe, 30 May 1908; IB/5/18/64, Olivier to Crewe, 27 May 1909.

33. Roberts, *Population of Jamaica.*

34. Report on the Blue Book, 1901–2; 1902–3.

35. Report on the Blue Book, 1899–1900, 82.

36. Clyde Hoyte, *The Life and Times of Willie Henry* (Kingston: Institute of Jamaica, 1975), 2.

37. See James, *Holding Aloft the Banner.*

38. Theophilus Saunders, interview by the author, Panama, July 1976.

39. Claude McKay, *My Green Hills of Jamaica* (Kingston: Heinemann Caribbean, 1979); Eric Walrond, *Tropic Death* (1926; New York: Collier, 1972).

40. H.G. de Lisser, *Susan Proudleigh* (London: Methuen, 1915).

41. Personal communication (family stories recounted to author). See also Carmen Hutchinson Miller, "Female Migrants in Port Limón, Costa Rica 1872–1890", in *Regional Footprints,* ed. Annette Insanally, Mark Clifford and Sean Sheriff (Kingston: Latin American–Caribbean Centre, University of the West Indies, 2006), 277.

42. ICC Annual Report, 1899–1901, 114.

43. ICC Annual Report, 1904, 13.

44. His pig-headedness gave rise to a new though short-lived coinage in America – "swettenhamming" (*New York World*, quoted in *Colón Starlet,* 23 March 1907), after what was perceived as his insulting behaviour in 1907 towards the rear admiral of the US Navy who brought supplies to the city of Kingston when it was devastated by earthquake and fire. The admiral had also landed armed marines to assist in the relief effort without Swettenham's permission. The governor ordered them back to their boat. Criticism of his conduct led to his resignation as governor, but that was three years in the future.

    For a more rounded account of his personality and tenure, see Jackie Ranston, *Behind the Scenes at King's House, 1873–2010* (Kingston: Jamaica National Building

Society, 2011). The world's press vilified Swettenham, and misleadingly reported riots and disorder among the black population when none occurred, claiming as well that in 1907 he abandoned his responsibilities. But the governor was in fact very much in charge of the situation following the earthquake. In a secret dispatch to London, Swettenham later cited his concern regarding armed white Americans using their guns. "I was not in a position to know whether all the American squadron could be trusted to get on well with the City populace. I deemed it prudent to avoid a possibility I dreaded, viz., that of having an American sailor or marine arrested by Negro police or Negro soldiers." He noted that the only instance of a shot being fired since the earthquake "was by an American naval officer" who drew his revolver "when surrounded by some half dozen black men whom he thought entertained some sinister design against him – a belief which I do not share". Quoted in Ranston, *Behind the Scenes*, 101.

45. *Daily Gleaner*, 3 and 27 January 1905.

46. *New York Sun*, 19 December 1905.

47. Despatches, Governor to Secretary of State, IB/5/18/59, Swettenham to Lyttelton, 10 December 1904. In the post-emancipation period, large numbers of indentured workers were brought to the West Indies from India, China and Africa to replace local workers who would not work for the low wages offered.

48. Canal Zone Records 2-E-2 Jamaica, part 4, Jackson Smith to J.F. Stevens, 2 December 1906.

49. Despatches, Governor to Secretary of State, IB/5/18/59, Swettenham to Lyttelton, 10 December 1904.

50. Mallet's experience of dealing with Jamaicans in Panama included his lengthy stint from 1884 as vice-consul, Panama; vice-consul, Colón, 1885; consul, Colón, 1888; he was appointed minister plenipotentiary of Panama 1914–19.

51. Despatches, Secretary of State to Governor, IB/5/26/42, Lyttelton to Swettenham, 27 January 1905.

52. *Jamaica Gazette*, 14 December 1904.

53. Law 10 of 1885 and subsequent amending laws passed in 1893, 1894 and 1899.

54. *Jamaica Gazette*, 14 December 1904.

55. *Daily Gleaner*, 23 January 1905.

56. *Daily Gleaner,* 3 January, 27 January 1905.

57. "Correspondence in Relation to the Emigration of Jamaicans to the Isthmus of Panama", *Jamaica Gazette*, 20 December 1905.

58. Canal Zone Records, 2-E-2, Jamaica, 27 November and 30 November 1905.

59. *Jamaica Gazette*, 20 December 1905.

60. Such "caution and repression" must have been extremely galling for Smith, whose abrasive manner made him unpopular with everyone on the Zone and forced his resignation in 1908.

61. Canal Zone Records 2-E-2 Jamaica, part 3, Jackson Smith to J.F. Stevens, 18 October 1906.

62. Ibid., and cable, Smith to Stevens, 18 October 1906.

63. Ibid. Letter Smith to Stevens, Canal Zone Records 2-E-2, Jamaica, part 4, 2 December 1906, urging Congress to consider a bill to put a tariff on bananas so as to threaten Jamaica.

64. Henry Burnett to John Stevens, chief engineer. 28 November 1905. Canal Zone Records 2-E-2, Jamaica, part 1.

65. Quoted in *Colón Telegram*, 17 February 1906.

66. The phrase "Glad to go but sorry to leave" comes from James, *Holding Aloft the Banner*, 38.

67. Bullard, *Panama*, 31.

68. Bonham C. Richardson, *Panama Money in Barbados, 1900–1920* (Knoxville: University of Tennessee Press, 1985), 117.

69. Ibid., 106.

70. Ibid., 136.

71. G.W. Roberts, "Emigration from the Island of Barbados", *Social and Economic Studies* 4, no. 3 (September 1955), 267.

72. Quoted in Richardson, *Panama Money*, 17.

73. Ibid., 18.

74. Ibid., 16.

75. Ibid., 137

76. Roberts, "Emigration from Barbados".

77. Richardson, *Panama Money*, 125.

78. George H. Martin, "True Stories".

79. ICC Annual Report, 1906, 15.

80. R.E. Wood, "The Working Force of the Panama Canal", *Transactions of the International Engineering Congress, 1915*, vol. 1, *The Panama Canal* (San Francisco, 1916), 195.

81. For instance, the *Canal Record* (28 July 1909) noted the arrival of several schooners from Barbados with men, women and children as immigrants, which meant they paid their own way and everyone over twelve years old could show the equivalent of fifteen dollars to satisfy Panamanian immigration laws. In one case, the schooner *Viola* brought 106.

82. John Angus Martin, *A–Z of Grenadian Heritage* (London: Macmillan, 2007). Yet no Grenadians (except for ninety-three in 1912) are in the list of contract labourers (table 5.1). It is possible that, like many others, they sailed to Panama from Barbados or Trinidad and were listed among those islanders.

83. The ads also promised that since there were no special qualifications, only "solid muscles and good health" were needed to make a fortune. Jos, *Guadeloupéens*, 15.

84. Ibid., 12.

85. Testimony, ibid., 222.

86. *Canal Record*, 25 March 1908, 236.

87. Bullard, *Panama*, 28.

88. Ibid., 29.

89. Ibid.

90. *Canal Record*, 14 July 1909.

91. Bullard, *Panama*, 29.

92. Harrigan Austin, "True Stories".

93. Edgar Simmons, "True Stories".

94. Ibid.

95. ICC Annual Report, 1905, 56.

96. *Canal Record*, 6 July, 19 July, 6 August 1910; 2 August 1911.

97. Quoted in Richardson, *Panama Money*, 119.

98. Daniel Reckord, interview by the author, Almirante, Panama, July 1976.

99. A lotion from the West Indies made of bay leaves steeped in rum, once widely used for external medicinal purposes and to revive oneself.

100. Winifred James, *The Mulberry Tree*, 2nd ed. (London: Chapman and Hall, 1913), 190.

101. *Colón Starlet*, 27 September 1906.

102. Ibid.

103. Mary Couloote, "True Stories".

104. *Daily Gleaner*, 9 July 1904.

105. Jos, *Guadeloupéens*, 217–18.

106. Ibid., 218.

107. Daniel T. Lawson, "True Stories".

Chapter 5

1. Rose van Hardeveld, *Make the Dirt Fly!* (Hollywood: Pan Press, 1956). The book and the van Hardevelds' story were featured in the PBS documentary *The American Experience: Panama Canal* (2011).

2. Hardeveld, *Make the Dirt Fly*, 8–9.

3. Thomas B. Gittens, "True Stories".

4. W. Leon Pepperman, *Who Built the Panama Canal?* (New York: E.P. Dutton, 1915), 49

5. Edwin Slosson and Gardner Richardson, "Life on the Canal Zone", *Independent*, 22 March 1906.

6. Ibid.

7. See McCullough, *Path between the Seas,* for details regarding the ingenuity which went into solving engineering and other technical problems.

8. Gorgona.

9. Amos E. Clarke, "True Stories".

10. *Canal Record*, 26 May 1909.

11. Amos E. Clarke, "True Stories".

12. ICC Annual Reports, 1905, 1906.

13. Hardeveld, *Make the Dirt Fly*, 9. The Canal Zone census of 1908 showed 583 Chinese (including twenty-three women) established along the route of canal construction, many engaged in agriculture and shop keeping.

14. Ibid.

15. *Washington Post*, n.d. Newspaper clipping file, 1905, Canal Zone Library.

16. ICC Annual Report, 1905, 48.

17. Interview with Theodore Shonts, ICC chairman, *Washington Evening Star*, 28 October 1905.

18. Albert Banister, "True Stories".

19. Jamaican carpenter in Slosson and Richardson, "Two Panama Life Stories".

20. Henry Barclay, interview by the author, Colón, Panama, July 1976.
21. Hardeveld, *Make the Dirt Fly*, 18
22. David Crawford, interview by the author, Panama, July 1976.
23. *Daily Gleaner,* 13 April 1904.
24. H.G. de Lisser, *Jamaicans in Colón and the Canal Zone, 1906* (Kingston: Gleaner Company), 5.
25. Ibid., 5–6.
26. "Five Years of Canal Work", *Canal Record,* 19 May 1909.
27. Alfred Banister, "True Stories".
28. Miles P. DuVal, *And the Mountains Will Move* (1947; repr., Westport, CT: Greenwood, 1975), 176.
29. "Mrs. Mattie J. Morrison Tells of Pioneer Days on the Zone", from the *Canal Record,* 1989, http://www.czbrats.com/Builders/morrison.htm.
30. Ross, a Nobel laureate for his work, is remembered today chiefly for the lines he penned to celebrate his discovery:

    I know this little thing
    A myriad men will save.
    O Death, where is thy sting?
    Thy victory, O grave?

31. "Yellow Eyes", in James Stanley Gilbert, *Panama Patchwork*, 3rd ed. (Panama: Star and Herald, 1906), 26.
32. Lindsay-Poland, *Emperors in the Jungle*, 33.
33. Although the ICC supplied these services to the cities, the cost with interest was to be repaid by the Panamanian government from water rates to be collected within fifty years. Shortfalls in rates at any period would be made up by the Panamanian government. When paid for, the municipal works would become the property of the Panamanian government. *Canal Record,* 7 October 1908.
34. Alfonso Suazo, "True Stories".
35. Sometimes the campaign got a little out of hand. When fire ripped through a poor section of Colón destroying about thirty houses, the owners, mostly West Indians, claimed compensation from the ICC on the grounds that fire had started in a building that was sealed up for fumigation and was caused by the carelessness of the sanitation crews. Despatches, Secretary of State to Governor, IB/5/26/46, Lyttelton to Swettenham, 25 January 1906 (with enclosure); and IB/5/26/52, Elgin to Olivier, 6 August 1907 (with enclosure).
36. Quoted in Mack, *Land Divided*, 536.
37. Leslie Carmichael, "True Stories".
38. DDT was not in fact used until the 1940s.
39. Quoted in Jos, *Guadeloupéens*, 224.
40. Lindsay-Poland, *Emperors in the Jungle*, notes some of the environmental impacts on the land and people.
41. Joseph Pennell, *Pictures of the Panama Canal* (Philadelphia: J.B. Lippincott, 1912), 10.
42. *Canal Record,* 10 March 1909.
43. *Canal Record,* 21 April 1915.

44. Conniff, *Black Labor*, 31.

45. Weston Chamberlain, *Twenty-five Years of American Medical Activity on the Isthmus of Panama, 1904–1929: A Triumph of Preventive Medicine* (Mount Hope, CZ: Panama Canal Press, 1929).

46. Aaron Clarke, "True Stories".

47. John F. Prescod, "True Stories".

48. Clifford Hunt, "True Stories".

49. *Canal Record*, 19 May 1905; 16 September, 26 August 1908.

50. George H. Martin, "True Stories".

51. Rufus E. Forde, "True Stories".

52. Leslie Carmichael, "True Stories".

53. Gorgas, *Sanitation in Panama*, 220–21.

54. Albert Banister, "True Stories".

55. George H. Martin, "True Stories".

56. Rufus E. Forde, "True Stories".

57. John F. Prescod, "True Stories".

58. Albert Banister, "True Stories".

59. Alfred E. Dottin, "True Stories".

60. Amos Parks, "True Stories".

61. "The savvy young businessman soon recognized the marketing potential of making his products available to Jamaicans abroad and, in a stroke of marketing genius set out to acquire customers, among them Jamaicans at work on the construction of the Panama Canal." The company still operates in Jamaica under the P.A. Benjamin Company name, as a leading manufacturer and exporter producing a wide range in personal care products, food additives and medicinal products. http://www.paben jamin.com/aboutbenjaminshistory.htm.

62. *Colón Starlet*, 12 March 1904.

63. Although all refer to "alligators", the reptile in Panama is actually the American crocodile.

64. Recalled by Gracelyn Cassells, Montserrat, as told to Jean Handscombe.

65. Rosemary Kavanagh, as told to Olive Senior.

66. Nelson, *Five Years at Panama*, 59. So would the wild boar hunted by the Maroons in Jamaica.

67. Joseph Edwin, "Long-Time Employee considers passage money was well spent", *Panama Canal Review,* 4 May 1954, http://www.czbrats.com. Mr Edwin started work in 1907 and survived almost forty-seven years of working on the Canal Zone. When interviewed, he was leaving with his wife to return to Grenada "thankful that I am going home without scratches".

68. The tapir is called "mountain cow" in Panama.

69. Constantine Parkinson, "True Stories".

70. George H. Martin, "True Stories".

71. Ibid.

72. Ibid.

73. Albert Banister, "True Stories".

74. *Canal Record*, 18 June 1913.

75. Bullard, *Panama*, 552.
76. *Handbook of the Panama Canal*, 1913.
77. *Canal Record*, 28 October 1908.
78. *Handbook of the Panama Canal,* 1913.
79. Rufus E. Forde, "True Stories".
80. *Daily Gleaner*, 11 March 1904.
81. ICC Annual Report, 1912.
82. James A. Williams, "True Stories".
83. Constantine Parkinson, "True Stories".
84. *Canal Record*, 14 August 1909.
85. Greene, *Canal Builders*, 136–37.
86. *Canal Record*, 3 November 1909, 3 August 1910.
87. John Garner, "True Stories".
88. *Canal Record*, 29 July 1908.
89. James A. Williams, "True Stories". Subsequent quotes from Williams in this section are from his contribution to "True Stories".
90. Franck, *Zone Policeman*, 49.
91. Hardeveld, *Make the Dirt Fly*, 51.
92. Alfred E. Dottin, "True Stories".
93. Reginald Beckford, "True Stories".
94. Charles F. Williams, recorded 1958. Roosevelt Medal Holders, transcription, Canal Zone Library.
95. Albert Peters, "True Stories".
96. For example, Hardeveld, *Make the Dirt Fly*, 49.
97. West Indians were themselves in the profitable mortuary business. In Maryse Condé's novel *Tree of Life* (New York: Ballantyne, 1992), that trade scandalized Albert's compatriots: "That Albert had turned himself into a transporter of stiffs was profoundly shocking. The job is an unhealthy one. The spirits of the dead cling to those who handle their bodies" (32).
98. Aaron Clarke, "True Stories".
99. ICC Annual Report, 1905, 120.
100. ICC Annual Report, 1907, 43.
101. *Daily Gleaner*, letters from workers in Mexico, 12 March 1883.
102. ICC Annual Report, 1905.
103. *Star and Herald*, 29 April 1905.
104. *Daily Gleaner*, 2 May 1905.
105. Rufus E. Forde, "True Stories".
106. Helon I. Allick, "True Stories".
107. Alfred E. Dottin, "True Stories".
108. Crawford, interview; also Bullard, *Panama,* and Biesanz and Biesanz, *People of Panama*, 56.
109. *Colón Starlet*, 1 February 1905; 11 January, 27 March, 26 May 1906.
110. Conniff, *Black Labor*, 38.
111. Walrond, *Tropic Death*.
112. Frequently mentioned in "True Stories".

113. Although Goethals's strong leadership during construction years led to his being admired by everyone including the silver workers (who incorporated his name in their chanteys), he himself was a product of American racism and was responsible for maintaining white supremacy both during construction days and after. Asked about the silver-gold system and the colour line, he explained that "it is not compatible with the white man's pride of race to do the work which it is traditional for the Negroes to do". Conniff, *Black Labor*, 43.

114. Vaughan Cornish, *Travels of Ellen Cornish* (London, 1913), 167.

115. See, for example, Richardson, *Panama Money*.

116. Sibert and Stevens, *Construction*, 114.

117. Farnham Bishop, *Panama Past and Present* (New York: D. Appleton-Century, 1913), 203.

118. Greene, *Canal Builders*, 124.

119. *Colón Starlet*, 7 June 1904.

120. De Lisser, *Jamaicans*.

121. Franck, *Zone Policeman*, 20.

122. ICC Annual Report, 1905, 70.

123. *Colón Starlet*, frequent reports, 1904–6.

124. Harrigan Austin, "True Stories".

125. Greene, *Canal Builders*, deals in some detail with law and order on the Zone.

126. ICC Annual Reports, 1907, 1911.

127. Albert Banister, "True Stories".

128. Jamaican carpenter in Slosson and Richardson, "Two Panama Life Stories".

129. Condé, *Tree of Life*, 25–26.

130. Albert Banister, "True Stories".

131. Quoted in Trevor O'Reggio, *Between Alienation and Citizenship: The Evolution of Black West Indian Society in Panama, 1914–1964* (Washington, DC: University Press of America, 2006), 167.

132. Enrique Plummer, "True Stories".

133. Poultney Bigelow, "Why Labour Shuns Panama", *Colón Independent*, part 2, 5 October 1906.

134. Franck, *Zone Policeman*, 37.

135. Bennett, *History of the Panama Canal*, 163.

136. Quoted in *Panama Journal*, 9 December 1906.

137. See Conniff, *Black Labor*.

138. For example, a stamp to honour silver workers on the initiative of George Westerman and the foundation of La Día de la Etnia Negra, first celebrated on 30 May 2001 (http://diadelaetnia.homestead.com/home.html). Rhonda Frederick has noted that "in a late-twentieth-century context, little has changed with regard to representations of laborers from the Caribbean. Despite the plethora of newspaper and magazine articles emanating from the 31 December 1999 transfer of the Panama Canal, there has been little mention of the presence and impact of Caribbean workers. This recent erasure is not surprising, however, since it followed a trend that consigned Colón Men to less than supporting roles in isthmian work and life". Frederick, "*Colón Man*", 15n8.

139. Wood, "Working Force", 199.

140. McCullough, *Path between the Seas*, 476–77.

141. *Workman*, 31 July 1920.

142. *Workman,* 25 May 1920.

143. See, for example, Conniff, *Black Labor.*

144. Ibid., 22.

145. Quoted in *Star and Herald*, 19 January 1905.

146. Panama Collection, Canal Zone Library, newspaper clippings file.

147. The first drug prohibition law of the United States was named after Harrison, who supported the view that "cocaine gave Negroes superhuman strength, criminal drive and hatred of white authority". www.nndb.com/people/ "Francis Burton Harrison".

148. *Colón Telegram*, 15 March 1906.

149. ICC Annual Report, 1908.

150. Ibid.

151. *Canal Record*, 9 February 1910.

152. *Panama Journal,* 16 May 1906; ICC Annual Report, 1906, 14.

153. A federal law of 1882 (with subsequent revisions) prohibited immigration of Chinese to the United States and barred those already there from citizenship. It was finally repealed in 1943.

154. *Panama Journal*, 7 September 1906.

155. According to McCullough, *Path between the Seas*, 475, "in reaction to the success of Chinese merchants in Colón and Panama City, many of them descendants of Chinese laborers left over from earlier projects", the Republic of Panama also enacted its own Chinese exclusion law.

156. Ibid., 471.

157. ICC Annual Report, 1906, 6.

158. *Canal Record*, 4 September 1907, 2.

159. *Canal Record,* 29 January 1908. For comments see, for example, Joseph Bucklin Bishop, *The Panama Gateway* (New York: Charles Scribner's Sons, 1913), 302.

160. *Canal Record*, 28 April 1909.

161. *Canal Record*, 28 July 1909.

162. Albert Banister, "True Stories".

163. See Newton, *Silver Men*, for a detailed discussion of the silver pay structure.

164. *Canal Record*, 28 April 1909.

165. Conniff, *Black Labour*, 36.

166. Executive order dated 8 February 1908 (*Canal Record*, 23 December 1908).

167. Conniff, *Black Labor*, 33.

168. *Canal Record*, 14 April 1909.

169. *Canal Record*, 28 July 1909 (circular 229A).

170. Frank Rose, "Reminiscences of Panama in the Days of the Canal Diggers" (typescript, n.d., Panama Collection, Canal Zone Library), 91–92.

171. *Canal Record*, 25 March 1914.

172. Rose, "Reminiscences".

Chapter 6

1. George Westerman, *Pioneers in Canal Zone Education* (La Boca: Occupational High School Shop, 1949).

2. Cecil Haynes, born in Panama of Barbadian ancestry, was to work on the Panama Canal for seventy-one years. He was honoured by President Clinton as the longest-serving employee of the US federal government. Born in 1913, he began work at the age of fourteen in 1928. Latin American–Caribbean Centre, University of the West Indies, "Reflection on Seventy-one Years of Service in the Panama Canal Zone", in *West Indian Participation in the Construction of the Panama Canal* (publication of the proceedings of a symposium held at the University of the West Indies, Kingston, Jamaica, 15–17 June 2000). Haynes died in 2012.

3. "Money Brought Him to Panama: He Counted It for 36 years", *Panana Canal Review*, 7 August 1953, http://www.czbrats.com/Builders/money.htm.

4. "They Wanted Young Men", *Panama Canal Review*, October 1953, http://www.czbrats.com/Builders/messen.htm.

5. Albert Peters, "True Stories".

6. John Garner, "True Stories".

7. Franck, *Zone Policeman*, 65.

8. *Canal Record*, 23 April 1913.

9. Slightly different versions appear in "Chanties and Worksongs of Canal Zone Employees", Panama Collection, Canal Zone Library, and Core, *Maid in Panama*.

10. John O. Butcher, "True Stories".

11. Rufus E. Forde, "True Stories".

12. John Garner, "True Stories".

13. Fitz H. Thomas, "True Stories".

14. Albert Banister, "True Stories".

15. Albert Peters, "True Stories".

16. *Canal Record*, 27 March 1912.

17. Alfred E. Dottin, "True Stories".

18. Jeremiah Waisome, "True Stories".

19. Slosson and Richardson, "Two Panama Life Stories".

20. George H. Martin, "True Stories". The woman's name is given as "Mattie" in a later version of the song (Cramer, *Songs*).

21. "Spirit of Good Old Days Preserved in Chanteys of West Indian Workers", from the *Panama American*, 15 August 1939, http://cbrats.com/Builders/chantey.htm.

22. The red-headed turkey buzzard *Cathartes aura* ranges from southern Canada to the tip of South America.

23. "West Indian Folk Songs", Panama Collection, Canal Zone Library.

24. Frederic J. Haskin, *The Panama Canal* (Garden City, NJ: Doubleday Page, 1916).

25. Joseph Brewster, "True Stories".

26. *Colón Starlet*, 22 November 1906.

27. Reginald Beckford, "True Stories".

28. Young, "A Few Will Remember".

29. Rufus E. Forde, "True Stories".

30. Young, "A Few Will Remember".

31. George H. Martin, "True Stories".

32. Hardeveld, *Make the Dirt Fly*, 39.

33. Rufus E. Forde, "True Stories".

34. Rose, "Reminiscences of Panama".

35. Rufus E. Forde, "True Stories".

36. Edgar L. Simmons, "True Stories".

37. George H. Martin, "True Stories".

38. *Canal Record*, 6 December 1911.

39. Ibid.

40. Rufus E. Forde, "True Stories".

41. "Spirit of Good Old Days" utilizes some of the words of a song that was composed by West Indians Joseph Haynes and Jonah Dean, who wrote and set it to music:

> You've heard about the locks and dams,
> Done by the men of fate
> They even had to emigrate
> Contractors from the States,
> England, France and Germany
> They all will have to pass
> The Atlantic and Pacific route
> Is almost shorter now
>
> *Chorus*:
> Goethals, Goethals, your name shall e'er be called!
>
> The principal contractors who came from the States
> Was McClintock and Marshall who hung the gates.
> They're seventy and five feet high – the truth you can't deny
> When the water display itself through spillway
> Through your locks and dams.

(The lock gates were built by the US contractor McClintic-Marshall.)

42. *Canal Record*, various issues.

43. *Canal Record*, 8 April 1913.

44. Lancelot Kavanagh, "True Stories".

45. Nehemiah Douglas, "True Stories".

46. *Canal Record*, 25 December 1912.

47. *Canal Record*, 21 May 1913.

48. *Canal Record*, 25 December 1912.

49. *Canal Record*, 25 March 1914.

50. Jekyll, *Jamaican Song*.

51. "Chanties and Worksongs of Canal Zone Employees", Panama Collection, Canal Zone Library.

52. Young, "A Few Will Remember".

53. Franck, *Zone Policeman*, 64.

54. Ibid.

55. Bullard, *Panama*, 550.

56. James, *Mulberry Tree*, 242.
57. Young, "A Few Will Remember".
58. Ibid.
59. Bullard, *Panama,* 552–53.
60. John K. Baxter, "Chantey of the Ditch Diggers", http://www.czbrats.com/Builders/chaney.htm.
61. George Peters, "True Stories".
62. Panama Canal, *Official Handbook*, 1913.
63. Reed E. Hopkins, "A Trip Down Memory Lane", Roosevelt Medal Holders, Isthmian Historical Society, recorded 1958, transcription Canal Zone Library.
64. Gertrude B. Hoffman, "A Trip Down Memory Lane", Roosevelt Medal Holders, Isthmian Historical Society, recorded 1958, transcription Canal Zone Library.
65. Mrs Bruce Saunders, "Men Dug the Canal . . . but Women Played a Vital Role", *Panama Canal Review* (Spring 1976), http://www.czbrats.com/Builders/women.htm.
66. *Canal Record*, 14 October 1908.
67. *Canal Record*, 23 April 1913.
68. *Canal Record*, 15 July 1914.
69. *Canal Record*, 8 July 1914.
70. *Colón Starlet*, 15 December 1908; *Canal Record*, 16 December 1908.
71. Amos E. Clarke, "True Stories".
72. Reginald Beckford, "True Stories".
73. George Hodges, "True Stories".
74. *Canal Record*, 14 October 1908.
75. *Canal Record*, 28 February 1912.
76. *Canal Record,* 23 July 1913.
77. Bullard, *Panama,* 551.
78. *Canal Record*, 6 January 1909.
79. *Canal Record*, 1 June 1910.
80. Ibid.
81. This includes the 4,850 workers who died in Canal Zone hospitals during the US construction years and the estimated 20,000 during the French effort.
82. The name was changed back to Culebra Cut in 2000.

Chapter 7

1. Philip McDonald, "True Stories".
2. Rufus E. Forde, "True Stories".
3. ICC Annual Report, 1905.
4. *Times*, London, 26 September 1912, quoted in J.S. Mills, *The Panama Canal: A History and Description of the Enterprise* (London: Thomas Nelson and Sons, 1913), 170.
5. Jos, *Guadeloupéens*, 48.
6. Quoted in Mills, *Panama Canal,* 170.
7. Franck, *Zone Policeman*, 29.

8. Ibid., 28.

9. *Canal Record*, 25 December 1907.

10. *Canal Record*, 16 October 1907, 5.

11. Thomas B. Gittens, "True Stories".

12. Jamaican carpenter in Slosson and Richardson, "Two Panama Life Stories".

13. *Canal Record*, 29 March 1911.

14. De Lisser, *Jamaicans*, 13.

15. ICC Annual Report, 1905, 46.

16. *Canal Record*, 22 July 1908, 370

17. *Canal Record*, 27 May 1908.

18. Ibid.

19. Ibid.

20. Arthur E. Phillips, "True Stories".

21. John O. Butcher, "True Stories".

22. Quoted in Greene, *Canal Builders*, 148.

23. John Butcher, "True Stories".

24. Philip McDonald, "True Stories".

25. Jamaican carpenter in Slosson and Richardson, "Two Panama Life Stories".

26. Albert Banister, "True Stories".

27. *Canal Record*, 27 May 1908.

28. The mess kitchens, like all catering establishments and hotels owned by the ICC, made a profit. In fiscal year 1910–11, for instance, common labourers' kitchens showed a profit of $14,462.

29. ICC Annual Report, 1911.

30. *Canal Record*, 9 February 1910.

31. Jamaican carpenter in Slosson and Richardson, "Two Panama Life Stories".

32. "Chanties and Worksongs of Canal Zone Employees". Panama Collection, Canal Zone Library.

33. Songs collected by Louise Cramer in the 1940s, after another set of West Indians came to construct a third set of locks in 1939, were equally derisive of the women (Cramer, "Songs", 270):

> Since de locks start to issue book,
> All de young gals start to cook. (*Rep*)
> They walk about pullin' dem style
> They got they way given away wild,
> All you can hear dem say,
> "Yes, m'child, today is m'man payday."

> Seven fifty book they walk with it in the hand
> Five dolla book they fan their face.
> Two fifty book they put it in the purse.
> All you can hear dem say,
> "Yes, m'child, today is m'man payday."

A Trinidad-style calypso of the era poured scorn on the "Commissary Gals" (Cramer, "Songs", 271):

> Commissary gals, them taking a chance
> Violet she disgrace the rest,
> She try to be dress better than the rest,
> But the government put her under arrest.
> She went to Colón to spend a few weeks,
> Boy, she put in a champion gold teeth.
> A jasper boy saw, and took her to a dance
> But to me she is nothing but a slot machine.

34. George H. Martin, "True Stories".
35. Walrond, *Tropic Death*, 45–46. Mr Poyer had a peg leg from his Panama days.
36. Cramer, "Songs", 257.
37. Trevor Marshall, Peggy McGeary and Grace Thompson, *Folk Songs of Barbados* (Kingston: Ian Randle, 1996), 61–62.
38. Reginald Beckford, "True Stories".
39. Elizabeth Thomas-Hope, *Explanation in Caribbean Migration: Perception and the Image: Jamaica, Barbados, St Vincent* (London: Macmillan, 1992), 4–5.
40. Patrick Bryan, "The Black Middle Class in Nineteenth-Century Jamaica", in *Caribbean Freedom*, ed. Hilary Beckles and Verene Shepherd (Kingston: Ian Randle, 1996), 293.
41. Putnam, *Company They Kept*, 52–53.
42. Juan Tam, "Matachin. El Primer 'Chinatown' de Panama".
43. Walrond, *Tropic Death*, 90.
44. Ibid., 92.
45. De Lisser, *Susan Proudleigh*.
46. For example, Core, *Maid in Panama*; Elizabeth Kittredge Parker, *Panama Canal Bride: A Story of Construction Days* (New York: Exposition, 1955).
47. Core, *Maid in Panama*, 194.
48. Ibid., 121.
49. "Men Dug the Canal . . . but Women Played a Vital Role", *Panama Canal Review* (Spring 1976), http://www.czbrats.com/Builders/women.htm.
50. Ibid.
51. For example, Core, *Maid in Panama*; Parker, *Panama Canal Bride*; Mary A. Chatfield, *Light on Dark Places at Panama* (New York: Broadway, 1908); Hardeveld, *Make the Dirt Fly!*
52. "Men Dug the Canal".
53. Jules E. LeCurrieux, "True Stories".
54. *Canal Record*, 27 January 1909.
55. ICC Annual Report, 1908.
56. Abbot, *Panama*, 344.
57. James, *Mulberry Tree*, 232.
58. John F. Prescod, "True Stories".
59. *Colón Starlet*, 30 April 1908.
60. Alfred Banister, "True Stories".
61. *Canal Record*, 18 November 1908.
62. Walrond, *Tropic Death*.

63. Lennie Ruddock, *With the Sound of the Steam Korchie* (Kingston: Arawak, 2002), 74.

64. See, for example, Olive Senior, "All Clear", in *Gardening in the Tropics* (Toronto: Insomniac, 2005), 57.

65. *New York Herald*, 19 December 1905.

66. *New York Tribune*, reproduced in *Panama Journal*, 26 January 1906.

67. Martinique woman in Slosson and Richardson, "Two Panama Life Stories".

68. Parker, *Panama Canal Bride*, 22–23.

69. Winifred James, *A Woman in the Wilderness* (London: Chapman and Hall, 1915), 107.

70. Putnam, *Company They Kept*, 11.

71. Jos, *Guadeloupéens*.

72. Simon A. Clarke, "The Status of the West Indian Worker in the Panama Canal Zone", in *Regional Footprints: The Travels and Travails of Early Caribbean Migrants*, ed. Annette Insanally, Mark Clifford and Sean Sheriff (Kingston: Latin American–Caribbean Centre, University of the West Indies, 2006), 92–93.

73. Alfred Mitchell, "True Stories".

74. Edward Howell, "Money Brought Him to Panama: He Counted It for 36 Years", *Panama Canal Review*, 7 August 1953, http://www.czbrats.com/Builders/money.htm.

75. Cecil Haynes, interview by Ifeoma Kiddoe Nwankwo, March 2007, Voices from Our America Digital Library.

76. ICC Annual Report, 1905.

77. Delia Goetz, *Education in Panama*, bulletin no. 12 (Washington, DC: Government Printing Office, 1948).

78. ICC Annual Report, 1906; Conniff, *Black Labor*, 39–40.

79. Westerman, *Pioneers*.

80. *Canal Record*, 2 July 1909.

81. *Canal Record*, 18 January 1911.

82. George Westerman (born in Colón of Barbadian and St Lucian parentage) was a newspaperman and diplomat and advocate for the silver workers. The George Westerman papers are now in the Schomburg Centre for Research in Black Culture, New York Public Library.

83. The colleges were the offshoot of Mico Schools that were established throughout the West Indies after emancipation to educate the children of the formerly enslaved. They were funded by the Lady Mico Trust, from monies originally earmarked in the seventeenth century to free English sailors captured by Barbary pirates. Over time, the focus of the Mico institutions turned to teacher training with colleges in Jamaica and Antigua. Mico College in Kingston is now Mico University.

84. The policy was changed in 1927.

85. Westerman, *Pioneers*, 17.

86. *Canal Record*, 18 January 1911.

87. *Colón Starlet*, 1904–7.

88. *Canal Record*, 15 June 1910.

89. ICC Annual Report, 1919.

90. Goetz, *Education in Panama*.

91. Ibid.
92. *Colón Starlet*, 1 August 1905.
93. Haynes, interview.
94. *Colón Starlet*, 19 June 1906.
95. *Canal Record*, 29 March 1911.
96. Bigelow, "Why Labour Shuns Panama".
97. *Canal Record*, 21 April 1915. For comments on the spread of venereal disease, see former governor Lord Olivier, *Jamaica, the Blessed Island* (London: Faber and Faber, 1936); *Report on the Condition of the Juvenile Population*; Despatches, Governor to Secretary of State, Olivier to Crewe, IB/5/18/16. The issue was prominent in the enquiry by a commission into the economic conditions of drought-stricken south Manchester and south-eastern St Elizabeth parishes and a link was made with emigration. One of its recommendations was that all returning emigrants should be examined before landing and that all cases of dangerous infective venereal disease should be isolated and treated.
98. *Canal Record*, 29 March 1911.
99. *Canal Record*, 21 April 1915.
100. *Workman*, 2 June 1921. See also Carlos Reid, *Memorias de un Criollo Bocatoreño*, Monografías antropólogicas, no. 1 (Panama: Asociación Panameña de antropología, 1980). Reid recalls the first mule and donkey were brought to the settlement of Old Bank (Bocas del Toro) by a Jamaican (p. 112). A Panamanian resident of the town of Bocas pointed out to this writer in 1976 trees that had been introduced by West Indians. See also Palmer, *"What Happen?"*.
101. *Canal Record*, 5 October 1910.
102. *Canal Record*, 2 June 1909.
103. *Canal Record*, 2 August 1911.
104. *Canal Record*, 21 May 1913.
105. ICC Annual Report, 1920.

Chapter 8

1. For example, Biesanz and Biesanz, *People of Panama*. See also, the author's interviews.
2. See, for example, Steeve O. Buckridge, *The Language of Dress: Resistance and Accommodation in Jamaica, 1760–1890* (Kingston: University of the West Indies Press, 2004).
3. Walrond, *Tropic Death*, 189.
4. Haynes, interview.
5. Clifford Allen, Jamaica Memory Bank interview, tape no. T 790.
6. Biesanz and Biesanz, *People of Panama*, 269.
7. Franck, *Zone Policeman*, 20.
8. James, *Woman in the Wilderness*, 103.
9. "Spirit of Good Old Days Preserved in Chanteys of West Indian Workers", *Panama American*, 15 August 1939, http://www.czbrats.com/Builders/chantey.htm.
10. Ibid.

11. ICC Annual Report, 1905.

12. *Canal Record*, "Five Years of Canal Work", 2 June 1909.

13. James, *Woman in the Wilderness*, 98. The Americans had in fact planned an elaborate celebration which was cancelled because of the war. But in 1915, the completion of the canal and American technology that made it possible was celebrated at the World's Fair in San Francisco – the Panama-Pacific International Exposition, which attracted eighteen million visitors, and the Panama-Pacific Exposition in San Diego.

14. Franck, *Zone Policeman*, 125.

15. Lamming, *In the Castle*, 85.

16. Crawford, interview; E.W. Martinez, "True Stories"; The Colón Jockey Club was advertising in the *Colón Starlet* (17 May 1906) its first race meet at New Road and Ninth Street for the Fourth of July 1906.

17. Charles Harcort Forbes-Lindsay, *Panama and the Canal Today* (Boston: L.C. Page, 1912), 307–8.

18. Abbot, *Panama*, 245.

19. *Colón Starlet*, 18 October 1904; *Workman*, 26 April 1924.

20. *Workman*, 3 December 1921.

21. La Beach's brothers were also noted athletes, including Byron La Beach who was an alternate member of Jamaica's 4 × 400-metre relay team that won that event at the 1952 Olympic Games in Helsinki, Finland.

22. Philip McDonald, "True Stories".

23. E.W. Martineau, "True Stories".

24. One in Colón in 1905 was run by R.A. Heslop (*Colón Starlet*, 3 August 1905)

25. *Canal Record*, 3 August 1910.

26. *Canal Record*, 29 March 1911.

27. *Canal Record*, 3 August 1910.

28. *Canal Record*, 14 December 1910.

29. *Canal Record*, 14 December 1910.

30. For an account, see Jos, *Guadeloupéens*, 226–30.

31. See, for example, Richardson, *Panama Money*, 226–28.

32. Jamaica Provident and Benevolent Society Silver Jubilee programme, 1952.

33. George Westerman, "Historical Notes on West Indians in the Isthmus of Panama", *Phylon* 22 (Winter 1961).

34. West Indian journalists and printers have a long history in Panama. Isaac Lawton went from Jamaica to Panama in 1868 and founded the short-lived *Panama Mail* and later established the *South Pacific Times* in Peru. He was also at one time editor of the *Star and Herald*. Obituary, *Daily Gleaner*, 6 January 1905.

    James McCraw Reeves came to Panama in 1883 to work on the *Star and Herald* and transferred to Colón to take charge of the *Starlet* and Edward Lopez of Kingston became manager. *Colón Starlet*, 6 September 1906.

    Benjamin P. Wynter first left Jamaica in 1899 for Bocas del Toro and later settled in Colón, was active in West Indian social and civic life and organized the Friendly Societies War Contingent; his long newspaper career included stints with the *Jamaica Post* (1895–98), *Central American Express* in Bocas, *Panama Morning Journal* (1918–19) the *Star and Herald* and the *Workman* (death announcement in the *Workman*, 25 July 1925). The latter paper was owned and operated by Barbadian

H.L. Walrond. Still later, the community was served by the *Panama Tribune*, which was founded by Sidney Young in 1928 and lasted for forty-four years.

35. *Colón Starlet*, 22 January 1907.

36. *Canal Record*, 5 October, 1910.

37. Westerman, "Historical Notes", 343.

38. In Walrond, *Tropic Death*.

39. Walrond, "Tropic Death", in *Tropic Death*, 187–89.

40. See "Bishop Ephraim S. Alphonse: A Giant of Love", http://thesilverpeople-heritage.wordpress.com and citation on the award of an honorary doctorate by the University of the West Indies, Jamaica, in 1982.

41. *Canal Record*, 18 June 1913.

42. *Colón Telegram*, 2 September 1906.

43. Despatches, Secretary of State to Governor, IB/5/26/48, Elgin to Swettenham, 20 September 1906, enclosure from Mallet, 13 August re Episcopal Mission.

44. O. Collins, *The Panama Guide* (Mount Hope, CZ: ICC Press, Quartermaster's Department, 1912).

45. Methodist Church, *"For Ever Beginning": Two Hundred Years of Methodism in the Western Area* (Kingston: Literature Department of the Methodist Church, Jamaica District, 1960).

46. *Colón Starlet*, 9 September 1904.

47. *Canal Record*, 25 June 1913.

48. A Christian Mission church building erected by Barbadians 1909–10 is now the home of the Museo Afro-Antillano de Panamá.

49. *Canal Record*, 27 July 1910.

50. *Canal Record*, 5 August 1908.

51. See *Workman*, 19 July, 26 July, 2 August, 9 August 1919.

52. Core, *Maid in Panama*, 168.

53. *Canal Record*, 10 June 1911.

54. *Workman*, 29 January 1927.

55. It was reproduced in the *Daily Gleaner*, 2 February 1927.

56. George Eaton, "Trade Union Development in Jamaica", *Caribbean Quarterly* 8, nos. 1–2 (1962): 71.

57. Louis J. Parascandola, *"Winds Can Wake Up the Dead": An Eric Walrond Reader* (Detroit: Wayne State University Press, 1998), 280.

58. "The Forgotten People: A Report on the Condition of the British West Indians on the Isthmus of Panama". British Vice Consulate, Colón, Republic of Panama, March 1943, CO318, 447/71004 6497.

59. In 1919, professionals in Panama City formed the West Indian Committee with representatives from all the islands and the motto "One and inseparable, now and forever". Members included Dr F.E. Lowe, Dr D.O. Johnson and Dr A.G. Connell (a dentist). *Workman*, 17 May 1919.

60. *Workman*, 13 December 1924.

61. Core, *Maid in Panama*, 93–94.

62. Slightly different versions appear in "Chanties and Worksongs of Canal Zone Employees", Panama Collection, Canal Zone Library, and Core, *Maid in Panama*.

Chapter 9

1. Conniff, *Black Labor*, traces this path.
2. PC Annual Report, 1937.
3. *Canal Record*, 6 October 1915.
4. Albert Banister, "True Stories".
5. George Westerman quoted in Conniff, *Black Labor*, 72.
6. PC Annual Report, 1916.
7. PC Annual Report, 1933.
8. PCWIEA Annual Report, 1928.
9. Core, *Maid in Panama*, 28.
10. PC Annual Report, 1919.
11. *Workman*, 17 January 1920.
12. PC Annual Reports.
13. PCWIEA Annual Report, 1928.
14. ICC Annual Reports, 1917, 1920; *Canal Record*, 23 March 1911, 5 May 1915.
15. Conniff, *Black Labor*, 51.
16. Ibid.
17. Ibid. See Conniff, *Black Labor*, for a more detailed account.
18. For example, in "True Stories".
19. Saunders, interview.
20. Haynes, interview.
21. *New York Times*, quoted in Greene, *Canal Builders*, 381–82.
22. *Canal Record*, 18 June 1913.
23. *Canal Record*, 3 December 1913.
24. *Workman*, 18 October 1919.
25. PCWIEA Annual Report, 1942.
26. A wave of strikes throughout the "banana belt" of Central America at this time led to violent repression against the local populations. The Colombian writer Gabriel García Márquez, in his monumental novel *One Hundred Years of Solitude*, gives a fictionalized account of the effects of the *bananero* on the lives of the local population and of one such strike in 1928 and its repercussions.
27. PCWIEA Annual Report, 1942; *Workman*, 24 May 1919.
28. Following the strike of United Fruit Company workers, thirty-three arrested in Costa Rica were all West Indians and mainly Jamaicans. The ringleaders were not company employees but petty traders and also included, for example, one minister of religion, two barbers and a tailor. CO318/9603/1919.
29. PC Annual Report, 1920.
30. Ibid.
31. Ibid.
32. *Workman*, 24 April 1920.
33. Biesanz and Biesanz, *People of Panama*.
34. Ibid. In 1930 the West Indian birth rate in the Zone was eighteen per thousand, substantially below that of Panamanians.
35. Representing American union interests.
36. *Workman*, 24 July, 7 August 1920.

37. Translation of article published in *Workman*, 25 June 1921.
38. Quoted in *Workman*, 2 June 1921.
39. *Workman*, 25 March 1922, 15 April 1922.
40. PCWIEA, quoting census of Panama.
41. *Workman*, 9 October 1926.
42. Conniff, *Black Labor*, 66.
43. Quoted ibid., 139.
44. Ibid., 70.
45. PCWIEA Annual Report, 1927, 46–49.
46. PC Annual Report, 1923.
47. PC Annual Report, 1928.
48. PCWIEA Annual Report, 1930.
49. PCWIEA Annual Report, 1936.
50. Clarke, "Status of the West Indian Worker", 96–97.
51. PCWIEA Annual Report, 1930.
52. Biesanz and Biesanz, *People of Panama*, 342.
53. See Rupert Lewis, *Marcus Garvey: Anti-Colonial Champion* (London: Karia, 1987).
54. Mrs Clarice Arthurs, Colón, Panama, and Mrs E. Campbell, Bocas del Toro, Panama, interviews by the author, July 1976.
55. Clarke, "Status of the West Indian Worker", 93.
56. Campbell, interview by the author, Bocas del Toro, 1976,
57. *Workman*, 20 September 1919. PRO CO 318/350/37003/1919.
58. *Workman*, 20 December, 27 December 1919; 2 January 1920.
59. *Workman*, 4 September 1920.
60. *Workman*, 30 April, 7 May 1921.
61. *Workman*, 26 March 1922.
62. *Workman*, 10 December 1927.
63. Arthurs, interview by the author.
64. Campbell, interview by the author.

Chapter 10

1. Louise Bennett, "Amy Son", in *Jamaica Labrish* (Kingston: Sangster's, 1966), 204.
2. Richardson, *Panama Money*, 143.
3. Jorge L. Giovannetti, "Black British Caribbean Migrants in Cuba", in *Regional Footprints: The Travels and Travails of Early Caribbean Migrants,* ed. Annette Insanally, Mark Clifford and Sean Sheriff (Kingston: Latin American–Caribbean Centre, University of the West Indies, 2006), 103–4.
4. Roberts, *Population of Jamaica*, 133–41.
5. According to the collector of taxes, 5,665 visas were issued by the US consulate in Kingston in the fiscal year 1923–24 alone. Quoted in Ken Post, *"Arise Ye Starvelings": The Jamaican Labour Rebellion of 1938 and Its Aftermath* (The Hague: Martinus Nijhoff, 1978), 50n78.
6. Song by returnees from Cuba, transcribed by Lester Bernard and quoted in Marguerite R. Curtin, *The Story of Hanover* (Kingston: Marguerite Curtin, 2007), 158.

7. Calculated from the start of the Panama Railroad in 1850 to the Wall Street crash of 1929.

8. See, for example, Thomas-Hope, *Explanation in Caribbean Migration*; Olive Senior, *Working Miracles: Women's Lives in the English-speaking Caribbean* (Bloomington: Indiana University Press, 1991).

9. Paule Marshall, *Triangular Road: A Memoir* (New York: Basic Civitas Books, 2009), 66–67.

10. Herbert G. de Lisser, "The Six Brothers: When Enterprise Waits on Skill", *Planters Punch* (1925–26).

11. Kingston Industrial Garage has changed ownership a number of times but continues to operate the Ford dealership. Henriques family legend has it that the brothers sold so many cars in the first year of operation that Henry Ford himself cabled to ask, "Please advise if I should enlarge my operations to take care of your requirements."

12. Fenton's *Who's Who* entry (*Jamaica: Who's Who and Why 1934–5*, 27) notes that he had two pieces of furniture included in the British Empire Exhibition at Wembley in 1924–25. Both were sold and one piece was presented by its purchaser, Viscount Hersdale, to the Manchester Museum.

13. Lancelot Kavanagh is one of those who contributed to the "True Stories" competition. Information on both brothers supplied by their descendant Rosemary Kavanagh.

14. Quoted in Harmsen, Ellis and Devaux, *History of St Lucia*.

15. *Canal Record*, 4 September 1907.

16. *Canal Record*, 15 December 1909.

17. G. St J. Orde-Browne, *Labour Conditions in the British West Indies* (London: HMSO, 1939).

18. Roberts, "Emigration from Barbados", 282.

19. *Colón Starlet*, 5 July 1905.

20. *Colón Starlet*, 2 February 1905.

21. *Colón Starlet*, 5 June 1906.

22. Quoted in Post, *"Arise Ye Starvelings"*, 132.

23. For example, "The savings of these labourers are . . . to a considerable extent remitted or brought to Jamaica for investment in the Government Savings Bank or in purchase of land". Report on the Blue Book, 1884; *Report on Government Savings Bank*, 1908; *Daily Gleaner*, 16 February, 21 February 1905; 16 March 1905; entries in *Who's Who* and the *Red Book of the West Indies* for individual achievements.

24. See, for example Jean Besson, *Martha Brae's Two Histories* (Chapel Hill: University of North Carolina Press, 2002) on family land in Jamaica.

25. Richardson, *Panama Money*, 193.

26. *Daily Gleaner*, 16 February 1905.

27. Post, *"Arise Ye Starvelings"*, 39.

28. Trevor Burrowes and Angus McDonald, "Old West Indian Dwelling Houses in Panama", *Jamaica Journal* 10, no. 2 (1976).

29. Richardson, *Panama Money*, 193.

30. Ibid., 199.

31. I met several persons in Canada in 2012 who told me of recent searches in Panama

for grandfathers or fathers who had gone there and simply "disappeared" but whose descendants have never lost the desire to know what they did there or what had happened to them. Similarly, several elderly Jamaicans interviewed in Panama in the 1970s yearned to re-establish contact with relatives with whom they had not corresponded since leaving Jamaica in the early years of the twentieth century.

32. Harmsen, Ellis and Devaux, *History of St Lucia*.
33. Richardson, *Panama Money*.
34. Lowenthal, "Population of Barbados". Migration figures are approximations only as no accurate figures on the scope of the migration are available. In Jamaica, for instance, for the earlier years data on emigrants were kept only for the port of Kingston though many left from the outports. Children counted as half and no records were kept of the many small craft that plied between Jamaica and the Central American mainland and – later – Cuba. Although more accurate data were kept after 1910, travellers on small boats still continued to escape official notice. Demographers have arrived at the figures quoted here by extrapolating from other data.
35. Roberts, "Emigration from Barbados".
36. Report on the Blue Book, 1884, 305.
37. Roberts, *Population of Jamaica*.
38. Ibid.
39. Roberts, "Emigration from Barbados".
40. Lowenthal, "Population of Barbados", 455.
41. Roberts, *Population of Jamaica*.
42. Ibid.
43. Such sums (and names of deceased emigrants) were regularly published by the administrator general in the *Jamaica Gazette*.
44. See Senior, *Working Miracles*.
45. See, for example, Annual Reports, Jamaica, 1880–89; Olivier, *Jamaica*; *Report on the Condition of the Juvenile Population*, especially 16, 17.
46. See, for example, Senior, "All Clear", 57; Walrond, "Tropic Death".
47. Olivier, *Jamaica*.
48. An initiative to record life stories, through the African-Caribbean Institute of Jamaica, Kingston, where the tapes are stored.
49. Mrs W. Robertson, Jamaica Memory Bank Tape no. 678.
50. Cleveland Stanhope, Jamaica Memory Bank interview, transcript 6–7.
51. Richardson, *Panama Money*, 184.
52. Clifford Allen, Jamaica Memory Bank tape T790 transcript, 16–17.
53. Dudley Thompson, *From Kingston to Kenya: The Making of a Pan-Africanist Lawyer* (Dover, MA: Majority Press, 1993), 5
54. Ibid., 4, 6.
55. Stanhope, Jamaica Memory Bank.
56. The fact that some of this American influence also came directly to Jamaica through the tourist and banana trades should not be overlooked or that many emigrants travelled back and forth to the United States. The Spanish influence came not only from Panama but from sojourns in many other places in Latin America, especially Cuba.
57. Condé, *Tree of Life*, 26.

58. Ibid., 56.

59. Ibid., 57.

60. Ibid., 67.

61. Though the story, perhaps apocryphal, is that Lady Musgrave Road in Kingston was cut so that the snooty wife of the English Governor who occupied the official residence next door (King's House) would not have to go past Stiebel's house.

62. Richardson, *Panama Money*, 153.

63. See Senior "All Clear", and "Window" in *Discerner of Hearts and Other Stories* (Toronto: McClelland and Stewart, 1995); Frederick, *"Colón Man"*, looks at the figure of the Colón Man in Caribbean literature.

64. McKay, *My Green Hills*, 113–14.

65. Ibid., 132.

66. Ibid., 153.

67. McKay, *Banana Bottom*, 65–66.

68. *Report on the Condition of the Juvenile Population*, 96. No less striking to the beholder was the appearance still later in time of another, now more famous returning émigré: Alexander Bustamante, Jamaica's most flamboyant populist leader and first prime minister at independence, who claimed to have worked in Panama as well as in Cuba and New York. Alex Clarke (as he was then) had been a rather wild young man when he left home, but as his cousin and political rival, Norman Manley, recalled from a visit from him around 1923, he returned "such a dandy! Oh, dressed with the most immaculate care – with all the airs and graces of a Cuban grandee. His ties matched the handkerchief in his pocket and that matched his socks – his hair was pomaded and he was full of airs and graces – he was real la-d-da." Wayne Brown, ed., *Edna Manley: The Private Years 1900–1938* (London: André Deutsch, 1975), 128.

69. McKay, *Banana Bottom*, 67.

70. Ibid., 34–35.

71. Note that from the late 1920s, it was Marcus Garvey and his influence that was blamed for lack of "manners". James Carnegie, *Social Aspects of Jamaica's Politics 1918–1938* (Kingston: Institute of Jamaica, 1973), 138.

72. Pullen-Burry, *Ethiopia in Exile,* quoted in Post, *"Arise Ye Starvelings"*, 97.

73. Though an anecdote about Bustamante shows him turning these attitudes on their head when he was about to be arrested during the 1938 riots. Facing a squad of police with rifles drawn, Bustamante urged the mob behind him to sing "God Save the King", which they did, forcing the policemen to stand at attention while he and the mob melted away.

74. McKay, *Banana Bottom*, 147.

75. Ibid., 70.

76. Such contradictions probably reached their zenith in the real life "badman" James Joseph Gordon, twenty-two years old, of St Thomas, Jamaica, who terrorized Port Limón, Costa Rica, and outlying districts around 1907 before he was finally captured and killed by the police. At the height of his exploits, Gordon wrote to the *Daily Telegraph* newspaper to explain his side of the story. Referring to himself in the third person, Gordon wrote a long poem praising the exploits of "the great boy, James Gordon", in these terms:

I am a true born British boy, my island I will own

The flag I own I'll never sell, God bless red, white and blue

Her cloth can never tear, her colours never fade

The staff that bears the Union Jack will break the Spaniard's head

God bless the good old England, the home of mighty men

I am the true Joe Gordon, that all the Spaniards dread

But if a bird could whisper in this Joe Gordon's ear

A battleships arrived here to secure the noble boy

Oh, then I would bless old England and sing this joyful song

I will fight for my old England and die beneath her gun

But I say not for Spanish dogs, for I am a true red white and blue . . .

Quoted in *Workman*, 13 April 1907.

77. Report on the Blue Books, 1885–86, 34.
78. For example, Carnegie, *Social Aspects.*
79. Richardson, *Panama Money.*
80. For example, *Star and Herald*, 10 July 1905.
81. *Report of the West India Royal Commission, 1938* (Moyne Commission) (London: HMSO, 1945), 216.
82. Colin G. Clarke, *Kingston, Jamaica: Urban Development and Social Change, 1692–1962* (Berkeley: University of California Press, 1975), 54.
83. Olivier, *Jamaica*, 335.
84. Orde-Browne, *Labour Conditions*, 12.
85. For example, R.F. Williams, *R.F. Looks Back* (Jamaica: R.F. Williams, n.d., c. 1968).
86. Olivier, *Jamaica.*
87. Kingston Charity Organization Society, Annual Reports, 1933, 1939.
88. Brinsley Samaroo, "The Trinidad Workingman's Association and the Origins of Popular Protest in a Crown Colony", *Social and Economic Studies* 21, no. 2 (July 1972).
89. Richard Hart,"Labour Rebellions of the 1930s", in *Caribbean Freedom*, ed. Hilary Beckles and Verene Shepherd (Kingston: Ian Randle, 1996), 370–75.
90. Frank Hill, *Bustamante and His Letters* (Kingston: Kingston Publishers, 1976), 49–50.
91. Post, "*Arise Ye Starvelings*".
92. Hill, *Bustamante.*
93. The 1917 Socialist Revolution in Russia was to have a profound impact on people of African ancestry everywhere.
94. C.L. Joseph, "The British West Indies Regiment, 1914–1918", *Journal of Caribbean History* 2 (May 1971).
95. CO 318/350/37004.
96. "Views of a Negro during 'The Red Summer' of 1919", *Journal of Negro History* 51, no. 3 (July 1966).
97. Joseph,"The British West Indies Regiment".
98. Tony Martin, "Marcus Garvey, the Caribbean, and the Struggle for Black Jamaican Nationhood", in *Caribbean Freedom*, ed. Hilary Beckles and Verene Shepherd (Kingston: Ian Randle, 1996), 360.

99. In 1930 there were four hundred Chinese groceries in the Corporate Area (Kingston and suburbs). Clarke, *Kingston*, 45.

100. The "Syrians" were a small number of mainly Christian Arabs from Lebanon and Palestine who were in the dry-goods trade.

101. A small group of business people distinct from the majority of East Indians who were descendants of indentured workers and at the time were working mainly in agriculture and market gardening.

102. Carnegie, *Social Aspects of Jamaica's Politics*, 149.

103. Ibid., 151.

104. Ibid., 150.

105. For example, the role of Boukman Dutty in the Haitian Revolution and Myalists in uprisings of enslaved Africans in Jamaica.

106. Gordon, *Our Cause for His Glory*, 1–2.

107. See note on "Israelites" in Robert Hill, "Leonard P. Howell and Early Rastafari", *Jamaica Journal* 16, no. 1 (1983): 32.

108. Richardson, *Panama Money*, 221.

109. Ibid., 222.

110. Though with a perceptible deradicalization of the churches' message.

111. For the history see Diane J. Austin-Broos, *Jamaica Genesis: Religion and the Politics of Moral Orders* (Kingston: Ian Randle, 1997).

112. Hill, "Leonard P. Howell and Early Rastafari".

113. For Bedward's story see Brooks, *History of Bedwardism*; Veront M. Satchell, "Colonial Injustice: The Crown v. the Bedwardites, 27 April 1921", in *The African-Caribbean Worldview and the Making of Caribbean Society*, ed. Horace Levy (Kingston: University of the West Indies Press). Satchell notes that Bedward's movement, in its heyday from 1891 to 1921, had over thirty-three thousand adherents in mission stations and camps throughout Jamaica and overseas.

114. Hill, "Leonard P. Howell and Early Rastafari", 30.

115. Numerous studies of Rastafari have been published. For good overviews see Barry Chevannes, *Rastafari: Roots and Ideology* (Syracuse: Syracuse University Press, 1994) and Barry Chevannes, ed., *Rastafari and other African-Caribbean World Views* (London: Macmillan, 1995).

116. Post, *"Arise Ye Starvelings"*, 168–71. Abyssinia was another name for Ethiopia.

117. For a brief overview see W. Arthur Lewis, "The 1930s Social Revolution", in *Caribbean Freedom*, ed. Hilary Beckles and Verene Shepherd (Kingston: Ian Randle, 1996), 376–92.

118. Ibid., 376.

119. *Report of the Commission Appointed to Enquire into the Disturbances which Took Place in Barbados on the 27th July 1937 and Subsequent Days* (Bridgetown: Advocate, 1937).

120. Report of the West India Royal Commission, 1938 (Moyne Commission) HMSO, 1945.

121. Letter to *Plain Talk,* quoted in Post, *"Arise Ye Starvelings"*, 133.

122. Carnegie, *Social Aspects of Jamaica's Politics*.

123. Olivier, *Jamaica*.

124. Ken Post, "The Politics of Protest in Jamaica, 1938: Some Problems of Analysis and Conceptualisation", *Social and Economic Studies* 18, no. 4 (December 1969): 386.

125. George Eaton, *Alexander Bustamante and Modern Jamaica* (Kingston: Kingston Publishers, 1975).

SELECTED BIBLIOGRAPHY

Note that the material cited at the Canal Zone Library where my research took place was transferred to the United States following the signing of the 1977 treaty to transfer ownership of the canal to Panama. This material is now known as the Panama Collection of the Canal Zone Library-Museum, Library of Congress, Washington, DC.

Oral Sources

Canal Zone Library. Panama Collection. Frank Rose, "Reminiscences of Panama in the Days of the Canal Diggers". Typewritten ms., n.d.

———. "West Indian Folk Songs".

———. "Chanties and Worksongs of Canal Zone Employees".

Haynes, Cecil. Interviewed by Ifeoma Kiddoe Nwankwo. March 2007. Voices from Our America Digital Library.

Isthmian Historical Society. "Letters in a Competition for the Best True Stories of Life and Work on the Isthmus of Panama during Construction of the Canal". Typewritten manuscript. Balboa, Panama, 1963. (Cited in the text as "True Stories".)

———. Roosevelt Medal Holders Tape Recorder Guest Book. "The Word-for-Word Reminiscences of 35 Old Timers Who Helped to Build the Panama Canal". Recorded on tape, 17 November 1958, in connection with the Theodore Roosevelt centennial observances in the Canal Zone (transcripts). Canal Zone Library.

Jamaica Memory Bank interviews: Clifford Allen, tape no. T790; Mrs W. Robertson, tape no. 678; Cleveland Stanhope, transcript. African-Caribbean Institute of Jamaica.

Olive Senior interviews: David Crawford, Theophilus Saunders, Oscar Savage, Panama; Clarice Arthurs, Henry Barclay, Colón; G. Campbell, Enos Fleming, Namen Gosling, Bocas del Toro; Daniel Reckord, Samuel Whyte, Almirante. July 1976.

Official Documents

Jamaica Archives. Despatches. Governors of Jamaica to the Secretary of State for the Colonies, 1882–89, 1904–20, 1922–27.

———. Secretary of State for the Colonies to the Governors of Jamaica, 1880–1914.

Jamaica. Colonial Reports. Governors Reports on the Blue Books, including Departmental Reports, various titles. 1880–1938.

Jamaica Gazette, 1884–1885, 1904–30.

Report of the Commissioners of Inquiry upon the Condition of the Juvenile Population of Jamaica with the evidence taken and an appendix. Presented October 1879. Kingston: Government Printer, 1879.

Report of the Hon. Edward Wood, Under Secretary of State for the Colonies on His Visit to the West Indian Colonies. London: HMSO, 1922.

Report (with Appendices) of the Commission Appointed to Enquire into the Disturbances which Occurred in Jamaica between 23rd May and 8th June 1938. Kingston: Government Printer, 1938.

Report (with Appendices) of the Commission Appointed to Enquire into the Disturbances which Occurred on Frome Estates in Westmoreland on 2nd May 1938. Kingston: Government Printer, 1938.

Report of the Commission Appointed to Enquire into the Disturbances which Took Place in Barbados on the 27th July 1937 and Subsequent Days. Bridgetown: Advocate, 1937.

Report of the West India Royal Commission, 1938 (Moyne Commission). London: HMSO, 1945.

"The Forgotten People: A Report on the Condition of the British West Indians on the Isthmus of Panama". British Vice Consulate, Colón, Republic of Panama, March 1943. CO 318, 447/71004 6497.

Panama Canal. Isthmian Canal Commission. Annual Reports, 1889–1914.

Panama Canal. Annual Reports, 1915–40.

———. *Canal Record.* Ancón, CZ, September 1907–40.

———. *Official Handbook.* 1913.

———. Report of the Department of Health, 1904–18.

———. Report of Joseph L. Bristow, Special Panama Railroad Commissioner to the Secretary of War, 24 June 1905.

———. *Twenty-fifth Anniversary, 15 August 1939.* Balboa: Panama Canal Company.

———. *Fiftieth Anniversary: The Story of a Great Conquest.* Balboa: Panama Canal Company, 1964.

Panama Canal Archives. Canal Zone Records, 2-E-2 Jamaica.

Panama Canal West Indian Employees Association. Annual Reports (PCWIEA), 1927–45.

Newspapers and Periodicals

Panama Collection, Canal Zone Library. Newspaper clippings file 1904–9.

Star and Herald (published as *Panama Star* 2 March 1849–30 April 1854; *Panama Herald*, 1850–54; combined as the *Star and Herald* from 1854).

Colón Telegram.

Colón Starlet.

Independent (Colón).

Workman (Panama).

Daily Advertiser (Jamaica).

Daily Gleaner (Jamaica).

Falmouth Post and General Advertiser (Jamaica).

Planters Punch (Jamaica).

Spotlight (Jamaica).

Books and Journals

Abbot, Willis J. *Panama and the Canal in Picture and Prose.* London: Syndicate, 1913.

Adams, F.U. *Conquest of the Tropics: The Story of the Creative Enterprises Conducted by the United Fruit Company.* New York: Doubleday Page, 1914.

Anon. "Views of a Negro During 'The Red Summer' of 1919". *Journal of Negro History* 51, no. 3 (July 1966).

Armytage, Frances. *The Free Port System in the British West Indies.* London: Longman, 1953.

Augier, F.R., and S.C. Gordon. *Sources of West Indian History.* London: Longman, 1971.

Austin-Broos, Diane J. *Jamaica Genesis: Religion and the Politics of Moral Orders.* Kingston: Ian Randle, 1997.

Bacon, E.M., and E. Aaron. *The New Jamaica.* New York: Walbridge, 1890.

Beckles, Hilary, and Verene Shepherd, eds. *Caribbean Freedom: Economy and Society from Emancipation to the Present.* Kingston: Ian Randle, 1996.

Belize, Lynn-Rose, and Loïs Hayot. *Costumes Créoles: Modes et Vêtements Traditionnels des Antilles Françaises de 1635 à 1948.* Fort-de-France, Martinique: Editions Fabre Domergue, 1999.

Bennett, Ira E. *History of the Panama Canal: Its Construction and Builders.* Washington, DC: Historical Publishing Company, 1915.

Bennett, Louise. *Jamaica Labrish.* Kingston: Sangster's, 1966.

Besson, Jean. *Martha Brae's Two Histories.* Chapel Hill: University of North Carolina Press, 2002.

Bidwell, C.T. *The Isthmus of Panama.* London: Chapman and Hall, 1865.

Biesanz, John. "Cultural and Economic Factors in Panamanian Race Relations". *American Sociological Review* 14 (1949).

Biesanz, John, and Mavis Biesanz. *The People of Panama.* New York: Columbia University Press, 1955.

Bigelow, John. *The Panama Canal.* New York: Press of the Chamber of Commerce, 1886.

Bigelow, Poultney. "Why Labour Shuns Panama". *Colón Independent,* part II, 5 October 1906.

Bishop, Farnham. *Panama Past and Present.* New York: D. Appleton-Century, 1913.

Bishop, Joseph Bucklin, *The Panama Gateway.* New York: Charles Scribner's Sons, 1913.

Brathwaite, Edward (Kamau). *Rights of Passage.* Oxford: Oxford University Press, 1967.

Brereton, Bridget. "The Development of an Identity: The Black Middle Class of Trinidad in the Later Nineteenth Century". In *Caribbean Freedom,* edited by Hilary Beckles and Verene Shepherd, 274–83. Kingston: Ian Randle, 1996.

Brooks, A.A. *History of Bedwardism.* Kingston: Gleaner, 1917.

Brown, Wayne, ed. *Edna Manley: The Private Years 1900–1938.* London: André Deutsch, 1975.

Bryan, Patrick. "The Background to the Canal". In *Regional Footprints: The Travels and Travails of Early Caribbean Migrants,* edited by Annette Insanally, Mark Clifford and Sean Sheriff, 43–51. Kingston: Latin American–Caribbean Centre, University of the West Indies, 2006.

———. "The Black Middle Class in Nineteenth-Century Jamaica". In *Caribbean Freedom,* edited by Hilary Beckles and Verene Shepherd, 284–95. Kingston: Ian Randle, 1996.

Buckridge, Steeve O. *The Language of Dress: Resistance and Accommodation in Jamaica, 1760–1890.* Kingston: University of the West Indies Press, 2004.

Bullard, Arthur. *Panama: The Canal, the Country and the People.* Rev. ed. New York: Macmillan, 1914.

Bunau-Varilla, Philippe. *Panama: The Creation, Destruction, and Resurrection.* New York: McBride, Nast, 1914.

Burrowes, Trevor, and Angus McDonald. "Old West Indian Dwelling Houses in Panama". *Jamaica Journal* 10, no. 2 (1976).

Bushell, T.A. *"Royal Mail": A Centenary History of the Royal Mail Line, 1839–1939.* London: Trade and Travel Publications, 1939.

Cameron, Ian. *The Impossible Dream: The Building of the Panama Canal.* New York: William Murrow, 1972.

Carnegie, James. *Social Aspects of Jamaica's Politics, 1918–1938.* Kingston: Institute of Jamaica, 1973.

Castillero, Ernesto J. *La isla que se transformó en cuidad: Historia de un siglo de la ciudad de Colón.* Panama: Imprenta Nacional, 1962.

Chamberlain, Weston. *Twenty-five Years of American Medical Activity on the Isthmus of Panama, 1904–1929: A Triumph of Preventive Medicine.* Mount Hope, CZ: Panama Canal Press, 1929.

Chatfield, Mary A. *Light on Dark Places at Panama.* New York: Broadway, 1908.

Chevannes, Barry, ed. *Rastafari and other African-Caribbean World Views.* London: Macmillan, 1995.

———. *Rastafari: Roots and Ideology.* Syracuse: Syracuse University Press, 1994.

Clarke, Colin G. *Kingston Jamaica: Urban Development and Social Change, 1692–1962.* Berkeley: University of California Press, 1975.

Clarke, Simon A. "The Status of the West Indian Worker in the Panama Canal Zone". In *Regional Footprints: The Travels and Travails of Early Caribbean Migrants,* edited by Annette Insanally, Mark Clifford and Sean Sheriff, 92–99. Kingston: Latin American–Caribbean Centre, University of the West Indies, 2006.

Collins, O. *The Panama Guide.* Mount Hope, CZ: ICC Press, Quartermaster's Department, 1912.

Condé, Maryse. *Tree of Life.* New York: Ballantyne, 1992.

Conniff, Michael L. *Black Labor on a White Canal: Panama, 1904–1981.* Pittsburgh: University of Pittsburgh Press, 1985.

Core, Sue. *Maid in Panama.* New York: Clermont Press, 1938.

Cornish, Vaughan. *Travels of Ellen Cornish.* London, 1913.

Cramer, Louise. "Songs of West Indian Negroes in the Canal Zone". *California Folklore Quarterly* 5, no. 3 (July 1946).

Curtin, Marguerite R. *The Story of Hanover*. Kingston: Marguerite Curtin, 2007.

De Lisser, H.G. *Jamaicans in Colón and the Canal Zone, 1906*. Pamphlet. Reprint of a series of articles published in the *Daily Gleaner*. Kingston: Gleaner Company.

———. "The Six Brothers: When Enterprise Waits on Skill". *Planters Punch* (1925–26).

———. *Susan Proudleigh*. London: Methuen, 1915.

DuVal, Miles P. *And the Mountains Will Move*. 1947. Reprint, Westport, CT: Greenwood, 1975.

———. *Cadiz to Cathay: The Story of the Long Diplomatic Struggle for the Panama Canal*. 1940. Reprint, Westport, CT: Greenwood, 1968.

Eaton, George. *Alexander Bustamante and Modern Jamaica*. Kingston: Kingston Publishers, 1975.

———. "Trade Union Development in Jamaica". Parts 1 and 2. *Caribbean Quarterly* 8, no. 1 (March 1962); 8, no. 2 (June 1962).

Eisner, Gisella. *Jamaica 1830–1930*. Manchester: University of Manchester Press, 1961.

Espino, Ovidio Diaz. *How Wall Street Created a Nation: J.P. Morgan, Teddy Roosevelt, and the Panama Canal*. New York: Four Walls Eight Windows, 2001.

Exquemelin, Alexandre-Olivier. *The History of the Buccaneers of America*. 1698; reprinted, Boston, 1853.

Eyre, Alan. "Dusky Doctress: A Jamaican Perspective on Mary Grant-Seacole". *Jamaica Journal* 30, nos. 1–2 (2006).

Forbes-Lindsay, Charles Harcort. *Panama and the Canal Today*. Boston: L.C. Page, 1912.

Ford, Isaac. *Tropical America*. London: Edward Stanford, 1893.

Franck, Harry. *Zone Policeman 88*. New York: Century Company, 1913.

Frederick, Rhonda D. *"Colón Man a Come": Mythographies of Panama Canal Migration*. Lanham, MD: Lexington, 2005.

Froude, J.A. *The English in the West Indies*. 1887. Reprint, New York: Charles Scribner's Sons, 1906.

Galeano, Eduardo. *Open Veins of Latin America*. New York: Monthly Review Press, 1974.

Gilbert, James Stanley. *Panama Patchwork*. 3rd ed. Panama: Star and Herald, 1906.

Giovannetti, Jorge L. "Black British Caribbean Migrants in Cuba: Resistance, Opposition, and Strategic Identity in the Early Twentieth Century". In *Regional Footprints: The Travels and Travails of Early Caribbean Migrants,* edited by Annette Insanally, Mark Clifford and Sean Sheriff, 103–20. Kingston: Latin American–Caribbean Centre, University of the West Indies, 2006.

Goetz, Delia. *Education in Panama*. Bulletin no. 12. Washington, DC: Government Printing Office, 1948.

Gordon, Shirley C. *Our Cause for His Glory: Christianisation and Emancipation in Jamaica*. Kingston: University of the West Indies Press, 1998.

Gorgas, William Crawford. *Sanitation in Panama,* New York: D. Appleton, 1916.

Greene, Julie. *The Canal Builders: Making America's Empire at the Panama Canal*. New York: Penguin, 2009.

Groh, George W. *Gold Fever: Being a True Account . . . of the Art of Healing . . . during the California Gold Rush*. New York: William Morrow, 1963.

Hardeveld, Rose van. *Make the Dirt Fly!* Hollywood: Pan Press, 1956.

Harmsen, Jolien, Guy Ellis and Robert Devaux. *A History of St Lucia*. Vieux Fort, St Lucia: Lighthouse Road, 2012.

Hart, Richard. "Labour Rebellions of the 1930s". In *Caribbean Freedom*, edited by Hilary Beckles and Verene Shepherd, 370–75. Kingston: Ian Randle, 1996.

Haskin, Frederic J. *The Panama Canal*. Garden City, NJ: Doubleday Page, 1916.

Higman, Barry. "Jamaicans in the Australian Gold Rushes". *Jamaica Journal* 10, no. 2 (1976).

Hill, Errol. *The Jamaican Stage 1655–1900: Profile of a Colonial Theatre*. Amherst: University of Massachusetts Press, 1992.

Hill, Frank. *Bustamante and His Letters*. Kingston: Kingston Publishers, 1976.

Hill, Robert. "Leonard P. Howell and Early Rastafari". *Jamaica Journal* 16, no. 1 (1983).

Hoyte, Clyde. *The Life and Times of Willie Henry*. Kingston: Institute of Jamaica, 1975.

Hutchinson Miller, Carmen. "Afro-Jamaican Female Migrants in Port Limón, Costa Rica, 1872–1890". In *Regional Footprints: The Travels and Travails of Early Caribbean Migrants,* edited by Annette Insanally, Mark Clifford and Sean Sheriff, 266–91. Kingston: Latin American–Caribbean Centre, University of the West Indies, 2006.

Insanally, Annette, Mark Clifford and Sean Sheriff, eds. *Regional Footprints: The Travels and Travails of Early Caribbean Migrants*. Kingston: Latin American–Caribbean Centre, University of the West Indies, 2006.

Jacobs, H.P. *Sixty Years of Change, 1806–1866: Progress and Reaction in Jamaica and the Countryside*. Kingston: Institute of Jamaica, 1973.

Jamaica Provident and Benevolent Society Silver Jubilee programme, 1952.

James, Winifred. *The Mulberry Tree*. 2nd ed. London: Chapman and Hall, 1913.

———. *A Woman in the Wilderness*. London: Chapman and Hall, 1915.

James, Winston A. *Holding Aloft the Banner of Ethiopia: Caribbean Radicalism in Early Twentieth-Century America*. London: Verso, 1998.

Jekyll, Walter, ed. *Jamaican Song and Story*. New York: Dover, 1904.

Jos, Joseph. *Guadeloupéens et Martiniquais au Canal de Panamá: Histoire d'une émigration*. Paris: L'Harmattan, 2004.

Joseph, C.L. "The British West Indies Regiment 1914–1918". *Journal of Caribbean History* 2 (May 1971).

Josephs, Aleric J. "More Than a Nurse: Mary Seacole as Wife, 'Mother' and Businesswoman". *Jamaica Journal* 30, nos. 1–2 (2006).

Kimball, W.W. *Special Intelligence Report on the Progress of the Work on the Panama Canal during the Year 1885*. 49th Congress, House of Representatives, 1st session, misc. doc. no. 395. Washington, DC: Government Printing Office, 1886.

Knight, Franklin W. "Migration and the American Experience". In *Regional Footprints: The Travels and Travails of Early Caribbean Migrants,* edited by Annette Insanally, Mark Clifford and Sean Sheriff, 5–19. Kingston: Latin American–Caribbean Centre, University of the West Indies, 2006.

Latin American–Caribbean Centre. *West Indian Participation in the Construction of the Panama Canal*. Publication of the Proceedings of Symposium held at the University of the West Indies, Kingston, Jamaica, 15–17 June 2000.

Lamming, George. *In the Castle of My Skin*. London: Longman Caribbean, 1970.

Lee, William S. *The Strength to Move a Mountain*. New York: G.P. Putnam's Sons, 1958.

Lewis, Rupert, *Marcus Garvey: Anti-Colonial Champion*. London: Karia, 1987.

Lewis, W. Arthur. "The 1930s Social Revolution". In *Caribbean Freedom*, edited by Hilary Beckles and Verene Shepherd, 274–83. Kingston: Ian Randle, 1996.

Lindsay-Poland, John. *Emperors in the Jungle: The Hidden History of the U.S. in Panama*. Durham: Duke University Press, 2003.

Livingstone, W.P. *Black Jamaica*. London: Sampson, Low, Marston, 1900.

Look Lai, Walton. *The Chinese in the West Indies, 1806–1995*. Kingston: University of the West Indies Press, 1998.

Lowenthal, David. "The Population of Barbados". *Social and Economic Studies* 6, no. 4 (December 1957).

McCullough, David. *The Path between the Seas*. New York: Simon and Schuster, 1977.

McGuinness, Aims. *Path of Empire: Panama and the California Gold Rush*. Ithaca: Cornell University Press, 2008.

McKay, Claude. *Banana Bottom*. 1933. Reprint, New York: Harcourt Brace Jovanovich 1961.

———. *My Green Hills of Jamaica*. Kingston: Heinemann Caribbean, 1979.

Mack, Gerstle. *The Land Divided*. New York: Octagon Books, 1944.

Mallet, Matilde Obarrio (Lady). *Sketches of Spanish-colonial Life in Panama*. New York: Sturgis and Walton, 1915.

Marshall, Paule. *Triangular Road: A Memoir*. New York: Basic Civitas Books, 2009.

Marshall, Trevor, Peggy McGeary and Grace Thompson. *Folk Songs of Barbados*. Kingston: Ian Randle, 1996.

Martin, John Angus. *A–Z of Grenadian Heritage*. London: Macmillan, 2007.

Martin, Tony. "Marcus Garvey, the Caribbean, and the Struggle for Black Jamaican Nationhood". In *Caribbean Freedom*, edited by Hilary Beckles and Verene Shepherd, 359–69. Kingston: Ian Randle, 1996.

Methodist Church. *"For Ever Beginning": Two Hundred Years of Methodism in the Western Area*. Kingston: Literature Department of the Methodist Church, Jamaica District, 1960.

Mills, J.S. *The Panama Canal: A History and Description of the Enterprise*. London: Thomas Nelson and Sons, 1913.

Minter, John Easter. *The Chagres: River of Westward Passage*. New York: Rinehart, 1948.

Moore, Brian L., and Michele A. Johnson, ed. *Neither Led nor Driven: Contesting British Cultural Imperialism in Jamaica, 1865–1920*. Kingston: University of the West Indies Press, 2004.

Nelson, Wolfred. *Five Years at Panama: The Trans-Isthmian Canal*. New York: Belford, 1889.

Newton, Velma. *The Silver Men: West Indian Labour Migration to Panama, 1850–1914*. Kingston: Institute of Social and Economic Research, University of the West Indies, 1984.

Olivier, Lord. *Jamaica, the Blessed Island*. London: Faber and Faber, 1936.

Orde-Browne, G. St J. *Labour Conditions in the British West Indies*. London: HMSO, 1939.

O'Reggio, Trevor. *Between Alienation and Citizenship: The Evolution of Black West Indian*

Society in Panama, 1914–1964. Washington, DC: University Press of America, 2006.

Otis, F.N. *Illustrated History of the Panama Railroad.* 2nd ed. New York: Harper and Bros., 1862.

Palmer, Paula. *"What Happen?" A Folk History of Costa Rica's Talamanca Coast.* San Jose, Costa Rica: Ecodesarrollos, 1979.

Parascandola, Louis J. *"Winds Can Wake Up the Dead": An Eric Walrond Reader.* Detroit: Wayne State University Press, 1998.

Parker, Elizabeth Kittredge. *Panama Canal Bride: A Story of Construction Days.* New York: Exposition, 1955.

Parker, Matthew. *Panama Fever: The Building of the Panama Canal.* New York: Doubleday, 2007.

Parkin, Andrew. *Flames of Panama: The True Story of a Forgotten Hero, Pedro Prestan.* London: Matador, 2006.

Payne-Jackson, Arvilla, and Mervyn C. Alleyne. *Jamaican Folk Medicine: A Source of Healing.* Kingston: University of the West Indies Press, 2004.

Pennell, Joseph. *Pictures of the Panama Canal.* Philadelphia: J.B. Lippincott, 1912.

Pepperman, W. Leon. *Who Built the Panama Canal?* New York: E.P. Dutton, 1915.

Pim, Commander Bedford. *Gates of the Pacific.* London: Lovel Reeve, 1863.

Porter, T.P. *The Railroad Handbook and Guide to the Isthmus, 1888–89.* London: Travel and Trade Publications.

Post, Ken. *"Arise Ye Starvelings": The Jamaican Labour Rebellion of 1938 and Its Aftermath.* The Hague: Martinus Nijhoff, 1978.

———. "The Politics of Protest in Jamaica, 1938: Some Problems of Analysis and Conceptualisation". *Social and Economic Studies* 18, no. 4 (December 1969).

Prebble, John. *The Darien Disaster.* London: Secker and Warburg, 1968.

Proudfoot, M. *Population Movements in the Caribbean.* Port of Spain: Caribbean Commission, 1950.

Putnam, Laura. *The Company They Kept: Migrants and the Politics of Gender in Caribbean Costa Rica, 1870–1960.* Chapel Hill: University of North Carolina Press, 2002.

Ranston, Jackie. *Behind the Scenes at King's House, 1873–2010.* Kingston: Jamaica National Building Society, 2011.

Rappaport, Helen. "The Lost Portrait". *Jamaica Journal* 30, nos. 1–2 (2006).

Reid, Carlos. *Memorias de un Criollo Bocatoreño.* Monografías antropólogicas, no. 1. Panama: Asociación Panameña de antropología, 1980.

Richardson, Bonham C. *Panama Money in Barbados, 1900–1920.* Knoxville: University of Tennessee Press, 1985.

Roberts, G.W. "Emigration from the Island of Barbados". *Social and Economic Studies* 4, no. 3 (September 1955).

———. *The Population of Jamaica.* Cambridge: Cambridge University Press, 1957.

Roberts, Sydney. "Silver and Gold". *Spotlight News Magazine* (Jamaica), March 1946.

Robinson, Jane. *Mary Seacole: The Most Famous Black Woman of the Victorian Age.* New York: Carroll and Graff, 2004.

Robinson, St John. "East Indians from Jamaica to Belize". In *Regional Footprints: The Travels and Travails of Early Caribbean Migrants,* edited by Annette Insanally, Mark Clifford and Sean Sheriff, 431–51. Kingston: Latin American–Caribbean Centre, University of the West Indies, 2006.

Robinson, Tracy. *Panama: A Personal Record of Forty-six Years, 1861–1907*. New York and Panama: Star and Herald, 1907.

Rogers, Charles C. *Intelligence Report of the Panama Canal*. Washington: Government Printing Office, 1889.

Ruddock, Lennie. *With the Sound of the Steam Korchie*. Kingston: Arawak, 2002.

Samaroo, Brinsley. "The Trinidad Workingman's Association and the Origins of Popular Protest in a Crown Colony". *Social and Economic Studies* 21, no. 2 (July 1972).

Satchell, Veront M., "Colonial Injustice: The Crown v. the Bedwardites, 27 April 1921". *The African-Caribbean Worldview and the Making of Caribbean Society*, edited by Horace Levy, 46–67. Kingston: University of the West Indies Press, 2009.

Schott, Joseph L. *Rails across Panama: The Story of the Building of the Panama Railroad, 1849–1855*. Indianapolis: Bobbs-Merrill, 1967.

Scott, Michael. *Tom Cringle's Log*. London, 1834.

Seacole, Mary. *Wonderful Adventures of Mrs. Seacole in Many Lands*. London: James Blackwood, 1857. Reprint, edited and with an introduction by Ziggi Alexander and Audrey Dewjee. Bristol: Falling Wall, 1984.

Senior, Olive. "All Clear". *Gardening in the Tropics*. Toronto: Insomniac Press, 2005.

———. "The Chinese Who Came from Panama". *Jamaica Journal* 44 (1980).

———. "The Colón People'. *Jamaica Journal* part 1, 11, no. 3 (1977) and part 2, 42 (1978).

———. "The Origins of 'Colón Man': Jamaican Emigration to Panama in the Nineteenth Century". In *Regional Footprints: The Travels and Travails of Early Caribbean Migrants*, edited by Annette Insanally, Mark Clifford and Sean Sheriff, 52–67. Kingston: Latin American–Caribbean Centre, University of the West Indies, 2006.

———. "The Panama Railway". *Jamaica Journal* 44 (1980).

———. "Window". *Discerner of Hearts and Other Stories*. Toronto: McClelland and Stewart, 1995.

———. *Working Miracles: Women's Lives in the English-speaking Caribbean*. Bloomington: Indiana University Press, 1991.

Sewell, W. *Ordeal of Free Labor in the British West Indies*. New York: Harper and Brothers, 1861.

Shepherd, Verene A. "Roots of Routes: Intra-Caribbean Trade Links since the Fifteenth Century". In *Regional Footprints: The Travels and Travails of Early Caribbean Migrants*, edited by Annette Insanally, Mark Clifford and Sean Sheriff, 20–39. Kingston: Latin American–Caribbean Centre, University of the West Indies, 2006.

Sibert, W.L., and J.F. Stevens. *The Construction of the Panama Canal*. New York: Appleton, 1915.

Simon, Maron J. *The Panama Affair*. New York: Charles Scribner's Sons, 1971.

Skinner, James M. *France and Panama: The Unknown Years, 1894–1908*. New York: Peter Lang, 1989.

Slosson, Edwin, and Gardner Richardson. "Life on the Canal Zone". *Independent*, 22 March 1906.

————. "Two Panama Life Stories". *Independent,* 19 April 1906.

Steward, Julian H., ed. *Handbook of South American Indians.* Bulletin 143, Bureau of American Ethnology, vol. 4. Washington, DC: Smithsonian Institution, 1948.

Sued-Badillo, Jalil. *UNESCO General History of the Caribbean.* Vol. 1, *Autochthonous Societies.* London and Paris: Macmillan and UNESCO, 2003.

Sullivan, Mark. *Our Times, 1900–1925.* Vol. 2, *America Finding Herself.* New York: Charles Scribner's Sons, 1936.

Thomas-Hope, Elizabeth. *Explanation in Caribbean Migration: Perception and the Image: Jamaica, Barbados, St Vincent.* London: Macmillan, 1992.

Thompson, Dudley. *From Kingston to Kenya: The Making of a Pan-Africanist Lawyer.* Dover, MA: Majority Press, 1993.

Tomes, Robert. *Panama in 1855.* New York: Harper Brothers, 1855.

Walrond, Eric. *Tropic Death.* 1926. Reprint, New York: Collier Books, 1972.

Watlington, Francisco. "The Physical Environment: Biogeographical Teleconnections in Caribbean Prehistory". In *UNESCO General History of the Caribbean.* Vol. 1, *Autochthonous Societies,* edited by Jalil Sued-Badillo, 30–92. London and Paris: Macmillan and UNESCO, 2003.

Weir, Hugh C. *The Conquest of the Isthmus.* New York: G.P. Putnam's, 1909.

Westerman, George. "Canal Zone Discrimination". *Crisis* 58, no. 4 (April 1951).

————. "Gold Men and Silver Men". *Crisis,* 54, no. 12 (December 1947).

————. "Historical Notes on West Indians in the Isthmus of Panama". *Phylon* 22 (Winter 1961).

————. "A Minority Group in Panama". 3rd ed. Liga Civica Nacional, 1950.

————. *Pioneers in Canal Zone Education.* (Published by students of La Boca and Silver City Occupational High School in observance of 1949 Negro History Week.) La Boca: Occupational High School Shop, 1949.

————. "School Segregation on the Panama Canal Zone". *Phylon,* n.d. c.1953.

————. "Towards a Better Understanding" (pamphlet), 2nd ed. July 1946.

Wilkins, Nadine. "The Medical Profession in Jamaica in the Post-Emancipation Period". *Jamaica Journal* 21, no. 4 (1989).

Williams, R.F. *R.F. Looks Back.* Jamaica: R.F. Williams, n.d., c.1968.

Wood, R.E. "The Working Force of the Panama Canal". *Transactions of the International Engineering Congress, 1915: The Panama Canal,* vol. 1. San Francisco, 1916.

Wynter, Sylvia ."Bernardo de Balbuena, Epic Poet and Abbot of Jamaica, 1562–1627". *Jamaica Journal* 3, no. 3 (1969); 3, no. 4 (1969); 4, no. 1 (1970); 4, no. 3 (1970).

Young, Edgar. "A Few Will Remember". *Excavating Engineer.* August 1921. http://www .czbrats.com/Builders/afew.htm.

INDEX

Note: Locations of notes are in the format 354n17, indicating note 17 on page 354. Page numbers in **bold** type refer to photograph captions.

Barclay, L. Horatio, 258
Barton, C.J., 258
Barton, J.T., 258
baseball, 274
Bas Obispo, 154, 252, 254; explosion at, 164, 219, 220–21
Beckford, Reginald, 13, 163–64, 198–99, 220–21, 238
Bedward, Alexander, 348–49
benevolent societies, 277–78, 308
Benjamin, P.A., 156
Bennett, Louise, 317
Bible, 279
Bidlack, Benjamin A., 22
Bidlack-Mallarino treaty (1846), 22, 84
Bigelow, John, 93
"Bishop Jack", 347
The Black Man (newspaper), 345
blacks: stereotyping of, 175, 177, 178–79, 338; whites *vs*, 104, 175. *See also* African Americans; West Indians
Black Star Line, 312–13, 314
Blake, Henry, 95, 96
Blanchet, Gaston, 74, 75
blasting, 159, 203, 218, 219–22, 223, 243
boatmen, 54–56, 206. *See also bungo boats*
La Boca, 95, 108, 301
Bocas del Toro, 17, 281, 283
Bolívar, Simón, 14, 22
Booth, Charles, 4
Boyer, Léon, 93
Isaac Brandon and Company, 64
Brathwaite, Viola, 241
Brewster, Joseph, 197
Britain: Colonial Office, 339–40, 347, 348, 350; and Panama, 22–23, 86, 285, 286; in Panama, 17; racial violence in, 344; War Office, 342
British and Foreign Bible Society, 279
British West Indies Regiment, 292, 300, 343–44. *See also* First World War
Brooke, Mark, 106
brothels, 64, 238
Bruckins Parties, 28
Bryan, Patrick, 240

bubonic plague, 140
Buchanan, Hugh, 350
Bullard, Albert, 214, 217–18, 222
Bunau-Varilla, Philippe, 22, 86, 92, 93, 118
bungo boats, 15, 26, 54–55, 206
Burke, Cespedes, 174
Burnett, Henry, 122, 123
"bush living", 229–34, 262, 263–66
Bustamante, Alexander, 338, 350, 351, 389n68
Butcher, John Oswald, 191, 234
Butler, Uriah, 351

Calabar College (Kingston), 65, 258
California, 23
California gold rush, 21, 25–28, 60; and Panama, 37–38, 44, 46
California (steamer), 25, 26–27
Canal Zone, 105–10; cost of living, 236–37; demographics, 245, 246, 247–48, 256, 309; education in, 256–58, 310; evictions from, 266, 296, 301, 302, 303; farming in, 263–66, 295; native Panamanians in, 228, 229; public health measures, 144, 147–52; racial tensions, 104, 284; segregation, 106–10, 134, 181, 228–29, 310; services available, 190, 191; social control efforts, 172, 238, 246, 249–52, 271–73; towns, 5–6, 107, 228, 229, 266, 271–72; women in, 238–45. *See also* Isthmian Canal Commission
cannabis, 362n10
Caribbean League, 344
Carib (Kalinago) people, 13
Carmichael, Leslie, 151
Carnegie, James, 345–46, 351
"Carta de Jamaica" (Bolívar), 14
Central America, 39; banana industry, 292, 300; Britain and, 17, 22; Garvey in, 312, 313–14, 345; Jamaica and, 17–18; West Indians in, 8, 9, 17, 63, 111, 263–64. *See also specific countries*
Chagres fever. *See* malaria
Chagres (port), 15–16, 26, 48, 50–51, 54, 56. *See also* Yankee Chagres

Chagres River, 2, 28, 202–3, 204; boats on, 15, 26, 54–55, 206; and construction projects, 38, 92
chanteys. *See* worksongs
Charles V, King of Spain, 10
Chauncey, Henry L., 25
children, 254–60; American, 255–56; deaths of, 262, 330; Panama- born, 331–33; as returnees, 331, 332; as workers, 91–92, 254–55. *See also* education
Chinese: antipathy towards, 33–34, 180, 304, 306, 345; as canal workers, 75, 124, 180, 368n47; deaths among, 30, 31, 33, 34, 180, 233; emigration from China, 31, 33; as food providers, 77, 141, 229, 234, 265; as gold seekers, 357n26, 357n31; in Jamaica, 34–35, 345; as Panamanians, 35, 180, 241, 265, 306; as railroad workers, 30, 31, 32–35. *See also* indentured workers
cholera, 42–43, 45–46
churches, 284, 298; and education, 258, 280, 281, 283; "native", 346; nonconformist, 279, 283; rebellion against, 346–47; segregation in, 108, 110, 282–83; social support roles, 279–80, 283, 284. *See also* religion; *specific churches*
Church of England, 282–83, 346
Cipriani, Arthur, 351
Clarke, Aaron, 154, 165
Clarke, Amos, 139, 220
Clarke, Frederick Alanzo, 311
Clarke, Simon, 253, 310
Clarke, Wesley, 4
Clayton-Bulwer treaty (1850), 22
clothing: of returnees, 68, 237, 336; for special occasions, 267–69; of women travellers, 360n78; for work, 154, 190, 236, 237
cohabitation, 110, 246, 249–50
Collins, John, 292
Colombia, 22; and Panama Railroad, 24, 29, 35; police force, 57, 85–86, 90; political turmoil, 58, 82–84, 99–100
Colón, 30, 67; amenities, 282–83; fires,

83, 84, 93, 296; French canal project and, 76, 79–81, 95–97; housing, 79, 260, 296; in ICC era, 143–44, 210, 296; as unhealthy, 48–49, 79, 147, 150, 296; UNIA in, 311, 313, 314–15; West Indians in, 64–65, 260–61, 262, 293, 306; workers in, 261, 302
Colón Coloured Comedy Company, 277
Colón Jockey Club, 110
"Colón Man" (Jamaica stereotype), 8, 63–64, 65–66, 333–40; impact, 68, 69, 317–18; in literature, 334–35; as scapegoat, 339, 346; as subversive, 334–35, 337–38. *See also* "Panama Man"; returnees
"Colón Man" (song), 63–64
Colón Negro Glee Club, 277
Coloured Cripples Association, 159
Columbus, Christopher, 30
commissaries, 52, 141, 234, 235–38, 334
Commission on the Condition of the Juvenile Population in Jamaica (1870s), 42, 70
Compagnie Nouvelle du Canal de Panama, 72–73, 99, 105–6, 139–40, 213
Compagnie Universelle du Canal Interocéanique, 71–74, 76; investment in, 71–72, 77, 94; problems encountered, 84, 92–95; recruitment practices, 86–87
Condé, Maryse, 241, 334–35
Connell, A.G., 384n59
Conniff, Michael, 153, 176, 178, 256, 296–97
Coombs, G.S., 350
Core, Sue, 242–43, 294–95
Cornwallis, Couba, 358n51
Costa Rica, 178, 300; West Indians in, 17, 63, 240, 253, 263–64
Couloote, Mary, 5, 134
Couvreaux and Hersent, 74, 77
Cox, S.A.G., 276
Cramer, Louise, 241
craneys, 216
Crawford, David, 143
cricket, 273

gold seekers, 37–38, 44, 46, 50, 54–55, 58, 206

gold workers: facilities for, 151, 246, 270; hardships encountered, 140–41; hierarchy, 107–8, 186; living conditions, 228, 296; as oligarchy, 296–97; performance, 179–80; preferential treatment, 8, 106–8, 109, 176, 186. *See also* Americans

Gomes, Albert, 351

Gordon, James Joseph, 389n76

Gordon, Shirley C., 346

Gorgas, William Crawford, 145–46, 147–48, 153, 155

Gorgona, 49, 51, 78

Government Savings Bank (Jamaica), 98–99, 324

Grant, St William, 350–51

Grant, Ulysses S., 46

Great Depression (1930s), 293, 318, 341

Green, Prince George, 6–7

Greene, Julie, 170

Grenada, 127, 278, 351

Groh, George W., 45

Guadeloupe, 127–28, 250–53

Guaymí (Valiente) people, 281

guns, 53, 89, 100, 339

Haile Selassie I, 349

Harrison, Francis Burton, 179

Harry family, 244, **325**

Hay–Bunau-Varilla Treaty (1903), 366n10

Haynes, Cecil, 254–55, 259–60, 268, 297, 376n2

Hay-Pauncefote treaty (1901), 23

Headley, George, 274

Hector-Connor, Franklin, 311

Henriques, A.N., 59

Henriques family, 320–21

Hewitt, Solomon, 348

Hibbert, Joseph, 349

higglers, 43, 52–53, 59, 252, 354n23. *See also* traders

Hill, Errol, 27–28

Hill, Frank, 342

Hilton, Isoline, **326**

Hodges, George, 221

Hoffman, Gertrude B., 219

holidays, 64–65, 67–68, 277; pay for, 176, 186

Honduras, 23, 263–64, 292, 339. *See also* Central America

Hopkins, Reed E., 219

horseracing, 273

hospitals, 161; in French canal era, 76, 80, 81; in ICC era, 147–48, 160–61; segregation in, 108, 110, 163

hotels, 50–51, 52

housing, 295–96; for families, 228, 229, 232, 246–49, 295; during French canal era, 79, 81; prefabricated, 50, 74; of returnees, 324–25, 327; shanty towns, 229–30, 265. *See also* "bush living"

Howell, Edward, 189, 254

Howell, Leonard, 349

Huertas, Esteban, 324

Humphrey, Sarah, 241

Hunt, Clifford, 7, 154

hurricanes, 113–14, 115–16

Hutchins and Company, 40

Hutin, Maurice, 92

ICC. *See* Isthmian Canal Commission

immigration. *See* emigration

Imperial Order of Good Samaritans and Daughters of Samaria, 277

indentured workers, 35, 132, 180, 361n3, 368n47

Independent Order of Odd Fellows, 277

Indians (East), 180, 361n2, 368n47

inflation, 81, 341–42

influenza, 154, 302

insanity, 160

insecticides, 148–49, 152–53

insects, 35, 37, 158. *See also* mosquitoes

Intercolonial Club, 276

intermarriage, 287

International Social and Literary Association, 276

In the Castle of My Skin (Lamming), 103, 272, 336

Irish, 33, 34, 35

Isthmian Canal Commission (ICC):

administration, 137, 138–39, 144, 147; and churches, 283–84; commissaries, 141, 234, 235–38, 334; facilities provided, 238, 270, 276, 283–84; foremen/superintendents, 166; meals provided, 23–24; pay system, 106–7, 141, 186–87, 262–63; racist attitudes, 309–10; recruitment methods, 118–24, 176, 180–83; and squatters, 265–66; treatment of workers, 128, 227. *See also* Canal Zone; Panama Canal project

Isthmian Dramatic Association, 277

Isthmian League of British West Indians, 299

Isthmus Guard, 58

Jamaica, 41–42; banana industry, 112, 113, 120, 340, 341; businessmen, 50–51, 320–23; and Central America, 17–18; as colony, 14–15, 119, 340; crime in, 53, 90–91, 97, 132, 339; demographics, 42, 68–70, 112, 116, 329, 340, 340–42; economy, 112–13, 116, 341–42; emigration from, 42, 63, 68–69, 93, 111, 112, 318, 328, 329; exports from, 65, 98, 324; farmers, 112–13, 325, 338, 341; former slaves, 39, 42, 43; housing, 324–25; middle class, 117, 124, 340; natural disasters, 113–16, 278–79; and Panama, 14–15, 65, 98; Portland parish, 116; privateers, 16–17; religion in, 347; rural population, 70, 112; St Ann parish, 116; St Elizabeth parish, 116; St Mary parish, 113–14, 116; St Thomas parish, 68; social and economic problems, 39, 40, 42, 68–69, 112–17, 329–30; unemployment, 40, 42, 69–70, 113, 116–17, 341; women, 69–70, 329, 341; xenophobia in, 345; young people, 42, 69–70, 91–92. *See also* Jamaica, Government of; Jamaicans; Kingston; returnees; West Indies

Jamaica, Government of: and canal worker recruitment, 93, 95–97, 119–24; and emigration, 119–20; and ICC,

119–24. *See also* Britain: Colonial Office

Jamaica Agricultural Society, 351

Jamaica Labour Party (est. 1937), 351

Jamaican Missionary Society, 283

Jamaicans: attachment to home, 65, 164–65, 278–79; *vs* Barbadians, 284; as carpenters, 39–40, 142, 322; *vs* Colombians, 53, 57, 78, 85–86, 88; as criminals, 57–58, 89, 90–91; diseases among, 47; as dissolute, 88–89; during French canal era, 63, 75; Jewish, 59, 64–65, 320–21; middle-class, 64, 124; occupations, 59, 64–65, 124; as Panamanians, 63, 143, 293–94, 307; in railroad era, 35, 39–43, 59–60; repatriation of, 84, 90, 95–97, 120, 318–19; violence among, 57–58, 88–89. *See also* silver workers; West Indians; *specific individuals*

Jamaica Permanent Development Convention, 351

Jamaica Protective League, 351

Jamaica Provident and Benevolent Society, 278

Jamaica Railway, 39

Jamaica Teachers Association, 351

James, Winifred, 133, 214, 249, 253, 269, 272

James, Winston, 112–13

Japanese, 180

Johnson, D.O., 384n59

Johnson, Theodore T., 54

Jos, Joseph, 128

Joseph, Edmee and Hortense, 134

Josephs, William, 272

justice system (Canal Zone), 58, 169, 172, 173–74; as unequal, 89–90, 303–4; and West Indians, 167–68, 172, 173–74, 298. *See also* police

Kalinago (Carib) people, 13

Karner, William J., 125, 132

Kavanagh, Austin, 157, 322

Kavanagh, Lancelot, 209, 322

Keith, Minor C., 63

Kimball, William, 93

144–47, 150, 151–53; eradication, 148–49, 150, 151–53

"Mother Abel" (missionary), 283

mules (animals), 15, 51, 58, 98, 175, 192

Murray, Andrew C., 65

Murray, Henry G., 65

music and dance, 277. *See also* songs

My Green Hills of Jamaica (McKay), 336

National Club of Kingston, 276

National Reform Association, 351

Native Defenders Committee (Jamaica), 345

Negro World, 298, 313, 345

Nelson, Wolfred, 77, 90, 157

New Granada. *See* Colombia

"New Negro", 298, 344

newspapers, 240, 303–4; in Jamaica, 345; Jamaican news in, 65, 278. *See also specific papers*

New York State, 23, 25

Nicaragua, 17, 22

Norman, Henry, 86

Nuñez, Rafael, 82

obeah, 156, 280, 284

Ocean Steam Navigation Company, 23

O'Connell, Thomas H., 122

Olano, Núflo de, 14

Olivier, Sydney, 341, 351

opium, 33, 34

Orde-Brown, St John, 341

Osborne, Alfred, 257–58

Osborne, David, 257–58

Otis, F.N., 28

Pacific Mail Steamship Company, 23, 26–27, 84

"The Palm Porch" (Walrond), 241

Pan African Club of London, 276

Panama: climate, 28–29, 35, 37, 44–45, 201–2; corruption in, 57, 89–90; cost of living, 81; crime in, 47, 57–58; demographics, 30–31, 79; entrepreneurs, 43, 50–51, 59; foreigners in, 14–18, 59; in French canal era, 79–81; geography, 10–13, 28, 35–36, 37; language issues, 104, 135, 174, 190, 259, 305–6, 310; law and order, 57, 89–90; native population, 38, 55, 281; natural disasters, 77, 92, 93; as part of New Granada (Colombia), 22, 30, 58; political tensions, 47; racial tensions, 47, 53–54, 56, 109–10, 171, 181, 293–94; transportation in, 21–22, 26, 51; transportation to, 40, 66, 67; wages in, 40, 99; in West Indian imagination, 8, 9, 103–4, 111, 118, 127; West Indians in, 8, 9, 264, 291, 302–3 (*see also* West Indians); West Indian women in, 238–45; and West Indies, 13–15; wildlife, 35, 37, 138, 157–58. *See also* Panama, Republic of; *specific towns*

Panama, Republic of, 276; Americanization of, 305, 347; Britain and, 285; citizenship laws, 306–7; demographics, 256, 261–62; independence declaration, 72, 100; nationalism, 259, 302, 306–7; public health, 148–49; restrictive laws, 271, 306–7; UNIA in, 311–15; United States and, 105, 148; West Indians in, 260–62

Panama Canal, 100; completion, 1–4, 225, 272; construction, 139–40, 199, 210–11; equipment used, 214–17, 222–23; land clearing, 203; locks, 199, 203–4, 207–10, 307; night crews, 222–23; opening, 1, 4, 272; planning, 73, 199–201; and tourism, 213. *See also* Canal Zone; French Canal project; Isthmian Canal Commission

Panama Canal West Indian Employees Association (PCWIEA), 308–9, 310

Panama City, 17, 74, 150; amenities, 74, 259, 283; destitute workers in, 96–97, 302; in railroad era, 48, 51; revolt (1885), 82–84; West Indians in, 262, 306

Panama Cricket Club, 273–74

Panama fever. *See* yellow fever; malaria

"Panama Gold" (Walrond), 237

"Panama Man" (Barbados stereotype), 8,

unions, 186, 286, 296, 297, 352, 353; American involvement, 300–301. *See also specific organizations*

United Brotherhood of Maintenance of Way Employees and Railroad Shop Laborers, 300–301

United Fruit Company, 120, 292, 300, 306

United States: blacks in, 8–9, 298, 344; California gold rush, 25–28, 37–38, 44, 46, 60; cholera in, 45; education policies, 310; and ICC recruitment, 119–24, 174; immigration laws, 180, 318; labour laws, 176; migration to, 8–9, 111, 320; and Panama, 22–23, 46, 83, 84; racism, 178, 179, 296–97, 307, 344; segregation, 178, 179; UNIA in, 344; xenophobia, 180. *See also* Americans; Canal Zone; Isthmian Canal Commission; Panama Canal

United States Mail Steamship Company, 23, 25, 26

Universal Negro Improvement Association (UNIA), 286, 298, 311–15, 344–45

Valiente (Guaymí) people, 281
Vampire (ship), 35
van Hardeveld, Jan, 137–38
van Hardeveld, Rose, 137–38, 141, 142, 201–2
venereal disease, 261
Vernon, Edward, 17
vigilantes, 58
violence: among Jamaicans, 57–58, 87–89; gun ownership and, 53, 89, 100, 339; importation to Jamaica, 87, 338–39, 346; in Panama, 53–58, 64, 78, 87–92, 339. *See also* crime

Waisome, Jeremiah, 100, 104, 194, 254
Waison, Leonard, 345
wakes, 89, 165. *See also* funerals
Walker, John G., 145
Walker, L.M., 308–9
Wallace, John F., 120, 145
Walrond, Eric, 118, 156, 169, 237, 241, 250, 280–81, 286

Walrond, H.N., 298–99, 383n34
War of a Thousand Days (1888–1902), 72, 99–100
War of Jenkins' Ear, 359n64
washerwomen, 65, **206**, **239**, 240, 252
water: aerated (soda), 275, 322; drinking, 52, 148, 150, 151
water boys, 254
"Watermelon War" (1856), 53
Webb, Arthur, 85
Webster, Hannah, 258
Webster, James C., 258
weddings, 267
Wesleyan-Methodist Church, 283
Westerman, George, 257, 258, 278, 280
West Indian Committee, 384n59
West Indian Protective League, 276
West Indians: as aliens, 302–7; Americanization of, 274, 327, 334; assimilation of, 307; attitudes towards, 83, 89, 160, 170, 171, 177–78, 183–85; in California gold rush, 27–28, 60; as carpenters, 76, 177; in Central America, 17, 263–64; citizenship problems, 253–54, 259; and civic projects, 148–50, 167–68; as criminals, 173; as culturally misunderstood, 104, 160, 170, 172, 242; as cultural nationalists, 259, 269–70, 285–87, 304, 305; divisions among, 286–87, 313; as entrepreneurs, 156, 275, 276, 302–3; flamboyance, 267–69; from French islands, 65, 127–28, 250–53, 277, 280, 292; in Latin America, 8–9, 63, 111, 318; leisure activities, 269–74, 277; middle-class, 276, 293, 352; as nomads, 292; occupations, 79, 189, 192; outside Canal Zone, 260–62; Panama-born, 307, 310–11; as Panamanians, 63, 143, 291, 293–94, 302, 307, 360n96; Panamanians and, 293–94, 298, 302–4; and Prestán revolt, 83, 84–85; radicalization of, 344, 349; restrictions on, 350; services operated by, 276; social life, 191, 275–78; from Spanish islands, 280; United States and, 174, 175; and US

West Indians (*continued*)
government, 297, 299–300; white, 59, 186. *See also* Barbadians; Jamaicans

West India Royal Commission, 350

West Indies, 13, 16; changes in, 330–31, 340–42, 344, 352; economic concerns, 39, 40–42, 324; former slaves in, 39, 42, 43; labour issues, 70, 263, 330–31; and Panama, 13–15; race relations in, 109, 117–18, 170, 345; religion in, 346–49. *See also* West Indians; *specific islands*

"The Wharf Rats" (Walrond), 280

Whyte, Samuel Horatio, 308–9

Williams, James, 160, 161–63

Wilson, Woodrow, 1, 224

women: abandoned, 329, 330; American, 238, 243–45; in Barbados, 328–29; in Canal Zone, 238–45; earnings, 240, 242, 331; as emigrants, 118, 128, 133, 239, 276; as family heads, 329, 330; in fiction, 241; as food sellers, 140, 141, 234–35, 275; from French islands, 250–53; in Jamaica, 69–70, 329, 341; living conditions, 243, 245; occupations, 51, 52–53, 69–70, 113, 240, 243; in Panama, 276; in songs, 235, 330; stresses on, 29, 160, 250, 330; as travellers, 360n78. *See also* families; *specific occupations*

Wood, R.E., 177

work camps, 228; barracks (French), 74, 75, 77; barracks (ICC), 142–43, 154, 228, 229–31, 232–33; commissaries, 52, 141, 234, 235–38, 334; eviction from, 296, 301; food supplies, 140–42, 143, 231–35; lack of privacy, 230, 231; life outside, 229–30, 231, 232–33, 234, 262; married quarters, 228, 229, 232, 246–49, 295; regulated life, 227; segregation, 228–29, 230, 233, 234

Workers and Tradesmen Union, 351

The Workman, 298–99, 302, 313, 314

work songs, 194–96, 212, 217, 218–19

world wars. *See* First World War; Second World War

Wynter, Benjamin P., 383n34

Yankee Chagres, 48, 50, 57

yellow fever, 46–47, 71, 75, 80–81, 92, 93, 144–47

Young, Edgar, 2–3, 201, 213, 216

Young, Sidney, 383n34

Young Men's Colored Institute, 276